OFFICIAL TOURIST B

Places to Stay and Visit

Northern England

visit Britain

Contents

Derwentwater, Cumbria

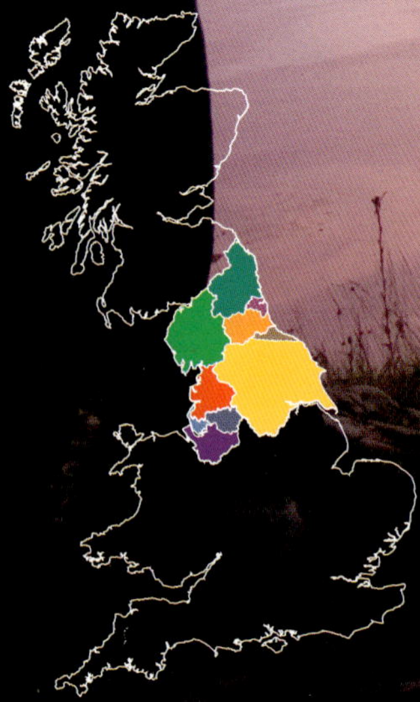

VisitBritain

VisitBritain is the organisation created to market Britain to the rest of the world, and England to the British.

Formed by the merger of the British Tourist Authority and the English Tourism Council, its mission is to build the value of tourism by creating world-class destination brands and marketing campaigns.

It will also build partnerships with – and provide insights to – other organisations which have a stake in British and English tourism.

This Enjoy England guide is packed with information from where to stay, to how to get there and what to see and do. **In fact, everything you need to know to enjoy Northern England.**

The guide that gives you more

Quality accommodation

Choose from a wide range of quality-assessed accommodation to suit all budgets and tastes. This guide contains an exclusive listing of hotels, B&B guest accommodation, self-catering properties, and camping & caravan parks in Northern England. Each establishment is a member of an Enjoy England Quality Rose assessment scheme – just look for the Quality Rose, the official marque of Enjoy England quality-assessed accommodation – or The British Graded Holiday Parks Scheme.

Regional information

Every region within Northern England has something unique and exciting to offer, whether it's coast or country, adventure or culture, retail therapy or romance you crave. There's something for everyone whatever their age and interests, from families to couples.

At the beginning of each regional section you can find a smattering of suggestions for eating out in the area. Inspirational ideas for memorable days out start on page 211 and if you turn to the back of the guide there's a selection of special offer vouchers for these attractions, together with a calendar of events. For more possibilities and ideas, turn to page 9 where you will find contact details for the different regions.

Tourist Information Centres

For local information phone or call into a Tourist Information Centre. Location and contact details can be found starting on page 289. Alternatively, you can text **TIC LOCATE** to 64118 to find your nearest Tourist Information Centre.

Ilkley, North Yorkshire

Head North

Blessed with magnificent landscapes, vibrant cities, hilltop castles and so much more – **make Northern England your next port of call.**

What's in the North?

Northern England, covering the area from Cheshire and Yorkshire up to the Scottish border, includes spectacular and varied scenery, a wealth of historic sites and lively cities, lots of popular attractions and some great beaches too. Turn to the county sections in this guide to find out more. With so much to offer, this part of the country is easy to tour and fascinating to explore.

Where to start?

If you're looking for accommodation, start right here with this guide. It gives details of a large selection of places to stay – from five-star hotels to B&Bs, from seafront apartments and country cottages to the open air of holiday parks.

What to do?

A beach holiday? Walking or cycling? High adventure? Heritage? Whatever you enjoy doing, you can do it in the North. Visit the websites opposite for more great ideas for memorable days out. Each site features useful searches so you can find exactly what you're looking for.

Blackpool, Lancashire

Find out **more**

North East England

One NorthEast Tourism Team
0870 160 1781
visitnortheastengland.co.uk

England's Northwest

England's Northwest
0845 600 6040
visitenglandsnorthwest.com

Visit Chester and Cheshire
(01244) 402111
visitchester.com

Cumbria Tourism
(015398) 22222
(brochure request – 0870 513 3059)
golakes.co.uk

Lancashire and Blackpool Tourist Board
(01257) 226600
lancashireandblackpool.com

Marketing Manchester
(0161) 237 1010
visitmanchester.com

The Mersey Partnership
0844 870 0123
visitliverpool.com

Yorkshire

Yorkshire Tourist Board
0870 609 0000
yorkshirevisitor.com

How to use this guide

In this brand new Northern England guide, you'll find a great choice of hotels, B&B guest accommodation, self-catering properties and camping & caravan parks.

Each property has been assessed by Enjoy England's assessors to nationally agreed standards so that you can book with confidence knowing your accommodation has been checked and rated for quality.

Detailed accommodation entries include descriptions, prices and facilities. You'll also find special offers and themed breaks to suit your tastes, interests and budget.

Finding accommodation is easy

Regional entries

The guide is divided into ten regional sections and accommodation is listed alphabetically by place name within each region.

Colour maps

Use the colour maps, starting on page 22, to pinpoint the location of all accommodation featured in the regional sections. Then refer to the place index at the back of the guide to find the page number.

Indexes

A place index at the back makes it easy to find accommodation in a particular area – and if you know the name of the establishment, use the property index.

Ratings and awards at a glance

Reliable, rigorous, easy to use – look out for the following ratings and awards to help you choose with confidence:

Ratings made easy

★	Simple, practical, no frills
★★	Well presented and well run
★★★	Good level of quality and comfort
★★★★	Excellent standard throughout
★★★★★	Exceptional with a degree of luxury

For full details of Enjoy England Quality Rose assessment schemes, go online at **enjoyengland.com/quality**

Guest accommodation – Diamond ratings

Establishments with a diamond rating were awaiting re-assessment under the new common standards star-rating scheme at the time of going to press.

rest assured with our official quality ratings

Star ratings

Establishments are awarded a rating of one to five stars based on a combination of quality of facilities and services provided. Put simply, the more stars, the higher the quality and the greater the range of facilities and level of service.

The process to arrive at a star rating is very thorough to ensure that when you book accommodation you can be confident it will meet your expectations. Enjoy England professional assessors visit establishments annually and work to strict criteria to rate the available facilities and service.

A quality score is awarded for every aspect of the experience. For hotels and guest accommodation this includes the comfort of the bed, the quality of the breakfast and dinner and, most importantly, the cleanliness. For self-catering properties the assessors also take into consideration the layout and design of the accommodation, the ease of use of all the appliances, the range and quality of the kitchen equipment, and the variety and presentation of the visitor information provided. Camping and caravan parks are awarded a rating following an assessment of the quality, cleanliness, maintenance and condition of the various facilities provided. The warmth of welcome and the level of care that each establishment offers its guests are noted, and places that go the extra mile to make every stay a special one will be rewarded with high scores for quality.

All the national assessing bodies (VisitBritain, VisitScotland, Visit Wales and the AA*) now operate to a common set of standards for rating hotels, guest accommodation and self-catering properties, giving holidaymakers and travellers a clear guide on exactly what to expect at each level. An explanation of all star ratings can be found on pages 272-274.

The range of accommodation within this guide differs greatly in style, so to help you make your choice, the rating scheme also includes categories that give an indication of the type of establishment. Descriptions of these can be found on the following pages.

*The AA does not assess self-catering properties.

Gold and Silver Awards

These Enjoy England awards are highly prized by proprietors and are only given to hotels and bed and breakfast accommodation offering the highest levels of quality within their star rating, particularly in areas of housekeeping, service and hospitality, bedrooms, bathrooms and food (see page 18).

Tourism Awards

The highly prized tourism awards in northern England showcase the very best in tourism in the area and celebrate the people whose contribution to its success is outstanding. A list of the winners for the accommodation categories can be found on page 16.

National Accessible Scheme

Establishments with a National Accessible rating provide access and facilities for guests with special visual, hearing and mobility needs (see page 20).

Walkers and Cyclists Welcome

Participants in these Enjoy England schemes actively encourage walking and cycling. Proprietors go out of their way to make special provision for guests who enjoy these activities to ensure they have a comfortable stay.

Caravan Holiday Home Award Scheme

VisitBritain runs an award scheme for individual holiday caravan homes on highly graded caravan parks. In addition to complying with standards for Holiday Parks, these exceptional caravans must have a shower or bath, toilet, mains electricity and water heating (at no extra charge) and a fridge (many also have a colour TV).

Categories explained

The following categories will help you decide which type of accommodation is right for you, whether you are seeking a non-stop, city-buzz holiday; a quiet weekend away; a home-from-home break or camping fun for all the family.

Hotels

Hotel	A minimum of six bedrooms, but more likely to have over 20.
Small Hotel	A maximum of 20 bedrooms and likely to be more personally run.
Country House Hotel	Set in ample grounds or gardens, in a rural or semi-rural location, with the emphasis on peace and quiet.
Town House Hotel	In a city or town-centre location, high quality with a distinctive and individual style. Maximum of 50 bedrooms, with a high ratio of staff to guests. Possibly no dinner served, but room service available. Might not have a dining room, so breakfast may be served in the bedrooms.
Metro Hotel	A city or town-centre hotel offering full hotel services, but no dinner. Located within easy walking distance of a range of places to eat. Can be of any size.
Budget Hotel	Part of a large branded hotel group, offering limited services. A Budget Hotel is not awarded a star rating.

Hotels awaiting re-assessment under the common standards rating scheme may have a category that is not entirely representative of the facilities and services they offer.

Guest Accommodation

Guest Accommodation Encompassing a wide range of establishments from one-room bed and breakfasts to larger properties, which may offer dinner and hold an alcohol licence.

Bed and Breakfast Accommodating no more than six people, the owners of these establishments welcome you into their home as a special guest.

Guest House Generally comprising more than three rooms. Dinner is unlikely to be available (if it is, it will need to be booked in advance). May possibly be licensed.

Farmhouse Bed and breakfast, and sometimes dinner, but always on a farm.

Restaurant with Rooms A licensed restaurant is the main business but there will be a small number of bedrooms, with all the facilities you would expect, and breakfast the following morning.

Inn Pubs with rooms, and many with restaurants as well.

Guest accommodation awaiting re-assessment under the common standards rating scheme may have a category that is not entirely representative of the facilities and services they offer.

Self Catering

Self Catering Choose from cosy country cottages, smart town-centre apartments, seaside villas, grand country houses for large family gatherings, and even quirky conversions of windmills, railway carriages and lighthouses. Most take bookings by the week, generally from a Friday or Saturday, but short breaks are increasingly offered, particularly outside the main season.

Serviced Apartments City-centre serviced apartments are an excellent alternative to hotel accommodation, offering hotel services such as daily cleaning, room service, concierge and business centre services, but with a kitchen and lounge area that allow you to eat in and relax when you choose. A telephone and Internet access tend to be standard. Prices are generally based on the property, so they often represent excellent value for money for families and larger groups. Serviced apartments tend to accept bookings for any length of period, and many are operated by agencies whose in-depth knowledge and choice of properties makes searching easier at busy times.

Camping and Caravan Parks

Camping Park These sites only have pitches available for tents.

Touring Park If you are planning to travel with your own caravan, motor home or tent, then look for a Touring Park.

Holiday Park If you want to hire a caravan holiday home for a short break or longer holiday, or are looking to buy your own holiday home, a Holiday Park is the right choice. They range from small, rural sites to larger parks with all the added extras, such as a pool.

Many parks will offer a combination of these categories.

Holiday Village Holiday Villages usually comprise a variety of types of accommodation, with the majority in custom-built rooms, chalets for example. The option to book on a bed and breakfast, or dinner, bed and breakfast basis is normally available. A range of facilities, entertainment and activities are also provided which may, or may not, be included in the tariff.

Holiday Villages must meet a minimum entry requirement for both the provision and quality of facilities and services, including fixtures, fittings, furnishings, decor and any other extra facilities. Progressively higher levels of quality and customer care are provided at each star level.

Quality visitor attractions

Enjoy England operates a Visitor Attraction Quality Assurance Service.

Participating attractions are visited annually by trained, impartial assessors who look at all aspects of the visit, from initial telephone enquiries to departure, customer service to catering, as well as all facilities and activities.

Only those attractions which have been assessed by Enjoy England and meet the standard receive the quality marque, your sign of a Quality Assured Visitor Attraction.

Look out for the quality marque and visit with confidence.

Accommodation entries explained

Each accommodation entry contains detailed information to help you decide if it is right for you. This has been provided by proprietors and our aim is to ensure that it is as objective and factual as possible.

1 Listing under town or village with map reference

2 Enjoy England star rating plus Gold or Silver Award where applicable

3 Category

4 Prices

Hotels – per room for bed and breakfast (B&B) and per person for half board (HB)

Guest accommodation – per room for bed and breakfast (B&B) and per person for evening meal

Self catering – per unit per week for low and high season

Camping and caravan parks – per pitch per night for touring pitches; per unit per week for caravan holiday homes

5 Establishment name and booking details

6 Indicates when the establishment is open

7 Accommodation details and payment accepted

8 Accessible rating where applicable

9 Walkers/Cyclists Welcome where applicable

10 Travel directions

11 Special promotions and themed breaks

12 At-a-glance facility symbols

A key to symbols can be found on the back-cover flap. Keep it open for easy reference.

Northern England Tourism Awards

Tourism awards in northern England are all about telling the world what a fantastic place the area is to visit, whether it's for a day trip, a weekend break or a fortnight's holiday.

England's Northwest Tourism Awards 2006

North East England Tourism Awards 2006 Passionate about tourism

Yorkshire Tourist Board White Rose Awards for Tourism 2006

The awards comprise several categories including Large and Small Visitor Attraction of the Year, Tourism Website of the Year and Tourist Information Centre of the Year and they were presented in autumn 2006.

All nominees for the accommodation categories had to demonstrate exceptionally high customer care and continual improvement of facilities. Other criteria included a commitment to recycling and the environment, accessibility for disabled customers and the use of local food and drink produce.

England's Northwest Tourism Award Winners 2006

Large Hotel of the Year
The Chester Grosvenor and Spa, Chester, *Cheshire*

Small Hotel of the Year
Stanley House, Mellor, *Lancashire*

Bed & Breakfast of the Year
Number One Blackpool, Blackpool, *Lancashire*

Self-Catering Holiday of the Year
Bridge End Farm Cottages, Eskdale, *Cumbria*

Caravan Holiday Park of the Year
Skelwith Fold Caravan Park, Ambleside, *Cumbria*

North East England Tourism Award Winners 2006

Large Hotel of the Year
GOLD **Malmaison,** NewcastleGateshead, *Tyne and Wear*

SILVER **De Vere Slaley Hall,** Slaley, *Northumberland*

Small Hotel of the Year
GOLD **Langley Castle,** Hexham, *Northumberland*

Bed & Breakfast of the Year
GOLD **The Old School Quality B&B,** Newton-on-the-Moor, *Northumberland*

SILVER **King's Head Hotel and Restaurant,** Great Ayton, nr Newton-under-Roseberry, *Tees Valley*

BRONZE **Tosson Tower Farm,** Rothbury, *Northumberland*

Self-Catering Holiday of the Year
GOLD **Beacon Hill Farm,** Longhorsley, *Northumberland*

SILVER **Dene House Farm,** Longframlington, *Northumberland*

BRONZE **The Mill Granary,** Ingleton, Darlington, *County Durham*

Caravan Holiday Park of the Year
GOLD **Ord House Country Park,** Berwick-upon-Tweed, *Northumberland*

SILVER **Haggerstone Castle Holiday Park,** Beal, *Northumberland*

BRONZE **Barnard Castle Camping & Caravanning Club Site,** Barnard Castle, *County Durham*

Yorkshire White Rose Awards for Tourism 2006

Large Hotel of the Year
Malmaison, Leeds, *South Yorkshire*

Small Hotel of the Year
Feversham Arms Hotel, Helmsley, *North Yorkshire*

Bed & Breakfast of the Year
The Moorlands Country House, Levisham, *North Yorkshire*

Self-Catering Holiday of the Year
Ashwell House, Bulmer, *North Yorkshire*

Caravan Holiday Park of the Year
Fell Grange Park & Golf Club, Skipsea, *East Riding of Yorkshire*

Above, left to right: The Chester Grosvenor and Spa; Malmaison, NewcastleGateshead; Langley Castle Hotel; Malmaison, Leeds

Gold and Silver Awards

Gold and Silver Awards are unique to Enjoy England and are given in recognition of **exceptional quality in hotel and guest accommodation.**

exceptional properties excelling in outstanding quality

enjoyEngland.com

Gold AWARD

enjoyEngland.com

Silver AWARD

Enjoy England professional assessors make recommendations for Gold and Silver Awards during assessments. They will look at the quality provided in all areas, in particular housekeeping, service and hospitality, bedrooms, bathrooms and food, to see if it meets the highest quality for the star level achieved. While star ratings are based on a combination of quality, range of facilities and level of service offered, Gold and Silver Awards are based solely on quality.

Here we list hotels and guest accommodation featured in this guide with a Gold or Silver Award. Use the property index starting on page 301 to find their page numbers.

Gold Award Hotels

Linthwaite House Hotel,
Windermere, *Cumbria*

Swinton Park,
Masham, *North Yorkshire*

Gold Award Guest Accommodation

17 Burgate,
Pickering, *North Yorkshire*

Alexander House,
York, *North Yorkshire*

Gallon House,
Knaresborough, *North Yorkshire*

Grinkle Lodge,
Staithes, *North Yorkshire*

Riggsacre,
Corbridge, *Northumberland*

Throapham House,
Dinnington, *South Yorkshire*

Tosson Tower Farm,
Rothbury, *Northumberland*

Waterford House,
Leyburn, *North Yorkshire*

West View Cottage,
Helmsley, *North Yorkshire*

Silver Award Hotels

Clare House,
Grange-over-Sands, *Cumbria*

The Coniston Hotel,
Skipton, *North Yorkshire*

The Devonshire Fell Hotel and Restaurant,
Burnsall, *North Yorkshire*

The Golden Fleece Hotel,
Thirsk, *North Yorkshire*

The Grasmere Hotel,
Grasmere, *Cumbria*

Lairbeck Hotel,
Keswick, *Cumbria*

Langley Castle,
Hexham, *Northumberland*

Netherwood Hotel,
Grange-over-Sands, *Cumbria*

Stanley House,
Mellor, *Lancashire*

Stanneylands Hotel,
Wilmslow, *Cheshire*

Waren House Hotel,
Bamburgh, *Northumberland*

Silver Award Guest Accommodation

Acorn House Hotel,
Keswick, *Cumbria*

The Alexander Hotel,
Scarborough, *North Yorkshire*

Amble House Guest House,
Keswick, *Cumbria*

Ascot House,
York, *North Yorkshire*

Ashmount Guest House,
Haworth, *West Yorkshire*

Augill Castle,
Kirkby Stephen, *Cumbria*

Barnes Fell Guest House,
Ambleside, *Cumbria*

Beach Court,
Beadnell, *Northumberland*

Beech Lodge,
Alnmouth, *Northumberland*

Bishops Hotel,
York, *North Yorkshire*

Borrowby Mill, Bed and Breakfast,
Thirsk, *North Yorkshire*

Bush Nook,
Gilsland, *Cumbria*

Capernwray House,
Carnforth, *Lancashire*

Carlton Lodge,
Helmsley, *North Yorkshire*

Cononley Hall Bed & Breakfast,
Skipton, *North Yorkshire*

Coole Hall Farm,
Nantwich, *Cheshire*

The Cornmill,
Kirkbymoorside, *North Yorkshire*

Cross Butts Stable Hotel and Restaurant,
Whitby, *North Yorkshire*

Dunsford Guest House,
Keswick, *Cumbria*

Elder Grove,
Ambleside, *Cumbria*

The Grange Country House,
Keswick, *Cumbria*

Haven Crest,
Whitby, *North Yorkshire*

The Hazelwood,
York, *North Yorkshire*

Hill House Farm Bed & Breakfast,
Rushton, *Cheshire*

The Hill on the Wall,
Gilsland, *Cumbria*

Kings Head Hotel and Restaurant,
Great Ayton, *North Yorkshire*

Locksley, Bed & Breakfast,
Stocksfield, *Northumberland*

The Old Barn
Thoralby, *North Yorkshire*

Scales Farm Country Guest House,
Threlkeld, *Cumbria*

Sharow Cross House,
Ripon, *North Yorkshire*

Sunny Bank,
Holmfirth, *West Yorkshire*

West Close Farmhouse,
Leyburn, *North Yorkshire*

Willow Run Bed & Breakfast,
Chester, *Cheshire*

National
Accessible Scheme

Finding suitable accommodation is not always easy, especially if you have to seek out ground-floor rooms or large print menus. Use the National Accessible Scheme to help you make your choice.

accessible accommodation for a comfortable stay

Proprietors of accommodation taking part in the National Accessible Scheme have gone out of their way to ensure a comfortable stay for guests with special hearing, visual or mobility needs. These exceptional places are full of extra touches to make everyone's visit trouble-free, from handrails, ramps and step-free entrances (ideal for buggies too) to level-access showers and colour contrast in the bathrooms. Members of the staff or owners may have attended a disability awareness course and will know what assistance will really be appreciated.

Appropriate National Accessible Scheme symbols are included in the guide entries (shown opposite). If you have additional needs or special requirements we strongly recommend that you make sure these can be met by your chosen establishment before you confirm your reservation.

tourismforall

The National Accessible Scheme forms part of the Tourism for All Campaign that is being promoted by VisitBritain and national/regional tourism organisations. Additional help and guidance on finding suitable holiday accommodation for those with special needs can be obtained from:

Tourism for All
c/o Vitalise, Shap Road Industrial Estate, Kendal LA9 6NZ

information helpline 0845 124 9971
reservations 0845 124 9973
(lines open 9-5 Mon-Fri)

f (01539) 735567

e info@tourismforall.org.uk

w tourismforall.org.uk

The criteria VisitBritain and national/regional tourism organisations have adopted do not necessarily conform to British Standards or to Building Regulations. They reflect what the organisations understand to be acceptable to meet the practical needs of guests with mobility or sensory impairments and encourage the industry to increase access to all.

Mobility Symbols

Typically suitable for a person with sufficient mobility to climb a flight of steps but who would benefit from fixtures and fittings to aid balance.

Typically suitable for a person with restricted walking ability and for those who may need to use a wheelchair some of the time and can negotiate a maximum of three steps.

Typically suitable for a person who depends on the use of a wheelchair and transfers unaided to and from the wheelchair in a seated position. This person may be an independent traveller.

Typically suitable for a person who depends on the use of a wheelchair in a seated position. This person also requires personal/mechanical assistance to aid transfer (eg carer, hoist).

Access Exceptional is awarded to establishments that meet the requirements of independent wheelchair users or assisted wheelchair users shown above and also fulfil more demanding requirements with reference to the British Standards BS8300:2001.

Visual Impairment Symbols

Typically provides key additional services and facilities to meet the needs of visually impaired guests.

Typically provides a higher level of additional services and facilities to meet the needs of visually impaired guests.

Hearing Impairment Symbols

Typically provides key additional services and facilities to meet the needs of guests with hearing impairment.

Typically provides a higher level of additional services and facilities to meet the needs of guests with hearing impairment.

Map 1

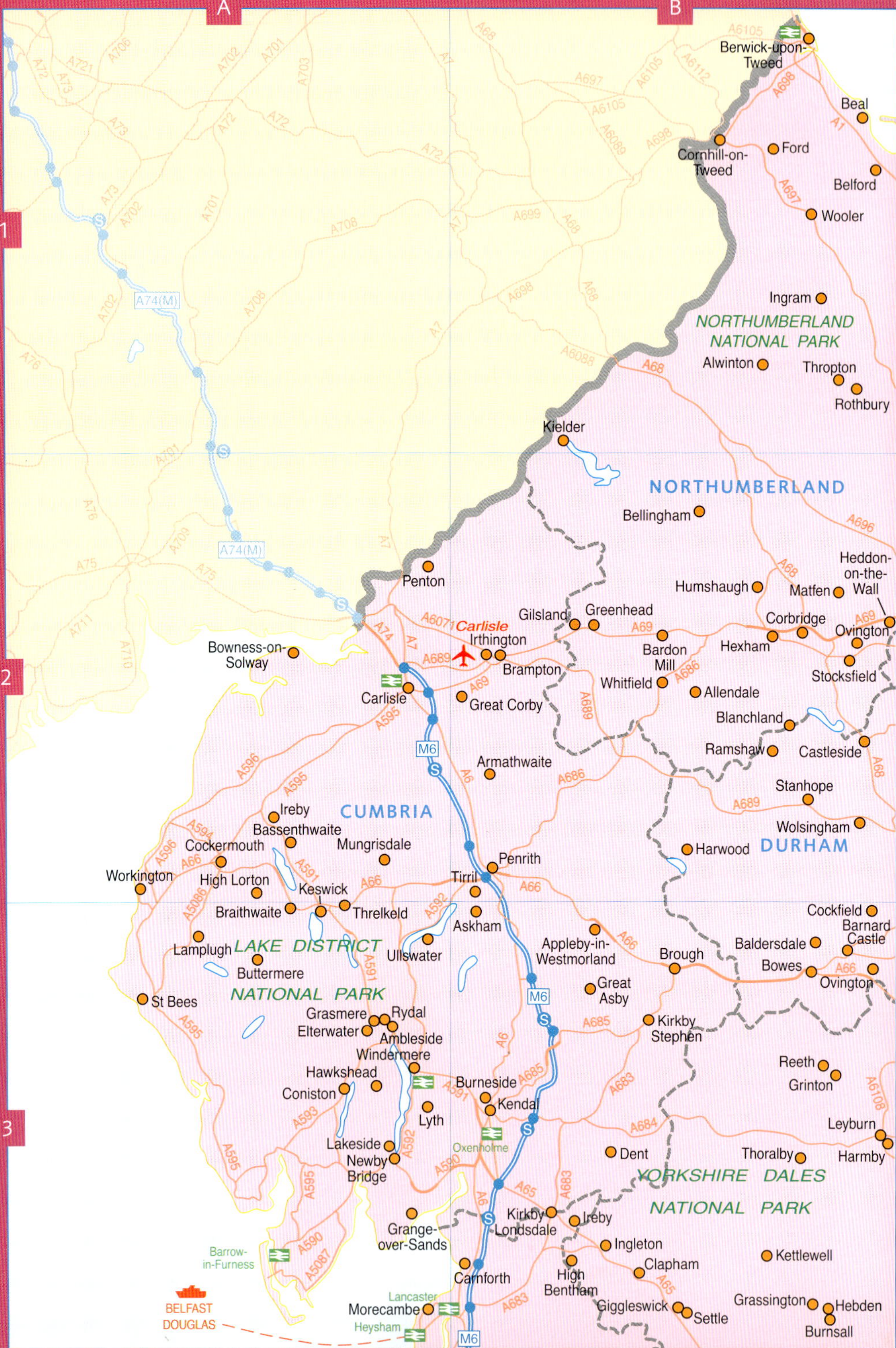
A
B
1
2
3
Berwick-upon-Tweed
Beal
Cornhill-on-Tweed
Ford
Belford
Wooler
Ingram
NORTHUMBERLAND NATIONAL PARK
Alwinton
Thropton
Rothbury
Kielder
NORTHUMBERLAND
Bellingham
Heddon-on-the-Wall
Humshaugh
Matfen
Penton
Gilsland
Greenhead
Carlisle
Irthington
Corbridge
Ovington
Bowness-on-Solway
Brampton
Bardon Mill
Hexham
Stocksfield
Whitfield
Allendale
Great Corby
Blanchland
Ramshaw
Castleside
Armathwaite
Stanhope
Ireby
CUMBRIA
Bassenthwaite
Wolsingham
Cockermouth
Mungrisdale
Harwood
DURHAM
Workington
High Lorton
Keswick
Penrith
Tirril
Braithwaite
Threlkeld
Askham
Cockfield
Barnard Castle
Lamplugh
LAKE DISTRICT NATIONAL PARK
Ullswater
Appleby-in-Westmorland
Baldersdale
Buttermere
Brough
Bowes
Ovington
St Bees
Great Asby
Grasmere
Rydal
Elterwater
Ambleside
Kirkby Stephen
Windermere
Hawkshead
Reeth
Grinton
Coniston
Burneside
Kendal
Lyth
Leyburn
Harmby
Lakeside
Newby Bridge
Oxenholme
Dent
Thoralby
YORKSHIRE DALES NATIONAL PARK
Kirkby Lonsdale
Ireby
Grange-over-Sands
Ingleton
Barrow-in-Furness
Clapham
Kettlewell
Carnforth
High Bentham
BELFAST
DOUGLAS
Lancaster
Morecambe
Giggleswick
Settle
Grassington
Hebden
Burnsall
Heysham
A74(M)
M6
A7
A68
A69
A66
A6
A591
A595
A590
A65
A683
A684
A685
A686
A689
A6071
A697
A698
A1
A696
A592
A593
A596
A594
A5086
A5087
A6108
A6105
A6112
A6089
A6088
A708
A701
A702
A703
A72
A73
A721
A706
A76
A75
A709
A711
A710
A699
A697

Location Maps

Every place name featured in the regional accommodation sections of this Enjoy England guide has a map reference to help you locate it on the maps which follow. For example, to find Blackpool, Lancashire, which has 'Map ref 2A1', turn to Map 2 and refer to grid square A1.

All place names appearing in the regional sections are shown in black type on the maps. This enables you to find other places in your chosen area which may have suitable accommodation – the place index (at the back of this guide) gives page numbers.

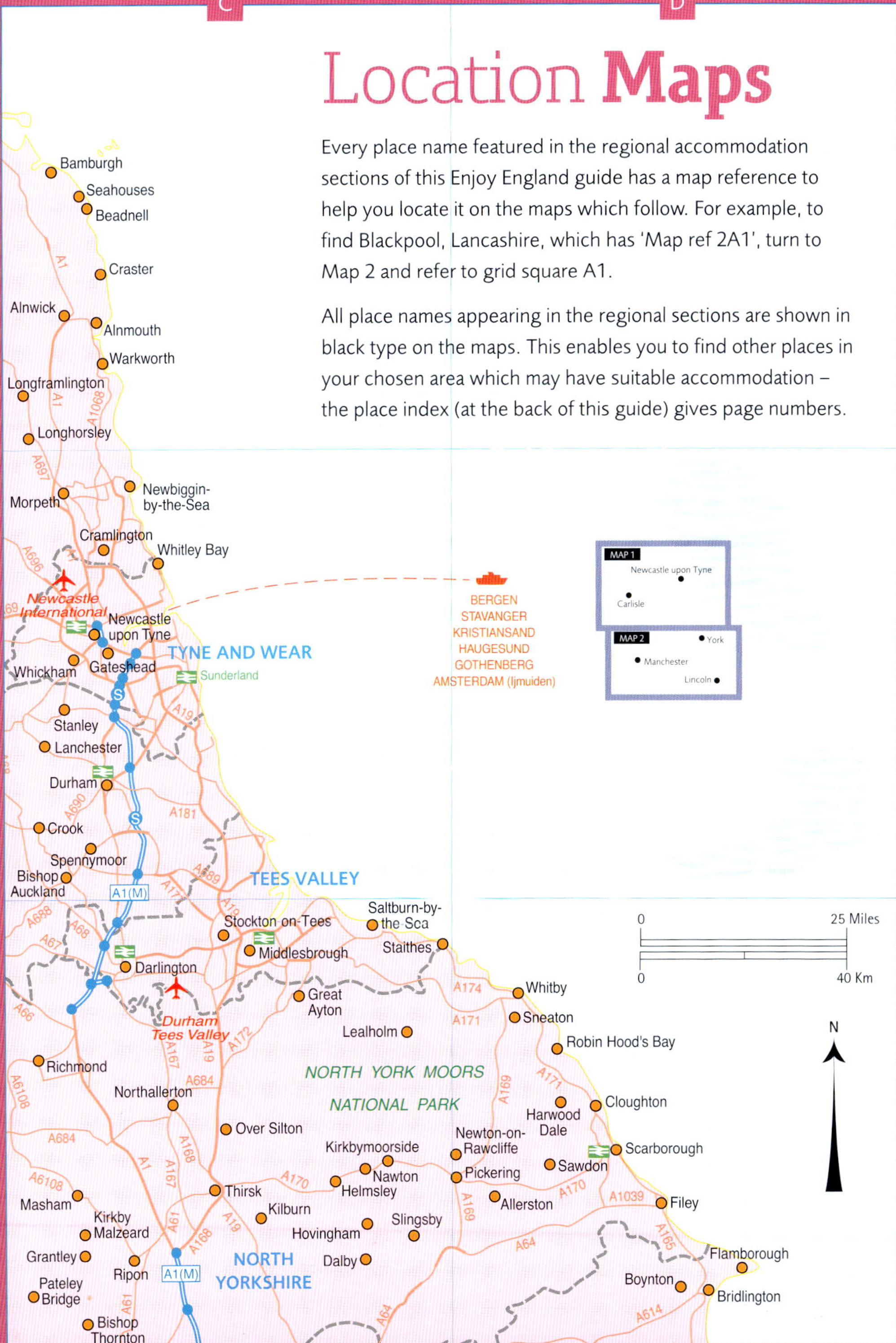

Map 2

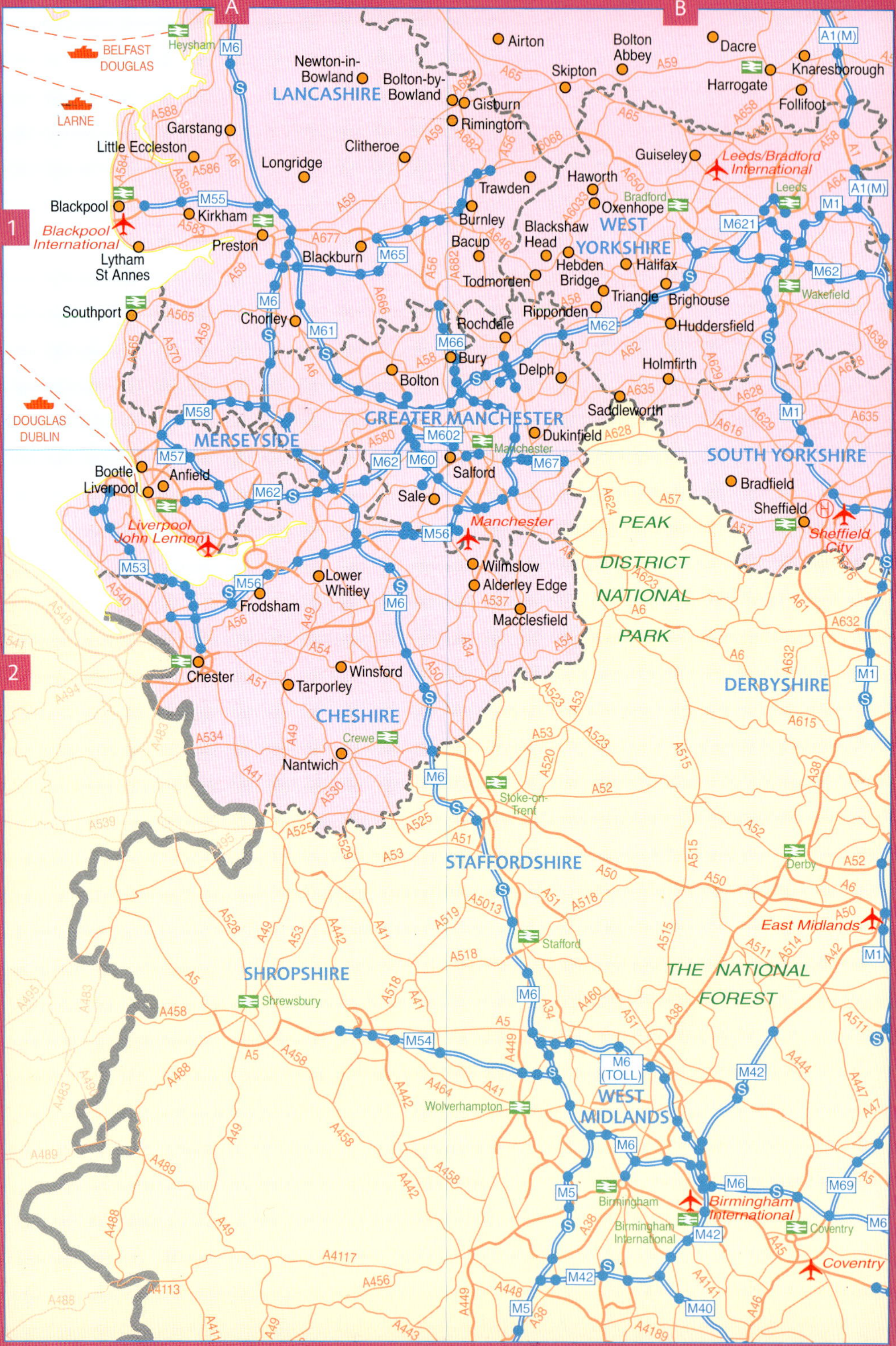
A
B
1
2
BELFAST
DOUGLAS
LARNE
DOUGLAS
DUBLIN
Heysham
LANCASHIRE
MERSEYSIDE
GREATER MANCHESTER
WEST YORKSHIRE
SOUTH YORKSHIRE
CHESHIRE
PEAK DISTRICT NATIONAL PARK
DERBYSHIRE
STAFFORDSHIRE
SHROPSHIRE
THE NATIONAL FOREST
WEST MIDLANDS
Airton
Bolton Abbey
Dacre
Knaresborough
Harrogate
Follifoot
Newton-in-Bowland
Bolton-by-Bowland
Gisburn
Rimington
Skipton
Garstang
Little Eccleston
Longridge
Clitheroe
Guiseley
Leeds/Bradford International
Haworth
Trawden
Bradford
Oxenhope
Leeds
Blackpool
Blackpool International
Kirkham
Preston
Lytham St Annes
Burnley
Blackshaw Head
Blackburn
Bacup
Hebden Bridge
Halifax
Todmorden
Triangle
Brighouse
Wakefield
Southport
Chorley
Rochdale
Ripponden
Huddersfield
Bury
Delph
Holmfirth
Bolton
Saddleworth
Dukinfield
Manchester
Bootle
Anfield
Liverpool
Salford
Bradfield
Sheffield
Sale
Sheffield City
Liverpool John Lennon
Manchester
Wilmslow
Lower Whitley
Alderley Edge
Frodsham
Macclesfield
Chester
Winsford
Tarporley
Crewe
Nantwich
Stoke-on-Trent
Derby
East Midlands
Stafford
Shrewsbury
Wolverhampton
Birmingham
Birmingham International
Coventry
M6
M55
M65
M61
M66
M62
M58
M57
M602
M60
M67
M621
M1
A1(M)
M56
M53
M54
M6 (TOLL)
M42
M69
M5
M40

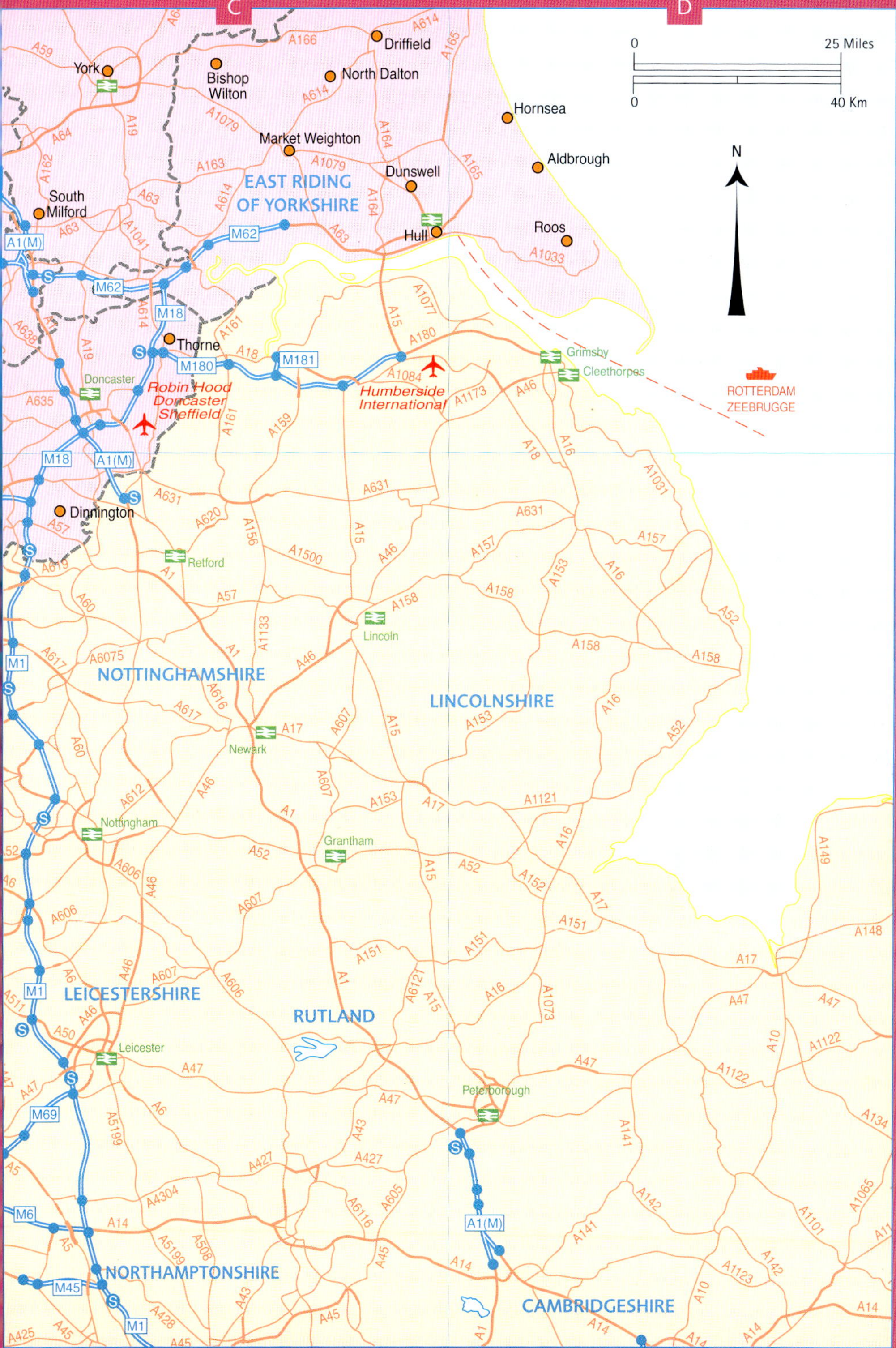
C
D
0
25 Miles
0
40 Km
N
York
Bishop Wilton
Driffield
North Dalton
Market Weighton
Hornsea
Aldbrough
Dunswell
Hull
Roos
South Milford
EAST RIDING OF YORKSHIRE
Thorne
Doncaster
Robin Hood Doncaster Sheffield
Humberside International
Grimsby
Cleethorpes
ROTTERDAM ZEEBRUGGE
Dinnington
Retford
Lincoln
NOTTINGHAMSHIRE
LINCOLNSHIRE
Newark
Nottingham
Grantham
LEICESTERSHIRE
RUTLAND
Leicester
Peterborough
NORTHAMPTONSHIRE
CAMBRIDGESHIRE

Relaxing on the Shropshire Union Canal, near Bunbury

colourful
canals,
idyllic
parkland,
Roman
heritage

Explore rounded hills and stretching plains, immerse yourself in rich Roman history and relax on idyllic inland waterways. Gaze towards the horizon at magnificent vistas and slow the pace of life to **enjoy this exceptional county.**

Explore Cheshire

Find retail heaven in The Rows, Chester

Roman riches

Begin your exploration in Chester, a city positively steeped in history, and discover its fabulous museums, galleries and restaurants. Recently voted one of the best cities in England for a spot of retail therapy, treat yourself to a unique keepsake in The Rows – Chester's medieval two-tier shopping streets framed in original black-and-white timber – or head to Mall Grosvenor and Rufus Court for the familiar high-street outlets.

Stroll down a reconstructed street at the Dewa Roman Experience and allow the sights, sounds and smells of a bygone age to play on your senses. Explore Saxon and medieval remains, once buried beneath modern-day Chester, and be sure to walk the city walls – a virtually complete two-mile circuit surrounding the city centre. Look skywards at the mighty spires of Chester Cathedral and take a moment to visit England's largest stone-built amphitheatre – can you picture the gladiator fights and public executions that took place here?

Time out

Let someone else do the work and relax while cruising Cheshire's waterways, or get stuck in and tackle the locks along the way. Skirt around the Peak District and take in stunning views of stone-built villages and the Cheshire Plains. Take a trip to the Anderton boat lift – the world's first and UK's only – where the River Weaver meets the Trent & Mersey Canal, and observe from the superb viewing deck.

Let the tension float away with a luxurious treat at the Grosvenor Spa in Chester. Awaken your senses with a herb sauna, leave your skin glowing with a trip to the crystal steam room and step under the ice fountain for a refreshing soak. The Scented Garden offers retail and physical therapy in one: peruse the shelves for your herbal needs and allow your every care to drift away during a 30-minute back and neck aromatherapy massage.

Search for inner peace at Tatton Park, Knutsford

Family days out at Chester Zoo

A sea of green

Lyme Park may look strangely familiar upon first sight: envisage Pemberley in the BBC adaptation of *Pride and Prejudice*. Lose yourself in the sways of romance in this idyllic setting of calm lakes and an Edwardian rose garden. Explore 1,000 acres of rolling parkland at Tatton Park in Knutsford, stroll down tree-lined avenues, past stunning lakes and grazing fallow deer, and find peace in the enchanting Japanese garden.

Capesthorne Hall in Siddington captures 18th-century Jacobean-style elegance set in acres of picturesque gardens, while spectacular views from Beeston Castle – atop a sheer rocky crag – will afford you sights over eight different counties.

Creatures great and small

Cheshire is brimming with action-packed and educational days out for visitors of all ages. Take a deep breath and swim with the sharks at the Blue Planet Aquarium in Ellesmere Port, and wander through the 70-metre Aquatunnel for a prime view of the fascinating marine life.

Learn a new skill and charm a few slimy friends out of the ground at the annual Worm-Charming Championships near Nantwich. Or head to Gulliver's Theme Park in Warrington for fast-paced adventures in both Smuggler's Wharf and Western World. At Chester Zoo spot endangered black rhinos and playful jaguars, hold on tight aboard a waterbus and admire wildfowl and beautiful woodland.

Food & drink

Fancy a bite to eat, a relaxing drink or some fresh local produce? Here's a selection of food and drink venues to get you started. For lots more ideas go online at **enjoyengland.com/taste**.

Restaurants

The Arkle Restaurant
Fine dining
The Chester Grosvenor,
East Gate Street, Chester CH1 1LT
t (01244) 324024
w chestergrosvenor.co.uk

Canvas Bar & Restaurant
European
93 King Street, Knutsford
WA16 6EQ
t (01565) 632669

Dilli
Indian
60 Stamford New Road,
Altrincham WA14 1EE
t (0161) 927 9219
w dilli.co.uk

Est Est Est – Alderley
Italian
75 London Road, Alderley Edge
SK9 7DY
t 0870 401 2101
w estestest.co.uk

Flamin' Nosh Restaurant
Italian/Mexican
97 Stamford Street, Stalybridge
SK15 1LH
t (0161) 338 5555
w flaminnosh.co.uk

Juniper
English
21 The Downs, Altrincham
WA14 2QD
t (0161) 902 4008
w juniper-restaurant.co.uk

La Taverna
Italian
52-54 Lower Bridge Street,
Chester CH1 1RU
t (01244) 350625
w la-taverna.org.uk

Oscar's Restaurant
English
31 Beam Street, Nantwich
CW5 5NA
t (01270) 620900

Pastarazzi
Fine Dining
29 Grosvenor Street, Chester
CH1 2DD
t (01244) 400029
w pastarazzi.com

Upstairs at the Grill
Fine dining
70 Watergate Street, Chester
CH1 2LA
t (01244) 344883
w upstairsatthegrill.co.uk

Pubs

Cabbage Hall
Forest Road, Little Budworth
Tarporley CW6 9ES
t (01829) 760292

The Davenport Arms
Manchester Road, Marton
SK11 9HF
t (01260) 224269

Mitchells Wine Bar & Brasserie
Lyndale House, High Street,
Tattenhall CH3 9PX
t (01829) 771477

Tearooms, coffee shops and cafes

The Harvest Store
Hopley House, Nantwich Road,
Wimboldsley CW10 0LN
t (01270) 526292
w harveststore.co.uk

Red House Farm Shop and Tearooms
Dunham Massey, Altrincham
WA14 5RL
t (0161) 941 3480
w redhousefarm.co.uk

Royal Stafford Factory Shop & Ceramic Cafe
Wedgewood Place, Burslem
ST6 4EE
t (01782) 525419
w royalstaffordtableware.co.uk

Delis

The Cheshire Smokehouse
Vost Farm, Morley Green,
Wilmslow SK9 5NU
t (01625) 548499
w cheshiresmokehouse.co.uk

Designasausage
12 Hibel Road, Macclesfield
SK10 2AB
t 0845 257 8884
w designasausage.com

Littlewoods Butchers
5 School Lane, Heaton Chapel,
Stockport SK4 5DE
t (0161) 432 1070
w littlewoodsbutchers.co.uk

Farm shops and local produce

Abbey Leys Farm
Peacock Lane, High Legh
WA16 6NS
t (01925) 753465
w abbeyleys.co.uk

Cheerbrook Quality Farm Foods
Cheerbrook Farm, Newcastle
Road, Nantwich CW5 7EL
t (01270) 666431
w cheerbrook.co.uk

Cheshire Farm Ice Cream
Tattenhall CH3 9NE
t (01829) 770446
w cheshirefarmicecream.co.uk

The Hollies Farm Shop
Forest Road, Little Budworth,
Tarporley CW6 9ES
t (01829) 760414
w theholliesfarmshop.co.uk

where to stay in

Cheshire

Maps
All place names in the blue bands are shown on the maps at the front of this guide.

Accommodation symbols
Symbols give useful information about services and facilities. Inside the back-cover flap you can find a key to these symbols. Keep it open for easy reference.

ALDERLEY EDGE, Cheshire Map ref 2B2 — **GUEST ACCOMMODATION**

♦♦♦
GUEST ACCOMMODATION

B&B per room per night
s Min £27.00
d Min £54.00

Mayfield

Wilmslow Road, Alderley Edge SK9 7QW **t** (01625) 583991 & 07703 289663

Bed and breakfast with optional dinner (notice required). If flying from Manchester Airport, car may be left (at owner's risk) with Sheila taking and picking up from the airport. No pets.

open All year
bedrooms 1 double, 1 twin, 2 single
payment Cash/cheques

Room General

CHESTER, Cheshire Map ref 2A2 — **HOTEL**

★★
HOTEL

B&B per room per night
s £65.00–£85.00
d £90.00–£120.00
HB per person per night
£60.00–£75.00

Curzon Hotel

52-54 Hough Green, Chester CH4 8JQ **t** (01244) 678581 **f** (01244) 680866
e curzon.chester@virgin.net **w** curzonhotel.co.uk

open All year except Christmas and New Year
bedrooms 8 double, 3 twin, 1 single, 2 family, 2 suites
bathrooms All en suite
payment Credit/debit cards, cash/cheques

The Curzon is a family-run, Victorian townhouse hotel. Unwind in the lounge bar and sample our excellent cuisine in the splendid restaurant. Sleep peacefully in one of the individually designed guest rooms. There is ample private parking, and we are within easy reach of the city centre.

⊕ *Junction of A55/A483 follow sign for Chester. At 3rd roundabout take 2nd exit A5104 signposted Saltney. Curzon Hotel 500yds on right-hand side.*

♥ *Deva Break: any 2 nights' DB&B £60pppn. Winter Warmers (from Nov): third night's DB&B half price. Special breaks our speciality.*

Room General Leisure

Check it out

Information on accommodation listed in this guide has been supplied by proprietors. As changes may occur you should remember to check all relevant details at the time of booking.

CHESTER, Cheshire Map ref 2A2 — **GUEST ACCOMMODATION**

★★★
GUEST ACCOMMODATION

B&B per room per night
s £42.00–£80.00
d £50.00–£95.00

Chester Brooklands

8 Newton Lane, Chester CH2 3RB **t** (01244) 348856 **f** 0871 236 9308
e enquiries@chester-bandb.com **w** chester-bandb.com

open All year except Christmas and New Year
bedrooms 2 double, 1 twin, 1 family
bathrooms All en suite
payment Credit/debit cards, cash/cheques, euros

Large bedrooms offering king, double, single and twin beds. Large en suite to every room with power shower. WI-FI Internet access available. Non-smoking establishment. Well located for Chester railway station, Chester races, Cheshire Oaks and Chester city centre.

⊕ *From M6 jct 19 to M56 (Queensferry, Chester), then jct 12 onto A56 to Chester. Turn right at All Saints Church.*

♥ *Stay 2 nights or more at £25pp based on twin room accommodation for 2 full-paying adults (excl Fri and Sat).*

Room General Leisure

CHESTER, Cheshire Map ref 2A2 — **GUEST ACCOMMODATION**

♦♦♦♦
GUEST ACCOMMODATION

B&B per room per night
s £28.00–£30.00
d £50.00

Kings Guesthouse

14 Eaton Road, Handbridge, Chester CH4 7EN **t** (01244) 671249 **e** king@kings.plus.com
w kingsguesthouse.co.uk

open All year except Christmas
bedrooms 2 double, 2 twin, 1 single, 2 family
bathrooms All en suite
payment Credit/debit cards, cash/cheques

The Kings is a lovely old Victorian guesthouse, family run and clean, with full English breakfast. Newly refurbished and just a few minutes' walk to river and city centre. Lounge. Car park. All rooms en suite.

⊕ *See website for full directions.*

Room General Leisure

CHESTER, Cheshire Map ref 2A2 — **GUEST ACCOMMODATION**

★★★★
BED & BREAKFAST

B&B per room per night
s Min £27.00
d £54.00–£56.00

Laurels

14 Selkirk Road, Curzon Park, Chester CH4 8AH **t** (01244) 679682
e howell@ellisroberts.freeserve.co.uk

Quiet residential area near racecourse and river. Within easy walking distance to the city centre. Parking on drive. Key to front door.

open All year except Christmas
bedrooms 1 double, 1 single, 1 family
bathrooms 1 en suite, 2 private
payment Cash/cheques

Room General Leisure

Key to symbols

Symbols at the end of each entry help you pick out the services and facilities which are most important for your stay. A key to the symbols can be found inside the back-cover flap. Keep this open for easy reference.

CHESTER, Cheshire Map ref 2A2 — **GUEST ACCOMMODATION**

★★★★
BED & BREAKFAST SILVER AWARD

B&B per room per night
s £45.00–£76.00
d £76.00–£86.00

Willow Run Bed & Breakfast

Barrow Lane, Tarvin Sands, Tarvin, Chester CH3 8JF **t** (01829) 749142 **f** (01829) 749142
e willowrun@btconnect.com **w** willowrun.co.uk

open All year except Christmas and New Year
bedrooms 2 double, 1 twin
bathrooms All en suite
payment Credit/debit cards, cash/cheques

A rural escape with city style. Executive-quality accommodation providing three very spacious bedrooms, with en suite facilities, furnished to the highest standards. Four miles from Chester; quick and easy access to motorways. Variety of restaurants within walking distance. A modern yet homely atmosphere awaits you at this truly unique gateway.

Approx 0.25 miles from Tarvin village, located just off the A54 at the Oscroft, Willington and Pryors Hayes crossroads. Four miles East of Chester.

Dec-Mar – 10% discount on 2 nights or more. Gift vouchers available, please call to discuss further.

Room General **P** Leisure

CHESTER, Cheshire Map ref 2A2 — **SELF CATERING**

★★★
SELF CATERING

Units **2**
Sleeps **2–4**
Low season per wk
£275.00–£375.00
High season per wk
£275.00–£375.00

City Walls Apartments, Chester

Thompson Cox Partnership
t (01244) 313400 **f** (01244) 313400 **e** admin@rufuscourt.co.uk

open All year
payment Credit/debit cards, cash/cheques, euros

Modern, second-floor apartments with courtyard and garden views, parking, near to everything. Large studio (one double bed) and two-bedroom (two doubles) in award-winning courtyard, half built in 1990, half in 1750, nestling on the city walls, housing craft shops, book shops, restaurants and Alexander's Jazz Bar. Everything included.

Chester city centre, 10 – 15 minutes' walk from railway station, 2 minutes' taxi ride. Served by any bus route which drops off at the main bus station.

Short breaks if late availability (3 weeks ahead) only. Ring for prices.

Unit
General **P** Shop < 0.5 miles Pub < 0.5 miles

CHESTER, Cheshire Map ref 2A2 — **SELF CATERING**

★★★
SELF CATERING

Units **1**
Sleeps **1–4**
Low season per wk
£150.00–£200.00
High season per wk
£200.00–£250.00

Kingswood Coach House, Chester

contact Mrs C Perry, Kingswood Coach House, Kingswood, Parkgate Road, Chester CH1 6JS
t (01244) 851204 **f** (01244) 851244 **e** caroline.m.perry@btopenworld.com

Ideal for couples. Large bedroom, fitted kitchen, living room, toilet and shower. Garden and patio, off-road parking. Close to bus route. Near Wales and Wirral.

open All year
payment Cash/cheques

Unit
General **P** Leisure

Check the maps

Colour maps at the front pinpoint all places in which you will find accommodation entries in the regional sections. Pick your location and then refer to the place index at the back to find the page number.

FRODSHAM, Cheshire Map ref 2A2 — **CAMPING & CARAVANNING**

★★★★
HOLIDAY PARK
(10) £209.00–£563.00

Ridgeway Country Holiday Park

The Ridgeway, Frodsham WA6 6XQ **t** (01928) 734981 **f** (01928) 734981 **e** sue@ridgewaypark.com
w ridgewaypark.com

An ideal base for exploring the scenic countryside, yet within close proximity to Liverpool and Chester. Prices weekly for the lodges and caravans. Open 1 March to 2 January. Short-break prices available.

payment Credit/debit cards, cash/cheques

General P Leisure

LOWER WHITLEY, Cheshire Map ref 2A2 — **GUEST ACCOMMODATION**

★★★
GUEST ACCOMMODATION

B&B per room per night
s £46.00–£50.00
d £46.00–£50.00

Tall Trees Lodge

Tarporley Road, Lower Whitley, Warrington WA4 4EZ **t** (01928) 790824 **f** (01928) 791330
e bookings@talltreeslodge.co.uk **w** talltreeslodge.co.uk

Set in the beautiful Cheshire countryside, a warm welcome awaits you at Tall Trees. The rooms are large, bright and have a TV, hairdryer, telephone and coffee-making facilities. All en suite.

open All year except Christmas
bedrooms 14 double, 1 twin, 5 family
bathrooms All en suite
payment Credit/debit cards, cash/cheques

Room TV General P

MACCLESFIELD, Cheshire Map ref 2B2 — **GUEST ACCOMMODATION**

Rating Applied For
GUEST ACCOMMODATION

B&B per room per night
s £35.00–£40.00
d £60.00

Moorhayes House

27 Manchester Road, Tytherington, Macclesfield SK10 2JJ **t** (01625) 433228 **f** (01625) 429878
e helen@moorhayes.co.uk **w** smoothhound.co.uk/hotels/moorhaye

Warm welcome. Comfortable home in mature gardens. About 0.5 miles north of town centre. Hearty breakfast with home-cooked food. Car park. Non-smoking.

open All year except Christmas and New Year
bedrooms 4 double, 1 twin, 1 single, 2 family
bathrooms All en suite
payment Credit/debit cards, cash/cheques

Room TV General 5 P Leisure

MACCLESFIELD, Cheshire Map ref 2B2 — **SELF CATERING**

★★★★
SELF CATERING

Units **2**
Sleeps **4–6**
Low season per wk
£180.00
High season per wk
£270.00

Lower Pethills Farm Cottage, Macclesfield

contact Mr & Mrs Greg Rowson, Lower Pethills Farm Cottage, Lower Pethills Farm, Sutton, Macclesfield SK11 0NJ
t (01260) 252410

Situated on a smallholding in a picturesque valley on the edge of the Peak District, the cottages provide a peaceful base for a relaxing or active holiday.

open All year
payment Cash/cheques

Unit TV
General P S Leisure Shop 3 miles Pub 1 mile

MANCHESTER AIRPORT

See under Alderley Edge, Wilmslow

NANTWICH, Cheshire Map ref 2A2 — **GUEST ACCOMMODATION**

★★★★
FARMHOUSE
SILVER AWARD

B&B per room per night
s £35.00–£40.00
d £60.00–£70.00
Evening meal per person
Min £12.00

Coole Hall Farm

Coole Pilate, Nantwich CW3 0JD **t** (01270) 811232 **f** (01270) 811232
e goodwin@coolehallfarm.plus.com

Come and enjoy the peace and quiet in our 200-year-old farmhouse, right in the middle of the beautiful Cheshire countryside. Local pubs three miles.

open All year except Christmas and New Year
bedrooms 1 double, 1 twin
bathrooms All en suite
payment Cash/cheques

Room TV General Leisure

TARPORLEY, Cheshire Map ref 2A2 — **GUEST ACCOMMODATION**

★★★★
FARMHOUSE
SILVER AWARD

B&B per room per night
s £35.00–£50.00
d £60.00–£90.00

Hill House Farm

Rushton, Tarporley CW6 9AU **t** (01829) 732238 **f** (01829) 733929
e info@hillhousefarm-cheshire.co.uk **w** hillhousefarm-cheshire.co.uk

open All year except Christmas
bedrooms 1 double, 1 twin, 1 family, 1 suite
bathrooms All en suite
payment Credit/debit cards, cash/cheques

Former farmhouse set in the middle of beautiful Cheshire countryside, surrounded by attractive gardens and horse paddocks. Stylish bedrooms tastefully decorated, well equipped and all en suite. One luxury suite with four-poster bed, own living room and kitchen. Spacious guest sitting room with log burner. Delicious Aga-cooked breakfasts.

⊕ *Two miles east of Tarporley. Off A51 or A49 to Eaton. Continue east to Rushton on Lower Lane. Right onto The Hall Lane, farm 0.5m right.*

♥ *Winter short-break packages.*

Room General P Leisure

WILMSLOW, Cheshire Map ref 2B2 — **HOTEL**

★★★★
HOTEL
SILVER AWARD

B&B per room per night
s £65.00–£110.00
d £90.00–£140.00
HB per person per night
£70.00–£90.00

Stanneylands Hotel

Stanneylands Road, Wilmslow SK9 4EY **t** (01625) 525225 **f** (01625) 537282
e enquiries@stanneylandshotel.co.uk **w** primahotels.co.uk

open All year
bedrooms 17 double, 11 twin, 2 single, 1 family
bathrooms All en suite
payment Credit/debit cards, cash/cheques

Exclusive country-house hotel set in several acres of beautiful gardens. All rooms en suite with satellite TV, radio, trouser-press and telephone. Rosettes for fine cuisine, in addition to many awards for excellence. Ideal base for exploring Cheshire and the Peak District. Twenty minutes from Manchester city centre and three miles from airport.

⊕ *From M56 jct 5 Manchester Airport, head for Cheadle/Wilmslow to traffic lights, right into Styal Road. Approx 1.5 miles left to Station Road, hotel on right.*

♥ *Park and fly – £65pp sharing (room only) including 15 days' free car parking, plus courtesy coach to airport between 0800 and 2300.*

Room General P Leisure

WINSFORD, Cheshire Map ref 2A2 — **GUEST ACCOMMODATION**

★★★
GUEST HOUSE

B&B per room per night
s £38.00–£43.00
d £48.00–£51.00
Evening meal per person
Min £15.00

The Winsford Lodge

85-87 Station Road, Winsford CW7 3DE **t** (01606) 862008 **f** (01606) 591822
e winsfordlodge@aol.com **w** winsfordlodge.co.uk

open All year
bedrooms 5 double, 3 twin, 2 single, 1 family
bathrooms All en suite
payment Credit/debit cards, cash/cheques

A comfortable guesthouse located in the heart of Cheshire. We pride ourselves on the fact we offer clean and comfortable, unparalleled, value-for-money accommodation.

⊕ *Follow A54 Chester. After roundabout at Winsford, next right at bottom of hill. Watch for brown tourist sign to Winsford Lodge.*

Room General P Leisure

Finding accommodation is as easy as 1 2 3

Enjoy England official guides to quality accommodation make it quick and easy to find a place to stay. There are several ways to use this guide.

1 PROPERTY INDEX

If you know the name of the establishment you wish to book, turn to the property index at the back where the relevant page number is shown.

2 PLACE INDEX

The place index at the back lists all locations with accommodation featured in the regional sections. A page number is shown where you can find full accommodation and contact details.

3 COLOUR MAPS

All the place names in black on the colour maps at the front have an entry in the regional sections. Refer to the place index for the page number where you will find one or more establishments offering accommodation in your chosen town or village.

High Force waterfall, a sight to behold

proud fortresses, unspoilt countryside, heritage city

Explore castles and cathedrals, immerse yourself in the fascinating history of the North East and enjoy breathtaking views across **sparsely populated dales and moors.**

Explore County Durham

City culture

Travel back through the Roman, Norman and medieval ages with a trip to 'the jewel in the North East's crown' – Durham. Find yourself spoilt for choice with an abundance of heritage and cultural attractions that fill this fasinating city. Enjoy a reminder of yesteryear as you pick your way through the Victorian Indoor Market. Or head to Fowlers Yard Creative Workspaces and watch artists at work in their studios. At the end of the day, wind down in one of the city's many bistros or prop up a stylish bar and enjoy the vibrant nightlife.

Explore the World Heritage Site at Durham Castle – one of England's largest and best-preserved Norman fortresses – and admire the impressive military memorabilia in the gallery of the Great Hall. Step into Durham Cathedral and find yourself overwhelmed by the mighty arches and incredible structure. Tentatively climb the tower and see for yourself why they call this one of 'the world's finest buildings'.

The majestic reflection of Durham Cathedral

The superb Bowes Castle and Museum, Barnard Castle

King of the castles

This county so rich in heritage is well stocked with proud fortresses. View the fabulous art collection within Raby Castle and wander its stunning grounds and beautiful parkland amid roaming deer. Feel the spray from powerful High Force, England's highest unbroken waterfall, part of the Raby Estate. Auckland Castle is an extremely magnificent and prestigious 800-year-old bastion, surrounded by glorious, peaceful countryside where Prince Bishops once hunted game.

Take a trip to Barnard Castle and wander the streets of the picturesque town that surround it, or visit Bowes Castle and Museum. Explore the ruins and greet The Bowes Museum Silver Swan, an intricately crafted music box that performs for visitors.

Step into a miner's shoes at Killhope: The North of England Lead Mining Museum

The history of the North

Whisk the kids into a world where the past comes to life at Beamish, The North of England Open Air Museum. Don a hard hat or cap lamp at Killhope: The North of England Lead Mining Museum and imagine yourself toiling underground in Victorian times; or children can dress as washer boys and hunt for lead ore.

Let off steam at Locomotion: the National Railway Museum in Shildon – aptly located where George Stephenson and Timothy Hackworth pulled the world's first steam-hauled passenger train in 1825. Or spot sculptures at Castle Eden Dene National Nature Reserve, near Peterlee, set in a stunning wooded ravine cut deep into the limestone.

The great outdoors

The North Pennines is one of the most peaceful and unspoilt areas of countryside in England, and a dream for walkers and cyclists alike. Spin your spokes in Hamsterley Forest – a veritable haven for mountain bikers. Varied colours mark routes in terms of difficulty, making this ideal for all abilities.

Spot an abundance of wildlife at The Otter Trust's North Pennines Reserve – observe grazing reindeer and tentatively spy birds from the safety of a hide. Get up close and meet lambs, chicks, pigs and donkeys at Hall Hill Farm, where over 1,000 sheep reside on the surrounding grassland. Or admire rare tree specimens at the arboretum at Houghall Gardens and relax in 25 acres of stunning scenery.

Food & drink

Fancy a bite to eat or a relaxing drink? Here's a selection of food and drink venues to get you started. For lots more ideas go online at **enjoyengland.com/taste**.

Restaurants

Bistro 21
Bistro
Aykley Heads, Aykley House, Durham DH1 5TS
t (0191) 384 4354
w bistrotwentyone.co.uk

Black Knight Restaurant – Lumley Castle
Fine dining
Chester-le-Street DH3 4NX
t (0191) 389 1111
w lumleycastle.com

Blagraves House
English
30-32 The Bank, Barnard Castle DL12 8PH
t (01833) 637668
w blagraves.com

Eggleston Hall
English
Eggleston Village, Barnard Castle DL12 OAG
t (01833) 650553
w egglestonhall.co.uk

Headlam Hall
Fine dining
Darlington DL2 3HA
t (01325) 730238
w headlamhall.co.uk

Hollanthan's
English
16-17 Elvet Bridge, Durham DH1 3AA
t (0191) 386 4618
w hollathans.co.uk

Knights Restaurant
Fine dining
Kingslodge Hotel, Waddington Street, Flass Vale, Durham DH1 4BG
t (0191) 370 9977
w kingslodge.info

The Morritt Arms Hotel
English
Greta Bridge, Barnard Castle DL12 9SE
t (01833) 627232
w themorritt.co.uk

Numjai Thai Restaurant
Thai
19 Millburngate Centre, Durham DS1 4SL
t (0191) 386 2020
w numjai.co.uk

Oldfields
English
18 Claypath, Durham DH1 1RH
t (0191) 370 9595
w oldfieldsrestaurants.com

The Pavilion Cantonese Restaurant
Cantonese
Iveston, Consett DH8 7TE
t (01207) 503388
w pavilioncantonese.co.uk

Seaham Hall Hotel – The White Room Restaurant, Ozone Restaurant
Fine dining
Lord Bryon's Walk, Seaham, Durham SR7 7AG
t (0191) 516 1400
w seaham-hall.com

Pubs

Collins
Global
183 Front Street, Chester-le-Street DH3 3AX
t (0191) 389 4900

The County
13 The Green, Aycliffe, Darlington DL5 6LX
t (01325) 312273
w the-county.co.uk

Inn on the Green
English
Waldridge, Chester-le-Street DH2 3LY
t (0191) 389 0439
w hollathans.co.uk

Rose and Crown
Romaldkirk, Barnard Castle DL12 9EB
t (01833) 650213
w rose-and-crown.co.uk

Whitworth Hall Country Park Hotel
Nr Spennymoor, Durham DL16 7QX
t (01388) 811772
w whitworthhall.co.uk

Tearooms, coffee shops and cafes

Beavers Tea Room
4 Market Place, Barnard Castle DL12 8ND
t (01833) 637634

Bowes Cafe
Bowes Musuem, Barnard Castle DL12 8NP
t (01833) 690606
w thebowesmuseum.org.uk

Castlegate Cafe
8 Market Place, Bishops Auckland DL14 7NJ
t (01388) 608770

Country Style Bakery & Tea Rooms
20 Market Place, Middleton DL12 0QS
t (01833) 640924

Durham Dales Centre
Castle Gardens, Stanhope, Weardale DL13 2SJ
t (01388) 527650
w durhamdalescentre.co.uk

The Market Place Tea Shop
29 Market Place, Barnard Castle, Durham DL12 8NE
t (01833) 690110

where to stay in

County Durham

Maps
All place names in the blue bands are shown on the maps at the front of this guide.

Accommodation symbols
Symbols give useful information about services and facilities. Inside the back-cover flap you can find a key to these symbols. Keep it open for easy reference.

BALDERSDALE, County Durham Map ref 1B3 — **SELF CATERING**

★★★
SELF CATERING

Units 1
Sleeps 4
Low season per wk
£200.00–£275.00
High season per wk
£275.00–£350.00

Clove Lodge Cottage, Barnard Castle

contact Mrs Caroline Carter, Clove Lodge Cottage, Baldersdale, Barnard Castle DL12 9UP
t (01833) 650030 **e** carolinecarter69@aol.com **w** clovelodge.co.uk

A stone-built Victorian cottage in a spectacular location on the Pennine Way. Ideal for sightseeing, walking, wildlife and relaxation.

open All year
payment Cash/cheques

Unit
General Leisure Shop 7 miles Pub 7 miles

BARNARD CASTLE, County Durham Map ref 1B3 — **GUEST ACCOMMODATION**

★★★★
BED & BREAKFAST

B&B per room per night
s £24.00–£28.00
d Max £48.00

Kirkstone

Marwood, Barnard Castle DL12 8QS **t** (01833) 690497 **f** (01833) 690497 **e** dstonekirk@aol.com

Kirkstone has one en suite double bedroom on the ground floor, and a conservatory for guests to relax in. Only 1.5 miles from Barnard Castle.

open All year except Christmas and New Year
bedrooms 1 double
bathrooms En suite
payment Cash/cheques

Room General Leisure

BARNARD CASTLE, County Durham Map ref 1B3 — **SELF CATERING**

★★★★
SELF CATERING

Units 1
Sleeps 4
Low season per wk
£275.00–£305.00
High season per wk
£380.00–£415.00

Boot and Shoe Cottage, Wycliffe, Barnard Castle

contact Mrs Rachel Peat, Waterside Cottage, Wycliffe, Barnard Castle DL12 9TR
t (01833) 627200 **f** (01833) 627200 **e** info@bootandshoecottage.co.uk **w** bootandshoecottage.co.uk

open All year
payment Cash/cheques

An idyllic cottage overlooking the River Tees. Once a cobbler's and a pub, it has been beautifully renovated with period features retained. Beamed sitting room with open fire, kitchen/dining with french windows on to garden and river. Welcome hamper. Ideal for exploring Durham and North Yorkshire.

Turn north off A66 at Greta Bridge. Two miles to Wycliffe. In village continue along private (concrete) road for 800yds to cottage.

Short breaks and late-booking offers. See website for details.

Unit
General Leisure Shop 2 miles Pub 0.5 miles

BARNARD CASTLE, County Durham Map ref 1B3 **SELF CATERING**

★★★★
SELF CATERING

Units 1
Sleeps 2–3
Low season per wk
£285.00–£295.00
High season per wk
£345.00–£395.00

Riverdale Cottage, Barnard Castle

contact Mrs Allyson Bunn, 2 Ridgeway Crescent, Barnes, Sunderland SR3 1YL
t (0191) 511 0555 & 07966 158127 **e** info@riverdale-cottage.co.uk **w** riverdale-cottage.co.uk

open All year
payment Cash/cheques

A perfect location for a memorable cottage holiday in Teesdale. Enjoy miles of fantastic woodland walks, see historic Barnard Castle and Bowes Museum, and have all the amenities of a market town that's full of life. Best of all, there are more pubs, restaurants and antique shops than you can shake a stick at!

Leave the A1(M) at Scotch Corner, join A66 West, take B6277 to Barnard Castle. Riverdale Cottage is close to the Tourist Information Centre and post office.

3-night stays available Nov-Feb (excl Christmas and New Year). Check our website for details.

Unit
General P Leisure Shop < 0.5 miles Pub < 0.5 miles

BISHOP AUCKLAND, County Durham Map ref 1C2 **SELF CATERING**

★★★★
SELF CATERING

Units 1
Sleeps 1–5
Low season per wk
£190.00–£240.00
High season per wk
£250.00–£350.00

Five Gables Cottage, Binchester, Bishop Auckland

contact Richard Lee and Allan Barker, Five Gables Cottage, Granville Terrace, Binchester, Bishop Auckland DL14 8AT
t (01388) 606898 **e** cottage@fivegables.co.uk **w** fivegables.co.uk

open All year
payment Credit/debit cards, cash/cheques

Traditional, Victorian, two-bedroom miner's cottage with country views, at edge of quiet hamlet. Tastefully restored and well appointed offering clean, quality comfort. Lawn, gardens and parking to the front and side. Ideal centre for north-east England – Durham, Beamish, Hadrian's Wall and railway heritage. Dogs welcome. Good country walks.

From A1(M) jct 60. Situated 300yds from A688 between Bishop Auckland and Spennymoor. In village, 1st left into cul-de-sac.

3-night breaks available in low season (excl Christmas and New Year). Special offers advertised on our website.

Unit
General 5 P Leisure Shop 0.5 miles Pub 1 mile

BOWES, County Durham Map ref 1B3 **SELF CATERING**

★★★★
SELF CATERING

Units 5
Sleeps 2–4
Low season per wk
£150.00–£200.00
High season per wk
£200.00–£270.00

Mellwaters Barn, Bowes, Barnard Castle

contact Mr Andrew Tavener, Mellwaters Barn, East Mellwaters Farm, Stainmore Road, Bowes, Barnard Castle DL12 9RH
t (01833) 628181 **f** (01833) 628020 **e** mellwatesbarn@aol.com **w** mellwatersbarn.co.uk

open All year
payment Cash/cheques

Wake up to wildlife on the edge of England's last wilderness, with quiet country roads and magnificent scenery. These spacious and airy cottages are fully equipped and are designed to give maximum possible access. Some cottages can be joined together for larger parties. Prices include linen, heating, electricity etc.

One mile west of Bowes, take a left-hand turn off the A66, trans-Pennine route.

Short breaks (3 nights) available from £110 for a 2-bedded cottage to £190 for a 4-bedded cottage.

Unit
General P Leisure Shop 1 mile Pub 1 mile

CASTLESIDE, County Durham Map ref 1B2 — **GUEST ACCOMMODATION**

★★★★
GUEST ACCOMMODATION

B&B per room per night
s £25.00–£30.00
d £45.00–£50.00

Dene View

15 Front Street, Consett DH8 9AR **t** (01207) 502925 **e** catherine@deneview.co.uk
w deneview.co.uk

open All year
bedrooms 1 double, 1 twin, 2 single
bathrooms All en suite
payment Cash/cheques

Superior accommodation in Castleside village on edge of beautiful Durham Dales. Situated on main A68 road to/from Scotland. The rooms are furnished to a high quality. Close to Beamish Museum, Durham City, Newcastle, Hexham.

Room General **P**

COCKFIELD, County Durham Map ref 1B3 — **SELF CATERING**

★★★
SELF CATERING

Units **1**
Sleeps **2**

Low season per wk
£245.00
High season per wk
£245.00

New Cottage, Bishop Auckland

contact Mrs Margaret Partridge, New Cottage, Hollymoor Farm, Cockfield, Bishop Auckland DL13 5HF
t (01388) 718567 **f** (01388) 718567

open All year
payment Cash/cheques

Relaxing break required? A warm hospitable welcome awaits guests to this delightful, cosy, comfortable, well-equipped cottage on a working farm. Relax amidst spectacular panoramic views from the lounge and witness truly magnificent sunsets. Good pub food within two miles. Towels, linen, electricity, oil-fired central heating included.

Unit
General **P** Leisure **Shop** 0.5 miles **Pub** 0.5 miles

CROOK, County Durham Map ref 1C2 — **HOTEL**

★★★
HOTEL

B&B per room per night
s £56.00
d £94.00
HB per person per night
£69.00

Helme Park Hall Hotel & Restaurant

Fir Tree, Bishop Auckland DL13 4NW **t** (01388) 730970 **f** (01388) 731799
e reception@helmeparkhotel.co.uk **w** helmeparkhotel.co.uk

open All year
bedrooms 9 double, 2 twin, 2 single
bathrooms All en suite
payment Credit/debit cards, cash/cheques

Comfortable, privately owned, recently refurbished hotel offering a welcoming atmosphere and incorporating our new acclaimed Elgees Restaurant. Food is of the highest quality with plentiful bar meals, table d'hote or a la carte meals. Spectacular views over the Dales. Easily accessible with good parking. With its two acres of grounds it offers a haven of peace and tranquillity.

On the main A68, between Corbridge and Darlington, 2 miles east of Tow Law, near Wolsingham and Fir Tree.

Weekend breaks from £109.95pp for 2 nights including accommodation, English breakfast and table d'hote evening meal. Christmas and New Year breaks.

Room General Leisure

DURHAM, County Durham Map ref 1C2 **HOTEL**

★★★★
HOTEL

B&B per room per night
s £89.00–£145.00
d £138.00–£175.00
HB per person per night
£85.00–£100.00

Ramside Hall Classic Hotel & Golf Club

Carrville, Durham DH1 1TD **t** (0191) 386 5282 **f** (0191) 386 0399 **e** mail@ramsidehallhotel.co.uk
w ramsidehallhotel.co.uk

open All year
bedrooms 47 double, 30 twin, 2 single, 2 suites
bathrooms All en suite
payment Credit/debit cards, cash/cheques, euros

Ramside Hall Hotel & Golf Club is all about quality, comfort and friendly service. Beautifully presented public areas/lounges, comfortable, spacious bedrooms, two bars, two eating areas, exceptional traditional food at value-for-money prices. Set in attractive gardens and surrounded by 27 holes of challenging scenic golf. Golf clubhouse, shop, floodlit range and Golf Academy.

Jct 62 off the main A1M. Travel 400m A690 towards Sunderland. Go under the railway bridge, turn right over the dual carriageway. You have arrived.

Room General Leisure

DURHAM, County Durham Map ref 1C2 **GUEST ACCOMMODATION**

★★
BED & BREAKFAST

B&B per room per night
s £50.00–£55.00
d £65.00–£75.00
Evening meal per person
£10.00–£15.00

WALKERS WELCOME

66 Claypath

Durham DH1 1QT **t** (0191) 384 3193 **f** (0191) 386 9989 **e** richard@66claypath.co.uk
w 66claypath.co.uk

open All year except Christmas
bedrooms 1 double, 1 single
payment Cash/cheques, euros

A Grade II Listed Georgian town house, with a delightful secluded garden. Comfortable rooms are beautifully decorated and furnished. Quality breakfasts are prepared fresh to order. A short walk from Durham's market square, castle, cathedral and riverside paths. Ideally located for exploring all the North East has to offer.

Room General Leisure

DURHAM, County Durham Map ref 1C2 **GUEST ACCOMMODATION**

♦♦–♦♦♦♦
GUEST ACCOMMODATION

B&B per room per night
s £28.50–£39.50
d £51.00–£80.00
Evening meal per person
£8.00–£16.00

Durham University

Conference and Tourism Office, Stockton Road, Durham DH1 3UP **t** (0191) 334 2887
f (0191) 334 2892 **e** event@durham.ac.uk

open All year except Christmas and New Year
bedrooms 24 double, 110 twin, 4000 single, 1 family, 1 suite
bathrooms 1500 en suite
payment Credit/debit cards, cash/cheques

Accommodation at Durham University is an excellent choice for both the single or group traveller. Our colleges are set in their own grounds each with unique character. Accommodation is available from only £25.50 per person sharing a twin room.

Turn off the A1(M) and onto the A690 to Durham City. Individual college locations will be confirmed at time of booking.

Room General Leisure

DURHAM, County Durham Map ref 1C2 — **GUEST ACCOMMODATION**

♦♦♦♦
GUEST ACCOMMODATION

B&B per room per night
s £35.00
d £60.00–£70.00

Hillrise Guest House

13 Durham Road West, Bowburn, Durham DH6 5AU **t** (0191) 377 0302 **f** (0191) 377 0898
e enquiries@hill-rise.com **w** hill-rise.com

Conveniently placed 200yds from junction 61 A1(M). Family, twin and double rooms with en suite facilities. Friendly atmosphere and a high standard of cleanliness.

open All year
bedrooms 2 double, 2 twin, 1 family
bathrooms All en suite
payment Credit/debit cards, cash/cheques, euros

Room General 12 Leisure

DURHAM, County Durham Map ref 1C2 — **CAMPING & CARAVANNING**

★★★★
TOURING PARK

(20) Min £16.00
(20) Min £16.00
Min £16.00
50 touring pitches

Finchale Abbey Caravan Park

Finchale Abbey Farm, Finchale Abbey, Durham DH1 5SH **t** (0191) 386 6528 & 07989 854704
f (0191) 386 1571 **e** godricawatson@hotmail.com **w** finchaleabbey.co.uk

open All year
payment Credit/debit cards, cash/cheques

Finchale Abbey (Priory) touring park is set in beautiful countryside overlooking the ruins, surrounded by the River Wear. Fishing, golf, riverside walks and the local bar are a short distance away. Durham is 0.75 miles away by bike along scenic bridle paths.

General P Leisure

DURHAM, County Durham Map ref 1C2 — **CAMPING & CARAVANNING**

★★★★★
TOURING & CAMPING PARK

(77) £12.50–£25.10
(77) £12.50–£25.10
77 touring pitches

See Ad on inside front cover

CENTENARY THE CARAVAN CLUB 1907 · 2007

Grange Caravan Club Site

Meadow Lane, Durham DH1 1TL **t** (0191) 384 4778 **w** caravanclub.co.uk

open All year
payment Credit/debit cards, cash/cheques

An open, level site, this is a lovely location for a short break and an ideal stopover en route to or from Scotland.

A1(M) jct 62, A690 towards Durham. Turn right after 50m. Signposted Maureen Terrace and brown caravan sign.

Special member rates mean you can save your membership subscription in less than a week. Visit our website to find out more.

General P Leisure

DURHAM, County Durham Map ref 1C2 — **CAMPING & CARAVANNING**

★★★★
HOLIDAY, TOURING & CAMPING PARK
ROSE AWARD

(35) £14.50–£16.50
(35) £14.50–£16.50
(10) £12.50–£16.50
(3) £295.00–£365.00
45 touring pitches

Strawberry Hill Farm Camping & Caravanning Park

Running Waters, Old Cassop, Durham DH6 4QA **t** (0191) 372 3457 **f** (0191) 372 2512
e howarddunkerley@strawberryhillfarm.freeserve.co.uk **w** strawberry-hill-farm.co.uk

Situated in open countryside with magnificent, panoramic views. Ideally situated to explore the World Heritage site of the castle and cathedral. For further details please see website. Open March to December.

payment Credit/debit cards, cash/cheques, euros

General P

HAMSTERLEY FOREST

See under Barnard Castle, Bishop Auckland, Crook, Stanhope, Wolsingham

HARWOOD, County Durham Map ref 1B2 — SELF CATERING

★★★★
SELF CATERING

Units 1
Sleeps 4
Low season per wk
Max £180.00
High season per wk
£280.00–£350.00

Frog Hall Cottage, Barnard Castle

contact Ms Kath Toward, Herd Ship Farm, Barnard Castle DL12 0YB
t (01833) 622215 **f** (01833) 622215 **e** kath.herdship@btinternet.com **w** herdship.co.uk

open All year
payment Cash/cheques

Secluded, stone-built dales cottage in spectacular setting in the centre of an award-winning environmental farm on the edge the Pennine moorland. Magnificent views of wading birds, flowering meadows, rare flowers and black grouse. Adjacent to National Nature Reserve. Private garden area.

Take the Alston Road (B6277) and follow for 10 miles. After passing Langdon Beck, left at next telephone box, follow lane until you reach Frog Hall.

Unit
General P Shop 10 miles Pub 3 miles

LANCHESTER, County Durham Map ref 1C2 — GUEST ACCOMMODATION

★★★
GUEST ACCOMMODATION

B&B per room per night
s Max £44.95
d Max £44.95

Kings Head Hotel

Station Road, Lanchester, Durham DH7 0EX **t** (01207) 520054 **e** info@accommodation-durham.com
w accommodation-durham.com

open All year
bedrooms 5 double/twin, 1 single
bathrooms All en suite
payment Credit/debit cards, cash/cheques

Situated in the beautiful village of Lanchester, overlooking the village green. An ideal location for visiting Durham, Newcastle, Consett and Gateshead, with local attractions such as Beamish Museum and country walks nearby.

From south: A1 jct 62. Left onto A690 for 2.3 miles, right onto A691 (Consett). From north: A1 south. Right onto A692 for 9.2 miles, left onto A691 for 3.6 miles.

Room General P

OVINGTON, County Durham Map ref 1B3 — GUEST ACCOMMODATION

★★★
INN

B&B per room per night
s £30.00
d £55.00
Evening meal per person
£7.00–£15.00

The Four Alls

Ovington, Richmond DL11 7BP **t** (01833) 627302

open All year
bedrooms 1 double, 2 twin, 2 single
bathrooms 3 en suite, 2 private
payment Credit/debit cards, cash/cheques

Privately run establishment offering quality accommodation and food in a quiet and beautiful village setting. Centrally located for exploring local area and places of interest.

From A1(M) Scotch Corner, take A66 towards Brough. After 6 miles, turn right to Hutton Magna, through village and on to Ovington.

2 nights' B&B £100 – based on 2 people sharing double or twin room. Subject to availability.

Room General 8 P Leisure

Key to symbols

Open the back flap for a key to symbols.

RAMSHAW, County Durham Map ref 1B2 **CAMPING & CARAVANNING**

★★★
HOLIDAY, TOURING & CAMPING PARK
(40) £12.00–£15.00
(40) £12.00–£15.00
40 touring pitches

Craggwood Caravan Park

Gordon Lane, Ramshaw, Bishop Auckland DL14 0NS **t** (01388) 835866 **f** (01388) 835866
e billy6482@btopenworld.com **w** craggwoodcaravanpark.co.uk

Craggwood Caravan Park is set in approximately 60 acres with lovely views, woodland and a river running through the park. Open 1 March to 31 October.

payment Credit/debit cards, cash/cheques

General Leisure

SPENNYMOOR, County Durham Map ref 1C2 **GUEST ACCOMMODATION**

★★★★
GUEST HOUSE
B&B per room per night
s Min £40.00
d Min £60.00

Highview Country House

Kirk Merrington, Spennymoor DL16 7JT **t** (01388) 811006 **f** (01388) 811006
e jayne@highviewcountryhouse.co.uk **w** highviewcountryhouse.com

Country house in one acre of gardens surrounded by countryside. Peace and tranquillity await. Safe parking. Situated on the edge of delightful village. Good pubs, Saxon church. Ten minutes from motorway/Durham.

open All year
bedrooms 5 double, 1 twin, 1 single, 1 family
bathrooms All en suite
payment Credit/debit cards, cash/cheques

Room General P Leisure

STANHOPE, County Durham Map ref 1B2 **SELF CATERING**

★★★
SELF CATERING
Units 2
Sleeps 4–9
Low season per wk
£150.00–£240.00
High season per wk
£240.00–£280.00

Stanhope Morningside, Bishop Auckland

contact Mr William Stobbs & Miss Donna Walton, Newfield Farm, East Lane, Stanhope, Bishop Auckland DL13 2YX
t (01388) 527045 **f** (01388) 527045 **e** williamstobbs@aol.com **w** stanhopemorningside.co.uk

Stanhope Morningside self-catering cottage is located in Stanhope at the heart of Weardale in the North Pennines. Recently renovated farm building comprising two units.

open All year
payment Cash/cheques

Unit
General P Shop < 0.5 miles Pub < 0.5 miles

STANLEY, County Durham Map ref 1C2 **GUEST ACCOMMODATION**

★★★
FARMHOUSE
B&B per room per night
s £30.00–£35.00
d £50.00

Bushblades Farm

Harperley, Stanley DH9 9UA **t** (01207) 232722

open All year except Christmas and New Year
bedrooms 1 double, 1 twin
bathrooms All en suite
payment Cash/cheques

60-acre livestock farm. Georgian farmhouse with large garden in rural setting. Both rooms en suite (one ground floor) with colour TV, tea/coffee facilities and comfortable chairs. Tasty breakfasts, separate tables. Ideal base or stopover. Close to Beamish Museum, Durham and A1(M). Hadrian's Wall and Alnwick under an hour.

Leave A1(M) at Chester-le-Street for Stanley on A693, then Consett. Half a mile after Stanley follow signs for Harperley. Farm is on right, 0.5 miles from crossroads.

Room General 12 P

Check it out

Please check prices, quality ratings and other details when you book.

STANLEY, County Durham Map ref 1C2 — **GUEST ACCOMMODATION**

♦♦♦
GUEST ACCOMMODATION

B&B per room per night
s £38.00–£52.00
d £54.00–£73.00
Evening meal per person
£4.95–£14.95

Harperley Hotel

Harperley Country Park, Stanley DH9 9TY **t** (01207) 234011 **f** (01207) 232325
e info@harperleyhotel.co.uk **w** harperleyhotel.co.uk

open All year
bedrooms 3 double, 2 single, 1 family
bathrooms All en suite
payment Credit/debit cards, cash/cheques

The hotel stands next to an old mill in a country park, offering a quiet and relaxing setting. The granary dates back to 1850 and is surrounded by 3.5 acres of ancient woodlands and walks.

A1(M) jct 61, take A693. At Stanley A6075 towards Tanfield. B6173 for 1 mile, take unmarked left turn opposite church. Approx 1 mile to Harperley.

♥ *Murder mystery/fright nights, incl 3-course meal, £15pp.*

Room General P Leisure

STANLEY, County Durham Map ref 1C2 — **SELF CATERING**

★★★
SELF CATERING

Units **1**
Sleeps **3**
Low season per wk
£175.00–£250.00
High season per wk
£250.00–£300.00

Bushblades Farm Cottage, Stanley

contact Mrs Pamela Gibson, Bushblades Farm, Harperley, Stanley DH9 9UA
t (01207) 232722

open All year except Christmas and New Year
payment Cash/cheques

Comfortable farm cottage with beamed ceilings, own private garden and patio. The cottage has one large bedroom with a double and a single bed. Nearest supermarket one mile. Ideal base. Close to Beamish Museum and Durham. Hadrian's Wall and Northumberland coast under an hour. A1(M) ten minutes.

Unit
General 5 P Shop 1 mile Pub 0.5 miles

WOLSINGHAM, County Durham Map ref 1B2 — **SELF CATERING**

★★★–★★★★
SELF CATERING

Units **4**
Sleeps **1–7**
Low season per wk
£190.00–£450.00
High season per wk
£280.00–£600.00

Bradley Burn Holiday Cottages, Bishop Auckland

contact Mrs Judith Stephenson, Bradley Burn Holiday Cottages, Bradley Burn Farm, Wolsingham, Bishop Auckland DL13 3JH
t (01388) 527285 **f** (01388) 527285 **e** jas@bradleyburn.co.uk **w** bradleyburn.co.uk

open All year
payment Cash/cheques, euros

Small complex of interesting barn conversions, with all modern amenities. Situated on our working farm in east Weardale. Ideal touring/walking base. Granary Cottage is ideal for families (three bedrooms, one en suite), whilst Stable Cottages and Harvest Cottage are perfect for couples.

Bradley Burn is adjacent to A689, the main road through Weardale, between A68 junction and Wolsingham.

Unit
General P Leisure

What's in a quality rating?

Information about ratings and awards can be found at the front of this guide.

Breathtaking views over Ullswater in The Lake District

Sail across rippling waters of picture-perfect lakes, gaze in awe at soaring peaks and roaming wildlife. Feel the adrenalin pumping with an array of outdoor pursuits and wind down by tucking in to some hearty local dishes.

Explore Cumbria – The Lake District

Take to the water

Be inspired by glorious watery scenes reflecting the mighty peaks in this stunning region. Climb aboard at the Windermere Outdoor Adventure Activities Centre where you can paddle a canoe, relax in a wayfarer or skim the waters on a powerboat.

Cruise across Coniston Water in The National Trust's steam-powered yacht – fusing classic Venetian gondola designs with Victorian steam technology. Meet Dolly, the oldest mechanically powered boat in the world, at Windermere Steam Boats & Museum and imagine her crew trawling the lakes over 100 years ago.

Prefer to stay on dry land? Ascend Scafell Pike, England's highest mountain, for magnificent views of Wastwater, England's deepest lake. Or clear your mind, wind down and be mesmerised by the setting sun seen from Friar's Crag beside Derwentwater.

Rowing peacefully across Windermere

Spinning spokes on the Eskdale Trail

Best foot forward

Pull your boots on and walk alongside Hadrian's Wall for spectacular views and reach a visitor centre detailing its 1,800-year history. Step up your pace: tackle the 190-mile Cumbria Coastal Way and pass by the fells, lakes, towns, villages and beaches of the Lake District National Park. Test your climbing skills or swing through the trees in Grizedale Forest on the Go Ape! Adventure Trail. For more adventure visit South Lakes Animal Park, where you can walk across treetops for a spectacular view of the park and watch tigers climbing trees to hunt for food.

Journey back in time with a ride aboard the miniature Ravenglass and Eskdale Railway. Store your bicycle on board and get the spokes spinning on the way back. Admire the beauty and tranquillity of Dalemain House, near Ullswater, or head south and stop to breathe in the scent of the immaculately kept, award-winning gardens at Holker Hall. Stroll around Long Meg and her Daughters near Penrith – one of the largest stone circles in the country – where you can almost hear the spirit of Wordsworth uttering his profound verse.

Let wonderful tales come to life at The World of Beatrix Potter, Bowness-on-Windermere

Finding inspiration

In a region where one is so easily transfixed by natural beauty, it is little wonder that so many literary geniuses have sought inspiration in Cumbria. Experience it for yourself as you wander around Dove Cottage in Grasmere, home of William Wordsworth and arguably where he wrote his finest romantic poetry.

Crawl into Mr McGregor's Greenhouse at The World of Beatrix Potter and imagine the fear poor Peter Rabbit felt creeping through the undergrowth! Or pay a visit to Hill Top, the delightful 17th-century farmhouse where the author devised many of her animal creations. Take time to wander around Brantwood in Coniston – one of the most beautifully located houses in the region and once home to John Ruskin, a champion of many aspects of civil society that remain in place today.

Treat your tastebuds

Garnering a reputation as one of the premier UK food destinations, here you'll find more Michelin-starred restaurants than anywhere outside of London. Sink your teeth into a juicy Cumberland sausage or a mouthful of traditional black pudding and wash it down with local ale or damson beer.

Stock up on fresh, local produce at Low Sizergh Barn near Kendal and feast your eyes on the vast array of tempting regional treats at Rheged Food Hall near Penrith. Seek out award-winning relish in Hawkshead and nibble on Sarah Nelson's historic gingerbread at Church Cottage in Grasmere.

Dine out in fine bistros and luxurious establishments, or settle down by the roaring fire in a cosy country pub and let the local delicacies both comfort and satisfy.

Food & drink

Fancy a bite to eat, a relaxing drink or some fresh local produce? Here's a selection of food and drink venues to get you started. For lots more ideas go online at **enjoyengland.com/taste**.

Restaurants

1 Park Road
Italian
Windermere LA23 2AW
t (015394) 42107
w 1parkroad.com

Appleby Manor Country House Hotel
Fine dining
Roman Road, Appleby-in-Westmorland CA16 6JB
t (01768) 351571
w applebymanor.co.uk

Bassenthwaite Lake
English
Ouse Bridge Hotel, Bassenthwaite Lake, Dubwath, Cockermouth CA13 9YD
t (01768) 776322
w ousebridge.com

The Glass House Restaurant
English
Rydal Road, Ambleside LA22 9AN
t (015394) 32137
w theglasshouserestaurant.co.uk

Jerichos Restaurant
European
Birch Street, Windermere LA23 1EG
t (015394) 42522
w jerichos.co.uk

The Jumble Room
Global
Langdale Road, Grasmere LA22 9SU
t (015394) 35188
w thejumbleroom.co.uk

The Waterhead
Fine dining
Lake Road, Ambleside LA22 0ER
t (015394) 32566
w elh.co.uk/restaurants

The Weary
Fine dining
Castle Carrock, Carlisle CA8 9LU
t (01228) 670230
w theweary.com

Winder Hall Hotel
Fine dining
Low Lorton, Cockermouth CA13 9UP
t (01900) 85107
w winderhall.co.uk

Pubs

The Bay Horse
Canal Foot, Ulverston LE12 9EL
t (01229) 583972
w thebayhorsehotel.co.uk

Drunken Duck Inn
Barnsgate, Ambleside LA22 0NG
t (015394) 36347
w drunkenduckinn.co.uk

Eagle & Child
Kendal Road, Staveley, Kendal LA8 9LP
t (01539) 821320
w eaglechildinn.co.uk

The Pooley Bridge Inn
Pooley Bridge, Lake Ullswater, Penrith CA10 2NN
t (01768) 486215
w pooleybridgeinn.co.uk

The Punch Bowl Inn
Crosswaite, Lyth Valley LA8 8HR
t (015395) 68237
w punchbowl.co.uk

The Woolpack Inn
Boot, Holmrook, Eskdale CA19 1TH
t (019467) 23230
w woolpack.co.uk

Tearooms, coffee shops and cafes

The Bridge Cafe & Bistro
Newby Bridge, Ulverston LA12 8ND
t (015395) 30667
w thebridgecafebistro.com

The Gincase
Mawbray Hayrigg, Silloth, Wigton CA7 4LL
t (016973) 32020
w gincase.co.uk

Hazelmere Cafe and Bakery
1 Yewbarrow Terrace, Grange-over-Sands LA11 6ED
t (015395) 32972
w hazelmerecafe.co.uk

High Head Sculpture Valley Tearoom
High Head Farm, Ivegill, Carlisle CA4 0PJ
t (016974) 73552
w highheadsculpturevalley.co.uk

Delis

Ainsworth Specialist Grocers
Kents Bank Road, Grange-over-Sands LA11 7EY
t (015395) 32946

Cranstons
Ullswater Road, Penrith CA11 7EH
t (01768) 868680
w cranstons.net

Farm shops and local produce

Greystone House Farm Shop and Tearoom
Stainton, Penrith CA11 0EF
t (01768) 866952
w greystonehousefarm.co.uk

Wellington Jersey's
Wellington Farm, Lamplugh Road Cockermouth CA13 0QU
t (01900) 822777
w wellingtonjerseys.co.uk

where to stay in
Cumbria – The Lake District

Maps
All place names in the blue bands are shown on the maps at the front of this guide.

Accommodation symbols
Symbols give useful information about services and facilities. Inside the back-cover flap you can find a key to these symbols. Keep it open for easy reference.

AMBLESIDE, Cumbria Map ref 1A3 — **GUEST ACCOMMODATION**

★★★★
GUEST ACCOMMODATION

B&B per room per night
s £26.00–£30.00
d £59.00–£69.00

3 Cambridge Villas

Church Street, Ambleside LA22 9DL **t** (015394) 32307 **e** cambridgevillas3@aol.com
w 3cambridgevillas.co.uk

Elegant stone Victorian house situated in the heart of Ambleside. Central to all amenities. Cyclists and walkers welcome. Secure lock-up available for mountain bikes.

open All year except Christmas
bedrooms 3 double, 2 twin/double/family, 2 single
bathrooms 5 en suite, 2 private
payment Credit/debit cards, cash/cheques

Room General Leisure

AMBLESIDE, Cumbria Map ref 1A3 — **GUEST ACCOMMODATION**

★★★★
GUEST HOUSE SILVER AWARD

B&B per room per night
s £35.00–£70.00
d £59.00–£75.00

Barnes Fell Guest House

Low Gale, Ambleside LA22 0BB **t** (015394) 33311 **f** (015394) 33311 **e** info@barnesfell.co.uk
w barnesfell.co.uk

open All year except Christmas
bedrooms 3 double
bathrooms All en suite
payment Cash/cheques

Lovely restored Victorian house with fabulous views. Delightful, non-smoking, Laura Ashley or four-poster bedrooms. Great choice of top-quality breakfasts. Quiet, but close to village centre.

From south, 1st right off A591 into Old Lake Road. Fork right into Low Gale. House on right. From north, left into Old Lake Road. 1st left.

Room General

AMBLESIDE, Cumbria Map ref 1A3 — **GUEST ACCOMMODATION**

★★★
GUEST HOUSE

B&B per room per night
s £25.00–£39.00
d £50.00–£70.00

Croyden House

Church Street, Ambleside LA22 0BU **t** (015394) 32209 **e** sylvia@croydenhouseambleside.co.uk
w croydenhouseambleside.co.uk

Croyden House is in a quiet area of Ambleside town centre close to bus stop and wide selection of eating establishments to suit all tastes. Time of arrival and early breakfasts can be arranged. Private car park.

open All year
bedrooms 4 double, 2 twin, 2 single, 2 family
bathrooms 8 en suite, 2 private
payment Credit/debit cards, cash/cheques

Room General P Leisure

AMBLESIDE, Cumbria Map ref 1A3 — **GUEST ACCOMMODATION**

★★★★ GUEST ACCOMMODATION SILVER AWARD

B&B per room per night
s £28.00–£85.00
d £56.00–£90.00

Elder Grove

Lake Road, Ambleside LA22 0DB **t** (015394) 32504 **f** (015394) 32251 **e** info@eldergrove.co.uk **w** eldergrove.co.uk

Our traditional Victorian house is ideally situated for restaurants, shops, walking and sightseeing. All rooms en suite, fantastic Cumbrian breakfasts, relaxing bar with free Internet access, lounge and car park. Non-smoking.

open All year except Christmas
bedrooms 6 double, 1 twin, 2 single, 1 family
bathrooms All en suite
payment Credit/debit cards, cash/cheques

Room General P Leisure

AMBLESIDE, Cumbria Map ref 1A3 — **GUEST ACCOMMODATION**

★★★ GUEST HOUSE

B&B per room per night
s £28.00–£32.00
d £58.00–£70.00

Thorneyfield Guest House

Compston Road, Ambleside LA22 9DJ **t** (015394) 32464 **f** 0870 167 1968 **e** info@thorneyfield.co.uk **w** thorneyfield.co.uk

open All year except Christmas
bedrooms 2 double, 1 twin, 2 family
bathrooms 4 en suite, 1 private
payment Credit/debit cards, cash/cheques

Charming Victorian property set in the heart of Ambleside and its many facilities. Thorneyfield sets a very high standard for its rooms (including two large family rooms), breakfasts and the quality of its service. We also offer our guests free parking. Strictly non-smoking for your convenience.

From A591 follow one-way system onto Compston Road. We are just past recreation ground and church on left-hand side, just before the cinema.

See our website for regular updates on our special offers.

Room General 5 Leisure

AMBLESIDE, Cumbria Map ref 1A3 — **GUEST ACCOMMODATION**

♦♦♦♦ GUEST ACCOMMODATION

B&B per room per night
s £30.00–£38.00
d £28.00–£32.00

Tock How Farm

High Wray, Ambleside LA22 0JF **t** (015394) 36106 **e** info@tock-how-farm.com **w** tock-how-farm.com

open All year except Christmas and New Year
bedrooms 1 double, 1 twin, 1 family
bathrooms All en suite
payment Credit/debit cards, cash/cheques

Family-run working farm set in a stunning location overlooking Lake Windermere and the surrounding fells. Separate dining-room and lounge with log fire. Ideal base for exploring the Lakes by car or on foot.

Take B5286 to Hawkshead and turn left for Wray Castle. After High Wray Farm take the next right and bear left at the bottom of the hill.

Room General P Leisure

Check it out

Information on accommodation listed in this guide has been supplied by proprietors. As changes may occur you should remember to check all relevant details at the time of booking.

AMBLESIDE, Cumbria Map ref 1A3 — **GUEST ACCOMMODATION**

♦♦♦♦
GUEST ACCOMMODATION

B&B per room per night
s £40.00–£50.00
d £80.00–£200.00
Evening meal per person
£8.95–£14.95

Wateredge Inn

Waterhead Bay, Ambleside LA22 0EP **t** (015394) 32332 **f** (015394) 31878
e stay@wateredgeinn.co.uk **w** wateredgeinn.co.uk

open All year
bedrooms 9 double, 6 twin, 3 single, 4 family
bathrooms All en suite
payment Credit/debit cards, cash/cheques

Delightfully situated family-run inn on the shores of Windermere at Waterhead Bay. Enjoy country-inn-style dining, freshly prepared gourmet bar food, real ales and fine wines, all served overlooking the lake. Pretty bedrooms, many with lake views, offer the best of Lakeland comfort.

From M6 jct 36 follow A591 through to Ambleside. At Waterhead bear left at traffic lights. Wateredge is on left at end of promenade.

3-night mid-week breaks from £105pp.

Room General Leisure

AMBLESIDE, Cumbria Map ref 1A3 — **SELF CATERING**

★★★
SELF CATERING

Units 1
Sleeps 2–6
Low season per wk
£200.00–£300.00
High season per wk
£300.00–£550.00

Hole House, Ambleside

contact Clare Irvine, Tock How Farm, High Wray, Ambleside LA22 0JF
t (015394) 36106 **e** info@tock-how-farm.com **w** tock-how-farm.com

open All year
payment Credit/debit cards, cash/cheques

Traditional 16thC longhouse and barn in peaceful location overlooking Blelham Tarn – with free fishing. The cottage has one double and two twin bedrooms. Lounge with open fire, kitchen/dining room and own garden.

Take B5286 to Hawkshead and turn left for Wray Castle. After High Wray Farm take the next right and carry straight on at bottom of the hill.

Unit
General Leisure Shop 2 miles Pub 2 miles

APPLEBY-IN-WESTMORLAND, Cumbria Map ref 1B3 — **HOTEL**

★★
HOTEL

B&B per room per night
s £39.00–£49.00
d £69.00
HB per person per night
Min £55.00

Royal Oak Inn

45 Bongate, Appleby-in-Westmorland CA16 6UN **t** (017683) 51463 **f** (017683) 52300
e jan@royaloakappleby.co.uk

open All year
bedrooms 4 double, 5 twin, 2 single, 1 family
bathrooms 11 en suite, 1 private
payment Credit/debit cards, cash/cheques

A charming 12thC coaching inn situated at the centre of the Eden Valley. Ideal for visiting the Lake District. Superb bar and restaurant guaranteed to serve only freshly prepared foods and quality cask ales. With nine en suite bedrooms and a holiday cottage The Royal Oak never fails to deliver.

From south-west: M6 jct 38, turn 12 miles to Appleby. Through town, right over bridge, 0.5 miles on left. From south-east: Appleby exit A66, 1.5 miles on left.

Bargain summer break mid-week 3 nights DB&B £152pp (standard room), £169pp (superior room). Bargain winter break – £149pp (standard room), £163pp (superior room).

Room General Leisure

APPLEBY-IN-WESTMORLAND, Cumbria Map ref 1B3 — **SELF CATERING**

★★★
SELF CATERING

Units **7**
Sleeps **2–7**
High season per wk
£220.00–£515.00

Milburn Grange Holiday Cottages, Appleby-in-Westmorland

Milburn Grange Holiday Cottages, Milburn Grange, Knock CA16 6DR
t (01768) 361867 **f** (01768) 362337 **e** holidays@milburngrange.co.uk **w** milburngrange.co.uk

open All year
payment Credit/debit cards, cash/cheques

Nestling at the foot of the Pennines and enjoying uninterrupted views of the Lakeland fells, our comfortable cottages offer a high standard of accommodation and are open all year. The seven cottages can sleep from two to six/seven people with large groups of up to 29 people possible.

⊕ *Exit jct 40 M6. Take the A66 towards Appleby and Scotch Corner. Turn left at Kirkby Thore to Milburn. See website for full directions.*

❤ *Short breaks available Oct-Mar and at other times subject to availability. Minimum 2-night stay. Contact us for prices.*

Unit
General P Leisure Shop 0.5 miles Pub 2 miles

APPLEBY-IN-WESTMORLAND, Cumbria Map ref 1B3 — **CAMPING & CARAVANNING**

★★★★★
HOLIDAY, TOURING & CAMPING PARK

(226) £15.50–£25.50
(157) £15.50–£25.50
(65) £15.50–£25.50
226 touring pitches

Wild Rose Park

Ormside, Appleby-in-Westmorland CA16 6EJ **t** (017683) 51077 **f** (017683) 52551

Friendly, family park in the lovely, unspoilt Eden Valley with mountain views. Within easy reach of the Lakes and the Dales. Spotless, super loos and private wash cubicles.

open All year
payment Credit/debit cards, cash

General P Leisure

ARMATHWAITE, Cumbria Map ref 1A2 — **CAMPING & CARAVANNING**

★★★★
TOURING PARK

(63) £8.50–£19.60
(63) £8.50–£19.60
63 touring pitches

See Ad on inside front cover

Englethwaite Hall Caravan Club Site

Armathwaite, Carlisle CA4 9SY **t** (01228) 560202 **w** caravanclub.co.uk

payment Credit/debit cards, cash/cheques

Tranquil site, scattered with rhododendrons. Walkers will love this beautiful, uncrowded area. Open March to November.

⊕ *Exit M6/A6 onto B6263, in 1.75 miles turn right. Site on right in about 2.75 miles.*

❤ *Special member rates mean you can save your membership subscription in less than a week. Visit our website to find out more.*

General P Leisure

Don't forget www.

Web addresses throughout this guide are shown without the prefix www. Please include www. in the address line of your browser. If a web address does not follow this style it is shown in full.

ASKHAM, Cumbria Map ref 1B3 — **SELF CATERING**

★★★★
SELF CATERING

Units 1
Sleeps 4
Low season per wk
Min £325.00
High season per wk
Max £500.00

Sycamore Barn Holiday Cottage, Ullswater

contact Ellen Pickup, Sycamore Barn Holiday Cottage, Sycamore House, Askham CA10 2PF
t (01931) 712410 **e** sycamorehousebarn@btinternet.com **w** sycamorehousebarn.com

open All year
payment Credit/debit cards, cash/cheques

Sycamore Barn is a high quality, beautifully furnished barn conversion attached to the owners' 18thC house situated in the pretty village of Askham, a conservation area on the Lowther Estate, in the Lake District National Park. Double bedroom (en suite shower room), twin bedroom (mezzanine with en suite bathroom). Excellent walking area.

⊕ *Travel directions can be viewed on the website and will also be sent with booking confirmation, Penrith railway station 5 miles.*

♥ *Short breaks (3 nights minimum) available.*

Unit
General Leisure Shop < 0.5 miles Pub < 0.5 miles

BASSENTHWAITE, Cumbria Map ref 1A2 — **SELF CATERING**

★★★★
SELF CATERING

Units 5
Sleeps 2–6
Low season per wk
£325.00–£700.00
High season per wk
£355.00–£730.00

Irton House Farm, Cockermouth

contact Mrs Almond, Irton House Farm, Isel, Cockermouth CA13 9ST
t (01768) 776380 **e** almond@farmersweekly.net **w** irtonhousefarm.com

Immaculate, spacious properties, all furnished to a high specification. Shopping at Keswick and Cockermouth. Superb views, walks and places of interest.

open All year
payment Credit/debit cards, cash/cheques

Unit
General Leisure Shop 1 mile Pub 3 miles

BOWNESS-ON-SOLWAY, Cumbria Map ref 1A2 — **GUEST ACCOMMODATION**

★★
BED & BREAKFAST

B&B per room per night
s £25.00
d £45.00

WALKERS WELCOME CYCLISTS WELCOME

The Old Chapel

Meadow View, Bowness-on-Solway, Wigton CA7 5BL **t** (01697) 351126
e oldchapelbowness@hotmail.com **w** oldchapelbownessonsolway.com

The Old Chapel is situated at the end of Hadrian's Wall and provides excellent facilities for walkers completing or starting the trail. Able to accommodate larger groups of visitors.

open All year
bedrooms 1 double, 2 twin, 1 family
bathrooms 1 en suite
payment Cash/cheques

Room General

BOWNESS-ON-SOLWAY, Cumbria Map ref 1A2 — **GUEST ACCOMMODATION**

★★★★
GUEST ACCOMMODATION

B&B per room per night
s £30.00–£40.00
d £56.00

Wallsend House, The Old Rectory

Church Lane, Bowness-on-Solway CA7 5AF **t** (01697) 351055 **f** (01697) 351010
e bill@wallsend.net **w** wallsend.net

open All year except Christmas and New Year
bedrooms 2 double, 2 single, 1 family
bathrooms All en suite
payment Cash/cheques

Peaceful, spacious and welcoming, The Old Rectory is located in its own wooded grounds at end of Hadrian's Wall in Solway Coast Area of Outstanding Natural Beauty. All rooms en suite. Picturesque village with local pub/restaurant 150yds. Easy access to historic city of Carlisle, North Lakes and Scotland.

From Carlisle B5307 towards Kirkbride. Pass hospital, 1km right towards Grinsdale, Kirk Andrews, Burgh, Bowness. Continue to Bowness-on-Solway. Left at Kings Arms, 100m on left.

20% reduction from third night onwards.

Room General 4 P Leisure

BRAITHWAITE, Cumbria Map ref 1A3 — **SELF CATERING**

★★★★
SELF CATERING

Units 2
Sleeps 4–6
Low season per wk
£190.00–£330.00
High season per wk
£340.00–£640.00

Highbridge Cottages, Keswick

contact Peter Rigg, Highbridge Cottages, Manor Crest, Manor Brow, Keswick CA12 4AW
t (01768) 780561 **e** riggpeter@tiscali.co.uk **w** braithwaite-cottage.co.uk

Located by the stream in Braithwaite, gateway to the north-western fells. Ideal for walkers. Quiet, comfortable, well-equipped. Dogs welcome.

open All year
payment Credit/debit cards, cash/cheques

Unit
General P Leisure Shop < 0.5 miles Pub < 0.5 miles

BRAMPTON, Cumbria Map ref 1B2 — **GUEST ACCOMMODATION**

★★★★
BED & BREAKFAST

B&B per room per night
s £30.00–£32.00
d £50.00–£55.00

Quarry Side

Banks, Brampton CA8 2JH **t** (01697) 72538 **e** elizabeth.harding@btinternet.com

On site of Hadrian's Wall, Vallum runs through the garden. Outstanding views over Irthing Valley. Close to Lanercost Priory. Home-made tea on arrival.

open All year except Christmas and New Year
bedrooms 2 double, 1 twin
bathrooms 1 en suite, 1 private
payment Cash/cheques, euros

Room General P Leisure

BRAMPTON, Cumbria Map ref 1B2 — **GUEST ACCOMMODATION**

★★★
FARMHOUSE

B&B per room per night
s £30.00–£35.00
d Min £50.00
Evening meal per person
Min £12.00

Walton High Rigg

Walton, Brampton CA8 2AZ **t** (01697) 72117 **f** (01697) 741697 **e** mounsey_highrigg@hotmail.com
w waltonhighrigg.co.uk

Spacious, comfortable, Grade II Listed Georgian building on a family-run dairy/beef/sheep farm. Animals, farm trail, chicken feeding, children any age. Home-made preserves, own or locally produced.

open All year except Christmas and New Year
bedrooms 1 family
bathrooms 1 private
payment Cash/cheques

Room General P Leisure

Key to symbols

Open the back flap for a key to symbols.

BROUGH, Cumbria Map ref 1B3 — GUEST ACCOMMODATION

★★★★
BED & BREAKFAST

B&B per room per night
d £45.00–£50.00

River View

Brough, Brough CA17 4BZ **t** (017683) 41894 **e** riverviewbb@btinternet.com **w** riverviewbb.co.uk

Converted barn by riverside. Historic village location near A66 makes convenient north/south stopover. Ideal base for visiting Lake District, Yorkshire Dales and North Pennines. A warm, friendly, homely welcome.

open All year except Christmas and New Year
bedrooms 1 double, 1 twin
bathrooms All en suite
payment Cash/cheques

Room General Leisure

BURNESIDE, Cumbria Map ref 1B3 — SELF CATERING

★★★★★
SELF CATERING

Units 2
Sleeps 2
Low season per wk
£210.00–£400.00
High season per wk
£320.00–£490.00

Mirefoot Cottages, Kendal

contact Kate Curwen, Mirefoot Cottages, Mirefoot, Burneside LA8 9AB
t (015397) 20015 **e** kate@mirefoot.co.uk **w** mirefoot.co.uk

Two properties in a converted 17thC Lakeland barn set in a picturesque, secluded, rural location within the Lake District National Park. The barn is surrounded by over an acre of mature private gardens.

open All year
payment Cash/cheques

Unit
General Leisure Shop 1.6 miles Pub 1.5 miles

BUTTERMERE, Cumbria Map ref 1A3 — SELF CATERING

★★★★
SELF CATERING

Units 6
Sleeps 2–6
Low season per wk
Min £240.00
High season per wk
Max £680.00

Bridge Hotel & Self Catering Apartments, Buttermere

contact John McGuire, Bridge Hotel & Self Catering Apartments, Buttermere, Nr Keswick CA13 9UZ
t (01768) 770252 **f** (01768) 770215 **e** enquiries@bridge-hotel.com **w** bridge-hotel.com

open All year
payment Credit/debit cards, cash/cheques, euros

Superbly situated, surrounded by fells in Area of Outstanding Natural Beauty. Each apartment is furnished to a high standard. All modern facilities. Dogs welcome.

Unit
General Leisure

BUTTERMERE, Cumbria Map ref 1A3 — SELF CATERING

★★★★
SELF CATERING

Units 1
Sleeps 2–4
Low season per wk
Min £290.00
High season per wk
Max £590.00

Lanthwaite Green Farm Cottage, Buttermere

contact John McGuire, Bridge Hotel & Self Catering Apartments, Buttermere, Nr Keswick CA13 9UZ
t (01768) 770252 **f** (01768) 770215 **e** enquiries@bridge-hotel.com **w** bridge-hotel.com

open All year
payment Credit/debit cards, cash/cheques, euros

Situated at the foot of Melbreak on a working farm. Looking towards Crummock Water, luxury, cosy 16thC cottage. Boasts all modern facilities.

Unit
General Leisure Shop 6 miles Pub 3 miles

CARLISLE, Cumbria Map ref 1A2 — **HOTEL**

★★
HOTEL

B&B per room per night
s £47.00–£50.00
d £60.00–£67.00

The Carlisle Pinegrove Hotel

262 London Road, Carlisle CA1 2QS **t** (01228) 524828 **f** (01228) 810941
e enquiries@pinegrovehotel.co.uk **w** pinegrovehotel.co.uk

Family-owned and -run hotel situated off junction 42 of the M6, one mile from the centre of the historic border city of Carlisle. Central for the Lakes and Hadrian's Wall.

open All year
bedrooms 13 double, 8 twin, 3 single, 7 family
bathrooms 29 en suite, 2 private
payment Credit/debit cards, cash/cheques

Room General Leisure

COCKERMOUTH, Cumbria Map ref 1A2 — **SELF CATERING**

★★★
SELF CATERING

Units 1
Sleeps 4–6
Low season per wk
£320.00–£390.00
High season per wk
£450.00–£680.00

The Stables, Dean, Workington

contact Veronica Roper, Sunnyside, Gib Lane, Hoghton PR5 0RS
t (01254) 852027 **e** veronica@vroper.fsnet.co.uk **w** vholidays.moonfruit.com

open All year
payment Cash/cheques, euros

Delightful 18thC, comfortable, well-equipped cottage with inglenooks, exposed beams and log fires – an excellent base at any time of year. Dean is a peaceful village, ideally situated for exploring the Northern Lakes, West Cumbria, Carlisle and the Scottish Borders. Secluded garden – perfect for a peaceful, relaxing holiday. Walking, cycling, golf, fishing. Ospreys nearby.

M6 jct 40, Workington. A66, Cockermouth. At roundabout, left (Egremont A5086), 4 miles right Dean, 1 mile right Dean. Pass Royal Yew. Left after barn conversion.

3-night breaks available Oct-Mar. 20% discount for 2 people, depending on season.

Unit
General Leisure Shop 5 miles Pub < 0.5 miles

CONISTON, Cumbria Map ref 1A3 — **HOTEL**

★★
HOTEL

B&B per room per night
s £40.00–£55.00
d £80.00–£120.00

Sun Hotel & 16th Century Inn

Coniston LA21 8HQ **t** (015394) 41248 **f** (015394) 41219 **e** mail@thesunconiston.com
w thesunconiston.com

open All year except Christmas
bedrooms 4 double, 2 twin, 1 single, 3 family
bathrooms 9 en suite, 1 private
payment Credit/debit cards, cash/cheques

The Sun in Coniston is a bit of a rarity these days: a comfortable, informal country hotel with an exceptionally good pub attached. We let the quality of our food, beers, wines and rooms speak for themselves, but it all adds up to a lovely place to stay. An excellent venue for wedding receptions and small parties.

Signposted from the bridge in the centre of the village, about 100yds up the hill.

Discounts available most months.

Room General Leisure

Check the maps

Colour maps at the front pinpoint all places in which you will find accommodation entries in the regional sections. Pick your location and then refer to the place index at the back to find the page number.

CONISTON, Cumbria Map ref 1A3 — GUEST ACCOMMODATION

◆◆◆
GUEST ACCOMMODATION

B&B per room per night
s £40.00–£60.00
d £60.00–£100.00
Evening meal per person
£7.50–£15.00

Yewdale Hotel

Yewdale Road, Coniston LA21 8DU **t** (015394) 41280 **f** (015394) 41871 **e** mail@yewdalehotel.com
w yewdalehotel.com

Small, family-run hotel situated in the centre of Coniston, within walking distance of the lake. Ideally positioned for walkers and cyclists. Children and pets welcome.

open All year
bedrooms 3 double, 4 family
bathrooms All en suite
payment Credit/debit cards, cash/cheques

Room General Leisure

CONISTON, Cumbria Map ref 1A3 — CAMPING & CARAVANNING

★★★★
TOURING & CAMPING PARK

(280) £11.00–£24.00
(280) £11.00–£24.00
280 touring pitches

See Ad on inside front cover

Park Coppice Caravan Club Site

Park Gate, Coniston LA21 8LA **t** (015394) 41555 **w** caravanclub.co.uk

payment Credit/debit cards, cash/cheques

Landscaped site set in 63 acres of National Trust woodland. Lake for watersports, on-site play areas, orienteering courses and Red Squirrel Nature Trail. Open March to November.

Follow A593, 1.5 miles south of Coniston village. Final approach from the north or south is narrow in places.

Special member rates mean you can save your membership subscription in less than a week. Visit our website to find out more.

General Leisure

DENT, Cumbria Map ref 1B3 — GUEST ACCOMMODATION

★★★
BED & BREAKFAST

B&B per room per night
s £30.00–£35.00
d £50.00–£65.00

Stone Close Tea Room & Guest House

Main Street, Dent, Sedbergh LA10 5QL **t** (015396) 25231 **e** stoneclose@btinternet.com
w dentdale.com

17thC listed building, once two separate cottages. Original features include flagstone floor, cast-iron range and exposed beams. Breakfast served in Tea Room, using local, organic and seasonal produce.

open All year
bedrooms 1 double, 2 twin
bathrooms 1 en suite
payment Cash/cheques

Room General Leisure

DENT, Cumbria Map ref 1B3 — SELF CATERING

★★★
SELF CATERING

Units 2
Sleeps 4
Low season per wk
£190.00–£245.00
High season per wk
£255.00–£310.00

Middleton's Cottage and Fountain Cottage, Sedbergh

contact Mr & Mrs Ayers, Middleton's Cottage and Fountain Cottage, The Old Rectory, Polegate BN26 5RB
t (01323) 870032 **f** (01323) 870032 **e** candpayers@mistral.co.uk **w** dentcottages.co.uk

open All year
payment Cash/cheques

Modernised mid-17thC cottages in centre of small, quaint village, comfortably furnished and decorated to high standards. Quiet, unspoilt Dentdale offers a good base for walking, touring and exploring the Yorkshire Dales or the Lake District, with Kendal and Hawes nearby. Brochure available. Open all year.

Dent is 10 miles from M6 jct 37. Follow A684 to Sedbergh, then minor road signposted to Dent, 5 miles. Cottages are in village centre.

Short breaks from Oct-Mar, weekend or mid-week. Any combination, subject to availability.

Unit
General

ELTERWATER, Cumbria Map ref 1A3 **SELF CATERING**

★★★
SELF CATERING

Units 2
Sleeps 3–4
Low season per wk
£325.00–£348.00
High season per wk
£376.00–£433.00

Wistaria Cottage and 3 Main Street, Elterwater

contact Mr G & Mrs D Beardmore, 2 Beech Drive, Stoke-on-Trent ST7 1BA
t (01782) 783170 **f** (01782) 783170 **e** geoff.doreen.beardmore@ntlworld.com

Traditional 18thC cottages near village centre. Tastefully renovated, well equipped. Serviced and maintained by owners. Warm and comfortable, off-peak heating, open fires. Fell and valley walking.

open All year
payment Cash/cheques

Unit
General 10 P Shop < 0.5 miles Pub < 0.5 miles

GILSLAND, Cumbria Map ref 1B2 **GUEST ACCOMMODATION**

♦♦♦♦
GUEST ACCOMMODATION
SILVER AWARD

B&B per room per night
s £28.00–£40.00
d £28.00–£35.00
Evening meal per person
£19.95–£23.00

Bush Nook

Upper Denton, Gilsland, Brampton CA8 7AF **t** (01697) 747194 **f** (01697) 747790
e info@bushnook.co.uk **w** bushnook.co.uk

open All year except Christmas and New Year
bedrooms 2 double, 2 twin, 2 single
bathrooms All en suite
payment Credit/debit cards, cash/cheques, euros

Set in superb open countryside, Bush Nook offers quality food and accommodation for the discerning individual or group. Overlooking Birdoswald Roman Fort on Hadrian's Wall, Bush Nook is close to the 'centre' section of the World Heritage site and some of the most stunning countryside to be found in England.

Low season special offers (excl Christmas and New Year). Ring for details. Discount for 3 or more nights all year.

Room General Leisure

GILSLAND, Cumbria Map ref 1B2 **GUEST ACCOMMODATION**

♦♦♦♦♦
GUEST ACCOMMODATION
SILVER AWARD

B&B per room per night
s £40.00–£50.00
d £60.00–£66.00
Evening meal per person
Min £15.00

The Hill on the Wall

Gilsland, Brampton CA8 7DA **t** (01697) 747214 **f** (01697) 747214
e info@hadrians-wallbedandbreakfast.com **w** hadrians-wallbedandbreakfast.com

open All year
bedrooms 1 double, 2 twin
bathrooms 2 en suite, 1 private
payment Cash/cheques

A 16thC farmhouse in one acre of gardens with outstanding views over the Irthing Valley and Hadrian's Wall at Birdoswald Roman Fort. Spacious, comfortable guest bedrooms/lounge. Delicious home cooking. Ideal centre for exploring Northumberland and the Borders. Once you have stayed at The Hill you will want to return time and again.

Leave A69 at Brampton, take turning for Lanercost and Hadrian's Wall. Past Tourist Centre (Birdoswald), right at T-junction, approximately 0.5 miles.

Off-season discounts apply – please phone for details.

Room General 10 P Leisure

GILSLAND, Cumbria Map ref 1B2 **SELF CATERING**

★★★★
SELF CATERING

Units 1
Sleeps 2
Low season per wk
£200.00–£300.00
High season per wk
£250.00–£350.00

Hay Barn Cottage, Gilsland

contact Paul & Judith Barton, Bush Nook, Upper Denton, Gilsland CA8 7AF
t (016977) 47194 **e** info@bushnook.co.uk **w** bushnook.co.uk

Set in wonderful open countryside, the cottage offers superb accommodation for two in a converted 18thC barn and is close to the centre section of Hadrian's Wall.

open All year except Christmas and New Year
payment Cash/cheques, euros

Unit
General P
Leisure
Shop 1 mile Pub 1 mile

GRANGE-OVER-SANDS, Cumbria Map ref 1A3 **HOTEL**

★
HOTEL
SILVER AWARD

HB per person per night
Min £69.00

Clare House

Park Road, Grange-over-Sands LA11 7HQ **t** (015395) 34253 **e** info@clarehousehotel.co.uk
w clarehousehotel.co.uk

bedrooms 3 double, 12 twin, 4 single
bathrooms All en suite
payment Credit/debit cards, cash/cheques

Charming hotel in its own grounds, with well-appointed bedrooms, pleasant lounges and super bay views, offering peaceful holidays to those who wish to relax and be looked after. Delightful meals, prepared with care and pride from fresh, local produce, will contribute greatly to the enjoyment of your stay. Open March to November.

From M6 jct 36 follow A590 through Grange, keep alongside sea. Clare House is on Park Road next to bandstand, between sea and road.

Early-season terms in Apr, mid-summer and autumn. Special 4-day breaks available all season.

Room
General 3 P

GRANGE-OVER-SANDS, Cumbria Map ref 1A3 **HOTEL**

★★★
HOTEL
SILVER AWARD

B&B per room per night
s £80.00–£115.00
d £150.00–£190.00
HB per person per night
£95.00–£130.00

Netherwood Hotel

Lindale Road, Grange-over-Sands LA11 6ET **t** (015395) 32552 **f** (015395) 34121
e enquiries@netherwood-hotel.co.uk **w** netherwood-hotel.co.uk

open All year
bedrooms 18 double, 7 twin, 1 single, 6 family
bathrooms All en suite
payment Credit/debit cards, cash/cheques

Built in 1893, a building of high architectural and historical interest, set in 14 acres of gardens and woodland overlooking Morecambe Bay estuary. Original oak-panelling, unique log fires in the public rooms. All bedrooms are furnished to extremely high, modern standards. The elevated restaurant maximizes the dramatic views of the estuary.

Take the M6, exit 36 then the A590 towards Barrow-in-Furness, then the B5277 into Grange-over-Sands. The hotel is on the right before the town.

Special mid-week short breaks available. Specialised holidays include bridge and gardening. Visit our website for late availability rates.

Room
General P
Leisure

Check it out

Please check prices, quality ratings and other details when you book.

GRANGE-OVER-SANDS, Cumbria Map ref 1A3 — **CAMPING & CARAVANNING**

★★★★★
TOURING PARK
(130) £12.50–£25.10
(130) £12.50–£25.10
130 touring pitches

See Ad on inside front cover

Meathop Fell Caravan Club Site

Meathop, Grange-over-Sands LA11 6RB **t** (015395) 32912 **w** caravanclub.co.uk

open All year
payment Credit/debit cards, cash/cheques

Peaceful site, ideal for exploring the southern Lake District. Kendal, famous for its mint cake, is within easy reach; Grange-over-Sands and Ulverston are close by.

M6 jct 36, A590 to Barrow. After about 3.25 miles take slip road and follow A590 to Barrow. At 1st roundabout follow International Camping signs. Steep approach.

Special member rates mean you can save your membership subscription in less than a week. Visit our website to find out more.

General P Leisure

GRASMERE, Cumbria Map ref 1A3 — **HOTEL**

★★
HOTEL
SILVER AWARD

HB per person per night
£55.00–£75.00

The Grasmere Hotel

Broadgate, Grasmere, Ambleside LA22 9TA **t** (015394) 35277 **f** (015394) 35277
e enquiries@grasmerehotel.co.uk **w** grasmerehotel.co.uk

open All year
bedrooms 9 double, 2 twin, 2 single
bathrooms All en suite
payment Credit/debit cards, cash/cheques

Our delightful Victorian hotel offers standards synonymous with larger hotels, providing modern levels of comfort and convenience. Sympathetically refurbished for 2006, the hotel boasts an elegant, award-winning restaurant which overlooks our gardens, the River Rothay and fells beyond. The friendly atmosphere encourages many guests to return.

Take A591 from Windermere, through Ambleside to Grasmere. Take 2nd turning signposted Grasmere Village. Hotel is 0.5 miles on the left, next to village hall.

Special 3- and 5-night mid-week breaks available throughout the year. Weekends from £120pp, DB&B.

Room General 10 P Leisure

GRASMERE, Cumbria Map ref 1A3 — **GUEST ACCOMMODATION**

★★★★
GUEST ACCOMMODATION

B&B per room per night
s £65.00–£105.00
d £110.00–£150.00
Evening meal per person
£30.00–£45.00

Dale Lodge Hotel & Tweedies Bar

Red Bank Road, Grasmere LA22 9SW **t** (015394) 35300 **f** (015394) 35570
e enquiries@dalelodgehotel.co.uk **w** dalelodgehotel.co.uk

Dale Lodge Hotel is situated in the centre of Grasmere village in three acres of mature gardens. Recently refurbished in a classic yet contemporary style, with the choice of two restaurants serving modern cuisine and outstanding gastro pub food.

open All year
bedrooms 7 double, 2 twin, 3 family
bathrooms All en suite
payment Credit/debit cards, cash/cheques

Room General P Leisure

Place index

If you know where you want to stay the index at the back of the guide will give you the page number which lists accommodation in your chosen town, city or village. Check out the other useful indexes too.

GRASMERE, Cumbria Map ref 1A3 — **SELF CATERING**

★★★★
SELF CATERING

Units 3
Sleeps 2–5

Low season per wk
£265.00–£300.00
High season per wk
£435.00–£600.00

Broadrayne Farm Cottages, Grasmere

contact Mr Bev Dennison & Mrs Jo Dennison Drake, Broadrayne Farm, Grasmere, Ambleside LA22 9RU
t (015394) 35055 **f** (015394) 35733 **e** bev@grasmerehostel.co.uk **w** grasmere-accommodation.co.uk

open All year
payment Cash/cheques

With dramatic mountains, rolling fells, glorious lakes and peaceful valleys, Broadrayne Farm is at the heart of the Lake District, superbly located for wonderful views. The traditional farm properties have been lovingly renovated with today's creature comforts, including open coal fires, central heating and off-street parking. Pets welcome by arrangement.

Our driveway is directly off the A591, we are 1.25 miles north of the village of Grasmere, 400m after the Travellers Rest Pub.

A week booked in the year allows 10% off a second week booked in Mar (excl Easter holidays).

Unit
General Leisure Shop 1.3 miles Pub 1.25 miles

GREAT ASBY, Cumbria Map ref 1B3 — **SELF CATERING**

★★★★
SELF CATERING

Units 3
Sleeps 2–5

Low season per wk
£240.00–£305.00
High season per wk
£336.00–£460.00

Scalebeck Holiday Cottages, Great Asby, Appleby-in-Westmorland

contact Mr K J Budding, Scalebeck Holiday Cottages, Scalebeck, Appleby-in-Westmorland CA16 6TF
t (01768) 351006 **f** (01768) 353532 **e** mail@scalebeckholidaycottages.com
w scalebeckholidaycottages.co.uk

Self-catering cottages in barn conversion. Secluded valley, abundant wildlife. Non-smokers, pets welcome, games room, open all year.

open All year
payment Credit/debit cards, cash/cheques

Unit
General Leisure Shop 5 miles Pub 1 mile

GREAT CORBY, Cumbria Map ref 1B2 — **SELF CATERING**

★★★★
SELF CATERING

Units 1
Sleeps 6

Low season per wk
Min £325.00
High season per wk
Max £750.00

Thackmoor House, Carlisle

contact Anne McDowall, Whitehall Properties, 3 Victoria Place, Carlisle CA1 1EJ
t (01228) 514004 **f** (01228) 536894 **e** anne_635@fsmail.net **w** northcumbriancottages.co.uk

Cosy, comfortable, well-equipped, two-storey Victorian cottage in the centre of Great Corby village in Lower Eden Valley. Ideal base for exploring the Lakes, Scottish Borders and Hadrian's Wall.

open All year
payment Cash/cheques

Unit
General Leisure Shop 1 mile Pub < 0.5 miles

HAWKSHEAD, Cumbria Map ref 1A3 — **GUEST ACCOMMODATION**

★★★★★
INN

B&B per room per night
s £71.25–£168.75
d £95.00–£220.00

The Drunken Duck Inn

Barngates, Ambleside LA22 0NG **t** (015394) 36347 **f** (015394) 36781

An old-fashioned inn amidst magnificent scenery, oak-beamed bars, cosy log fires and charming bedrooms. Excellent food and beers. Cumbria Dining Pub of the Year, Good Pub Guide 1999 and 2003.

open All year except Christmas
bedrooms 14 double, 2 twin
bathrooms All en suite
payment Credit/debit cards, cash/cheques

Room General Leisure

Rest assured
All accommodation in this guide has been rated, or is awaiting assessment, by a professional assessor.

HAWKSHEAD, Cumbria Map ref 1A3 — **GUEST ACCOMMODATION**

♦♦♦♦
GUEST ACCOMMODATION

B&B per room per night
s £33.00–£40.00
d £27.00–£45.00

Yewfield Vegetarian Guest House

Hawkshead Hill, Ambleside LA22 0PR **t** (015394) 36765 **f** (015394) 36096
e derek.yewfield@btinternet.com **w** yewfield.co.uk

open All year except Christmas and New Year
bedrooms 3 double, 2 twin
bathrooms All en suite
payment Credit/debit cards, cash/cheques

An impressive, Gothic, Victorian house set in over 30 acres of organic grounds with lovely walks to Tarn Hows and the surrounding fells.

One mile from Hawkshead, 4 miles from Ambleside, 2 miles past The Drunken Duck. See website for map.

Classical concerts throughout the year. See website for dates.

Room · General 9

HAWKSHEAD, Cumbria Map ref 1A3 — **SELF CATERING**

★★★
SELF CATERING

Units **1**
Low season per wk
£229.00–£274.00
High season per wk
£324.00–£448.00

Meadow View, Ambleside

Blakes Cottages, Earby, Barnoldswick BB94 0AA
t 0870 336 7777 **w** blakes.cottages.co.uk

Three-hundred-year-old cottage in the centre of Hawkshead. Entrance hall, bathroom, twin bedroom, double bedroom with wash basin and separate wc, kitchen and living accommodation. Central heating.

payment Credit/debit cards, cash/cheques

Unit · General 11 P · Leisure · Shop < 0.5 miles · Pub < 0.5 miles

HIGH LORTON, Cumbria Map ref 1A3 — **SELF CATERING**

★★★
SELF CATERING

Units **3**
Sleeps **2–8**
Low season per wk
£195.00–£420.00
High season per wk
£320.00–£745.00

High Swinside Holiday Cottages, High Lorton

contact Jacques Hankin, High Swinside Holiday Cottages, High Swinside Farm, High Lorton CA13 9UA
t (01900) 85206 **f** (01900) 85451 **e** bookings@highswinside.demon.co.uk
w highswinside.demon.co.uk

open All year
payment Credit/debit cards, cash/cheques

Former hill farm, overlooking Lorton Vale with stunning views and offering peace and tranquillity. Well-equipped cottages. Large groups (up to 14) can be catered for. Children welcome. Beams and log fires, together with meal service, make for a wonderful stay. Full details on our website.

A66 to Braithwaite, Whinlatter Pass, past visitor centre, left along small road to Hopebeck and narrow-gated road. Left at fork, through gate, property below 1st gate.

Unit · General P · Leisure · Shop 2 miles · Pub 2 miles

Using map references

The map references refer to the colour maps at the front of this guide. The first figure is the map number; the letter and figure that follow indicate the grid reference on the map.

IREBY, Cumbria Map ref 1A2 — **GUEST ACCOMMODATION**

★★★★
GUEST HOUSE

B&B per room per night
d £76.00–£110.00
Evening meal per person
£22.00–£25.00

Woodlands Country House

Ireby, Nr Bassenthwaite CA7 1EX **t** (01697) 371791 **f** (01697) 371482
e stay@woodlandsatireby.co.uk **w** woodlandsatireby.co.uk

open All year
bedrooms 3 double, 1 twin, 3 family
bathrooms All en suite
payment Credit/debit cards, cash/cheques

Woodlands offers fine food, good wines and very comfortable accommodation. Relax and unwind in our welcoming lounges and bars, or wander in our lovely garden, surrounded by beautiful countryside and watch the wild birds. The perfect location to explore The North Western lakes and fells and The South Solway coast.

⊕ *Twelve miles from Keswick: follow A591 towards Carlisle then signs for Ireby. Last house in the village on the left, just past the church.*

❤ *3 night DB&B package from £160pp. Telephone for special rates for party bookings.*

Room · General · Leisure

IRTHINGTON, Cumbria Map ref 1B2 — **GUEST ACCOMMODATION**

★★★★
BED & BREAKFAST

B&B per room per night
s £35.00–£40.00
d £56.00–£60.00

Corbett House

Irthington, Carlisle, Brampton CA6 4NN **t** (01697) 741533 **e** corbetthouse@tiscali.co.uk
w corbetthouse.co.uk

open All year
bedrooms 1 double, 1 twin
bathrooms All en suite
payment Cash/cheques

Relax in our comfortable, converted-forge cottage. Enjoy our charming garden or unwind in our conservatory. In a tranquil village only minutes from Carlisle and M6. Ideal for Hadrian's Wall Trail (0.4 miles) and the Roman sites, north/south stopovers, or the lovely Border countryside. Great food at the village pub.

⊕ *Exit M6 jct 44, Carlisle North. Exit to A689 (Hexham/Carlisle Airport). Follow A689 for approx 5.5 miles, turn left (Carlisle Airport/Irthington).*

❤ *Discounts for stays of 3 nights or more.*

Room · General · Leisure

IRTHINGTON, Cumbria Map ref 1B2 — **GUEST ACCOMMODATION**

★★★
FARMHOUSE

B&B per room per night
s £35.00
d £28.00
Evening meal per person
£12.00

Newtown Farm

Newtown, Irthington, Carlisle CA6 4NX **t** (01697) 72768 **e** susangrice@tiscali.co.uk

Susan and Malcolm welcome you to Newtown Farm bed and breakfast, a family-run working farm located directly on Hadrian's Wall Path. The stone buildings on the farm date back to 1722.

open All year except Christmas and New Year
bedrooms 1 double, 1 family
bathrooms All en suite
payment Cash/cheques

Room · General · Leisure

WALKERS WELCOME · WELCOME WALKERS

Best foot forward

Walkers feel at home in accommodation participating in our Walkers Welcome scheme. Look out for the symbol. Consider walking all or part of a long-distance route – go online at nationaltrail.co.uk.

KENDAL, Cumbria Map ref 1B3 — **SELF CATERING**

★★★
SELF CATERING

Units 1
Sleeps 2–4
Low season per wk
£250.00–£300.00
High season per wk
£300.00–£350.00

Barkinbeck Cottage, Kendal

contact Mrs Ann Hamilton, Barkinbeck Cottage, c/o Barkin House Barn, Gatebeck, Kendal LA8 0HX
t (015395) 67122 **e** barkinhouse@yahoo.co.uk **w** barkinbeck.co.uk

Converted barn in beautiful, peaceful countryside between Lakes and Dales, an ideal base for touring and walking. Log fire, owner maintained. Adapted for disabled.

open All year
payment Cash/cheques

Unit
General 12 P Shop 5 miles Pub 5 miles

KESWICK, Cumbria Map ref 1A3 — **HOTEL**

★★
SMALL HOTEL
SILVER AWARD

B&B per room per night
s £42.00–£48.00
d £84.00–£112.00
HB per person per night
£61.50–£75.50

Lairbeck Hotel

Vicarage Hill, Keswick CA12 5QB **t** (017687) 73373 **f** (017687) 73144
e ct@lairbeckhotel-keswick.co.uk **w** lairbeckhotel-keswick.co.uk

open All year except Christmas and New Year
bedrooms 7 double, 2 twin, 4 single, 1 family
bathrooms All en suite
payment Credit/debit cards, cash/cheques

Ten minutes' walk into Keswick old town. Secluded location with mountain views. Fourteen en suite bedrooms including superior, four-poster and ground-floor rooms all with colour TV, hairdryer, direct-dial telephone and tea/coffee-making facilities. No single-room supplement. Traditional, award-winning dining and hospitality. Log fires. WI-FI broadband. Spacious garden and parking. Totally non-smoking.

From M6 jct 40 follow A66 until roundabout then turn left towards Keswick then 1st right into Vicarage Hill. Hotel a few hundred yards on right.

3-day weekend, 4-day mid-week and 7-day DB&B special breaks available (excl Easter and Bank Holiday weekends).

Room General 5 P Leisure

KESWICK, Cumbria Map ref 1A3 — **GUEST ACCOMMODATION**

★★★★
GUEST HOUSE
SILVER AWARD

B&B per room per night
s £45.00–£60.00
d £60.00–£76.00

Acorn House

Ambleside Road, Keswick CA12 4DL **t** (017687) 72553 **e** info@acornhousehotel.co.uk
w acornhousehotel.co.uk

Detached Georgian house set in well-maintained gardens. Spacious rooms, all tastefully refurbished. Four-poster beds available. Quietly situated, yet close to the town centre and lake. Real log fires.

open All year except Christmas
bedrooms 7 double, 2 family
bathrooms All en suite
payment Credit/debit cards, cash/cheques

Room General 6 Leisure

KESWICK, Cumbria Map ref 1A3 — **GUEST ACCOMMODATION**

★★★★
GUEST ACCOMMODATION
SILVER AWARD

B&B per room per night
s £25.00–£45.00
d £52.00–£60.00

Amble House Guest House

23 Eskin Street, Keswick CA12 4DQ **t** (017687) 73288 **e** info@amblehouse.co.uk
w amblehouse.co.uk

Richard and Judy extend a warm and friendly welcome to you from Amble House. Quietly located, close to town centre, lake and fells. Come and visit our magical Lake Derwentwater.

open All year except Christmas
bedrooms 4 double, 1 twin
bathrooms All en suite
payment Credit/debit cards, cash/cheques

Room General Leisure

KESWICK, Cumbria Map ref 1A3 — **GUEST ACCOMMODATION**

★★★★
GUEST HOUSE
SILVER AWARD

B&B per room per night
d £56.00–£62.00

Dunsford Guest House

16 Stanger Street, Keswick CA12 5JU **t** (017687) 75059 **e** enquiries@dunsford.net **w** dunsford.net

open All year except Christmas and New Year
bedrooms 4 double
bathrooms All en suite
payment Cash/cheques

Dunsford is a beautifully restored Victorian house providing high-quality accommodation and creating a homely, friendly atmosphere exclusively for couples and non-smokers. All rooms have double beds, colour televisions, clock radios, hairdryers and tea-/coffee-making facilities, and are fully en suite. Private parking at rear of property.

Exit M6 jct 40. Take A66 to Keswick and follow sign for town centre. After 2nd set of traffic lights Stanger Street is 1st right.

Room TV General P

KESWICK, Cumbria Map ref 1A3 — **GUEST ACCOMMODATION**

★★★★
GUEST HOUSE

B&B per room per night
d £48.00–£60.00

Ellergill Guest House

22 Stanger Street, Keswick CA12 5JU **t** (017687) 73347 **e** stay@ellergill.co.uk **w** ellergill.co.uk

open All year
bedrooms 2 double, 2 twin
bathrooms 3 en suite, 1 private
payment Cash/cheques

An informal and relaxed atmosphere is assured at our recently refurbished, Lakeland-stone, Victorian guesthouse where period features meet modern design. Ellergill is situated in the heart of Keswick, yet in a quiet cul-de-sac, with well-appointed, spacious rooms and high standards of comfort and cleanliness.

M6 jct 40, A66 west for 17 miles. 2nd roundabout left to T-junction, left again then over mini-roundabout. 1st left into Stanger Street.

Reduced rates for stays of 4 or more nights.

Room TV General 12

KESWICK, Cumbria Map ref 1A3 — **GUEST ACCOMMODATION**

★★★★★
GUEST ACCOMMODATION
SILVER AWARD

B&B per room per night
s £41.00–£51.00
d £72.00–£92.00

The Grange Country House

Manor Brow Ambleside Road, Keswick CA12 4BA **t** (017687) 72500 **e** info@grangekeswick.com **w** grangekeswick.com

The Grange Country House is set in its own grounds overlooking Keswick-on-Derwentwater and the surrounding fells. Lovely bedrooms, spacious lounges, ample parking and quality and style at affordable prices. Open February to November.

bedrooms 6 double, 3 twin, 1 single
bathrooms All en suite
payment Credit/debit cards, cash/cheques

Room TV General 7 P Leisure

Friendly help and advice

Tourist Information Centres offer friendly help with accommodation and holiday ideas as well as suggestions of places to visit and things to do. You'll find contact details at the back of the guide.

KESWICK, Cumbria Map ref 1A3 — **GUEST ACCOMMODATION**

★★★★
GUEST ACCOMMODATION

B&B per room per night
s £29.00–£60.00
d £58.00–£100.00

Keswick Park Hotel

33 Station Road, Keswick CA12 4NA **t** (017687) 72072 **f** (017687) 74816
e reservations@keswickparkhotel.com **w** keswickparkhotel.com

open All year
bedrooms 7 double, 5 twin, 2 single, 2 family
bathrooms All en suite
payment Credit/debit cards, cash/cheques

We are a small, family-run hotel in the heart of Keswick. All our rooms are newly decorated and are en suite. We also have two rooms with beautiful four-poster beds.

From jct 40 M6 follow A66 15 miles, take 1st exit to Keswick. Follow signs to Keswick. After 1 mile, park and river then hotel on right.

Room General P Leisure

KESWICK, Cumbria Map ref 1A3 — **GUEST ACCOMMODATION**

★★★★
GUEST HOUSE

B&B per room per night
s £35.00–£40.00
d £70.00–£80.00
Evening meal per person
£15.00

Rickerby Grange Country House

Portinscale, Keswick CA12 5RH **t** (017687) 72344 **f** (017687) 75588 **e** stay@rickerbygrange.co.uk
w rickerbygrange.co.uk

Peaceful location, overlooked by Skiddaw, and only a short walk into Keswick. Family-run, quality accommodation offering a warm, relaxed, friendly atmosphere, home-cooked food and personal service without undue formality.

open All year except Christmas
bedrooms 5 double, 2 twin, 1 single, 2 family
bathrooms 9 en suite, 1 private
payment Credit/debit cards, cash/cheques

Room General 5 P Leisure

KESWICK, Cumbria Map ref 1A3 — **GUEST ACCOMMODATION**

★★★★
GUEST HOUSE

B&B per room per night
s £35.00–£40.00
d £56.00–£70.00
Evening meal per person
£12.50–£15.00

WALKERS WELCOME · CYCLISTS WELCOME

Sunnyside Guest House

25 Southey Street, Keswick CA12 4EF **t** (017687) 72446 **e** enquiries@sunnysideguesthouse.com
w sunnysideguesthouse.com

Comfortable Victorian house providing well-equipped and tastefully furnished rooms, most en suite. Relaxing guest lounge. Central location. Parking for eight cars. Non-smoking. No children under 12. Ref enjoy.

open All year except Christmas
bedrooms 4 double, 2 twin, 1 family
bathrooms 6 en suite, 1 private
payment Credit/debit cards, cash/cheques

Room General 12 P Leisure

KESWICK, Cumbria Map ref 1A3 — **SELF CATERING**

★★★
SELF CATERING

Units 1
Sleeps 1–4
Low season per wk
£240.00–£335.00
High season per wk
£360.00–£460.00

13 Greta Grove House, Keswick

contact Jean Pechartscheck, Leethwaite Cottage, Powter How, Thornthwaite CA12 5SQ
t (017687) 78325 & 07876 407 995 **e** info@chaucer-selfcatering.co.uk **w** chaucer-selfcatering.co.uk

Recently redecorated and refurbished to a very high standard, this comfortable, welcoming flat is close to Keswick's main attractions and lake. Always immaculate. Small patio.

open All year
payment Cash/cheques

Unit
General P Leisure Shop < 0.5 miles Pub < 0.5 miles

If you have access needs...
Look for the National Accessible Scheme symbols if you have special hearing, visual or mobility needs.

KESWICK, Cumbria Map ref 1A3 — **SELF CATERING**

★★★★
SELF CATERING

Units **5**
Sleeps **1–4**
Low season per wk
£365.00–£435.00
High season per wk
£525.00–£685.00

Low Briery Cottages, Keswick

contact Michael Atkinson, Low Briery Holiday Village, Penrith Road, Keswick CA12 4RN
t (01768) 772044 **w** keswick.uk.com

open All year
payment Credit/debit cards, cash/cheques

Our timber-faced lodges are superbly sited right on the bank of the River Greta. Lounges have sliding patio doors onto the bank and the view down the river and the friendly (and ever hungry) ducks make the location idyllic. Lodges have their own private patio with furniture.

⊕ *Low Briery is clearly signed on the slip road off the A66 into Keswick.*

Unit
General Leisure Shop 1 mile Pub 1 mile

KIRKBY LONSDALE, Cumbria Map ref 1B3 — **CAMPING & CARAVANNING**

★★★★★
HOLIDAY, TOURING & CAMPING PARK

(17) £10.00–£22.00
£10.00–£22.00
(12) £12.00–£14.00
17 touring pitches

Woodclose Caravan Park

Kirkby Lonsdale LA6 2SE **t** (01524) 271597 **f** (01524) 272301 **e** info@woodclosepark.com
w woodclosepark.com

payment Cash/cheques

A quiet, picturesque, exclusive site situated between the Lakes and the Dales, a short walk from Kirkby Lonsdale. All pitches are supplied with electric and TV hook-up points. The camping field is sheltered and secluded. Children's play area and shop. David Bellamy Gold Award. Open March to October.

⊕ *M6 jct 36, follow A65 for approx 6 miles. The park entrance can be found just past Devil's Bridge on the left-hand side.*

General Leisure

KIRKBY STEPHEN, Cumbria Map ref 1B3 — **GUEST ACCOMMODATION**

◆◆◆◆◆
GUEST ACCOMMODATION
SILVER AWARD

B&B per room per night
s £100.00–£140.00
d £120.00–£140.00
Evening meal per person
£35.00–£40.00

Augill Castle

Kirkby Stephen CA17 4DE **t** (017683) 41937

open All year except Christmas
bedrooms 6 double, 4 twin
bathrooms All en suite
payment Credit/debit cards, cash/cheques, euros

A neo-Gothic Victorian fantasy. Romantic, quirky, laid back and utterly beguiling. Anything goes except hushed tones or a false formality. The ultimate escape or the ultimate house party. A real family home where children aren't just tolerated, but welcomed. Be part of the family or keep yourself to yourself.

⊕ *From M6 take jct 38 onto A685 to Brough. Turn right 0.5 miles before village. Exit A66 at Brough then left 0.5 miles outside village.*

Room General Leisure

Rest assured

All accommodation in this guide has been rated, or is awaiting assessment, by a professional assessor.

LAKESIDE, Cumbria Map ref 1A3 — GUEST ACCOMMODATION

★★★
INN

B&B per room per night
s £45.00–£59.00
d £70.00–£120.00
Evening meal per person
£8.95–£21.00

Boathouse Hotel

Lakeside, Newby Bridge LA12 8AS **t** (015395) 31381 **f** (015395) 31129
e enquiries@boathousehotel.co.uk **w** boathousehotel.co.uk

open All year except Christmas
bedrooms 5 double, 5 twin
bathrooms All en suite
payment Credit/debit cards, cash/cheques

The Boathouse Hotel offers a unique combination of excellent accommodation and a sense of homeliness. We are a family-run business, and our main aim is to provide all of our guests with exceptional service from their initial enquiry. Live music. Conference facilities.

⊕ *From the A590 follow signs to Newby Bridge. One mile to Lakeside.*

♥ *3 nights for the price of 2. Mid-week breaks: £199pp.*

Room General Leisure

LAMPLUGH, Cumbria Map ref 1A3 — CAMPING & CARAVANNING

★★★★
TOURING PARK
(53) £8.50–£19.60
(53) £8.50–£19.60
53 touring pitches

See Ad on inside front cover

Dockray Meadow Caravan Club Site

Lamplugh CA14 4SH **t** (01946) 861357 **w** caravanclub.co.uk

payment Credit/debit cards, cash/cheques

Site close to lesser-known lake beauties including Cogra Moss and Ennerdale. Within easy reach of Keswick. Open March to November.

⊕ *From A66 turn onto A5086. In 6.5 miles turn left at signpost for Lamplugh Green. Turn right at signpost for Croasdale. Site on left.*

♥ *Special member rates mean you can save your membership subscription in less than a week. Visit our website to find out more.*

General P Leisure

LYTH, Cumbria Map ref 1A3 — SELF CATERING

★★★
SELF CATERING

Units **2**
Sleeps **2–4**
Low season per wk
£280.00–£350.00
High season per wk
£345.00–£450.00

Fellside Farm, Lyth Valley, Kendal

contact Mrs R Bell, Fellside, Lyth, Kendal LA8 8DA
t (015395) 68312

Orchard Barn and Fellside Barn date back 400 years and have been renovated to a high standard, retaining their old world charm. Both properties sleep four. Double and single bedrooms.

open All year
payment Cash/cheques

Unit
General P Shop 2.5 miles Pub 0.75 miles

A holiday on two wheels

For a fabulous freewheeling break seek out accommodation participating in our Cyclists Welcome scheme. Look out for the symbol and plan your route online at nationalcyclenetwork.org.

MUNGRISDALE, Cumbria Map ref 1A2 — **GUEST ACCOMMODATION**

★★★★
GUEST ACCOMMODATION

B&B per room per night
s £30.00–£40.00
d £50.00–£70.00

Near Howe Hotel and Cottages

Mungrisdale, Troutbeck, Penrith CA11 0SH **t** (017687) 79678 **f** (017687) 79678
e enquiries@nearhowe.co.uk **w** nearhowe.co.uk

open All year
bedrooms 2 double, 1 twin, 2 family
bathrooms 3 en suite, 2 private
payment Cash/cheques, euros

The ideal answer for a stress-free, away-from-it-all holiday. Set amidst 350 acres of open moorland. All bedrooms have spectacular views over the Cumbrian fells. The comfortable residents' lounge and bar both have real coal/log fires. Easily accessible, yet isolated enough to ensure peace and tranquillity.

From M6 jct 40 travel west towards Keswick (A66). After 9 miles pass Troutbeck. After 1 mile turn right to Mungrisdale/Caldbeck. Drive is 1 mile on right.

Room General Leisure

MUNGRISDALE, Cumbria Map ref 1A2 — **SELF CATERING**

★★★★
SELF CATERING

Units **5**
Sleeps **2–7**
Low season per wk
£250.00–£375.00
High season per wk
£350.00–£575.00

Near Howe Cottages, Penrith

contact Steve & Jill Woolley, Near Howe Hotel and Cottages, Near Howe, Mungrisdale, Penrith CA11 0SH
t (01768) 779678 **f** (01768) 779462 **e** wswoolley@tiscali.co.uk **w** nearhowe.co.uk

open All year
payment Cash/cheques, euros

The ideal answer for a stress-free, away-from-it-all holiday, set amidst 350 acres of open moorland. All cottages have spectacular views over the Cumbrian Fells. Comfortable bar with real fire. Large garden with relaxation areas. Easily accessible, yet isolated enough to ensure peace and tranquillity.

From M6 jct 40, travel west towards Keswick (A66). Pass Troutbeck after 9 miles. After 1 mile, turn right to Mungrisdale/Caldbeck. Near Howe is 1 mile on the right.

Unit
General Leisure Shop 5 miles Pub 2 miles

NEWBY BRIDGE, Cumbria Map ref 1A3 — **HOTEL**

★★★
HOTEL

B&B per room per night
s £85.00–£105.00
d £100.00–£195.00
HB per person per night
£75.00–£120.00

The Whitewater Hotel

Backbarrow, Newby Bridge, Ulverston LA12 8PX **t** (015395) 31133 **f** (015395) 31881
e enquiries@whitewater-hotel.co.uk **w** whitewater-hotel.co.uk

open All year
bedrooms 15 double, 3 twin, 2 single, 15 family
bathrooms All en suite
payment Credit/debit cards, cash/cheques, euros

Enviable Lake District location on the banks of the River Leven, 20 minutes from the M6. Superb leisure facilities. Our health and fitness club, Cascades, provides every opportunity to unwind in the pool, sauna, steam room and whirlpool or pamper yourself in our exclusive health spa which offers a full range of treatments.

From jct 36 of M6 follow A590 towards Ulverston for approx 16 miles. Whitewater Hotel is 1 mile past Newby Bridge on the right.

Pamper breaks available. Special mid-week breaks. Family Christmas holiday. Winter jazz festivals. Romantic weekend packages.

Room General
Leisure

PENRITH, Cumbria Map ref 1B2 — **GUEST ACCOMMODATION**

★★★★
GUEST HOUSE

B&B per room per night
s £30.00–£45.00
d Min £60.00

Norcroft Guest House

Graham Street, Penrith CA11 9LQ **t** (01768) 862365 **f** (01768) 210425
e info@norcroft-guesthouse.co.uk **w** norcroft-guesthouse.co.uk

open All year
bedrooms 2 double, 3 twin, 1 single, 3 family
bathrooms All en suite
payment Credit/debit cards, cash/cheques

A large Victorian house conveniently situated for the M6, five minutes from the town centre. Renowned for the delicious Cumbrian breakfasts and a warm, friendly atmosphere. Bike storage and drying facilities provided. Cyclists welcome. Private off-road parking.

Room General P Leisure

PENRITH, Cumbria Map ref 1B2 — **SELF CATERING**

★★★★
SELF CATERING

Units **1**
Sleeps **6**
Low season per wk
£210.00–£280.00
High season per wk
£320.00–£420.00

Chapel House, Penrith

contact Mr Lowis, Chapel House, c/o Drovers Ghyll, Glassonby CA10 1DU
t (01768) 898747 **e** enquiries@glassonbycottages.co.uk **w** glassonbycottages.co.uk

Cosy, well-equipped detached three-bedroom cottage in rural Eden Valley setting. Sleeps up to six (two double, one twin). Open fires. Dog kennel/run.

open All year
payment Cash/cheques

Unit
General P Leisure Shop 2 miles Pub 2 miles

PENRITH, Cumbria Map ref 1B2 — **SELF CATERING**

★★★★
SELF CATERING

Units **3**
Sleeps **2–3**
Low season per wk
£280.00–£340.00
High season per wk
£310.00–£390.00

Stonefold, Ullswater

contact Gill Harrington, Stonefold Cottages, Newbiggin, Stainton CA11 0HP
t (01768) 866383 **f** (01768) 866383 **e** gill@stonefold.co.uk **w** stonefold.co.uk

open All year
payment Credit/debit cards, cash/cheques

These superbly appointed self-catering holiday cottages offer the comfort you'd expect in a modern hotel, but with the addition of all the personal touches which go to make them a home from home. Situated in a beautiful panoramic position bordering the Lake District, Eden Valley and the majestic Pennines. Leisure facilities available nearby.

Leave M6 at jct 40, take A66 Keswick road. Straight over roundabout at Rheged centre and turn right at sign, for Newbiggin. Stonefold one minute's drive on left.

Unit
General P Leisure Shop 1 mile Pub 1 mile

It's all quality-assessed accommodation

VisitBritain's commitment to quality involves wide-ranging accommodation assessment. Ratings and awards were correct at the time of going to press but may change following a new assessment. Please check at the time of booking.

PENRITH, Cumbria Map ref 1B2 — **SELF CATERING**

★★★★
SELF CATERING

Units **5**
Sleeps **3–8**
Low season per wk
£230.00–£450.00
High season per wk
£430.00–£780.00

Wetheral Cottages, Penrith

contact Mr & Mrs J Lowrey, Wetheral Cottages, Great Salkeld, Penrith CA11 9NA
t (01768) 898779 **e** wetheralcottages@btopenworld.com **w** wetheralcottages.co.uk

open All year
payment Credit/debit cards, cash/cheques, euros

Charming, well-equipped sandstone cottages clustered amongst attractive gardens with large grassed area. Situated in Eden Valley on the edge of a quiet country village with pub. Easy access to the amenities of the Lake District, northern England and southern Scotland. Walking, cycling, golf, swimming and fishing nearby. Prices fully inclusive.

From the A686 take the road signed Great Sakeld. In the village take the turning opposite the telephone box, after 200yds turn right.

Short breaks available Nov 07-Easter 08. 3-night weekend breaks or 4-night mid-week breaks.

Unit
General P Leisure Shop 2 miles Pub < 0.5 miles

PENRITH, Cumbria Map ref 1B2 — **CAMPING & CARAVANNING**

★★★★★
HOLIDAY &
TOURING PARK

(45) £15.00–£18.00
(7) £15.00–£18.00
52 touring pitches

Flusco Wood Caravan Park

Flusco, Penrith CA11 0JB **t** (017684) 80020 **e** admin@fluscowood.co.uk **w** fluscowood.co.uk

payment Cash/cheques

A very high-standard and quiet woodland touring caravan park with fully serviced pitches and centrally heated amenity building. Short drive to many attractions and places of interest in the Lake District. Open April to October.

M6 jct 40, travel west on A66 towards Keswick. After about 4 miles turn right (signposted Flusco). Entrance along lane on the left.

Luxury pine holiday lodges for sale. Reduction on prices for pre-booked stays of 1 week or more.

General P Leisure

PENTON, Cumbria Map ref 1A2 — **SELF CATERING**

★★★
SELF CATERING

Units **2**
Sleeps **2–4**
Low season per wk
£230.00–£280.00
High season per wk
£310.00–£395.00

Liddel Park Country Cottages, Carlisle

contact Brian Wicklow, Liddel Park Country Cottages, Catlowdy, Penton, Carlisle CA6 5QW
t (01228) 577440 **e** holiday@liddelpark.co.uk **w** liddelpark.co.uk

Peace and tranquillity in a forest setting, abundance of wildlife. Ideal base for exploring England's Border Country, Hadrian's Wall and the Northern Lake District. Fishing available on local rivers.

open All year
payment Cash/cheques

Unit
General P Leisure Shop 7 miles Pub 2 miles

It's all in the detail

Please remember that all information in this guide has been supplied by the proprietors well in advance of publication. Since changes do sometimes occur it's a good idea to check details at the time of booking.

RYDAL, Cumbria Map ref 1A3 — **SELF CATERING**

★★★
SELF CATERING

Units 1
Sleeps 2–6
Low season per wk
£250.00–£300.00
High season per wk
£450.00–£575.00

Hall Bank Cottage – Rydal Estate, Ambleside

contact Janet Horne, Carter Jonas, 52 Kirkland, Kendal LA9 5AP
t (01539) 814902 **f** (01539) 814902 **e** janet.horne@carterjonas.co.uk

open All year
payment Cash/cheques

Delightful 17thC detached cottage set centrally within a large rural estate, held by one family since 1480. Spacious, yet cosy with log fire. Large private garden and ample off-road parking. Superb location at foot of Nab Scar. Historic Rydal Mount, Rydal Hall and gardens immediately adjacent.

Rydal is midway between Ambleside and Grasmere on A591. Hall Bank Cottage is situated on side road halfway up Rydal Hill opposite entrance to Rydal Hall.

Short breaks available.

Unit
General   Leisure

ST BEES, Cumbria Map ref 1A3 — **GUEST ACCOMMODATION**

★★★★★
GUEST ACCOMMODATION

B&B per room per night
s £45.00–£55.00
d £70.00–£80.00

Fleatham House

High House Road, St Bees CA27 0BX **t** (01946) 822341 **f** (01946) 820862
e fleathamhouse@aol.com **w** fleathamhouse.com

Victorian country house set in seven acres of secluded garden overlooking St Bees Head and Solway Firth. Fleatham House offers a personal service in a peaceful setting. All rooms are spacious and en suite.

open All year except Christmas and New Year
bedrooms 3 double, 3 single
bathrooms All en suite
payment Credit/debit cards, cash/cheques

Room   General   Leisure

THRELKELD, Cumbria Map ref 1A3 — **GUEST ACCOMMODATION**

★★★★
INN

B&B per room per night
s £30.00–£35.00
d £60.00–£70.00
Evening meal per person
£7.00–£16.50

Horse and Farrier Inn

Threlkeld, Keswick CA12 4SQ **t** (017687) 79688 **f** (017687) 79823 **e** info@horseandfarrier.com
w horseandfarrier.com

open All year
bedrooms 3 double, 7 double/twin, 1 single
bathrooms 9 en suite, 2 private
payment Credit/debit cards, cash/cheques

The Horse and Farrier Inn is situated beneath Blencathra and is ideally located for walking or touring the Lake District. All bedrooms are en suite, with TV, tea- and coffee-making facilities and hairdryer. Our head chef has recently won the Cumbria Tourist Board's Most Inspiring Chef of the Year 2005/2006.

Room   General   Leisure

A holiday for Fido?

Some proprietors welcome well-behaved pets. Look for the symbol in the accommodation listings. You can also buy a copy of our new guide – Pets Come Too! – available from good bookshops and online at enjoyenglanddirect.com.

THRELKELD, Cumbria Map ref 1A3 — **GUEST ACCOMMODATION**

★★★★
GUEST HOUSE
SILVER AWARD

B&B per room per night
s £33.00–£38.00
d £56.00–£74.00

Scales Farm Country Guest House

Scales, Threlkeld, Keswick CA12 4SY **t** (017687) 79660 **f** (017687) 79510 **e** scales@scalesfarm.com
w scalesfarm.com

open All year except Christmas
bedrooms 3 double, 2 twin, 1 family
bathrooms All en suite
payment Credit/debit cards, cash/cheques

A warm welcome awaits you at our beautifully renovated 17thC farmhouse. The farm is set on the lower slopes of Blencathra, just ten minutes from Keswick by car. Wonderful open views to the south. Ideal location for touring and walking. Lakeland inn/restaurant next door.

Turn off A66 at Scales, White Horse Inn. Eleven miles jct 40 M4, 6 miles Keswick. Nearest train station Penrith 12 miles.

Winter breaks – see website for details. Discount on 7 nights or more.

Room General Leisure

TIRRIL, Cumbria Map ref 1B2 — **SELF CATERING**

★★★★
SELF CATERING

Units **5**
Sleeps **1–9**
Low season per wk
£120.00–£470.00
High season per wk
£220.00–£890.00

Tirril Farm Cottages, Penrith

contact David Owens, Tirril Farm Cottages, Tirril View, Penrith CA10 2JE
t (01768) 864767 **f** (01768) 864767 **e** enquiries@tirrilfarmcottages.co.uk **w** tirrilfarmcottages.co.uk

open All year
payment Cash/cheques

Easily accessible, two miles from Ullswater, these tasteful barn conversions enjoy a quiet courtyard setting with outstanding views over the fells. Tirril is an attractive village with prize-winning pub/restaurant. Ideal for visiting the Lakes and Eden Valley. Short breaks welcome.

M6 jct 40, A66 Scotch Corner for 1 mile then A6 Shap for 0.5 miles. Right onto B5320 to Tirril. Left at village green – Tirril Farm Cottages 100m.

Unit
General Leisure Shop 2 miles Pub < 0.5 miles

ULLSWATER, Cumbria Map ref 1A3 — **GUEST ACCOMMODATION**

★★★★
GUEST ACCOMMODATION

B&B per room per night
s £30.00–£40.00
d £56.00–£60.00

Tymparon Hall

Newbiggin, Penrith CA11 0HS **t** (017684) 83236 **f** (017684) 83236
e margaret@tymparon.freeserve.co.uk **w** tymparon.freeserve.co.uk

open All year except Christmas and New Year
bedrooms 1 double, 1 twin, 1 family
bathrooms 2 en suite, 1 private
payment Cash/cheques

Spacious and very comfortable 18thC manor-house situated on fringe of quiet village, a ten-minute drive to Lake Ullswater and close to M6 junction 40. En suite rooms available and excellent home cooking. Cosy residents' lounge with log fire. Ample private parking.

M6 jct 40, take A66 towards Keswick, in approx 1.75 miles turn right for Newbiggin. Tymparon Hall is at end of village on the right.

Reductions for 3-night, mid-week breaks.

Room General

ULLSWATER, Cumbria Map ref 1A3 — **SELF CATERING**

★★★
SELF CATERING

Units **4**
Sleeps **1–5**
Low season per wk
£290.00–£550.00
High season per wk
£350.00–£560.00

Land Ends Cabins, Watermillock

contact Mrs B Murphy, Land Ends Country Lodge, Watermillock, Ullswater CA11 0NB
t (01768) 486438 **f** (01768) 486903 **e** infolandends@btinternet.com **w** landends.co.uk

open All year
payment Cash/cheques, euros

For those seeking total relaxation, Land Ends is ideal. Only one mile from Ullswater, our detached log cabins have a peaceful, fellside location in 25-acre grounds with two pretty lakes and wonderful wildlife. Inside, exposed logs and comfortable furnishings give a cosy, rustic appeal. Dogs welcome. Guest accommodation also available.

M6 jct 40, A66 towards Keswick for 4 miles. Left at 1st sign for Hutton. Keep straight on for 2 miles, entrance is on the right.

Short breaks available.

Unit
General Leisure Shop 3 miles Pub 1.5 miles

ULLSWATER, Cumbria Map ref 1A3 — **SELF CATERING**

★★★
SELF CATERING

Units **5**
Sleeps **6–14**
Low season per wk
£195.00–£668.00
High season per wk
£245.00–£1,430.00

Swarthbeck Farm Holiday Cottages, Howtown-on-Ullswater, Penrith

contact Mr & Mrs W H Parkin, Swarthbeck Farm Holiday Cottages, Swarthbeck Farm, Howtown-on-Ullswater, Penrith CA10 2ND
t (017684) 86432 **e** whparkin@ukonline.co.uk

Properties on 160-acre farm overlooking Ullswater. Private access to lake. Visitors may bring own boats and horses. Owners' boats and mountain bikes available for visitors' use.

open All year
payment Cash/cheques

Unit
General Leisure Shop 2 miles Pub 2 miles

ULLSWATER, Cumbria Map ref 1A3 — **CAMPING & CARAVANNING**

★★★★★
HOLIDAY & TOURING PARK

(38) £15.00–£21.50
£15.00–£21.50
38 touring pitches

Waterfoot Caravan Park

Pooley Bridge, Penrith CA11 0JF **t** (017684) 86302 **f** (017684) 86728
e enquiries@waterfootpark.co.uk **w** waterfootpark.co.uk

payment Cash/cheques

Situated in the grounds of a Georgian mansion overlooking Ullswater. The park has an excellent touring area with a mix of hardstanding and lawned areas. The reception and shop are open daily. Licensed bar and games room with pool table. Children's play area. David Bellamy Gold Award. Open March to November.

M6 jct 40, follow signs marked Ullswater Steamers. West on A66 for 1 mile. Left at roundabout onto A592 (Ullswater). Pass Dalemain; Waterfoot is under 2 miles on right.

Private boat-launching area available.

General Leisure

Looking for a little luxury?

VisitBritain's unique Gold and Silver Awards are given to hotels and B&B guest accommodation achieving the highest levels of quality and service. There's more information at the front of the guide.

WINDERMERE, Cumbria Map ref 1A3 **HOTEL**

★★
HOTEL

B&B per room per night
s £40.00–£80.00
d £52.00–£110.00
HB per person per night
£39.00–£85.00

Cranleigh Hotel

Kendal Road, Bowness-on-Windermere, Windermere LA23 3EW **t** (015394) 43293
f (015394) 47283 **e** rooms@thecranleigh.com **w** thecranleigh.com

open All year
bedrooms 11 double, 2 twin, 2 family
bathrooms 14 en suite, 1 private
payment Credit/debit cards, cash/cheques

Our hotel is friendly and comfortable, two minutes' walk to lake and village centre. Ample breakfasts, good-value dinners, bar, garden. Free leisure facilities for that rainy day! Four-poster beds available. Ideal base for exploring. For full details phone for our colour brochure.

⊕ *From A592 turn up Kendal Road in Bowness village, opposite St Martin's Church. The hotel is situated a further 150m on right.*

Room General Leisure

WINDERMERE, Cumbria Map ref 1A3 **HOTEL**

★★★
COUNTRY HOUSE HOTEL GOLD AWARD

B&B per room per night
s £120.00–£150.00
d £145.00–£320.00
HB per person per night
£85.00–£180.00

Linthwaite House Hotel

Crook Road, Bowness-on-Windermere, Windermere LA23 3JA **t** (015394) 88600 **f** (015394) 88601
e stay@linthwaite.com **w** linthwaite.com

open All year
bedrooms 19 double, 4 twin, 2 single, 1 family, 1 suite
bathrooms All en suite
payment Credit/debit cards, cash/cheques

Spectacular views over Lake Windermere, friendly, unstuffy staff, award-winning food and eclectic wine list all make Linthwaite a great place to unwind. Attractions include the Lake District, Muncaster and Sizergh Castles, Levens and Holker Halls. Antiques, galleries and quality shopping widely available. Fourteen acres of peace and tranquillity, including private tarn for fishing.

⊕ *From M6 jct 36 follow A590 towards Kendal for 8 miles to large roundabout. Take 1st left onto B5284 (Crook Road). Hotel 6 miles on left.*

❤ *Romantic breaks: chilled champagne, handmade chocolates and flowers in your room ready for your arrival. Just add £68.*

Room General Leisure

WINDERMERE, Cumbria Map ref 1A3 **HOTEL**

★★★
HOTEL

B&B per room per night
s £65.00–£150.00
d £130.00–£250.00
HB per person per night
£85.00–£125.00

The Old England

Church Street, Bowness-on-Windermere, Windermere LA23 3DF **t** (015394) 42444
f (015394) 43432 **e** general@macdonald-hotels.co.uk **w** macdonald-hotels.co.uk

open All year
bedrooms 39 double, 18 twin, 8 single, 5 family, 6 suites
bathrooms All en suite
payment Credit/debit cards, cash/cheques

Arguably the best location on the shores of Lake Windermere. Take in the stunning views from the elegant Vinard Restaurant, serving fine cuisine, and the outdoor terrace bar. Ideal for exploring Bowness and all of the National Park attractions.

Room General Leisure

WINDERMERE, Cumbria Map ref 1A3 — GUEST ACCOMMODATION

♦♦♦
GUEST ACCOMMODATION

B&B per room per night
s £25.00–£35.00
d £46.00–£60.00

Brooklands

Ferry View, Bowness-on-Windermere, Windermere LA23 3JB **t** (015394) 42344
e enquiries@brooklandsguesthouse.net **w** brooklandsguesthouse.net

Brooklands is built of Lakeland stone with fine views of Lake Windermere and fells. There is off-road, private parking. We have no age limits on children.

open All year
bedrooms 2 double, 1 twin, 1 single, 1 family
bathrooms All en suite
payment Credit/debit cards, cash/cheques

Room General P Leisure

WINDERMERE, Cumbria Map ref 1A3 — GUEST ACCOMMODATION

★★★★
GUEST HOUSE

B&B per room per night
s £29.00–£37.00
d £58.00–£94.00
Evening meal per person
£20.50

Fairfield Garden Guesthouse

Brantfell Road, Bowness Bay LA23 3AE **t** (015394) 46565 **f** (015394) 46564
e relax@the-fairfield.co.uk **w** the-fairfield.co.uk

open All year except Christmas
bedrooms 5 double, 2 twin, 1 single, 1 family, 2 suites
bathrooms 10 en suite, 1 private
payment Credit/debit cards, cash/cheques, euros

Secluded Georgian house set in own grounds with beautiful garden and private car park. Informally run B&B with exceptional breakfasts. King-size four-poster bedrooms available. All rooms en suite, some with state-of-the-art, deluxe bathrooms. Guest lounge with Internet access. Located central Bowness – close to Lake Windermere, restaurants, shops and pubs.

M6 jct 36. Follow signs Kendal, Windermere. Through Windermere town to Bowness. 1st left after roundabout and left in front of Spinnery restaurant.

Reduced prices for 3 nights during weekdays, or extended weekends in low season. DB&B available Nov-Mar.

Room General 5 Leisure

WINDERMERE, Cumbria Map ref 1A3 — GUEST ACCOMMODATION

★★★★
GUEST ACCOMMODATION

B&B per room per night
s £26.00–£36.00
d £50.00–£60.00

Holly Lodge

6 College Road, Windermere LA23 1BX **t** (015394) 43873 **f** (015394) 43873
e anneandbarry@hollylodge6.fsnet.co.uk **w** hollylodge20.co.uk

Traditional Lakeland, family-run guesthouse in a quiet location close to shops, restaurants, buses and trains. Friendly atmosphere. Hearty English breakfast. Each bedroom individually furnished.

open All year except Christmas
bedrooms 4 double, 1 single, 4 family
bathrooms All en suite
payment Credit/debit cards, cash/cheques

Room General P Leisure

Country Code

Always follow the Country Code

- Be safe – plan ahead and follow any signs
- Leave gates and property as you find them
- Protect plants and animals, and take your litter home
- Keep dogs under close control
- Consider other people

WINDERMERE, Cumbria Map ref 1A3 — **GUEST ACCOMMODATION**

★★★
GUEST HOUSE

B&B per room per night
s £20.00–£40.00
d £40.00–£70.00

St John's Lodge

Lake Road, Windermere LA23 2EQ **t** (015394) 43078 **f** (015394) 88054
e mail@st-johns-lodge.co.uk **w** st-johns-lodge.co.uk

open All year except Christmas
bedrooms 9 double, 1 twin, 2 single, 2 family
bathrooms 12 en suite, 2 private
payment Credit/debit cards, cash/cheques, euros

Attractive guesthouse between Windermere and lake, exclusively for non-smokers. Comfortable, clean, en suite rooms. Large breakfast menu including traditional English, veggie/vegan, fresh fish and some house-speciality dishes. Free internet access including radio connectivity for laptops. Free use of nearby leisure club. Parking. Option to book online using our secure server.

A591 to Windermere, left at Windermere Hotel, follow signs Bowness and lake. New Road/Lake Road. We are 100m after Catholic church on left.

3-day breaks (price per person): low season from £57, mid-season from £69, high season from £78.

Room General 6 P Leisure

WINDERMERE, Cumbria Map ref 1A3 — **SELF CATERING**

★★★
SELF CATERING

Units **2**
Sleeps **2–6**
Low season per wk
£195.00–£295.00
High season per wk
£295.00–£455.00

The Abbey Coach House, Windermere

contact Mrs P Bell, The Abbey Coach House, St Mary's Park, Windermere LA23 1AZ
t (015394) 44027 **f** (015394) 44027 **e** abbeycoach@aol.com **w** abbeycoachhouse.co.uk

open All year
payment Cash/cheques

This former Victorian coach house offers an excellent location of a ground-floor apartment and bungalow in quiet, private grounds. Only a short walk to the lake and Windermere town. Extensive gardens with ample parking. Within easy reach of all amenities. Ideal for families and the retired.

M6 jct 36, A590/A591 towards Windermere. Pass 2 Windermere town turnings on A591. Approx 200m after 2nd turning, St Mary's church. Immediately left into St Mary's Park. 3rd left driveway into Abbey Coach House.

Short breaks available throughout the year (excl Christmas and New Year).

Unit
General P Leisure Shop < 0.5 miles Pub < 0.5 miles

WINDERMERE, Cumbria Map ref 1A3 — **CAMPING & CARAVANNING**

★★★★★
HOLIDAY & TOURING PARK

(43) £10.00–£26.00
£10.00–£26.00
43 touring pitches

Hill of Oaks and Blakeholme Caravans

Tower Wood, Windermere LA23 3PJ **t** (015395) 31578 **f** (015395) 30431
e enquiries@hillofoaks.co.uk **w** hillofoaks.co.uk

payment Cash/cheques

Award-winning caravan park situated on the shores of Windermere. Very much family orientated, the park has a play area and nature walks through the woodland. The site has six jetties, boat launching and access to watersport activities. Shop and disabled facilities. Children's play area. David Bellamy Gold Award. Open March to November.

M6 jct 36, head west on A590 towards Barrow and Newby Bridge. At roundabout turn right, onto A592. Park is approx 3 miles on the left-hand side.

General P Leisure

WORKINGTON, Cumbria Map ref 1A2 — **GUEST ACCOMMODATION**

★★★
GUEST ACCOMMODATION

B&B per room per night
s £28.00–£32.00
d £48.00–£50.00

Morven Guest House

Siddick Road, Workington CA14 1LE **t** (01900) 602118 & 07718 864 7196 **f** (01900) 602118
e cnelsonmorven@aol.com **w** morvenguesthouse.gbr.cc

Detached house north-west of town. Near start of C2C cycleway. On Reivers and Hadrian's cycle routes. You may leave your car until you return. Car park, secure cycle storage.

open All year
bedrooms 1 double, 4 twin, 1 single
bathrooms All en suite
payment Cash/cheques

Room General P Leisure

WORKINGTON, Cumbria Map ref 1A2 — **GUEST ACCOMMODATION**

★★★★
INN

B&B per room per night
s £45.00–£55.00
d £60.00–£100.00

The Old Ginn House

Moor Road, Great Clifton, Workington CA14 1TS **t** (01900) 64616 **f** (01900) 873384
e enquiries@oldginnhouse.co.uk **w** oldginnhouse.co.uk

The Old Ginn House has been successfully converted from a 17thC farm into a charming village inn and offers quality accommodation, great food and a warm welcome. Ideal for exploring the Western Lake District.

open All year except Christmas
bedrooms 10 double, 4 twin, 4 family, 1 suite
bathrooms All en suite
payment Credit/debit cards, cash/cheques

Room General P Leisure

Spot the matchstick men at the Lowry Gallery

Immerse yourself in the culture, entertainment and nightlife of one of the most vibrant modern cities in England. Step outside its boundaries and explore winding rivers, black-and-white timber houses and **the sweet sound of jazz.**

Explore Greater Manchester

The striking B of the Bang sculpture

Head for the city

Discover the Manchester waterfront at the impressive Quays. Enjoy a play, wander the galleries or dine out in a restaurant at The Lowry, a veritable centre of culture and entertainment. Marvel at the impressive B of the Bang sculpture – the tallest in the UK – and discover how Mancunians lived a hundred or so years ago at the Museum of Science & Industry in Manchester.

Visit the 'Theatre of Dreams' and imagine days filled with glory at the famous Old Trafford football ground. Admire the impressive trophies, strut down the players' tunnel and take a moment to sit in the home team's dressing room. Feel part of the drama and enjoy a spot of street theatre or an evening of music at The Bridgewater Hall, an outstanding piece of architecture and Manchester's premier concert venue.

Paint the town red and sample the vibrant Manchester nightlife, from clubs to stylish bars, restaurants to cosy pubs, this modern city is packed with after-dark entertainment. Laugh the night away at one of the many comedy clubs and on the way home catch a glimpse of The Lowry Bridge – not just a stunning walkway, but also the finish line for the Commonwealth Games – lit up for a true night-time spectacle.

All that jazz...

Explore 30 miles of rivers and canals in Salford. Drop a penny in the water and make a wish at the Victorian ornamental fountain in Worsley village – built from the old factory's chimney stacks – and admire the charming 18th- and 19th-century black-and-white timber buildings.

Learn about the world's largest working mill steam engine on a trip to Wigan Pier or relax to a host of soothing sounds during the Jazz Festival in the summer months. Feel the lively buzz of entertainment in Rochdale, where street parties, performing arts, markets and live music are guaranteed to interest and amuse.

Get a piece of the action at Old Trafford

Explore the enlightening exhibits at The Imperial War Museum North

Time travel

Manchester's museums not only contain fascinating and contemporary exhibitions, but the buildings themselves are fantastic examples of modern-day architecture. Click your heels and take a walk through urban culture at the magnificent glass-walled Urbis museum where you can experience interactive exhibits and gen up on the city. Make sure the impressive Imperial War Museum North – designed by Daniel Libeskind – is on your 'to do' list and learn how people are affected by war and conflict.

Soak up four centuries of history with a visit to Wythenshawe Hall – a magnificent half-timbered Tudor house that now serves as an art gallery and its grounds a public park. Step back to 1940s Britain at the Stockport Air Raid Shelters where you can experience the sights and sounds of a country at war, and imagine yourself taking refuge after dark.

Make time for a visit to Bolton Museum, Art Gallery & Aquarium to see gnashing piranhas among a vast array of colourful marine life. Remember to check out the events too before you go.

Food & drink

Fancy a bite to eat, a relaxing drink or some fresh local produce? Here's a selection of food and drink venues to get you started. For lots more ideas go online at **enjoyengland.com/taste**.

Restaurants

Choice Bar & Restaurant
English
Castle Quay, Castlefield, Manchester M15 4NT
t (0161) 833 3400
w choicebarandrestaurant.co.uk

Est Est Est – Didsbury
Italian
756 Wilmslow Road, Didsbury, Manchester M20 2DW
t 0870 401 2107
w estestest.co.uk

The Establishment
Fine dining
43-45 Spring Gardens, Manchester M2 2BG
t (0161) 839 6300
w establishmentrestaurant.com

The Fat Loaf
English
62 Green Lane, Ashton-on-Mersey, Sale M33 5PG
t (0161) 972 0397
w thefatloaf.co.uk

The Gaucho Grill
English
2A St Marys Street, Manchester M3 2LB
t (0161) 833 4333
w gaucho-grill.com

Isinglass English Dining Rooms
English
46 Flixton Road, Urmston M41 5AB
t (0161) 749 8400
w isinglassrestaurant.co.uk

Le Mont
French
Levels 5&6, The Urbis, Cathedral Gardens, Manchester M4 3BG
t (0161) 605 8282
w urbis.org.uk

Little Yang Sing
Cantonese
17 George Street, China Town, Manchester M1 4HE
t (0161) 228 7722
w littleyangsing.co.uk

Midland Hotel
French
Peter Street, Manchester M60 2DS
t (0161) 236 3333
w e-travelguide.info/midland

Nutters
European
Edenfield Road, Norden, Rochdale OL12 7TT
t (01706) 650167
w nuttersrestaurants.co.uk

Pacific China
Chinese
58-60 George Street, Manchester M1 4HF
t (0161) 228 6668

Pearl City Cantonese Restaurant
Cantonese
33 George Street, Manchester M1 4HQ
t (0161) 228 7683

Ramson's
Italian
18 Market Place, Ramsbottom, Bury BL0 9HT
t (01706) 825070
w ramsons.org.uk

San Carlo Restaurant
Italian
40-42 King Street West, Manchester M3 2WY
t (0161) 834 6226
w sancarlo.co.uk

Shimla Pinks
Indian
Dolefield, Crown Square, Manchester M3 3HA
t (0161) 831 7099
w shimlapinksmanchester.co.uk

Watersreach Restaurant
European
Golden Tulip, Trafford Park, Manchester M171 1WS
t (0161) 868 1900

Yang Sing
Chinese
34 Princess Street, Manchester M1 4JY
t (0161) 236 2200
w yang-sing.com

Delis

Barbakan Continental Delicatessen
67-71 Manchester Road, Chorlton M21 9PW
t (0161) 881 7053
w barbakan-deli.co.uk

Carnival Organics
24 Lever Street, Manchester M1 1DW
t (0161) 228 6600
w carnivalorganics.co.uk

The Cheese Hamlet
706 Wilmslow Road, Didsbury M20 2DW
t (0161) 434 4781
w cheesehamlet.co.uk

Love Saves The Day
345 Deansgate Knott Mill, Knott Mill M3 4LG
t (0161) 834 2266
w lovesavestheday.co.uk

PJ Howarth Butchers of Flixton
304 Flixton Road, Flixton M41 5DP
t (0161) 748 0199
w pjhowarthbutcher.com

Unicorn Grocery
89 Albany Road, Chorlton M21 0BN
t (0161) 861 7675
w unicorn-grocery.co.uk

where to stay in
Greater Manchester

Maps
All place names in the blue bands are shown on the maps at the front of this guide.

Accommodation symbols
Symbols give useful information about services and facilities. Inside the back-cover flap you can find a key to these symbols. Keep it open for easy reference.

BOLTON, Greater Manchester Map ref 2A1 — **GUEST ACCOMMODATION**

★★★
GUEST HOUSE

B&B per room per night
s £27.00
d £40.00–£60.00

Highgrove Guest House

63 Manchester Road, Bolton BL2 1ES **t** (01204) 384928 **e** thehighgrove@btconnect.com
w highgroveguesthouse.co.uk

We are a family-run, welcoming guesthouse. Modern, comfortable, well-appointed rooms. A short walk to the town centre and station. A perfect base for your stay in Bolton.

open All year
bathrooms 3 twin, 4 single, 3 family
bathrooms All en suite
payment Credit/debit cards, cash/cheques

Room General P

BURY, Greater Manchester Map ref 2B1 — **SELF CATERING**

★★★★
SELF CATERING

Units 1
Sleeps 2

Low season per wk
Min £350.00
High season per wk
Min £350.00

Top o' th' Moor Cottage, Bury

contact Mrs Michelle Richardson, Moorbottom Road, Holcombe, Bury BL8 4NR
t 07976 034196 **e** info@topofthemoorcottage.com **w** topofthemoorcottage.com

One-bedroom self-contained cottage, attached to farmhouse, on the edge of the West Pennine Moors.

open All year
payment Cash/cheques

Unit
General P Leisure Shop 2 miles Pub 0.5 miles

BURY, Greater Manchester Map ref 2B1 — **CAMPING & CARAVANNING**

★★★★★
TOURING PARK
(75) £12.50–£25.10
(75) £12.50–£25.10
75 touring pitches

See Ad on inside front cover

Burrs Country Park Caravan Club Site

Woodhill Road, Bury BL8 1BN **t** (0161) 761 0489 **w** caravanclub.co.uk

payment Credit/debit cards, cash/cheques

On a historic mill site, Burrs has much to offer, including relaxing river and countryside walks as well as easy access into Manchester. Open March to November.

From A676 (signposted Ramsbottom), follow signs for Burrs Country Park.

Special member rates mean you can save your membership subscription in less than a week. Visit our website to find out more.

General P

DELPH, Greater Manchester Map ref 2B1 — **SELF CATERING**

★★★★
SELF CATERING

Units 2
Sleeps 2–6
Low season per wk
£250.00–£350.00
High season per wk
£250.00–£350.00

The Stables, Delph, Oldham

contact Mrs G Whipp, Sandbed Farm Cottage, Sandbed Lane, Delph, Oldham OL3 5UZ
t (01457) 871668 **f** (01457) 871668 **e** gwynethwhipp@btinternet.com **w** saddleworthcottages.co.uk

Luxury modern conversion of stables into two self-contained units in a rural and historic area known as Saddleworth. One family room plus sofa bed and two twin rooms plus sofa bed.

open All year
payment Cash/cheques

Unit
General Leisure Shop 0.5 miles Pub 0.5 miles

DUKINFIELD, Greater Manchester Map ref 2B1 — **GUEST ACCOMMODATION**

♦♦♦
GUEST ACCOMMODATION

B&B per room per night
s £30.00–£35.00
d £50.00–£55.00

Barton Villa Guest House

Crescent Road, Dukinfield SK16 4EY **t** (0161) 330 3952 **f** (0161) 285 8488 **e** harrott4@aol.com
w bartonvilla.co.uk

Large, detached house in own grounds with car park and separate annexe. Within easy reach of town centre.

open All year
bedrooms 3 double, 4 twin, 8 single, 3 family
bathrooms 15 en suite
payment Credit/debit cards, cash/cheques

Room General

MANCHESTER AIRPORT

See under Sale, Salford

ROCHDALE, Greater Manchester Map ref 2B1 — **GUEST ACCOMMODATION**

♦♦♦♦
GUEST ACCOMMODATION

B&B per room per night
s £30.00
d £39.95

WALKERS WELCOME CYCLISTS WELCOME

Fernhill Barn B&B

Fernhill Lane, Lanehead, Rochdale OL12 6BW **t** (01706) 355671 **f** (01706) 868405
e info@fernhillbarn.com **w** fernhillbarn.com

Fernhill Barn is set in countryside surrounded by beautiful views. Separate entrance for guests, own kitchen. All rooms have a luxury en suite, digital TV/DVDs. Well placed for shops, restaurants etc. Easy motorway access.

open All year
bedrooms 2 double, 2 twin, 1 single, 2 family
bathrooms All en suite
payment Credit/debit cards, cash/cheques

Room General Leisure

ROCHDALE, Greater Manchester Map ref 2B1 — **SELF CATERING**

★★★★
SELF CATERING

Units 1
Sleeps 6
Low season per wk
Min £450.00
High season per wk
Max £600.00

Butterworth Hall, Milnrow, Rochdale

contact Mrs Judith Hirst, The Gatehouse, Ogden Lane, Newhey, Rochdale OL16 3TQ
t (01706) 882781 **f** (01706) 882781 **e** judyhirst@btinternet.com **w** springmill.co.uk

open All year
payment Credit/debit cards, cash/cheques, euros

Tucked away in a little row just two doors down from the friendly local, this extremely well decorated and refurbished end weaver's cottage offers a high standard of living. Lounge with gas 'woodburner' stove. Spacious, well-equipped kitchen with range cooker. Penthouse-style bedroom/lounge and three further bedrooms.

On M62 jct 21, follow A640 towards Shaw. Take 1st left signed Milnrow. Opposite BP petrol station, turn right up New Street.

Unit
General Leisure Pub < 0.5 miles

Key to symbols

Open the back flap for a key to symbols.

ROCHDALE, Greater Manchester Map ref 2B1 — **SELF CATERING**

★★★
SELF CATERING

Units 1
Sleeps 5
Low season per wk
£220.00–£250.00
High season per wk
£240.00–£300.00

Pennine Cottages, Wardle, Rochdale

contact Mrs Joy Mitchell, 2 Pennine Cottages, Lower House Lane, Wardle, Rochdale OL12 9PL
t (01706) 379632 **w** hometown.aol.co.uk/penninecottage/myhomepage/business.html

Stone-built farm cottage on a working sheep farm. Three bedrooms. Baby facilities on request, at no extra charge.

open All year
payment Cash/cheques, euros

Unit
General Leisure Shop 1 mile Pub 1 mile

ROCHDALE, Greater Manchester Map ref 2B1 — **CAMPING & CARAVANNING**

★★★
HOLIDAY, TOURING & CAMPING PARK

(30) £10.00–£14.00
(10) £10.00–£14.00
(10) £8.00–£14.00
50 touring pitches

Hollingworth Lake Caravan Park

Roundhouse Farm, Hollingworth Lake, Littleborough OL15 0AT **t** (01706) 378661

open All year
payment Cash/cheques

A popular, five-acre park adjacent to Hollingworth Lake, at the foot of the Pennines, within easy reach of many local attractions. Backpackers walking the Pennine Way are welcome at this family-run park.

From M62. Jct 21 Milnrow. Follow Hollingworth Lake Country Park signs to the Fishermans Inn/The Wine Press. Take Rakewood Road then 2nd on right.

General Leisure

SADDLEWORTH, Greater Manchester Map ref 2B1 — **HOTEL**

★★★
HOTEL

B&B per room per night
s £45.00–£65.00
d £62.00–£77.00

La Pergola Hotel

Rochdale Road, Denshaw, Oldham OL3 5UE **t** (01457) 871040 **f** (01457) 873804
e reception@lapergola.freeserve.co.uk **w** hotel-restaurant-uk.com

A hotel offering a warm and friendly atmosphere. Our restaurant serves authentic Italian cuisine, with a traditional Sunday lunch. The Peacock Suite is licensed for civil ceremonies.

open All year except Christmas
bedrooms 11 double, 7 twin, 2 single, 4 family, 2 suites
bathrooms All en suite
payment Credit/debit cards, cash/cheques

Room General Leisure

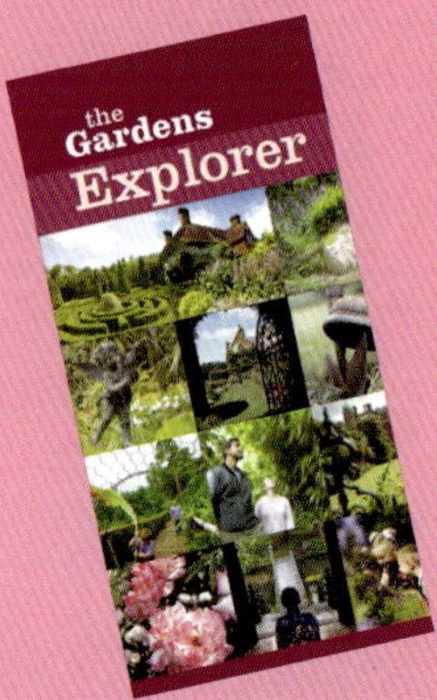

The great outdoors

Discover Britain's green heart with this easy-to-use guide. Featuring a selection of the most stunning gardens in the country, The Gardens Explorer is complete with a handy fold-out map and illustrated guide. You can purchase the Explorer series from good bookshops and online at visitbritaindirect.com.

SALE, Greater Manchester Map ref 2A2 — **HOTEL**

★★
HOTEL

B&B per room per night
s £35.95–£55.95
d £55.95–£75.95
HB per person per night
£50.00–£80.00

Lennox Lea Hotel

Irlam Road, Sale M33 2BH **t** (0161) 973 1764 **f** (0161) 969 6059 **e** info@lennoxlea.co.uk
w lennoxlea.co.uk

open All year
bedrooms 11 double, 1 twin, 14 single, 1 family, 1 suite
bathrooms All en suite
payment Credit/debit cards, cash/cheques

An attractive Victorian building set in its own grounds with ample free parking. Privately run, offering a warm welcome, comfortable accommodation and excellent food. Situated on a peaceful, tree-lined road while conveniently located for many North West attractions. One mile from the motorway network and 0.3 miles from the tram.

Arriving at Sale Metrolink station, turn right and walk along Northenden Road. Irlam Road is the 3rd road on the left.

Fri & Sat DB&B for 2, £90 per room (sharing a double or twin).

Room General P Leisure

SALFORD, Greater Manchester Map ref 2B1 — **GUEST ACCOMMODATION**

★★
GUEST ACCOMMODATION

B&B per room per night
s £30.00–£37.00
d £46.00–£50.00

Lyndale Court

1-2 The Drive, Bury New Road, Salford M7 3ND **t** (0161) 792 7270 **f** (0161) 792 7270

Situated in a leafy suburb, just 2.5 miles north of Manchester city centre and two miles south of junction 17, M60. Providing easy access to all destinations.

open All year
bedrooms 1 double, 1 twin, 2 single, 1 family
bathrooms 3 en suite
payment Credit/debit cards, cash/cheques

Room General Leisure

sunset sands, literary legends, superb countryside

Having a blast at Blackpool Pleasure Beach

Tighten your grip as you plummet down a Blackpool rollercoaster, or recharge your batteries whilst admiring unspoilt scenery from the garden of a cosy country pub and **just take it easy.**

Explore Lancashire

Never-ending fun

Cruise peacefully through the River Caves at Blackpool's Pleasure Beach, or feel your heart thumping as you speed down the traditional big dipper and imagine one World Record breaker riding it solidly for three months! Pick out your favourite amongst the sparkling Autumn Illuminations, enjoy high tea in the glitzy Blackpool Tower Ballroom or get down to the beach and feel the sand between your toes.

Step back in time to the Jurassic period at Blackpool Zoo & Dinosaur Safari where you can even see an impressive erupting volcano! Get your adrenalin pumping as you speed round the track at the Blackpool Karting Centre. Feel ten feet tall as you tower over the model village at Stanley Park or discover contemporary sculpture at the Grundy Art Gallery.

Stroll along five miles of promenade at Morecambe, shop for souvenirs at the Festival Market and gaze at the horizon as the sun sets spectacularly across stunning Morecambe Bay. Take a trip to The Wildfowl and Wetland Trust Martin Mere, near Ormskirk, to watch strutting flamingos, endangered ducks and nestling geese and swans.

The Wildfowl and Wetland Trust Martin Mere

Hot on the trail in the Forest of Bowland

Natural creations

Relax in one of Lancashire's superb Areas of Outstanding Natural Beauty: spot rare birds in the Forest of Bowland, hunt for datestones and stroll through 65 acres of grass and woodland. Breathe in the crisp country air at Arnside or catch a glimpse of the picturesque Lindeth Tower at Silverdale.

Visit the beautifully preserved National Trust properties that Lancashire has to offer. Rufford Old Hall is a quaint 16th-century black-and-white timbered building with an abundance of charm. Study the intricately carved wooden screen in the Great Hall and don't forget to visit the armour collection. Enjoy the tranquillity in the stunning grounds of Gawthorpe Hall, and steal a precious moment of peace and quiet.

Watch top-level golf at Royal Lytham and St Annes

Magical games

Let the magic take hold at Camelot Theme Park: watch Merlin perform his legendary illusions, get a soaking on Pendragon's Plunge and watch from the sidelines as jousting knights and jesters put on a show. Discover secret rooms, hidden until a hundred years ago, at Lancaster Castle and allow its fascinating history to unravel before your eyes.

For sporting fans, The National Museum of Football in Preston is a must. Stroll through illuminated galleries and test your skills at GoalStriker – the interactive penalty shoot-out experience. Golfing enthusiasts can enjoy breathtaking views whilst playing on one of the many courses in the region.

A literary connection

Sup a pint in the Golden Lion, where the legendary Pendle Witches savoured their last drink before being led to the gallows. Gaze wistfully into the ruins of Wycoller Hall, in the village of Wycoller, and conjure up images of Ferndean Manor from Charlotte Brontë's *Jane Eyre* – for which it was allegedly the inspiration.

Walk the corridors of Stonyhurst College – one of the largest buildings in the North West – and imagine Sherlock Holmes novelist Sir Arthur Conan Doyle treading its boards as a schoolboy. Or visit Houghton Tower, where William Shakespeare was once a resident.

Food & drink

Fancy a bite to eat, a relaxing drink or some fresh local produce? Here's a selection of food and drink venues to get you started. For lots more ideas go online at **enjoyengland.com/taste**.

Restaurants

Bombay Brasserie
Indian
2 Oxcliffe Road, Heysham,
Morecambe LA3 1PS
t (01524) 850088

De Vere Heron's Reach
English
East Park Drive, Blackpool FY3 8LL
t (01253) 838866
w devere.co.uk

Kwizeen Restaurant
European bistro
47-49 King Street, Blackpool
FY1 3EJ
t (01253) 290045
w kwizeen.co.uk

The Longridge Restaurant
English
104-106 Higher Road, Longridge,
Preston PR3 3SY
t (01772) 784969
w heathcotes.co.uk

Northcote Manor
English
Northcote Road, Langho,
Blackburn BB6 8BE
t (01254) 240555
w northcotemanor.com

Imperial Hotel
Fine dining
North Promenade, Blackpool
FY1 2HB
t (01253) 623971
w paramount-hotels.co.uk

Seniors Fish Bar & Restaurant
Seafood
106 Normoss Road, Blackpool
FY3 8QP
t (01253) 393529
w seniorsfishexperience.com

The Spread Eagle
Fine dining
Sawley, Forest of Bowland,
Clitheroe BB7 4NH
t (01200) 441202
w the-spreadeagle.co.uk

Stanley House – Cassis Restaurant
Fine dining
Preston New Road, Mellor,
Blackburn BB2 7NP
t (01254) 769200
w stanleyhouse.co.uk

Winckley Square Chop House
English
23 Winkley Square, Preston
PR1 3JJ
t (01772) 252732
w heathcotes.co.uk

Pubs

The Derby Arms
Chipping Road, Longridge,
Preston PR3 2NB
t (01772) 782623

Fence Gate Inn
Wheatley Lane Road, Fence,
Nr Burnley BB12 9EE
t (01282) 618101
w fencegate.co.uk

The Hest Bank Hotel
2 Hest Bank Lane, Hest Bank,
Lancaster LA2 6DN
t (01524) 824339

The Millstone at Mellor
Church Lane, Mellor BB2 7JR
t (01254) 813333
w millstonehotel.co.uk

The Three Fishes
Mitton Road, Mitton,
Nr Whalley BB7 9PQ
t (01254) 826888
w thethreefishes.com

Tearooms, coffee shops and cafes

Artisan cafe
296 Marine Road Central,
Morecambe LA4 5BY
t (01524) 417954

Cafe Artisan
1 Brook Street, Bury Road,
Rawtenstall BB4 6AA
t (01706) 211114

Delis

Bashall Eaves Farm Shop
Bashall Eaves, Clitheroe BB7 3LQ
t (01200) 428964

Culinary Herbs
The Herbarium, Rawcliffe Lodge,
Bodkin Lane, Preston PR3 6TL
t (01253) 700311

Todderstaffes of Lytham
13 Park Street, Lytham Street,
Lytham St Annes FY8 5LU
t (01253) 735325

Farm shops and local produce

Conder Green Farm Shop
Conder Green, Lancaster
LA2 0AN
t (01524) 752174

Mansergh Hall Farm Shop
Kirkby Lonsdale, Carnforth
LA6 2EN
t (015242) 71397
w manserghhall.co.uk

Walling's Meats
Higher Crookhey Farm,
Cockerham LA2 OHA
t (01524) 792162
w traditional-breeds-meats.co.uk

where to stay in
Lancashire

Maps
All place names in the blue bands are shown on the maps at the front of this guide.

Accommodation symbols
Symbols give useful information about services and facilities. Inside the back-cover flap you can find a key to these symbols. Keep it open for easy reference.

BACUP, Lancashire Map ref 2B1 — **GUEST ACCOMMODATION**

♦♦♦♦
GUEST ACCOMMODATION

B&B per room per night
s £30.00
d £50.00

Rossbrook House

New Line, Bacup OL13 0BY **t** (01706) 878187 **f** (01706) 878099 **e** rossbkhouse@aol.com
w a1touristguide.com/rossbrookhouse

Spacious former vicarage set in own grounds with ample parking. Refurbished to retain the charm of its Victorian past and providing excellent facilities for guests.

open All year except Christmas
bedrooms 3 double, 1 twin
bathrooms All en suite
payment Cash/cheques

Room General P Leisure

BLACKBURN, Lancashire Map ref 2A1 — **HOTEL**

Rating Applied For
COUNTRY HOUSE HOTEL

B&B per room per night
s £120.00–£155.00
d £155.00–£190.00

Northcote Manor Hotel

Northcote Road, Blackburn BB6 8BE **t** (01254) 240555 **f** (01254) 246568
e sales@northcotemanor.com **w** northcotemanor.com

open All year except Christmas and New Year
bedrooms 10 double, 4 twin
bathrooms All en suite
payment Credit/debit cards, cash/cheques, euros

Northcote Manor is an award-winning restaurant with highly individual rooms offering total luxury and comfort. Elegant wood panelling, warm welcoming lounges with sumptuous leather sofas and impressive staircases add to the atmosphere. Enjoy the gardens and grounds, with breathtaking views of the Ribble Valley.

Leave the M6 at jct 31, take the A59 to the village of Langho. Approximately 9 miles at the edge of Ribble Valley.

Gourmet Breaks available from £105pp – includes: Champagne, 5-course gourmet dinner, overnight stay and stunning Lancashire breakfast.

Room General P Leisure

Check it out

Information on accommodation listed in this guide has been supplied by proprietors. As changes may occur you should remember to check all relevant details at the time of booking.

BLACKBURN, Lancashire Map ref 2A1 — **HOTEL**

★★★★
COUNTRY HOUSE HOTEL
SILVER AWARD

B&B per room per night
s £190.00–£220.00
d £190.00–£250.00
HB per person per night
£122.50–£167.50

Stanley House

Preston New Road, Mellor, Blackburn BB2 7NP **t** (01254) 769200 **f** (01254) 769206
e info@stanleyhouse.co.uk **w** stanleyhouse.co.uk

Stanley House is a 17thC manor-house, which has undergone major restoration and sympathetic enhancement, leaving it to rank amongst the country's finest contemporary country-house hotels, and a perfect venue for events.

open All year
bedrooms 8 double, 4 twin
bathrooms All en suite
payment Credit/debit cards, cash/cheques

Room General 3 P

BLACKPOOL, Lancashire Map ref 2A1 — **GUEST ACCOMMODATION**

♦♦♦
GUEST ACCOMMODATION

B&B per room per night
s £22.00–£35.00
d £44.00–£60.00
Evening meal per person
Max £10.00

Poldhu Hotel

330 Queens Promenade, Blackpool FY2 9AB **t** (01253) 356918 **f** (01253) 354911
e info@poldhu-hotel.co.uk **w** poldhu-hotel.co.uk

Family-run small hotel quietly situated on the Queens Promenade, overlooking the sea, with walks along the seafront.

open All year except Christmas and New Year
bedrooms 4 double, 1 twin, 1 single, 1 family
bathrooms 5 en suite
payment Credit/debit cards, cash/cheques

Room General P

BLACKPOOL, Lancashire Map ref 2A1 — **GUEST ACCOMMODATION**

★★★
GUEST ACCOMMODATION

B&B per room per night
s £20.00–£22.00
d £44.00–£50.00
Evening meal per person
£6.00–£8.00

St Ives Hotel

10 King George Avenue, Blackpool FY2 9SN **t** (01253) 352122 **f** (01253) 352122
e enquiries@stiveshotel-blackpool.co.uk **w** stiveshotel-blackpool.co.uk

open All year
bedrooms 3 double, 2 single, 4 family
bathrooms 5 en suite
payment Credit/debit cards, cash/cheques

A highly recommended non-smoking hotel, situated adjacent to Queens Promenade. All rooms with TV, tea-/coffee-making facilities and full central heating throughout. Good food and cleanliness assured.

Take M55 to central promenade. Turn right and keep sea on left to reach large roundabout. Stay on promenade and take 2nd right past roundabout.

Mid-week breaks: 4 nights' B&B from £74 – £82.

Room General

BLACKPOOL, Lancashire Map ref 2A1 — **GUEST ACCOMMODATION**

★★★
GUEST ACCOMMODATION

B&B per room per night
s £20.00–£30.00
d £40.00–£60.00
Evening meal per person
£5.50–£9.00

Sandalwood

3 Gynn Avenue, Blackpool FY1 2LD **t** (01253) 351795 **f** (01253) 351795
e peter.gerald@btconnect.com **w** sandalwoodhotel.co.uk

Small family-run guest accommodation in quiet part of Blackpool, close to seafront, offering a friendly service and good home-cooked meals. Tower, shows and attractions 20 minutes' walk away.

open All year except Christmas
bedrooms 5 double, 2 twin, 2 family
bathrooms 7 en suite
payment Cash/cheques

Room General

Check the maps

Colour maps at the front pinpoint all places in which you will find accommodation entries in the regional sections. Pick your location and then refer to the place index at the back to find the page number.

BLACKPOOL, Lancashire Map ref 2A1 — **GUEST ACCOMMODATION**

★★★★
GUEST HOUSE

B&B per room per night
s £22.00–£26.00
d £44.00–£52.00

Tudor Rose Original

5 Withnell Road, Blackpool FY4 1HF **t** (01253) 343485 **e** tudor_rose@onetel.com
w tudorroseoriginal.co.uk

The Tudor Rose is perfectly situated for all that Blackpool has to offer. A two-minute walk from the Pleasure Beach and South Pier. A warm welcome guaranteed.

open All year
bedrooms 8 double, 2 twin, 1 single
bathrooms All en suite
payment Cash/cheques

Room General

BLACKPOOL, Lancashire Map ref 2A1 — **SELF CATERING**

★★–★★★
SELF CATERING

Units 4
Sleeps 1–4
Low season per wk
£85.00–£140.00
High season per wk
£140.00–£200.00

Donange Holiday Flats, Blackpool

contact Mr M Hasson, Donange Holiday Flats, 29 Holmfield Road, Blackpool FY2 9TB
t (01253) 355051 **e** donange@msn.com **w** donangeblackpoolaccomodation.co.uk

Select holiday apartments 150yds from Queens Promenade. High standard of cleanliness assured. Tea/sugar/towels provided. Standard beds. A friendly welcome awaits. Families, couples, senior citizens, small pets welcome.

open All year
payment Cash/cheques

Unit
General Shop < 0.5 miles Pub < 0.5 miles

BOLTON-BY-BOWLAND, Lancashire Map ref 2B1 — **GUEST ACCOMMODATION**

♦♦♦♦
GUEST ACCOMMODATION

B&B per room per night
s £35.00–£45.00
d £56.00–£65.00
Evening meal per person
£22.00–£28.00

Middle Flass Lodge

Forest Becks Brow, Clitheroe BB7 4NY **t** (01200) 447259 **f** (01200) 447300
e info@middleflasslodge.fsnet.co.uk **w** middleflasslodge.co.uk

open All year
bedrooms 4 double, 2 twin, 1 family
bathrooms All en suite
payment Credit/debit cards, cash/cheques

Tastefully converted barn/cow byre, set in idyllic countryside location of Forest of Bowland. Ideal touring base on Lancashire/Yorkshire border. Always personal and professional attention with neat and cosy bedrooms. Lounge with stove, dining room with chef-prepared cuisine. Licensed. Gardens and ample parking.

From M65 – Clitheroe – Skipton A59. Take Sawley turning. Follow signpost for Bolton-by-Bowland. Just before village take signpost for Settle. Two miles on the right.

Room General Leisure

BURNLEY, Lancashire Map ref 2B1 — **GUEST ACCOMMODATION**

♦♦♦♦
GUEST ACCOMMODATION

B&B per room per night
s £24.00
d £48.00
Evening meal per person
£10.00–£12.00

Higher Cockden Farm

Todmorden Road, Briercliffe, Burnley BB10 3QQ **t** (01282) 831324 **f** (01282) 831324
e j.hodkinson_bb@tiscali.co.uk **w** highercockdenfarm.com

Working farm on the edge of the Pennine Way Mary Towneley Loop. Ideal for walkers, cyclists and horse-riders. Fishing, clay-pigeon shooting and stabling available. Luggage transfers. Dales and lakes within easy reach.

open All year
bedrooms 3 double, 2 twin, 1 single, 1 family
bathrooms 4 en suite
payment Cash/cheques

Room General Leisure

Key to symbols

Open the back flap for a key to symbols.

CARNFORTH, Lancashire Map ref 1B3 — **GUEST ACCOMMODATION**

★★★★
GUEST ACCOMMODATION
SILVER AWARD

B&B per room per night
s £27.50–£37.50
d £52.00–£55.00
Evening meal per person
£12.50

Capernwray House

Borrans Lane, Capernwray, Carnforth LA6 1AE **t** (01524) 732363 **e** mel@capernwrayhouse.com
w capernwrayhouse.com

open All year except Christmas and New Year
bedrooms 2 double, 1 twin, 1 single
bathrooms 3 en suite
payment Credit/debit cards, cash/cheques

Country house in 12 acres of rolling countryside. Beautiful views. Residents' lounge. Ideal for Lake District, Dales, Lancaster. Totally non-smoking. A warm welcome guaranteed. Ideal stopover North/South. Well worth seeking out!

M5 jct 35. Follow signs for Over Kellett. Left at village green. We are 2 miles down road on right.

Room General 6 Leisure

CARNFORTH, Lancashire Map ref 1B3 — **GUEST ACCOMMODATION**

★★★★
BED & BREAKFAST

B&B per room per night
s £27.50–£30.00
d £44.00–£50.00

Dale Grove

162 Lancaster Road, Carnforth LA5 9EF **t** (01524) 733382

open All year
bedrooms 2 double, 1 twin
bathrooms 1 en suite
payment Cash/cheques

Delightful Victorian house. Ideally situated for M6 (five minutes), railway station, Lancaster and Morecambe. Lake District 30 minutes away. Opposite the house there are canal and country walks with stunning scenery. RSPB Leighton Moss and golf five miles. Ample off-road parking.

2 miles from M6, jct 35. One mile south of Carnforth town centre.

Room General Leisure

CARNFORTH, Lancashire Map ref 1B3 — **GUEST ACCOMMODATION**

★★★★
FARMHOUSE

B&B per room per night
d £48.00

Grisedale Farm

Leighton, Carnforth LA5 9ST **t** (01524) 734360 **w** grisedalefarm.co.uk

Comfortable farmhouse on working family farm set in scenic Area of Outstanding Natural Beauty. Location rich in wildlife adjacent to Leighton Moss RSPB Reserve. Ideally situated for visiting Lakes and Dales.

open All year except Christmas and New Year
bedrooms 1 double, 1 twin
bathrooms 2 private
payment Cash/cheques

Room General Leisure

CHORLEY, Lancashire Map ref 2A1 — **GUEST ACCOMMODATION**

★★★★
GUEST ACCOMMODATION

B&B per room per night
s £35.00–£45.00
d £60.00–£70.00

Parr Hall Farm

Parr Lane, Eccleston, Chorley PR7 5SL **t** (01257) 451917 **f** (01257) 453749 **e** parrhall@talk21.com

open All year
bedrooms 7 double, 2 twin
bathrooms All en suite
payment Credit/debit cards, cash/cheques

Georgian farmhouse built in 1721 and tastefully restored. Quiet, rural location within easy walking distance of good public houses, restaurants and village amenities. Conveniently situated for Lancashire coast and countryside, Lake District and Yorkshire Dales. Manchester Airport 45 minutes, M6 junction 27 five miles north on B5250.

⊕ *M6 jct 27, take A5209 to Parbold, turn immediately onto B5250 to Eccleston. Parr Lane is on right after 4.8 miles. Parr Hall Farm 1st property on left.*

Room · General · Leisure

CLITHEROE, Lancashire Map ref 2A1 — **SELF CATERING**

★★★
SELF CATERING

Units **3**
Sleeps **2–6**
Low season per wk
£190.00–£230.00
High season per wk
£250.00–£400.00

Harrop Fold Cottages, Harrop Fold, Nr Clitheroe

contact Mr Frank Robinson, Harrop Fold, Bolton-by-Bowland, Clitheroe BB7 4PJ
t (01200) 447665 **e** robinsonharrop@aol.com

open All year
payment Cash/cheques

Three well-furnished period cottages with gardens, in the small hamlet of Harrop Fold. Situated in a recognised Area of Outstanding Natural Beauty, its history dating back to the 12th century. The character of this ancient hamlet has been preserved; the result is an ideal location for a relaxing holiday.

⊕ *Harrop Fold is situated off the Grindleton to Slaidburn road, near its junction with the road from Holden and Bolton-by-Bowland.*

❤ *Low season and last-minute breaks from £20pppn (min 3 nights).*

Unit
General · Leisure · Shop 3 miles · Pub 2 miles

GARSTANG, Lancashire Map ref 2A1 — **GUEST ACCOMMODATION**

♦♦♦♦
GUEST ACCOMMODATION

B&B per room per night
s £51.56–£74.00
d £56.12–£80.00
Evening meal per person
£5.00–£30.00

Guy's Thatched Hamlet

Canalside, St Michael's Road, Bilsborrow, Preston PR3 0RS **t** (01995) 640010 **f** (01995) 640141
e info@guysthatchedhamlet.com **w** guysthatchedhamlet.com

open All year except Christmas
bedrooms 48 double, 10 twin, 7 family
bathrooms All en suite
payment Credit/debit cards, cash/cheques

A canalside haven of thatched-roof buildings, just off the A6 at Bilsborrow near Garstang. Here you will find Guy's Lodge, Owd Nell's Tavern, Guy's Restaurant and Pizzeria, craft shops, bowling green and cricket ground. Guy's Lodge offers rooms from only £49.50. All rooms have Sky TV, tea/coffee etc.

⊕ *M55 jct1, just off the A6 at Garstang.*

❤ *Rooms with spas available. Champagne weekend, from £160. Sunday saver only £65 for 2 people, DB&B.*

Room · General · Leisure

Check it out

Please check prices, quality ratings and other details when you book.

GISBURN, Lancashire Map ref 2B1 — **HOTEL**

★★★
HOTEL

B&B per room per night
s £45.00–£75.00
d £90.00–£150.00

Stirk House Hotel

Gisburn Road, Gisburn BB7 4LJ **t** (01200) 445581 **f** (01200) 445744

A 16thC country manor with modern leisure facilities, log fires and excellent restaurant. Easy to find, yet secluded.

open All year
bedrooms 28 double, 16 twin, 1 single, 2 family, 3 suites
bathrooms All en suite
payment Credit/debit cards, cash/cheques, euros

Room General Leisure

IREBY, Lancashire Map ref 1B3 — **SELF CATERING**

★★★★
SELF CATERING

Units 1
Sleeps 4
Low season per wk
£350.00
High season per wk
£350.00

Springfield, Carnforth

contact Miss Heather Bavin, Bainbridge House, Ireby LA6 2JQ
t (01524) 242501 **e** heather.bavin@btinternet.com

Renovated 19thC cottage with two double bedrooms, situated in quiet hamlet. Ideal for away-from-it-all holidays. Open fire. Sun lounge. Welcome hamper for stays of one week or more. Offpeak short breaks.

open All year
payment Cash/cheques

Unit
General Leisure Shop 1.5 miles Pub 2 miles

KIRKHAM, Lancashire Map ref 2A1 — **CAMPING & CARAVANNING**

★★★★★
HOLIDAY PARK
(2) £240.00–£400.00

Mowbreck Holiday and Residential Park

Mowbreck Lane, Preston PR4 3HA **t** (01772) 682494 **f** (01772) 672986

No noisy amusement arcades. Relax in this picturesque setting. Mowbreck Park is family run to the highest standards. Ideal location to enjoy the Fylde coast. Just one hour from Manchester and North Yorkshire.

open All year except Christmas
payment Cash/cheques

General Leisure

LITTLE ECCLESTON, Lancashire Map ref 2A1 — **SELF CATERING**

★★★★
SELF CATERING

Units 1
Sleeps 4
Low season per wk
£320.00–£355.00
High season per wk
£355.00–£390.00

Barn Owl Cottage, Little Eccleston, Near Preston

contact Mr & Mrs J. A. Garnett, 27 The Hermitage, Thornton-Cleveleys FY5 2TH
t (01253) 858293 **e** garnett.j@virgin.net

open All year
payment Cash/cheques

Close to the River Wyre, our charming cottage is ideally situated for exploring the Fylde villages and coastal resorts of Fleetwood, Blackpool, St Anne's and Lytham. Personally run to a high standard of cleanliness, its accommodation comprises one double, two single bedrooms, lounge, dining room, well-equipped kitchen. Welcome pack.

M55 jct 3. A585 Fleetwood. Right at lights, A586. After 2 miles right Blackpool Old Road. Left into Cartford Lane. Barn Owl on left.

Unit
General Leisure Shop 1 mile Pub < 0.5 miles

LONGRIDGE, Lancashire Map ref 2A1 — **CAMPING & CARAVANNING**

★★★
HOLIDAY, TOURING & CAMPING PARK

(45) £5.00–£24.90
(5) £5.00–£24.90
(10) £5.00–£24.90
(30) £100.00–£500.00
55 touring pitches

Beacon Fell View

Higher Road, Longridge, Preston PR3 2TF **t** (01772) 783233 **f** (01772) 784204

Peaceful family park, indoor heated pool, clubhouse, entertainment and the bright lights of Blackpool only 30 minutes away.

open All year
payment Credit/debit cards

General Leisure

LYTHAM ST ANNES, Lancashire Map ref 2A1 — **HOTEL**

★★★★
HOTEL

B&B per room per night
s £70.00–£130.00
d £90.00–£160.00
HB per person per night
£65.00–£100.00

The Grand Hotel

South Promenade, Lytham St Annes FY8 1NB **t** (01253) 721288 **f** (01253) 714459
e book@the-grand.co.uk **w** the-grand.co.uk

open All year except Christmas
bedrooms 43 double/twin, 2 family, 10 suites
bathrooms All en suite
payment Credit/debit cards, cash/cheques

55 superbly appointed bedrooms, all individually designed and all with fine linen bedding. The hotel's Cafe Grand is a modern bar/restaurant with a wide range of beers and wines from around the world. Local specialist suppliers provide most of the ingredients that create the menu's innovative dishes.

From M6, jct 32 onto M55 to Lytham St Annes. Follow signs to the Promenade. We are 500yds south of the pier.

All our special offers are to be found on our website – updated daily!

Room General Leisure

LYTHAM ST ANNES, Lancashire Map ref 2A1 — **HOTEL**

★★
HOTEL

B&B per room per night
s £30.00–£45.00
d £60.00–£85.00
HB per person per night
£35.00–£55.00

Lindum Hotel

63-67 South Promenade, Lytham St Annes FY8 1LZ **t** (01253) 722516 & (01253) 721534
f (01253) 721364 **e** info@lindumhotel.co.uk **w** lindumhotel.co.uk

open All year
bedrooms 25 double, 25 twin, 12 single, 16 family
bathrooms All en suite
payment Credit/debit cards, cash/cheques

A warm welcome awaits at this family-run, seafront hotel opposite all promenade amenities including cinemas, casino, swimming pools and mini-golf. The hotel is renowned for its excellent food and comfortable accommodation. Close to fine shops and championship golf courses. Five miles from Blackpool centre.

From end M55 take A5230 (Blackpool Airport) past airport to traffic lights at the seafront, turn left. Right at 2nd lights, then left to seafront. We are 250yds on left.

Theatre trips, racing weekends, bridge holidays, Christmas/New Year breaks, weekend and mid-week offers throughout the year. Tailor-made golfing holidays.

Room General Leisure

Take a break

Look out for special promotions and themed breaks. This could be your chance to indulge an interest, find a new one, or just relax and enjoy exceptional value! Offers are highlighted in colour (and are subject to availability).

LYTHAM ST ANNES, Lancashire Map ref 2A1 — **HOTEL**

★★
HOTEL

HB per person per night
£25.00–£57.50

St Ives Hotel

7 South Promenade, Lytham St Annes FY8 1LS **t** (01253) 720011 **f** (01253) 722873
e book@st-ives-hotel.co.uk **w** st-ives-hotel.co.uk

open All year except Christmas
bedrooms 16 double, 4 twin, 1 single, 45 family
bathrooms All en suite
payment Credit/debit cards, cash/cheques

Warm and friendly family hotel with a reputation for excellent food, facilities and entertainment. We offer many special weekend/mid-week packages throughout the year. Overlooking the beach, pier and promenade and just a short stroll from the elegant town centre, the St Ives occupies one of the best seafront locations in St Annes.

See website or contact hotel for directions.

Weekend breaks from £90.00 – £106.00, 2 nights min, full family entertainment. Children free on some weekends.

Room General Leisure

MORECAMBE, Lancashire Map ref 1A3 — **CAMPING & CARAVANNING**

★★★★
HOLIDAY, TOURING & CAMPING PARK

Min £14.45
Min £14.45
(10)
(12) £180.00–£350.00
56 touring pitches

Venture Caravan Park

Langridge Way, Westgate, Morecambe LA4 4TQ **t** (01524) 412986 **f** (01524) 422029
e mark@venturecaravanpark.co.uk **w** venturecaravanpark.co.uk

Family-run park, 0.75 miles from the sea. Local amenities and restaurants just a walk away. Easy access to the Lake District, Yorkshire Dales and Blackpool.

open All year
payment Credit/debit cards, cash/cheques

General Leisure

NEWTON-IN-BOWLAND, Lancashire Map ref 2A1 — **SELF CATERING**

★★★★
SELF CATERING

Units 1
Sleeps 5

Low season per wk
Min £250.00
High season per wk
Max £470.00

Stonefold Holiday Cottage, Clitheroe

contact Mrs Helen Blanc, Stonefold Farm, Slaidburn Road, Newton-in-Bowland BB7 3DL
t 07966 582834 **w** stonefoldholidaycottage.co.uk

open All year
payment Cash/cheques

Idyllic, recently renovated barn with spectacular views. Beautifully maintained throughout with exposed beams and flagged floors. Spacious open-plan lounge with well-equipped oak kitchen, ground-floor twin bedroom and shower/wet room, first-floor en suite double bedroom and a cosy single bedroom. Ideally situated for walking, cycling and touring.

From Clitheroe, take the B6478 (signposted Waddington). On reaching Waddington, follow signs to Newton. After approx 4 miles turn left at 'Stonefold' sign. Property 1 mile.

Unit
General Leisure Shop 5 miles Pub 3 miles

PRESTON, Lancashire Map ref 2A1 — **HOTEL**

★★★
SMALL HOTEL

B&B per room per night
s Min £55.00
d £80.00–£90.00
HB per person per night
£50.00–£70.00

Springfield House Hotel & Restaurant

Wheel Lane, Pilling, Preston PR3 6HL **t** (01253) 790301 **f** (01253) 790907
e recep@springfieldhousehotel.co.uk **w** springfieldhousehotel.co.uk

open All year except Christmas
bedrooms 5 double, 3 family
bathrooms All en suite
payment Credit/debit cards, cash/cheques

Manor-house, built in 1840, in its own grounds. Award-winning gardens, full facilities in all rooms. Enjoy the tranquillity of surrounding countryside. Well renowned for superb food and value for money. Within striking distance of The Lakes, Lancaster, Preston and Blackpool.

Only 20 minutes from Lancaster, Preston and Blackpool. See website for location map and directions.

Mid-week and weekend breaks; romantic night breaks; gourmet nights; psychic nights.

Room General Leisure

RIBBLE VALLEY

See under Clitheroe, Newton-in-Bowland, Rimington

RIMINGTON, Lancashire Map ref 2B1 — **CAMPING & CARAVANNING**

★★★★★
HOLIDAY, TOURING & CAMPING PARK

(2) Min £16.00
(2) Min £16.00
39 touring pitches

Rimington Caravan Park

Hardacre Lane, Gisburn, Nr Clitheroe BB7 4EE **t** (01200) 445355
e rimingtoncaravanpark@btinternet.com

Quiet, family-run site with clean, modern facilities. Set in picturesque countryside, just off the beaten track. Open March to October.

payment Cash/cheques

General Leisure

TRAWDEN, Lancashire Map ref 2B1 — **SELF CATERING**

★★★
SELF CATERING

Units 1
Sleeps 5

Low season per wk
£250.00–£300.00
High season per wk
£300.00–£420.00

Far Wanless Farm Stable Cottage, Colne

contact Mrs V M or Paul Johnson, Far Wanless Farm Stable Cottage, Far Wanless Farm, Hollin Hall, Colne BB8 8QE
t (01282) 867514 & 07974 822028

Converted from a stable and piggery on a sheep and beef farm. One double, one twin, plus z-bed. Ideal walking area close to the Brontë village of Haworth and the Yorkshire Dales.

open All year
payment Cash/cheques

Unit General Leisure Shop 2 miles Pub 2 miles

Friendly help and advice

Did you know there are more than 500 Tourist Information Centres throughout England? It adds up to a lot of friendly help and advice. You'll find contact details at the back of the guide.

Making musical connections in Liverpool

Speed across a beach in a kite buggy or immerse yourself in vibrant city life. With its rich maritime and musical history, nearby coastal retreats and floral spectacles, this northern haven of culture will **leave you wanting more.**

Explore Merseyside

Capital culture

Take a ferry across the Mersey and visit Liverpool – the European Capital of Culture for 2008. Hop off at Albert Dock, stroll into the Tate Liverpool and be enthralled by the vast and intriguing array of modern art. Listen to stories of Liverpool's seafaring heritage at the Merseyside Maritime Museum and take a trip down memory lane at The Beatles Story – an exhibition dedicated to the life and times of the Fab Four, including a full-size replica of the notorious Cavern Club.

Musical re-enactments at The Cavern Club, Liverpool

Indulge in some retail therapy and treat yourself at one of the numerous shopping havens throughout the city. Browse elegant rows of exquisite designer clothing at The Cavern Designer Shopping Centre or head to St John's for all the high-street outlets. At the Liverpool Palace and Quiggins, find yourself rummaging through stylish vintage clothes, unique sparkling jewellery and unusual keepsakes of every description. Round off the day with a visit to the highly acclaimed 60 Hope Street where modern European cuisine will both delight and satisfy.

Take a trip from Albert Dock, Liverpool

A sea of colour

Explore the spectacular coastline of the Wirral Peninsula on two legs, four legs or two wheels! Enjoy stunning views across the Irish Sea and take time to discover just how much there is to do. Bask in the Victorian beauty of Port Sunlight Village and catch the scent of the colourful flowers scattered all around. Visit Ness Botanical Gardens – residing in their own microclimate – and delight in the picturesque surroundings awash with dazzling colours and idyllic waterfalls. Work your way around one of the 14 golf courses in the area and relax in the peaceful surroundings.

Stroll through beautiful countryside at Speke Hall, Garden and Estate. Gaze out over the Mersey Basin towards Wales, and admire the picturesque black-and-white-timber Tudor Manor House from afar. Or lose yourself in the tranquillity of the National Wildflower Centre; saunter along the rooftop walkway and look down on the remarkable Victorian park, ablaze with colour.

Kite-buggying across wide-open spaces in Southport

Sport and space

Hedge your bets at the famed Haydock Park Racecourse in St Helens: dine in the bistro overlooking the course or celebrate a momentous occasion in the Park Suite and relish panoramic views of the action. Sing your heart out from the stand at Knowsley Road, St Helens, home of The Saints – the most successful British team in the Super League.

Do we have lift-off? Head to Spaceport and explore all corners of the universe in this fantastic virtual space adventure. Discover the secret world beneath the River Mersey at Seacombe Aquarium or hop aboard a tram at Woodside – home to the first tramway – and journey to the Wirral Transport Museum to see a superb collection of restored public transport.

Plenty to do

Try kite-buggying on the expansive sandy beaches at Southport, wonder at the spectacles in the sky during the September air show or get in rhythm at the jazz festival in July. With some of the cleanest beaches around, spend a carefree day with the kids splashing in the sea, building sandcastles, playing cricket and picnicking on the golden sands.

Wander thoughtfully through the intimate art experience at 5athegallery in St Helens. This unique shop-turned-gallery features the intriguing abstract works of 'the fifth Beatle', Stuart Sutcliffe, who famously chose art over fame and fortune. Don a hard hat at the nearby World of Glass and squeeze through the Victorian tunnels, watch glass being blown before your eyes and try your hardest not to get lost in the Maze of Mirrors!

Food & drink

Fancy a bite to eat or a relaxing drink? Here's a selection of food and drink venues to get you started. For lots more ideas go online at **enjoyengland.com/taste**.

Restaurants

60 Hope Street
English/bistro
Liverpool L1 9BZ
t (0151) 707 6060
w 60hopestreet.com

Alma De Cuba
European
St Peters Church, Seel Street, Liverpool L1 4AZ
t (0151) 709 7097
w alma-de-cuba.com

Auberge Brasserie
French
1b Seabank Road, Southport PR9 0EW
t (01704) 530671
w auberge-brasserie.com

Blue Bar and Grill
English
Unit17 Edward Pavilion, Albert Dock, Liverpool L3 4AF
t (0151) 702 5831
w blue-venue.co.uk

Charlie Parker's Restaurant
European
47 Crosby Road North, Liverpool L22 4QB
t (0151) 928 1101

The Courtyard
European
Rigby's Building, 19 Dale Street, Liverpool L2 2EZ
t (0151) 236 5556
w courtyard-restaurant.co.uk

Fraiche
French
11 Rose Mount, Oxton Village, Wirral CH43 5SG
t (0151) 652 2914
w restaurantfraiche.com

The Gulshan
Indian
544-548 Aigburth Road, Liverpool L19 3QG
t (0151) 427 2273
w gulshan-liverpool.com

Il Forno
Italian
132 Duke Street, Liverpool L1 5AG
t (0151) 709 4002
w ilforno.co.uk

The London Carriageworks
English
40 Hope Street, Liverpool L1 9DA
t (0151) 705 2222
w tlcw.co.uk

St Petersburg Russian Restauant
Russian
7a York Street, Liverpool L1 5BN
t (0151) 709 6676
w russian-cuisine.com

Sapporo Teppanyaki Restaurant
Japanese
134 Duke Street, East Village, Liverpool L1 5AG
t (0151) 705 3005
w sapporo.co.uk

The Side Door
English
29a Hope Street, Liverpool L1 9BQ
t (0151) 707 7888
w thesidedoor.co.uk

Simply Heathcotes
Modern English
Beechtham Plaza, 25 The Strand, Liverpool L2 0XL
t (0151) 236 3534
w heathcotes.co.uk

Warehouse Brasserie
Global
30 West Street, Southport PR8 1QN
t (01704) 544662
w warehouse-brasserie.co.uk

Zucchini's
European
107 Market Street, Hoylake, Wirral CH47 5AA
t (0151) 632 2277

Pubs

The Devon Doorway
2 Telegraph Road, Heswall, Wirral CH60 2SA
t (0151) 348 4462
w thedevondoorway.co.uk

The Pan American Club
22 Britannia Pavillion, Albert Dock, Liverpool L3 4AE
t (0151) 702 5840
w panam-venue.co.uk

Red Cat
8 Red Cat Lane, Crank, St Helens WA11 8RU
t (01744) 882422

Ring O' Bells
Old Chester Road, Daresbury, Runcorn WA4 4AJ
t (01925) 740256

The Unicorn Inn
405 Cronton Road, Widnes WA8 5QF
t (0151) 495 1304

Tearooms, coffee shops and cafes

Darcys Tea & Dining Rooms
52 Eastbank Street, Southport PR8 1ES
t (01704) 543290
w darcystearooms.co.uk

Roses Tea Rooms
23 Milner Road, Heswall CH60 5RT
t (0151) 342 9912

where to stay in

Merseyside

Maps

All place names in the blue bands are shown on the maps at the front of this guide.

Accommodation symbols

Symbols give useful information about services and facilities. Inside the back-cover flap you can find a key to these symbols. Keep it open for easy reference.

ANFIELD, Merseyside Map ref 2A2 — **GUEST ACCOMMODATION**

★★
GUEST ACCOMMODATION

B&B per room per night
s Min £30.00
d Min £50.00

Carey's B&B

89 Walton Breck Road, Anfield, Liverpool L4 0RD **t** (0151) 286 7965

A small family-run B&B. Warm and friendly atmosphere, clean comfortable rooms, with separate TV lounge for additional comfort.

open All year
bedrooms 2 twin
payment Cash/cheques

Room General

BOOTLE, Merseyside Map ref 2A2 — **HOTEL**

★★★
HOTEL

B&B per room per night
s Min £50.00
d Min £65.00
HB per person per night
Min £65.00

The Park Hotel

Dunningsbridge Road, Liverpool L30 6YN **t** (0151) 525 7555 **f** (0151) 525 2481
e info@theparkhotel.biz **w** theparkhotel.biz

open All year
bedrooms 37 double, 18 twin
bathrooms All en suite
payment Credit/debit cards, cash/cheques, euros

Fifty-five bedrooms newly refurbished to the highest standard. Ideally located at the end of the M57/M58. The hotel offers tremendous value for money for the business traveller and tourist alike.

⊕ *Situated 1 mile from jct 7 of M57 and end of M58. Take A5036 at 3rd set of lights, turn right, hotel on right.*

Room General Leisure

Check the maps

Colour maps at the front pinpoint all the cities, towns and villages for which you will find accommodation entries in the regional sections. Pick your location and then refer to the place index at the back to find the page number.

LIVERPOOL, Merseyside Map ref 2A2 — **GUEST ACCOMMODATION**

★★★
GUEST ACCOMMODATION

B&B per room per night
s £35.00–£45.00
d £54.00–£65.00

Aachen Hotel

89-91 Mount Pleasant, Liverpool L3 5TB **t** (0151) 709 3477 **f** (0151) 709 1126
e enquiries@aachenhotel.co.uk **w** aachenhotel.co.uk

open All year except Christmas
bedrooms 5 double, 5 twin, 2 single, 4 family
bathrooms 9 en suite
payment Credit/debit cards, cash/cheques

Award-winning hotel situated in the heart of the city convenient for all road, rail and air links. Within walking distance of all attractions, and famous for the 'eat as much as you like' breakfast. Late bar.

⊕ *Follow City Centre signs towards Catholic cathedral. The Aachen is situated 100yds on the left of the main entrance.*

Room General Leisure

LIVERPOOL, Merseyside Map ref 2A2 — **SELF CATERING**

★★★★
SELF CATERING

Units **2**
Sleeps **4–6**
Low season per wk
Min £309.00
High season per wk
£490.00–£515.00

Port Sunlight Village Trust, Port Sunlight, Wirral

contact Mrs Sandra Nicholls, 95 Greendale Road, Port Sunlight, Wirral CH62 4XE
t (0151) 644 4801 **f** (0151) 645 8973 **e** sandra.psvt@btconnect.com **w** portsunlightvillage.com

Grade II Listed cottages located in the heart of Port Sunlight garden village amid picturesque surroundings. Within easy reach of Chester, Liverpool and North Wales.

open All year
payment Credit/debit cards, cash/cheques

Unit
General P Leisure Shop 0.5 miles Pub 0.5 miles

SOUTHPORT, Merseyside Map ref 2A1 — **SELF CATERING**

★★★★
SELF CATERING

Units **2**
Sleeps **1–6**
Low season per wk
£285.00–£350.00
High season per wk
£325.00–£410.00

Martin Lane Farmhouse Holiday Cottages, Burscough

contact Mrs Stubbs, Martin Lane Farmhouse Holiday Cottages, Ormskirk L40 8JH
t (01704) 893527 **f** (01704) 893527 **e** mlfhc@btinternet.com
w martinlanefarmhouse.btinternet.co.uk

open All year
payment Cash/cheques, euros

Beautiful, award-winning country cottages, nestling in the rich arable farmland of West Lancashire and just four miles from Southport and the seaside. Our cottages have a friendly, relaxed, family atmosphere. The ideal base for visiting all the North West's major attractions.

⊕ *From A59 take B5242. After 2 miles turn right (Drummersdale Lane). 1st right (Merscar Lane). Right onto Martin Lane, over canal, 200yds.*

❤ *10% discount on 2-week bookings.*

Unit
General P Leisure

dramatic castles, tempting beaches, evocative moorland

Clambering over the rocks leading to Lindisfarne Castle, Holy Island

Dramatic cliff-top castles and magnificent panoramas, evocative moorland and immaculately preserved heritage. A trip to this region will **transport you far away** from the world of nine to five.

Explore Northumberland

Roman connection

Start your journey at Morpeth – 'the gateway to Northumberland' – and join in the hubbub of this attractive, bustling market town. Stroll the delightful gardens at Belsay Hall and admire a riot of colour throughout the grounds of this castle-turned-mansion. At Wallington, admire the huge pre-Raphaelite paintings adorning the walls and creep around the enchanting hidden garden. Or take in the dramatic landscapes at Bolam Lake and spot grazing Highland cattle in Plessey Woods.

Explore 84 miles of history along Hadrian's Wall

The most impressive and best preserved of the Roman forts can be found at Housesteads. Explore the only example of a Roman hospital that remains in existence and marvel at some of the earliest known flushing toilets! The ongoing excavation at the Vindolana and Roman Army Museum is fascinating and you can see ancient artefacts on display. Stride alongside Hadrian's Wall and enjoy breathtaking panoramic views over heather-clad moorland. Then explore the finest Roman bathhouse in England at Chesters and imagine soldiers relaxing in the steam thousands of years ago.

Coastal classics

Northumberland's stunning coastline offers sights and sounds beyond the realms of imagination. The smouldering skies and vast, stretching sands alone will draw you to this region and castles peppered across the skyline will drive you to explore. Climb the tower at Alnwick Castle to follow in the footsteps of Harry Potter or spend a day at The Alnwick Garden for a truly magical experience. Here you can dine out in the extraordinary Treehouse Restaurant linked by suspended walkways.

Devour a famous oak-smoked kipper in the pretty fishing village of Craster and visit the dramatic ruins of Dunstanburgh Castle; imagine yourself the protagonist of an English classic as waves crash over the rocks below. Observe nesting puffins in their thousands and watch Atlantic grey seals on the Farne Islands. Let the tide slip away from the Berwick coast and walk the causeway to Holy Island and Lindisfarne Castle. While there, savour a glass of honey and grape-infused Holy Island mead.

Experience the magic at The Alnwick Garden

Exploring the beautiful Cheviot Hills

Active adventures

Get into gear, head out along Hadrian's Cycleway, and feel the fresh breeze on your face as you traverse some of the most historical countryside in England. Pedal through Kielder Forest and around magnificent Kielder Water – the largest man-made lake in Western Europe. With a 27-mile shoreline, this is a watersports enthusiast's dream! Take a cruise across the water, strap on some water skis, or cast off and catch a bite for supper. Be inspired by the impressive visual arts and sculpture trail and enjoy a picnic in this beautiful setting.

Discover how your winter woollens are made at the historic Otterburn Mill and buy some new ones for the coming season. Wander the streets of this quaint village and envisage the bloody moonlit battle that took place in the 14th century between the English and the Scots.

Get a taste for it

Savour a slice of succulent Cheviot lamb accompanied by juicy, local redcurrant jelly. For afters, satisfy your sweet tooth with a generous helping of award-winning Doddington Dairy ice cream – made from all-natural ingredients.

Whatever you do, be sure not to pass up your turn at the cheese board. With the Northumberland Cheese Company producing a phenomenal range of textures and flavours, you'll want to have your crackers at the ready!

Food & drink

Fancy a bite to eat, a relaxing drink or some fresh local produce? Here's a selection of food and drink venues to get you started. For lots more ideas go online at **enjoyengland.com/taste**.

Restaurants

Al Ponte
Italian
18 Front Street, Corbridge
NE45 5AP
t (01434) 634214

Anglers Arms
English
Weldon Bridge, Longframlington
NE65 8AX
t (01665) 570271
w anglersarms.fsnet.co.uk

The Beadnell Towers Hotel
Seafood/English
Beadnell NE67 5AU
t (01665) 721211
w beadnelltowers.com

Cafe Lowrey
Bistro
35 The Broadway, Darras Hall, Ponteland
NE20 9PW
t (01661) 820357
w cafelowrey.co.uk

De Vere Slaley Hall
English
Hexham NE47 0BY
t (01434) 673350
w devere.co.uk

General Havelock Inn
English
9 Ratcliffe Road, Haydon Bridge
NE47 6ER
t (01434) 684376

Henri's Brasserie & Cafe Bar
Cafe/bistro
59 Bridge Street, Morpeth
NE61 1PQ
t (01670) 516205
w henris.co.uk

Il Porto Di Mare
European
Kings Arms Hotel, Hide Hill, Berwick-upon-Tweed TD15 1EJ
t (01289) 307454
w kingsarms-hotel.com

Lord Crewe Arms Hotel
English
Blanchland, Nr Consett DH8 9SP
t (01434) 675251
w crewearms.freeserve.co.uk

Tillmouth Park Country House Hotel
Fine dining
Cornhill-on-Tweed TD12 4UU
t (01890) 882255
w tillmouthpark.co.uk

The Treehouse Restaurant
English
The Alnwick Garden, Denwick Lane, Alnwick NE66 1YU
t (01665) 511350
w alnwickgarden.com

The Valley
Indian
Old Station House, Station Road, Corbridge NE45 5AY
t (01434) 633434

The Victoria Hotel
Fine dining
Front Street, Bamburgh NE69 7BP
t (01668) 214431
w victoriahotel.net

Pubs

Manor House Inn
Carterway Heads, Nr Shotley Bridge DH8 9LX
t (01207) 255268
w manorhouse-a68.co.uk

The Queen's Head Inn
Great Whittington NE19 2HP
t (01434) 672267

Ridley Arms
Stannington, Nr Morpeth
NE61 6EL
t (01670) 789216

The Tankerville Arms Hotel
22 Cottage Road, Wooler
NE71 6AD
t (01668) 287581
w tankervillehotel.co.uk

Tearooms, coffee shops and cafes

Brocksbushes Farm Shop and Tea Room
Stocksfield, Corbridge NE43 7UB
t (01434) 633100
w brocksbushes.co.uk

Doxford County Store
Doxford Farm, Chathill, Alnwick
NE67 5DY
t (01665) 579477
w doxfordfarmcottages.com

Millfield Country Cafe
Main Road, Millfield, Wooler
NE71 6JD
t (01668) 216323

Roseden Farm Shop
Wooperton, Alnwick NE66 4XU
t (01668) 217271
w roseden.com

Farm shops and local produce

New Barns Farm Shop
New Barns, Warkworth, Morpeth
NE65 0TR
t (01665) 710035

Northumberland Cheese Company
The Cheese Farm, Green Lane, Blagdon NE13 6BZ
t (01670) 789798
w northumberland-cheese.co.uk

L Robson & Sons
Craster NE66 3TR
t (01665) 576223
w kipper.co.uk

The Sportsman Inn
Sean Lane, Embleton, Alnwick
NE66 3XF
t (01665) 576588
w sportsmanhotel.co.uk

where to stay in **Northumberland**

Maps
All place names in the blue bands are shown on the maps at the front of this guide.

Accommodation symbols
Symbols give useful information about services and facilities. Inside the back-cover flap you can find a key to these symbols. Keep it open for easy reference.

ALLENDALE, Northumberland Map ref 1B2 — GUEST ACCOMMODATION

★★★★
BED & BREAKFAST

B&B per room per night
s £32.00–£34.00
d £54.00–£56.00
Evening meal per person
£18.00

Thornley House

Thornley Gate, Hexham NE47 9NH **t** (01434) 683255 **e** e.finn@ukonline.co.uk
w http://web.ukonline.co.uk/e.finn

Country house in spacious grounds with two lounges, one with plasma TV and Steinway grand piano. Home baking. Gorgeous walks – maps provided. Near Hadrian's Wall. Two resident Maine Coons. Original feline paintings.

open All year
bedrooms 2 double, 1 twin
bathrooms 2 en suite, 1 private
payment Cash/cheques

Room General Leisure

ALNMOUTH, Northumberland Map ref 1C1 — GUEST ACCOMMODATION

♦♦♦♦
GUEST ACCOMMODATION SILVER AWARD

B&B per room per night
d £60.00–£68.00

Beech Lodge

8 Alnwood, Alnwick NE66 3NN **t** (01665) 830709 **e** beechlodge@hotmail.com **w** alnmouth.com

bedrooms 2 double
bathrooms 1 en suite, 1 private
payment Cash/cheques

A warm and friendly welcome awaits guests at our spacious, detached, modern bungalow in a quiet woodland setting, close to village shops, pubs and restaurants. Our en suite rooms are decorated and furnished to a high and modern standard. An ideal base for exploring all the wonderful coast and countryside. Open April to October.

Take A1068 from Alnwick, follow via Lesbury to Hipsburn. Take B1338 to Alnmouth, cross bridge, turn right into Alnwood. Last bungalow on left is Beech Lodge.

Room General Leisure

Check it out

Information on accommodation listed in this guide has been supplied by proprietors. As changes may occur you should remember to check all relevant details at the time of booking.

ALNWICK, Northumberland Map ref 1C1 — **HOTEL**

★★
HOTEL

B&B per room per night
s £50.00
d £80.00

The Oaks Hotel

South Road, Alnwick NE66 2PN **t** (01665) 510014 **f** (01665) 603219
e kentheoakshotel@alncom.net **w** theoakshotel.co.uk

Comfortable accommodation minutes from the town centre. Every room in The Oaks Hotel is individually furnished to the highest standard and includes en suite facilities, television, telephone and tea-/coffee-making facilities.

open All year
bedrooms 5 double, 2 twin, 1 single, 4 family
bathrooms All en suite
payment Credit/debit cards, cash/cheques

Room General Leisure

ALNWICK, Northumberland Map ref 1C1 — **GUEST ACCOMMODATION**

★★★★
GUEST ACCOMMODATION

B&B per room per night
d £60.00–£70.00

Alndyke Bed and Breakfast

Alnmouth Road, Alnwick NE66 3PB **t** (01665) 510252 **e** alndyke@fsmail.net **w** alndyke.co.uk

Georgian farmhouse set in 500 acres of arable farmland with rural views. All rooms are en suite. Colour TV, tea and coffee facilities. Guest lounge with woodburner.

open All year except Christmas and New Year
bedrooms 3 double, 1 twin
bathrooms All en suite
payment Cash/cheques

Room General

ALNWICK, Northumberland Map ref 1C1 — **GUEST ACCOMMODATION**

★★★
BED & BREAKFAST

B&B per room per night
s £40.00
d £70.00–£100.00
Evening meal per person
£22.50–£27.50

Brunton House

Brunton, Alnwick NE66 3HQ **t** (01665) 589198 **f** (01665) 589199 **e** victoriajolliffe@tiscali.co.uk

Country-house B&B, spacious rooms, warm welcome. Well off main road, large garden and fine views. Wheelchair access to downstairs bedroom and shower.

open All year
bedrooms 2 double, 1 twin
bathrooms 2 en suite, 1 private
payment Cash/cheques

Room General Leisure

ALNWICK, Northumberland Map ref 1C1 **GUEST ACCOMMODATION**

★★★
FARMHOUSE

B&B per room per night
s £39.00
d £58.00

Rock Midstead Organic Farm House

Rock, Alnwick NE66 2TH **t** (01665) 579225 **f** (01665) 579326 **e** ian@rockmidstead.co.uk
w rockmidstead.co.uk

open All year
bedrooms 2 double, 1 family
bathrooms All en suite
payment Credit/debit cards, cash/cheques

Comfortable, spacious, family farmhouse set in peaceful organic farm with extensive views of surrounding countryside. Ideal for walking or cycling. Excellent home cooking, fresh-baked bread daily, afternoon tea on the lawn. Log fires. En suite rooms with colour TV and radio. Perfect base for exploring coastline, castles, hills and historic houses.

B6347 east off the A1, signposted Seahouses, Christan Bank Rock. Then 1st right (farm road) off the B6347.

Room General Leisure

ALNWICK, Northumberland Map ref 1C1 **GUEST ACCOMMODATION**

★★★★
BED & BREAKFAST

B&B per room per night
d £55.00–£70.00

Sherborne House B&B

9 Percy Street, Alnwick NE66 1AE **t** (01665) 605626 **e** helen@awod.co.uk **w** awod.co.uk

open All year
bedrooms 2 double, 1 twin
bathrooms All en suite
payment Cash/cheques

In a quiet courtyard setting within the centre of historic Alnwick, the recently converted 19thC barn boasts spacious and comfortable en suite rooms. We offer an excellent breakfast menu combining local and Fairtrade produce. A family-run B&B, we endeavour to make your stay both enjoyable and memorable.

From A1 north and south follow signs for town centre. Turn left before Bondgate Tower, 500yds turn left into Percy Street.

Discounts available for bookings of 3 nights or more.

Room General Leisure

ALNWICK, Northumberland Map ref 1C1 **GUEST ACCOMMODATION**

★★★
BED & BREAKFAST

B&B per room per night
s £25.00–£35.00
d £50.00–£65.00

Tate House

11 Bondgate Without, Alnwick NE66 1PR **t** (01665) 604661 **e** bookings@stayinalnwick.co.uk
w stayinalnwick.co.uk

open All year
bedrooms 2 double, 1 family
bathrooms 2 en suite, 1 private
payment Cash/cheques

Tate House is an attractive, three-storey, late Victorian townhouse built in 1885 and situated within the centre of Alnwick. The property has recently undergone an extensive upgrading and refurbishment programme.

Nearest train station: Alnmouth. 180yds from Bondgate Tower leading into the town centre. Opposite the Plough pub/hotel.

Discounts on stays of 3 or more days. Stay 3 days and 4th day is free during winter months (Oct-Mar).

Room General 5 P Leisure

ALNWICK, Northumberland Map ref 1C1 — **SELF CATERING**

★★★★
SELF CATERING

Units **2**
Sleeps **2–6**
Low season per wk
£250.00–£350.00
High season per wk
£350.00–£600.00

Alndyke Farm Cottages, Alnwick

contact Mrs Laura Davison, Alndyke Farm Cottages, Alndyke Farmhouse, Alnmouth Road, Alnwick NE66 3PB
t (01665) 510252 **e** alndyke@fsmail.net **w** alndyke.co.uk

Semi-detached stone-built cottages located in 500 acres of farmland. Two doubles and one twin. Lounge with woodburner, kitchen with all amenities. Open May to September.

payment Cash/cheques

Unit
General Leisure

ALNWICK, Northumberland Map ref 1C1 — **SELF CATERING**

★★★★
SELF CATERING

Units **1**
Sleeps **1–2**
Low season per wk
Min £190.00
High season per wk
Max £420.00

Barbican View, Alnwick

contact Mrs Frances Draper, Barbican View, 10 Springwood Road, Thongsbridge, Holmfirth HD9 7SJ
t (01484) 683705 **e** fran.draper@virgin.net **w** barbicanview.co.uk

Overlooking Alnwick Castle, beautifully furnished non-smoking apartment for two. Lovely, peaceful courtyard garden. Excellent location for exploring countryside and coast.

open All year
payment Cash/cheques

Unit
General Leisure Shop < 0.5 miles Pub < 0.5 miles

ALNWICK, Northumberland Map ref 1C1 — **SELF CATERING**

★★★
SELF CATERING

Units **1**
Sleeps **1–5**
Low season per wk
£247.00–£285.00
High season per wk
£350.00–£499.00

The Pebble, Alnwick

contact Mrs Clare Laughton, Okelands, Pickhurst Road, Chiddingfold GU8 4TS
t (01428) 683941 **e** clarelaughton@googlemail.com

Spacious, comfortable, warm, semi-detached cottage on family farm. Enclosed garden with barbecue, facing south over farmland. One double, one twin, one single. Ideal base for exploring Heritage Coast, beaches, castles and moors.

open All year
payment Cash/cheques

Unit
General 4 Leisure Shop < 0.5 miles Pub 2.5 miles

ALNWICK, Northumberland Map ref 1C1 — **SELF CATERING**

★★★–★★★★★
SELF CATERING

Units **12**
Sleeps **1–12**
Low season per wk
£150.00–£510.00
High season per wk
£270.00–£1,650.00

Village Farm, Alnwick

contact Mrs Crissy Stoker, Town Foot Farm, Shilbottle, Alnwick NE66 2HG
t (01665) 575591 **f** (01665) 575591 **e** crissy@villagefarmcottages.co.uk **w** villagefarmcottages.co.uk

open All year
payment Credit/debit cards, cash/cheques

17thC farmhouse, cottages and beautifully appointed chalets complemented by excellent facilities – indoor heated swimming pool, health club, steam room, sauna, sunshower, beauty therapist, games room, tennis, riding, fishing and adventure playground. Situated between Alnwick and Heritage Coast. A warm, personal welcome.

Travelling north – from A1 take Alnmouth/Shilbottle turn-off to right. Proceed for 1.5 miles to the village, take 1st right and 1st left. Proceed 200yds – near church.

2-/3-night stays available Nov-Easter (excl Christmas, New Year and half-terms).

Unit
General Leisure Shop < 0.5 miles Pub < 0.5 miles

ALWINTON, Northumberland Map ref 1B1 — **SELF CATERING**

★★★★
SELF CATERING

Units 1
Sleeps 3

Low season per wk
£195.00–£350.00
High season per wk
£400.00–£495.00

Fellside Cottage, Alwinton

contact Mrs Denise Straughan, Fellside Cottage, Bedlington Lane Farm, Bedlington NE22 6AA
t (01670) 823042 **f** (01670) 827230 **e** stay@fellsidecottcheviots.co.uk **w** fellsidecottcheviots.co.uk

open All year
payment Cash/cheques

Cosy country cottage nestling in tiny hamlet within the Upper Coquet Valley and Northumberland National Park. Fully furnished and equipped to a high standard. Open fire. Lovely garden and patio. Enjoy the peace and stunning views. Cheviot Hill country literally at your back door. A walkers' paradise. Country pub close by.

Short breaks available in low season.

Unit
General Leisure Shop 10 miles Pub < 0.5 miles

BAMBURGH, Northumberland Map ref 1C1 — **HOTEL**

★★★
COUNTRY HOUSE HOTEL
SILVER AWARD

B&B per room per night
d £145.00–£210.00
HB per person per night
£99.50–£132.00

Waren House Hotel

Waren Mill, Belford NE70 7EE **t** (01668) 214581 **f** (01668) 214484
e enquiries@warenhousehotel.co.uk **w** warenhousehotel.co.uk

open All year
bedrooms 6 double, 4 twin, 3 suites
bathrooms All en suite
payment Credit/debit cards, cash/cheques, euros

Traditional, beautifully restored and renovated, award-winning country-house hotel in six acres of wooded grounds and walled garden on edge of Budle Bay overlooking Holy Island. Superb accommodation, excellent food, choice of over 250 reasonably priced wines. Two miles Bamburgh Castle, five miles Farne Islands. Children over 14 welcome. Ground-floor suite with wheelchair access.

Midway between Belford and Bamburgh on B1342 and 2 miles from the A1 on which we have a sign from both north and south.

Short breaks – DB&B from £99.50pppn.

Room General 14 Leisure

BAMBURGH, Northumberland Map ref 1C1 — **SELF CATERING**

★★★–★★★★
SELF CATERING

Units 4
Sleeps 2–6

Low season per wk
£200.00–£400.00
High season per wk
£400.00–£600.00

Bradford Country Cottages, Bamburgh

contact Mr L W Robson, Bradford Country Cottages, Bradford House, Bamburgh NE70 7JT
t (01668) 213432 **f** (01668) 213891 **e** lwrob@tiscali.co.uk **w** bradford-leisure.co.uk

Stone-built cottages in a rural setting, two miles from Bamburgh village, full central heating and facilities, access to swimming pool included in tariff.

open All year
payment Credit/debit cards, cash/cheques

Unit
General Leisure Shop 2 miles Pub 2 miles

Check the maps

Colour maps at the front pinpoint all places in which you will find accommodation entries in the regional sections. Pick your location and then refer to the place index at the back to find the page number.

BAMBURGH, Northumberland Map ref 1C1 — **SELF CATERING**

★★★★
SELF CATERING

Units **16**
Sleeps **2–6**
Low season per wk
£247.00–£440.00
High season per wk
£402.00–£737.00

Outchester & Ross Farm Cottages, Belford

contact Mrs Shirley McKie, 1 Cragview Road, Belford NE70 7NT
t (01668) 213336 **f** (01668) 219385 **e** enquiry@rosscottages.co.uk **w** rosscottages.co.uk

open All year
payment Cash/cheques

Outchester and Ross are both in unique, secluded coastal locations in one of the most beautiful areas of Northumberland between Bamburgh and Holy Island. Our cottages are warm, comfortable and well equipped – each double glazed and with its own private garden. Relax completely and just enjoy being here.

Maps supplied on booking.

Unit
General Leisure Shop 3 miles Pub 3 miles

BAMBURGH, Northumberland Map ref 1C1 — **SELF CATERING**

★★★
SELF CATERING

Units **5**
Sleeps **5–17**
Low season per wk
£195.00–£255.00
High season per wk
£430.00–£490.00

Point Cottages, Bamburgh

contact Mrs Sanderson, 30 The Oval, Benton, Newcastle upon Tyne NE12 9PP
t (0191) 266 2800 **f** (0191) 215 1630 **e** info@bamburgh-cottages.co.uk **w** bamburgh-cottages.co.uk

Cluster of cottages, with fine sea views, located next to golf course. Furnished to a high standard with log fires and large garden.

open All year
payment Cash/cheques

Unit
General Leisure Shop 1 mile Pub 1 mile

BAMBURGH, Northumberland Map ref 1C1 — **SELF CATERING**

★★★★–★★★★★
SELF CATERING

Units **3**
Sleeps **2–28**
Low season per wk
£221.00–£1,666.00
High season per wk
£394.00–£2,362.00

Waren Lea Hall, Bamburgh

contact Carolynn and David Croisdale-Appleby, Abbotsholme, Hervines Road, Amersham HP6 5HS
t (01494) 725194 **f** (01494) 725474 **e** croisdaleappleby@aol.com **w** selfcateringluxury.co.uk

open All year
payment Cash/cheques

Imposing, spacious country house on shore of Budle Bay at Waren Mill near Bamburgh in two acres of waters-edge parkland. Breathtaking, panoramic views of Lindisfarne and the Cheviots. The holiday homes can be booked individually or together. Waren Lea Hall enjoys an unrivalled location with easy access for walking, golf, fishing etc.

From A1, 15 miles north of Alnwick, turn towards Belford Station on B1342. On reaching Waren Mill turn towards Bamburgh. Cross bridge over river. Property is 100yds on left.

Short breaks available from Nov-Mar. Weekend breaks, 3 nights, Fri-Mon. Mid-week breaks, 4 nights, Mon-Fri.

Unit
General Leisure Shop 1.5 miles Pub 1.5 miles

BAMBURGH, Northumberland Map ref 1C1 — **CAMPING & CARAVANNING**

★★
HOLIDAY, TOURING & CAMPING PARK
(80) £12.00–£15.00
(80) £12.00–£15.00
(80) £12.00–£15.00
80 touring pitches

Bradford Kaims Caravan Park

Bradford House, Bamburgh NE70 7JT **t** (01668) 213432 **f** (01668) 213891 **e** lwrob@tiscali.co.uk
w bradford-leisure.co.uk

Beautiful walking country. Close to Bamburgh, Seahouses, Wooler and Cheviot Hills. Pre-booking advised during school holidays. Open March to November. Bradford Kaims Caravan Park is signposted from the B1341.

payment Credit/debit cards, cash/cheques

General Leisure

BARDON MILL, Northumberland Map ref 1B2 — **GUEST ACCOMMODATION**

★★★★
BED & BREAKFAST
B&B per room per night
s £35.00
d £59.00–£65.00

Maple Lodge Bed and Breakfast

Birkshaw, Bardon Mill, Hexham NE47 7JL **t** (01434) 344365 **e** tonyarmstrong@tiscali.co.uk
w maplelodge-hadrianswall.co.uk

Maple Lodge is a 16thC Bastle House next to Vindolanda. An ideal base to visit Hadrian's Wall and Northumberland's many attractions. A warm welcome in comfortable surroundings.

open All year except Christmas
bedrooms 1 double, 1 single, 1 family
bathrooms All en suite
payment Cash/cheques

Room General P Leisure

BARDON MILL, Northumberland Map ref 1B2 — **GUEST ACCOMMODATION**

♦♦♦
GUEST ACCOMMODATION
B&B per room per night
s £25.00–£28.00
d £48.00–£70.00
Evening meal per person
£5.50–£14.75

Twice Brewed Inn

Bardon Mill, Hexham NE47 7AN **t** (01434) 344534 **e** info@twicebrewedinn.co.uk
w twicebrewedinn.co.uk

open All year except Christmas
bedrooms 4 double, 7 twin, 2 single, 1 family
bathrooms 6 en suite
payment Credit/debit cards, cash/cheques

Family-run inn situated 0.5 miles from Hadrian's Wall offering accommodation, a warm welcome, good food, real ales, breathtaking views and wide-open spaces. Centrally placed for visits to Scotland, Cumbria and the North East (all within one hour's drive).

Situated North of Bardon Mill on B6318 adjacent to youth hostel and National Park information centre. 7 miles east of Greenhead, 3 miles west of Housesteads.

Bi-annual bridge weekend held first weekend in Mar and first weekend in Nov.

Room General P Leisure

BARDON MILL, Northumberland Map ref 1B2 — **GUEST ACCOMMODATION**

★★★★
GUEST HOUSE
B&B per room per night
s £45.00–£50.00
d £66.00

Vallum Lodge

Twice Brewed, Bardon Mill NE47 7AN **t** (01434) 344248 **f** (01434) 344488
e stay@vallum-lodge.co.uk **w** vallum-lodge.co.uk

bedrooms 2 double, 3 twin, 1 family
bathrooms All en suite
payment Credit/debit cards, cash/cheques, euros

Comfortable house in lovely open countryside just half a mile south of Hadrian's Wall. Good central position for visiting Roman sites, touring and walking in the area. Well-appointed en suite bedrooms, ample parking and hearty breakfasts. Warm and welcoming. Open February to October.

From the A69 follow the signs for Once Brewed. Just past the Visitors Centre turn left, we are 400yds along.

Discounts available for stays of 4 days or more.

Room General P Leisure

BEADNELL, Northumberland Map ref 1C1 — GUEST ACCOMMODATION

◆◆◆◆◆
GUEST ACCOMMODATION
SILVER AWARD

B&B per room per night
s £54.50–£74.50
d £79.00–£119.00

Beach Court

Harbour Road, Beadnell NE67 5BJ **t** (01665) 720225 **f** (01665) 721499 **e** info@beachcourt.com
w beachcourt.com

open All year except Christmas
bedrooms 1 double, 1 twin, 1 suite
bathrooms All en suite
payment Credit/debit cards, cash/cheques, euros

Beach Court, our award-winning turreted beachside home, is on the very edge of the bay and harbour. The tide laps gently under your window seats from where you can catch up on your reading, paint or simply unwind as you gaze across the vast stretch of golden sands which form Beadnell Bay.

From A1 take B6347 just north of Alnwick. Follow signs for Beadnell Harbour. Beach Court is the last property before the North Sea!

Discounts on weekly and winter breaks available – see website for details.

Room General Leisure

BEADNELL, Northumberland Map ref 1C1 — SELF CATERING

★★★★
SELF CATERING

Units 1
Sleeps 5

Low season per wk
£225.00–£325.00
High season per wk
£450.00–£595.00

3 Alexandra House, Beadnell

contact Mr & Mrs Stephen & Ruth Lithgow, 3 Alexandra House, 16 Ashcroft Drive, Forest Hall, Newcastle upon Tyne NE12 9LN
t (0191) 266 6440 **e** ruthlithgow@yahoo.ie **w** beadnellholidays.co.uk

Newly refurbished, large and spacious, three-bedroom apartment (one en suite) in the heart of Beadnell village. Accommodation comprises: one double, one twin, one single, large fully equipped kitchen.

open All year
payment Cash/cheques

Unit
General Shop < 0.5 miles Pub < 0.5 miles

BEAL, Northumberland Map ref 1B1 — GUEST ACCOMMODATION

★★★★
GUEST ACCOMMODATION

B&B per room per night
s £30.00–£35.00
d £55.00–£60.00

Brock Mill Farmhouse

Brock Mill, Beal, Berwick-upon-Tweed TD15 2PB **t** (01289) 381283 **f** (01289) 381283
e brockmillfarmhouse@btinternet.com

open All year except Christmas
bedrooms 1 double, 1 twin, 1 family
payment Credit/debit cards, cash/cheques

A 220-acre mixed farm. Peaceful, idyllic surroundings, ideal as a base for touring North Northumberland and Scottish Borders. Quality accommodation with spacious, well-furnished rooms. Residents' lounge. Enjoy our superb English breakfasts or our tasty vegetarian alternatives. Golf and fishing nearby. A warm, friendly welcome awaits.

About 1.5 miles from A1 at Beal on the Holy Island road.

Mid-week deals – prices on request. Christmas and New Year packages. Discount for 1 or more nights.

Room General Leisure

To your credit

If you book by phone you may be asked for your credit card number. If so, it is advisable to check the proprietor's policy in case you have to cancel your reservation at a later date.

BELFORD, Northumberland Map ref 1B1 — **SELF CATERING**

★★★
SELF CATERING

Units 1
Sleeps 2–4
Low season per wk
£190.00
High season per wk
£320.00

Chillingham Cottage, Belford

contact Mr Scott Carruthers, Chillingham Cottage, 20 Richmond Terrace, Whitley Bay NE26 1SG
t (0191) 280 2484 **e** scarruthers@blueyonder.co.uk

open All year
payment Cash/cheques

Spacious, well-equipped, stone-built cottage close to all amenities. Two bedrooms (one double, one bunk beds) sleeping four. Full gas central heating, including solid fuel fire (fuel not included). Laundry facilities. Fully enclosed patio, barbecue area. Pets welcome. One mile from A1, 14 miles south of Berwick, 14 miles north of Alnwick.

A1 to Belford. At market cross in front of Bluebell Hotel, take B6349 to Wooler. Bluebell Farm is opposite Co-op. Follow road into farm; reception over the bridge.

Unit
General Leisure Shop 0.5 miles Pub 0.5 miles

BELFORD, Northumberland Map ref 1B1 — **SELF CATERING**

★★★–★★★★
SELF CATERING

Units 3
Sleeps 2–6
Low season per wk
£290.00–£500.00

Fenham-le-Moor Cottages and Lindisfarne Lookout, Belford

contact Mrs Katie Burn, Fenham-le-Moor, Belford NE70 7PN
t (01668) 213247 **f** (01668) 213247 **e** enquiries@fenham-le-moor.co.uk **w** fenham-le-moor.co.uk

Comfortably furnished cottages and open plan studio on working farm, overlooking the Lindisfarne Nature Reserve. A unique situation for bird-watching and walking, with views over to Holy Island.

open All year
payment Cash/cheques

Unit
General Leisure Shop 4 miles Pub 4 miles

BELLINGHAM, Northumberland Map ref 1B2 — **HOTEL**

★★
HOTEL

B&B per room per night
s £56.00–£65.00
d £98.00–£130.00
HB per person per night
£65.00–£85.00

Riverdale Hall Hotel

Bellingham, Hexham NE48 2JT **t** (01434) 220254 **f** (01434) 220457
e reservations@riverdalehallhotel.co.uk **w** riverdalehallhotel.co.uk

open All year
bedrooms 10 double, 9 twin, 4 single, 4 family, 3 suites
bathrooms All en suite
payment Credit/debit cards, cash/cheques

Spacious Victorian country hall in large grounds, on the banks of the North Tyne river, with splendid views southwards to Dunterley Fell (Pennine Way). All bedrooms en suite with TV, telephone and hospitality tray. Indoor swimming pool, sauna, fishing, cricket field and golf nearby. Award-winning restaurant. Kielder Water, Pennine Way and Hadrian's Wall nearby. The Cocker family's 29th year.

Golfing, fishing and cricketing breaks arranged. Free place for organiser for parties of 15 or more.

Room General Leisure

Use your i's

Tourist Information Centres provide a wealth of information and friendly advice, both before you go and during your stay. Refer to the back of the guide for a list of Tourist Information Centres in the region.

BERWICK-UPON-TWEED, Northumberland Map ref 1B1 **HOTEL**

★★★
HOTEL

B&B per room per night
s £84.00–£95.00
d £129.00–£149.00
HB per person per night
£79.50–£94.50

King's Arms Hotel

43 Hide Hill, Berwick-upon-Tweed TD15 1EJ **t** (01289) 307454 **f** (01289) 308867
e enquiries@kingsarms-hotel.com **w** kingsarms-hotel.com

open All year
bedrooms 17 double, 6 twin, 1 single, 1 family, 3 suites
bathrooms All en suite
payment Credit/debit cards, cash/cheques, euros

18thC Georgian coaching inn with beautiful en suite bedrooms, medieval walled garden and Il Porto di Mare seafood restaurant. An ideal centre for touring the Borders, Lindisfarne, Farne islands, Holy Island, castles, abbeys, barracks and museum with Burrell collection. Historic-weekend breaks within medieval town walls. A step back in history.

⊕ *Leave A1 from north or south into town centre, turn right at Guildhall and first right into Hide Hill.*

♥ *Short breaks to include visits to all major historical sites. Fishing arranged on Tweed tributaries. Golfing packages – choice of 4 courses.*

Room General Leisure

BERWICK-UPON-TWEED, Northumberland Map ref 1B1 **GUEST ACCOMMODATION**

♦♦♦
GUEST ACCOMMODATION

B&B per room per night
s £30.00
d £50.00
Evening meal per person
£4.85–£9.95

The Cat Inn

Great North Road, Cheswick, Berwick-upon-Tweed TD15 2RL **t** (01289) 387251 **f** (01289) 387251

Seven-bedroom inn situated five miles south of Berwick, providing accommodation, good food and range of ales and lagers.

open All year
bedrooms 1 double, 4 twin, 2 family
bathrooms All en suite
payment Credit/debit cards, cash/cheques

Room General 5 P Leisure

BERWICK-UPON-TWEED, Northumberland Map ref 1B1 **SELF CATERING**

★★★★★
SELF CATERING

Units 4
Sleeps 1–4
Low season per wk
£265.00–£330.00
High season per wk
£395.00–£490.00

Composers at Woodlands, Berwick-upon-Tweed

contact Mr & Mrs Martin & Dee Colam, Composers at Woodlands, Woodlands, Scremerston, Berwick-upon-Tweed TD15 2QU
t (01289) 332599 **f** (01289) 332559 **e** info@composers-woodlands.co.uk
w composers-woodlands.co.uk

open All year
payment Credit/debit cards, cash/cheques, euros

Luxury properties, tastefully furnished and immaculately maintained to highest standard. Fully fitted kitchens equipped with everything you could need, double and twin-bedded rooms, sumptuous bathroom suite with bath and walk-in shower. Lounge with leather sofas, writing desk, digital television and audio radio/CD. Warm welcome from on-site owners.

⊕ *Travel directions provided on booking/enquiry.*

♥ *Various special rates available for flexible short breaks, 2-person occupancy or group bookings. Details available on request.*

Unit
General P Leisure Shop 2 miles Pub 2 miles

Key to symbols

Open the back flap for a key to symbols.

BERWICK-UPON-TWEED, Northumberland Map ref 1B1 — **SELF CATERING**

★★★
SELF CATERING

Units 1
Sleeps 6
Low season per wk
£270.00–£514.00
High season per wk
£307.00–£536.00

Smiddy Cottage, Berwick-upon-Tweed

contact Mrs June Simpson, Smiddy Cottage, Forgeway, Main Street, Horncliffe, Berwick-upon-Tweed TD15 2XW
t (01289) 386411 **f** (01289) 386411 **e** june@smiddycottage.co.uk **w** smiddycottage.co.uk

Converted blacksmith's shop in quiet village on English/Scottish border. Five miles from coast. Ideal for walking and fishing.

open All year
payment Cash/cheques

Unit
General P Shop 4 miles Pub < 0.5 miles

BERWICK-UPON-TWEED, Northumberland Map ref 1B1 — **SELF CATERING**

★★★★
SELF CATERING

Units 1
Sleeps 1–5
Low season per wk
£207.00–£299.00
High season per wk
£350.00–£434.00

Tigh Na Rudh, Berwick-upon-Tweed

contact Dr Rosemary Evans, Tigh Na Rudh, Alderwood, Main Street, St Boswells, Melrose TD6 0AP
t (01835) 823031 **e** b.wynn.evans@care4free.net

Comfortable property in historic Berwick-upon-Tweed. A short stroll from the coast, river and town's amenities. Excellent base for Northumberland holiday. Holy Island ten miles, Alnwick 25 miles. One double, one twin, one single.

open All year
payment Cash/cheques

Unit
General 5 Shop < 0.5 miles Pub < 0.5 miles

BERWICK-UPON-TWEED, Northumberland Map ref 1B1 — **SELF CATERING**

★★★★
SELF CATERING

Units 1
Sleeps 6
Low season per wk
£250.00–£300.00
High season per wk
£350.00–£480.00

Whitecroft, Berwick-upon-Tweed

contact Mrs Moira Kay, Whitecroft, Tweed Cottage, Horncliffe, Berwick-upon-Tweed TD15 2XW
t (01289) 386066 **f** (01289) 386066 **e** enquiries@whitecroftcottage.co.uk **w** whitecroftcottage.co.uk

open All year
payment Cash/cheques

Adorable country cottage in peaceful salmon fishing village on River Tweed (the Scottish border). The cottage is beautifully furnished and well equipped. One double and two twin rooms, separate laundry room and shed for bicycles etc. Freshly cooked food from local produce available. Fresh flowers, fruit and a welcome hamper. Fully inclusive price.

From A1 at the East Ord roundabout take A698, direction Coldstream. Take 1st right signposted Horncliffe. In village pass pub, across square. 1st left.

Unit
General P Leisure Shop 4 miles Pub < 0.5 miles

BLANCHLAND, Northumberland Map ref 1B2 — **SELF CATERING**

★★★★
SELF CATERING

Units 1
Sleeps 4
Low season per wk
Min £195.00
High season per wk
Max £310.00

Boltslaw Cottage, Blanchland

contact Mrs Nicola Smith, Boltslaw Cottage, 6 Selborne Avenue, Gateshead NE9 6ET
t (0191) 487 9456 **f** (01670) 510300 **e** asmith6000@aol.com **w** cottageguide.co.uk/boltslaw

open All year
payment Cash/cheques

Set in beautiful moorland, this is our family retreat. Two-bedroom stone cottage with log stove, historic features and comfortable pine furnishings. Double bedroom recently refurbished. Central heating, telephone, DVD, garden with barbecue and stunning views. Sailing, fishing and golf nearby, 40 minutes to Beamish, Hadrian's Wall and Durham. Favourite honeymoon destination!

A68 at Kiln Pitt Hill, turning to Blanchland. Road to Stanhope, after about 2 miles right turn at cattle grid to Ramshaw. Last cottage on right.

Mid-week breaks outside school holidays £35 per night. 4 nights for price of 3 (1 winter break promotion).

Unit
General P S Leisure Shop 2 miles Pub 2 miles

CORBRIDGE, Northumberland Map ref 1B2 — **GUEST ACCOMMODATION**

♦♦♦
GUEST ACCOMMODATION

B&B per room per night
s £28.00–£42.00
d £56.00–£62.00

The Hayes

Newcastle Road, Corbridge NE45 5LP **t** (01434) 632010 **e** camon@surfree.co.uk
w hayes-corbridge.co.uk

Large, late-19thC country house with splendid views southwards. Set in spacious grounds, in historic village with easy access to Hadrian's Wall, A69 and A68. Family run.

open All year except Christmas and New Year
bedrooms 1 twin, 1 single, 2 family
bathrooms 2 en suite, 2 private
payment Credit/debit cards, cash/cheques

Room · General · Leisure

CORBRIDGE, Northumberland Map ref 1B2 — **GUEST ACCOMMODATION**

★★★★★
BED & BREAKFAST
GOLD AWARD

B&B per room per night
d £76.00

Riggsacre

Appletree Lane, Corbridge NE45 5DN **t** (01434) 632617 **e** atclive@supanet.com
w riggsacrebandb.co.uk

Lovely detached property within a half-acre site. Luxurious en suite rooms with feature beds. Peaceful lane, central village location. Private parking. Minimum two nights.

open All year except Christmas and New Year
bedrooms 2 double
bathrooms All en suite
payment Cash/cheques

Room · General P

CORBRIDGE, Northumberland Map ref 1B2 — **SELF CATERING**

★★★
SELF CATERING

Units 2
Sleeps 4–5
Low season per wk
£235.00–£300.00
High season per wk
£330.00–£410.00

The Hayes, Corbridge

contact Mrs Monica Matthews, The Hayes, Newcastle Road, Corbridge NE45 5LP
t (01434) 632010 **e** camon@surfree.co.uk **w** hayes-corbridge.co.uk

Two stone cottages, converted from former stables. Set in a small courtyard, in spacious grounds of large country house on the outskirts of the historic village of Corbridge. Easy access A68/A69.

open All year
payment Credit/debit cards, cash/cheques

Unit
General P · Leisure · Shop 0.5 miles · Pub 0.5 miles

CORBRIDGE, Northumberland Map ref 1B2 — **SELF CATERING**

★★★
SELF CATERING

Units 1
Sleeps 4
Low season per wk
£110.00–£150.00
High season per wk
£200.00–£260.00

West Fell Cottage, Corbridge

contact Mrs Joan Smith, West Fell Cottage, Ladycutter Lane, Corbridge NE45 5RZ
t (01434) 632044

Two-bedroom farm cottage near Dilston Castle, convenient for Corbridge and the Roman Wall.

open All year
payment Cash/cheques

Unit
General P · Leisure

CORNHILL-ON-TWEED, Northumberland Map ref 1B1 — **SELF CATERING**

★★★
SELF CATERING

Units 2
Sleeps 1–4
Low season per wk
£200.00–£220.00
High season per wk
£270.00–£300.00

Harelaw Cottages, Mindrum

contact Mr & Mrs Andy & Val Young, Harelaw, Mindrum TD12 4QP
t (01890) 850327 **f** (01890) 850327 **e** harelawcot@btinternet.com **w** harelaw.org

Harelaw is a rural property set in two acres of woodland gardens. Leveret and Hoolit are two-bedroom adjoining cottages. Ideal for touring and walking North Northumberland and the Scottish Borders.

open All year
payment Cash/cheques

Unit
General · Leisure · Shop 2 miles · Pub 2 miles

CRAMLINGTON, Northumberland Map ref 1C2 — **SELF CATERING**

★★★★
SELF CATERING

Units **9**
Sleeps **2–36**
Low season per wk
£270.00–£520.00
High season per wk
£430.00–£840.00

Burradon Farm Houses & Cottages, Cramlington

contact Mrs Judith Younger, Burradon Farm Houses & Cottages, Burradon Farm, Cramlington NE23 7ND
t (0191) 268 3203 **e** judy@burradonfarm.co.uk **w** burradonfarm.co.uk

open All year
payment Credit/debit cards, cash/cheques

Burradon Farm is located only a few miles from the spectacular Northumbrian coastline and within easy reach of the cultural heritage and dynamic centre which is Newcastle-upon-Tyne. The new barn conversions have become characterful, high-quality houses and cottages boasting every amenity and facility to ensure an enjoyable visit. Dishwasher in houses.

B1505 to Burradon. Travel 0.3 miles up hill and take 1st left onto Burradon Farm Road. Farmhouse is on right-hand side.

3-4-night stays welcomed, all year round.

Unit
General P Leisure Shop 0.5 miles Pub 0.5 miles

CRASTER, Northumberland Map ref 1C1 — **GUEST ACCOMMODATION**

★★★
FARMHOUSE

B&B per room per night
s Min £38.00
d Min £50.00

Howick Scar Farmhouse

Craster, Alnwick NE66 3SU **t** (01665) 576665 **f** (01665) 576665 **e** howick.scar@virgin.net
w howickscar.co.uk

250-acre mixed farm. Comfortable farmhouse with television lounge. Sea view from bedrooms. Shared bathroom. Seven miles from Alnwick between Craster and Howick on the coast. Lovely scenery and walks. Open April to October.

bedrooms 2 double
payment Cash/cheques

Room General 12 P Leisure

FORD, Northumberland Map ref 1B1 — **GUEST ACCOMMODATION**

GUEST ACCOMMODATION

B&B per room per night
s £35.00–£45.00
d £60.00–£70.00
Evening meal per person
£15.50–£18.50

The Estate House

Ford, Berwick-upon-Tweed TD15 2PX **t** (01890) 820668 & 07812 803516
e the.estate.house@btinternet.com **w** theestatehouse.co.uk

This elegant Edwardian home is located in Ford village in the heart of Northumberland's 'Secret Kingdom', between the A1 and A697. Ideally situated for a wide range of visitor attractions.

open All year
bedrooms 2 double, 2 single
bathrooms 3 en suite, 1 private
payment Credit/debit cards, cash/cheques

Room General P Leisure

GREENHEAD, Northumberland Map ref 1B2 — **GUEST ACCOMMODATION**

♦♦♦♦
GUEST ACCOMMODATION

B&B per room per night
s £34.00–£44.00
d £64.00–£68.00
Evening meal per person
£25.00

Holmhead Guest House

On Thirlwall Castle Farm, Hadrian's Wall, Greenhead, Haltwhistle CA8 7HY **t** (01697) 747402
f (01697) 747402 **w** holmhead.com

Standing on the foundations of Hadrian's Wall, the house was built from its stones in 1800. Your host was a former guide and is an expert on Hadrian's Wall.

open All year except Christmas and New Year
bedrooms 2 double, 2 twin
bathrooms All en suite
payment Credit/debit cards, cash/cheques, euros

Room General P Leisure

Check it out

Please check prices, quality ratings and other details when you book.

GREENHEAD, Northumberland Map ref 1B2 — **SELF CATERING**

★★★
SELF CATERING

Units **1**
Sleeps **2–4**
Low season per wk
£220.00–£295.00
High season per wk
£350.00–£398.00

Holmhead Cottage, Birdoswald

Holmhead Cottage, Hadrian's Wall, Birdoswald, Nr Greenhead, Via Brampton CA8 7HY
t (016977) 47402 **f** (016977) 47402 **w** holmhead.com

Surrounded by fields and footpaths, with stream and ruined castle. On Hadrian's Wall path near museum and most spectacular remains. Minimum age ten years. Arrival 1600 depart 1000. Ground floor rooms.

open All year except Christmas and New Year
payment Credit/debit cards, cash/cheques, euros

Unit
General 10 P Leisure Shop 1.5 miles Pub < 0.5 miles

HEDDON-ON-THE-WALL, Northumberland Map ref 1B2 — **GUEST ACCOMMODATION**

♦♦♦♦
GUEST ACCOMMODATION

B&B per room per night
d Min £65.00
Evening meal per person
£12.50–£20.00

Ironsign Farm B&B

Ironsign Farm, Heddon-on-the-Wall, Newcastle upon Tyne NE15 0JB **t** (01661) 853802
e lowen532@aol.com **w** ironsign.co.uk

Country farmhouse accommodation built to a high standard. Easily accessed, situated just off the A69 midway between Newcastle and Hexham. Please check website for further information and travel directions.

open All year except Christmas and New Year
bedrooms 1 double, 2 twin
bathrooms All en suite
payment Cash/cheques

Room General P

HEXHAM, Northumberland Map ref 1B2 — **HOTEL**

★★★★
HOTEL
SILVER AWARD

B&B per room per night
s £99.50–£184.50
d £119.00–£239.00
HB per person per night
£69.50–£124.50

Langley Castle

Langley-on-Tyne, Hexham NE47 5LU **t** (01434) 688888 **f** (01434) 684019
e manager@langleycastle.com **w** langleycastle.com

open All year
bedrooms 16 double, 3 family
bathrooms All en suite
payment Credit/debit cards, cash/cheques

A genuine 14thC castle set in own woodland estate. All en suite rooms with facilities, some with window seats set into seven-foot-thick walls. Sauna, four-poster beds. The magnificent drawing room, with blazing log fire, complements the intimate Josephine Restaurant. Perfect to explore Hadrian's Wall, Northumberland, Bamburgh Castle, Holy Island and the Borders.

⊕ *From A69 take A686 for 2 miles.*

♥ *Reserve a castle-view room and we will offer a 'feature' room in the main castle (if available) at check-in, at no extra charge.*

Room General P Leisure

HEXHAM, Northumberland Map ref 1B2 — **GUEST ACCOMMODATION**

★★★★★
GUEST HOUSE

B&B per room per night
s £60.00–£70.00
d £80.00–£90.00
Evening meal per person
£13.00–£18.00

Hallbank Guest House

Hallbank House, Hallgate, Hexham NE46 1XA **t** (01434) 605567 **f** (01434) 605567
e hallbank@freenetname.co.uk **w** hallbankguesthouse.com

Beautiful Edwardian house furnished to a high standard. Quiet location in the town centre.

open All year
bedrooms 4 double, 2 twin, 1 single, 1 family
bathrooms All en suite
payment Credit/debit cards, cash/cheques

Room General P

Travel update

Get the latest travel information – just dial the RAC on 1740 from your mobile phone.

HEXHAM, Northumberland Map ref 1B2 — **GUEST ACCOMMODATION**

★★★★
FARMHOUSE

B&B per room per night
s £30.00–£40.00
d £60.00–£70.00
Evening meal per person
£10.00–£15.00

Hallbarns B&B

Simonburn, Hexham NE48 3AQ **t** (01434) 681419 & 07788 998959
e enquiries@hallbarns-simonburn.co.uk **w** hallbarns-simonburn.co.uk

open All year
bedrooms 2 twin, 1 family
bathrooms 2 en suite, 1 private
payment Cash/cheques

A welcoming and friendly stay awaits you in a tranquil and peaceful setting, with scenic views near Hadrian's Wall, National Forest Park and historic town of Corbridge. Garden to relax and enjoy the sunsets in or have a barbecue. Log fire and comfortable, quality en suite rooms. Hearty breakfast.

⊕ *A69 to Hexham, A6079 at Acomb. At Low Brunton turn left B6320. Approx 4 miles left at Nunwirk into Simonburn, over bridge left. House up hill.*

❤ *Discounts on 4-day stays or more, excl Saturdays.*

Room General P Leisure

HEXHAM, Northumberland Map ref 1B2 — **GUEST ACCOMMODATION**

♦♦♦♦
GUEST ACCOMMODATION

B&B per room per night
s £35.00–£40.00
d £70.00–£80.00
Evening meal per person
Min £20.00

Loughbrow House

Dipton Mill Road, Hexham NE46 1RS **t** (01434) 603351 **f** (01434) 609774
e patricia@loughbrow.fsnet.co.uk **w** loughbrow.fsnet.co.uk

open All year except Christmas and New Year
bedrooms 2 double, 2 twin, 2 single
bathrooms 3 en suite, 2 private
payment Cash/cheques

Standing 600ft above the River Tyne and set in nine acres of garden. The house, built in 1780, is comfortably furnished with antique furniture, where all are given a friendly welcome and are well fed, using mostly local produce from the estate. Within easy distance of the Lake District, Durham and National Trust properties.

⊕ *From Hexham take B6303. After 0.25 miles take right-hand fork, Dipton Mill Road, go for further 0.25 miles. Turn into drive gates, house is 0.5 miles.*

Room General 5 P Leisure

HEXHAM, Northumberland Map ref 1B2 — **SELF CATERING**

★★★★
SELF CATERING

Units **3**
Sleeps **1–5**
Low season per wk
£180.00–£350.00
High season per wk
£250.00–£440.00

Old Church Cottages, Chollerton, Hexham

contact Mrs Marilyn Framrose, Old Church Cottage, Chollerton, Hexham NE46 4TF
t (01434) 681930 **e** oldchurch@supanet.com **w** http://chollerton.urscene.net

open All year
payment Cash/cheques, euros

Beautiful converted country church: two two-bedroom apartments and The Stable (studio apartment – double). Spacious gardens with patio, seating, pond and barbecue. Local bus. Superb restaurants within one to five miles. Wonderful countryside, two miles from Hadrian's Wall, convenient for Newcastle, Alnwick and the Scottish Borders.

⊕ *A69 west of Hexham, take A6079 (Rothbury). Go through Acomb and Wall, cross military road (B6320). Continue to Chollerton. Left fork towards Barrasford. Property on right.*

❤ *Weekend and mid-week breaks available out of season, or sometimes last minute.*

Unit
General P Leisure Shop 6 miles Pub 1 mile

HUMSHAUGH, Northumberland Map ref 1B2 — **GUEST ACCOMMODATION**

★★★
FARMHOUSE

B&B per room per night
s £20.00–£35.00
d £25.00–£40.00
Evening meal per person
£10.00–£15.00

Greencarts Farm

Humshaugh, Hexham NE46 4BW **t** (01434) 681320 **f** (01434) 681320 **e** sandra@greencarts.co.uk
w greencarts.co.uk

Working farm in Roman Wall Country. Magnificent views, log fires, comfortable and friendly atmosphere, ideal for exploring the area. Especially good for walkers and cyclists. Offers choice accommodation.

open All year except Christmas
bedrooms 1 double, 2 twin, 2 family
bathrooms 3 en suite, 2 private
payment Credit/debit cards, cash/cheques, euros

Room General Leisure

INGRAM, Northumberland Map ref 1B1 — **GUEST ACCOMMODATION**

♦♦♦
GUEST ACCOMMODATION

B&B per room per night
d £60.00–£70.00
Evening meal per person
£10.00–£15.00

Reaveley Farmhouse B&B

Ingram Valley, Powburn, Alnwick NE66 4LS **t** (01665) 578268 & 07766 834504
e reaveleyfarm@aol.com

Set in beautiful Ingram Valley, all rooms non-smoking and en suite. Residents' lounge available. Tea/coffee facilities. Children, walkers and cyclists welcome; sorry no pets.

open All year except Christmas and New Year
bedrooms 2 double, 1 twin
bathrooms All en suite
payment Cash/cheques

Room General Leisure

KIELDER, Northumberland Map ref 1B1 — **CAMPING & CARAVANNING**

★★★★
TOURING & CAMPING PARK

(83) £8.50–£19.60
(83) £8.50–£19.60
83 touring pitches

See Ad on inside front cover

Kielder Water Caravan Club Site

Leaplish Waterside Park, Falstone, Hexham NE48 1AX **t** (01434) 250278 **w** caravanclub.co.uk

payment Credit/debit cards, cash/cheques

This is a gently sloping site, with some pitches overlooking the beautiful Kielder Water – Britain's largest man-made lake. A fabulous site for an active holiday. Open March to October.

From east on A69. Past Hexham, right onto A6079. Approx 3 miles, left onto B6320. In Bellingham, left to Kielder Water. Right, signposted Leaplish Waterside Park. Site on right.

Special member rates mean you can save your membership subscription in less than a week. Visit our website to find out more.

General

KIELDER FOREST

See under Bellingham, Kielder

LONGFRAMLINGTON, Northumberland Map ref 1C1 — **GUEST ACCOMMODATION**

★★★★
INN

B&B per room per night
s £39.50
d £70.00–£80.00
Evening meal per person
£7.95–£19.50

The Angler's Arms

Weldon Bridge, Morpeth NE65 8AX **t** (01665) 570655 **f** (01665) 570041
e johnyoung@anglersarms.fsnet.co.uk **w** anglersarms.com

Grade II Listed Georgian country inn, by River Coquet amid Northumberland countryside. With character bar and Pullman restaurant.

open All year
bedrooms 5 double, 1 twin, 1 family
bathrooms All en suite
payment Credit/debit cards, cash/cheques, euros

Room General Leisure

Take a break

Look out for special promotions and themed breaks highlighted in colour. (Offers subject to availability.)

LONGHORSLEY, Northumberland Map ref 1C1 — **GUEST ACCOMMODATION**

★★
BED & BREAKFAST

B&B per room per night
s £20.00–£27.00
d £50.00–£55.00

Kington

East Linden, Morpeth NE65 8TH **t** (01670) 788554 **f** (01670) 788747
e clive@taylor-services.freeserve.co.uk **w** kington-longhorsley.com

Attractive converted farm building. Quiet rural location six miles north of the market town of Morpeth and a 15-minute drive to Alnwick Castle and Gardens. Friendly atmosphere and wonderful breakfasts.

open All year
bedrooms 1 double, 1 twin
bathrooms 2 private
payment Cash/cheques

Room General Leisure

MATFEN, Northumberland Map ref 1B2 — **HOTEL**

★★★★
HOTEL

B&B per room per night
s £115.00–£190.00
d £170.00–£265.00

Matfen Hall

Matfen, Newcastle upon Tyne NE20 0RH **t** (01661) 886500 **f** (01661) 886055
e info@matfenhall.com **w** matfenhall.com

open All year
bedrooms 34 double, 14 twin, 2 single, 3 family
bathrooms All en suite
payment Credit/debit cards, cash/cheques

Voted Large Hotel of the Year 2006 in the Excellence in England Awards, Matfen Hall, in Northumberland's beautiful countryside, is only 25 minutes from Newcastle's centre and 15 minutes from its international airport. The hotel offers luxurious bedrooms, award-winning restaurant, conference suites, golf and acclaimed spa and leisure club.

⊕ *From A1 take A69 signposted Hexham and Carlisle. Exit at Heddon and pick up B6318 towards Chollerford, for 7 miles. Turning for Matfen on left.*

♥ *Mid-week breaks from £180pp for 2 nights' DB&B. Special anniversary packages available.*

Room General Leisure

MORPETH, Northumberland Map ref 1C2 — **HOTEL**

★★★
HOTEL

B&B per room per night
s £45.00–£85.00
d £50.00–£108.00

Longhirst Hall

Longhirst, Morpeth NE61 3LL **t** (01670) 791348 **f** (01670) 791385 **e** enquiries@longhirst.co.uk
w longhirst.co.uk

open All year
bedrooms 54 double, 19 twin, 4 single
bathrooms All en suite
payment Credit/debit cards, cash/cheques

Nestled in rural Northumberland, Longhirst Hall is an early-19thC, John Dobson-designed building set in 75 acres of woodland and landscaped gardens. All en suite bedrooms in the hall, and 34 dormy houses, each able to accommodate up to eight guests. The perfect blend of business, adventure and tranquillity.

⊕ *Located just off the A1. Take turning marked Hebron, follow road, turn left at T-junction. Longhirst 1 mile along the B1337.*

♥ *Exclusive Alnwick Garden breaks, including tickets and brochure, £118 (£59pp).*

Room General Leisure

Tourist Information Centres

To find the nearest one during your stay refer to the pages at the back of the guide.

MORPETH, Northumberland Map ref 1C2 — SELF CATERING

★★★
SELF CATERING

Units 1
Sleeps 4
Low season per wk
£250.00–£300.00
High season per wk
£375.00–£400.00

Meldon Park, Morpeth

contact Mrs Janet Wilson, Flat 1, Meldon Park, Morpeth NE61 3SW
t (01670) 772622 **f** (01670) 772341 **e** mrscookson@compuserve.com
w cottageguide.co.uk/meldonpark

Stunning, unique and peaceful location in rural Northumberland, centrally located for city, hills and coast. One double and one twin room, log-burning stove, central heating, spacious gardens and unrivalled views.

open All year
payment Cash/cheques

Unit
General Leisure Shop 5 miles Pub 0.5 miles

MORPETH, Northumberland Map ref 1C2 — SELF CATERING

★★★
SELF CATERING

Units 1
Sleeps 4
Low season per wk
£240.00–£360.00
High season per wk
£330.00–£500.00

Netherwitton Hall Cottages, Morpeth

contact Mrs Anne-Marie Trevelyan, Netherwitton Hall Cottages, Netherwitton Hall, Netherwitton, Morpeth NE61 4NW
t (01670) 772249 & 07970 653258 **f** (01670) 772510 **e** anne-marie@netherwitton.com

Stone-built cottage in peaceful surroundings of historical Grade I Netherwitton Hall, comprehensively equipped and furnished to a high standard.

open All year
payment Cash/cheques

Unit
General

NEWBIGGIN-BY-THE-SEA, Northumberland Map ref 1C2 — SELF CATERING

SELF CATERING

Units 1
Sleeps 10
Low season per wk
£350.00–£650.00
High season per wk
£650.00–£900.00

Tahfay House, Newbiggin-by-the-Sea

contact Mr Stuart Dodds, 4 Fawdon House Farm, Longhirst, Morpeth NE61 3LQ
t (01670) 503597 **f** (01670) 503597 **e** cozydays@tiscali.co.uk **w** cozydays.co.uk

open All year
payment Cash/cheques

Tahfay House offers spacious accommodation just 50m from the sea, 30 minutes from Newcastle and is ideally located for exploring Northumberland. This refurbished, tastefully appointed Victorian town house has five bedrooms. Northumberland's Heritage Trail boasts wonderful castles and miles of exquisite beaches, bays and lovely seaside villages.

From Newcastle, follow the A1 north, exit A197 (Morpeth). A197 to Newbiggin-by-the-Sea. Tahfay House is located opposite public library on Windsor Road.

3-night stays available Oct-Mar (excl Christmas and New Year). Last-minute discounts available. Reduction for parties of up to 5 people.

Unit
General Leisure Shop < 0.5 miles Pub < 0.5 miles

Take a break

Many establishments offer special promotions and themed breaks. It's a golden opportunity to indulge an interest or find a new one, or just relax and enjoy exceptional value! Offers and promotions are highlighted in colour (and are subject to availability).

OVINGTON, Northumberland Map ref 1B2 — **GUEST ACCOMMODATION**

★★★★
BED & BREAKFAST

B&B per room per night
s £25.00–£30.00
d £50.00–£55.00

Evenwood Cottage

Ovington NE42 6DN **t** (01661) 832259 **e** stuartoram@btinternet.com

open All year except Christmas
bedrooms 1 double, 1 twin
bathrooms 1 en suite, 1 private
payment Cash/cheques

Comfortable, well-appointed, traditional Northumbrian cottage in attractive village location, midway between Newcastle and Hexham. Convenient for main attractions of the area, airport and North Sea ferries. Choice of good restaurants within easy reach.

Room General 3 P Leisure

ROTHBURY, Northumberland Map ref 1B1 — **GUEST ACCOMMODATION**

♦♦♦♦♦
GUEST ACCOMMODATION GOLD AWARD

B&B per room per night
s £50.00–£60.00
d £70.00–£75.00

Tosson Tower Farm

Rothbury, Morpeth NE65 7NW **t** (01669) 620228 **f** (01669) 620228 **e** stay@tossontowerfarm.com
w tossontowerfarm.com

open All year except Christmas and New Year
bedrooms 4 double, 1 twin
bathrooms All en suite
payment Cash/cheques

An idyllic setting for a restful holiday. King-size beds with goose-down duvets. En suite bathrooms and soft bath sheets. Breakfasts served in our Garden Room, with stunning views, using fresh local produce including Craster kippers. Near to National Trust Cragside, Alnwick Castle and beautiful beaches. Fishing available.

Room General P Leisure

ROTHBURY, Northumberland Map ref 1B1 — **SELF CATERING**

★★★–★★★★
SELF CATERING

Units **4**
Sleeps **4–21**
Low season per wk
£200.00–£300.00
High season per wk
£320.00–£495.00

Low Alwinton Cottages, Nr Rothbury

contact Mr & Mrs Eamonn and Susan Gribben, 12 Parkshiel, South Shields NE34 8BU
t (0191) 420 4919 **f** (0191) 420 4919 **e** eamonngribben@blueyonder.co.uk **w** lowalwinton.co.uk

open All year
payment Credit/debit cards, cash/cheques, euros

Luxury cottages nestling in a spectacular wooded valley, amidst the glorious National Park. Located beside the River Coquet and ten minutes from Caistron trout fishery. Stunning panoramic views. Otters, birds, squirrel and deer are just some of the wildlife found here. Ideal for nature lovers, walkers, fishermen, cyclists and families.

❤ *If 4 people or less in Byre Cottage (sleeps 8), £50 off.*

Unit
General P Leisure Shop 1.5 miles Pub 1 mile

Stay focused

Don't forget your camera. Take home shots of some of the greatest scenery, super seascapes and family fun.

ROTHBURY, Northumberland Map ref 1B1 — **CAMPING & CARAVANNING**

★★★
TOURING PARK
(84) £7.90–£17.10
(84) £7.90–£17.10
84 touring pitches

See Ad on inside front cover

Nunnykirk Caravan Club Site

Nunnykirk, Morpeth NE61 4PZ **t** (01669) 620762 **w** caravanclub.co.uk

payment Credit/debit cards, cash/cheques

The peace and tranquillity of this site makes it a haven for wildlife. Space, fresh air and open countryside abound. Hill-walkers will enjoy the splendour of the nearby Simonside Hills. Open April to October.

From B6342, cross bridge at foot of 1:8 hill and turn right into private road. Site on right in 0.25 miles.

Special member rates mean you can save your membership subscription in less than a week. Visit our website to find out more.

General P Leisure

SEAHOUSES, Northumberland Map ref 1C1 — **HOTEL**

★★★
HOTEL

B&B per room per night
s £45.95–£56.95
d £87.90–£105.00
HB per person per night
£61.47–£69.47

Bamburgh Castle Hotel

Seahouses NE68 7SQ **t** (01665) 720283 **e** bamburghcastlehotel@btinternet.com
w bamburghcastlehotel.co.uk

open All year except Christmas
bedrooms 11 double, 5 twin, 2 single, 2 family
bathrooms All en suite
payment Cash/cheques

Overlooking the harbour with magnificent views of the Farne Islands, Bamburgh Castle and Holy Island. Log fire in lounges, private garden and secure car parking. Oak-panelled restaurant serving quality food prepared from the best of fresh, local produce. Visit our website for tariffs, on-line reservations and details of offers.

Cap park entrance on mini-roundabout opposite Barclays Bank/left of Neptune Restaurant. Automatic barrier will rise as you approach.

Four-poster champagne breaks with DB&B and champagne on arrival for £70pppn.

Room TV General P Leisure

SEAHOUSES, Northumberland Map ref 1C1 — **GUEST ACCOMMODATION**

★★
BED & BREAKFAST

B&B per room per night
s Min £25.00
d Min £40.00

Leeholme

93 Main Street, Seahouses NE68 7TS **t** (01665) 720230 **e** lisaevans67@tiscali.co.uk

A warm welcome awaits you at this small, homely bed and breakfast. Five minutes' walk to Seahouses' harbour and shops. Farne Islands, Lindisfarne and castles within easy reach. Hearty breakfast assured. Open March to October.

bedrooms 1 double, 2 twin
bathrooms 1 en suite
payment Cash/cheques

Room TV General P Leisure

Ancient and modern

Experience timeless favourites or discover the latest must-sees. Whatever your choice, be inspired by the places of interest highlighted in the attractions section and the events listed towards the back of this guide.

SEAHOUSES, Northumberland Map ref 1C1 — **CAMPING & CARAVANNING**

★★★★★
HOLIDAY & TOURING PARK
ROSE AWARD

(18) £18.00–£35.00
(18) £18.00–£35.00
(37) £295.00–£620.00
18 touring pitches

Seafield Caravan Park

Seafield Road, Seahouses NE68 7SP **t** (01665) 720628 **f** (01665) 720088 **e** info@seafieldpark.co.uk **w** seafieldpark.co.uk

payment Credit/debit cards, cash/cheques

Luxurious holiday homes for hire on Northumberland's premier park. Fully appointed caravans. Superior, fully serviced touring pitches. Prices include full use of Ocean Club facilities (www.ocean-club.co.uk).

Take the B1340 from Alnwick for 14 miles. East to coast.

Seasonal discounts available on 3-, 4- and 7-day breaks.

General Leisure

STOCKSFIELD, Northumberland Map ref 1B2 — **GUEST ACCOMMODATION**

♦♦♦♦
GUEST ACCOMMODATION SILVER AWARD

B&B per room per night
s £27.50
d £55.00

Locksley Bed & Breakfast

45 Meadowfield Road, Stocksfield NE43 7PY **t** (01661) 844778 **f** (01661) 844778
e Josie@locksleybedandbreakfast.co.uk **w** locksleybedandbreakfast.co.uk

bedrooms 2 double, 1 twin
bathrooms 2 en suite, 1 private
payment Credit/debit cards, cash/cheques

Friendly, comfortable, centrally heated home set in one acre of lovely gardens, conveniently situated in the Tyne Valley. Large guest lounge with inglenook fireplace. Plenty of off-road parking. Ground-floor en suite double bedroom. Warm welcome assured. Closed at New Year.

Turn right off A695 (travelling west to east) just after bridal dress shop into Cadehill Road. Leads to Meadowfield Road. Nearest station, Stocksfield 1 mile.

WALKERS WELCOME CYCLISTS WELCOME

Room General 12 Leisure

STOCKSFIELD, Northumberland Map ref 1B2 — **GUEST ACCOMMODATION**

♦♦♦
GUEST ACCOMMODATION

B&B per room per night
s £30.00–£35.00
d £60.00

Old Ridley Hall

Stocksfield NE43 7RU **t** (01661) 842816 **e** josephinealdridge@oldridleyhall.force9.co.uk
w oldridley.co.uk

open All year except Christmas
bedrooms 2 twin, 1 single, 1 family
bathrooms 1 private
payment Cash/cheques

Country house with rambling garden, dovecote. Listed buildings. Easy reach of MetroCentre, places to eat, Prudhoe, Corbridge Roman Wall, Newcastle, railway.

From A68, south of Tyne at roundabout, east for Stocksfield. B6309 right, signed Hindley. 1st left, then biggest house at end.

Room General

Confirm your booking

It's always advisable to confirm your booking in writing.

THROPTON, Northumberland Map ref 1B1 — **SELF CATERING**

★★★★
SELF CATERING

Units 1
Sleeps 4
Low season per wk
£277.00–£293.00
High season per wk
£340.00–£484.00

Westfield Cottage, Thropton, Rothbury

contact Mr & Mrs Alastair & Catherine Hardie, Westfield Cottage, Westfield House Farm, Thropton, Rothbury, Morpeth NE65 7LB
t (01669) 640263 **e** info@westfield-cottage.co.uk **w** westfield-cottage.co.uk

open All year
payment Cash/cheques, euros

Former water bailiff's cottage at heart of owner's farm in a stunning location in Upper Coquetdale. Three miles from Rothbury yet completely secluded with magnificent views. Site of Special Scientific Interest hosts numerous birds, badgers, otters, deer and foxes. Generous accommodation includes en suite double and twin bedroom.

⊕ *Travel west from Rothbury on B6341. Pass through Thropton and after 0.75 miles you will see Westfield House Farm drive on your right.*

♥ *Winter breaks – please phone or email for details.*

Unit
General Leisure Shop 1 mile Pub 1 mile

WARKWORTH, Northumberland Map ref 1C1 — **GUEST ACCOMMODATION**

★★★★
BED & BREAKFAST

B&B per room per night
d £52.00–£56.00

West View Lodge

35 Watershaugh Road, Warkworth, Morpeth NE65 0TX **t** (01665) 711532 **e** smgunn@aol.com
w visitwarkworth.com

open All year except Christmas
bedrooms 2 double, 1 twin
bathrooms 2 en suite, 1 private
payment Cash/cheques

A large, attractive stone house with delightful views, good quality accommodation, a private garden and a relaxing guest lounge. Situated in lovely countryside yet only one mile from coast. A riverside walk leads to a medieval castle in the historic and picturesque village of Warkworth. Near to Alnwick Castle, Bamburgh, Holy Island and Cheviot Hills.

⊕ *Enter Warkworth on A1068 from north. With castle in front turn left. 2nd right onto Watershaugh Road. Follow round to left. 200yds on left.*

♥ *Please ring for details of off-peak special offers.*

WALKERS WELCOME CYCLISTS WELCOME

Room General 10 Leisure

WHITFIELD, Northumberland Map ref 1B2 — **GUEST ACCOMMODATION**

★★★
BED & BREAKFAST

B&B per room per night
d £45.00–£65.00

West Steel

Whitfield, Hexham NE47 8JE **t** (01434) 344096 **f** (01434) 344328 **e** a.dacosta@ukonline.co.uk

open All year except Christmas and New Year
bedrooms 1 double, 1 twin, 1 suite
bathrooms 2 en suite, 1 private
payment Cash/cheques

Bed and breakfast on working hill farm with outstanding views of Allen Valley. Visitors' lounge with open fire and TV. Spacious en suite bedrooms. Ideal location for Hadrian's Wall.

⊕ *Three miles off A69 trunk road. Take road signposted Ridley Hall and Beltingham.*

WALKERS WELCOME CYCLISTS WELCOME

Room General Leisure

WOOLER, Northumberland Map ref 1B1 — **SELF CATERING**

★★★
SELF CATERING

Units 1
Sleeps 1–5
Low season per wk £280.00–£305.00
High season per wk £350.00

Castle Hill Cottage, Alnwick

contact Mr James Nall-Cain, Castle Hill Cottage, Waterend House, Waterend Lane, Wheathampstead, St Albans AL4 8EP
t (01582) 831083 **f** (01582) 831081 **e** manussj@aol.com

Beautifully secluded cottage. Magnificent views of the Cheviots. It is a real home with open fire, dishwasher and microwave.

open All year
payment Cash/cheques

Unit
General Leisure Shop 1 mile Pub 3 miles

WOOLER, Northumberland Map ref 1B1 — **SELF CATERING**

★★★
SELF CATERING

Units 1
Sleeps 6
Low season per wk £220.00–£260.00
High season per wk £300.00–£350.00

Rose Cottage, Wooler

contact Mrs Christine Andrews, 1 Littleworth Lane, Esher KT10 9PF
t (01372) 464284 **f** (01372) 467715 **e** andrews@playfactors.demon.co.uk

payment Cash/cheques, euros

Old stone cottage with superb views over Glendale Valley, set amid farmland. Beautiful Northumberland beaches, castles and gardens. Edinburgh and Newcastle within easy reach, plus all the Scottish Border land. Log fires and efficient heating make it a good spring or autumn break. Open April to October.

⊕ *Short distance from A697 as it goes through Wooler.*

Unit
General Leisure Shop 1 mile Pub 1 mile

Finding accommodation
is as easy as 1 2 3

Enjoy England official guides to quality accommodation make it quick and easy to find a place to stay. There are several ways to use this guide.

1 PROPERTY INDEX

If you know the name of the establishment you wish to book, turn to the property index at the back where the relevant page number is shown.

2 PLACE INDEX

The place index at the back lists all locations with accommodation featured in the regional sections. A page number is shown where you can find full accommodation and contact details.

3 COLOUR MAPS

All the place names in black on the colour maps at the front have an entry in the regional sections. Refer to the place index for the page number where you will find one or more establishments offering accommodation in your chosen town or village.

maritime heritage, classic towns, watersport thrills

Surf's up at Saltburn-by-the-Sea

Watch lazing seals, paddle in soft waves and dine on hearty fresh fish suppers. Discover rich maritime and mining histories or enjoy a white-water quest on the River Tees. Adventure or relaxation, **it's up to you.**

Explore Tees Valley

Old and new

Amble through the cobbled streets of Yarm, nestling in the shadows of the mighty 43-arch railway viaduct, and feel a sense of quintessential Englishness. Stop off in a cosy tearoom and continue the 'old world' experience in this quaint Georgian town.

Retail therapy is in order at Darlington so treat yourself and enter designer heaven in the Imperial Quarter. Rummage through nick-nacks in the narrow lanes known as Yards and Wynds or hit the high street in Middlesbrough. Get caught up in the drama in the summer months and enjoy colourful street scenes, carnivals and parades.

It's a sailor's life at Hartlepool Historic Quay

Take to the waves

Pay the award-winning Hartlepool Historic Quay a visit, admire Britain's oldest floating warship HMS *Trincomalee* and enjoy an evening at one of the many organised events in the stylish marina. Dine on the fresh catch at one of the local fishing ports and visit the picture-postcard village of Staithes to see the colourful houses standing all askew at the base of the rugged cliffs.

Fun at the Four Seasons Teeside White Water Centre

Up the tempo and take your chances on the rapids at the Four Seasons Teesside White Water Centre: pick your way through the slalom in a canoe or jump aboard a raft and hold on tight! Sunbathing seals are a sight to behold on the banks of the Tees Estuary at Seal Sands; wander the nearby mudflats and look out for wading birds in the tidal creeks.

Saltburn-by-the-Sea is the renowned home of surfing in the North East, so surely this is the best time to don a wetsuit and board the waves! Roll up your jeans and splash about or relax on the inviting sandy beach. Hop in the cliff lift and gaze out to sea as you descend for a stroll along the recently refurbished Victorian pier to experience traditional English seaside life at its best.

Discovering tropical plants at Nature's World, Middlesbrough

Energy flow

Climb to the summit of magnificent Roseberry Topping for spectacular views across the Tees Valley and down to the evocative North Yorkshire Moors. Hop on your bike and follow the tracks of a disused railway line through Guisborough Forest. If you're on foot you can keep the little ones entertained on the Children's Activity Trail. Explore the surrounding parks and nature reserves to your heart's content, then lay out a chequered rug and picnic in the delightful setting at Broken Scar in Darlington.

A day out

Get to grips with 18th-century life atop treacherous waves at the Captain Cook Birthplace Museum on the outskirts of Middlesbrough. Try your hand at the interactive displays and peruse the artefacts from the pioneer's life and times. Learn the movements of the earth and stars at the Planetarium in Wynyard Country Park or give the kids a pioneering eco-experience at Nature's World in Middlesbrough.

Pull on a hard hat and explore underground at Cleveland Ironstone Mining Museum – the most important of its kind in Victorian and Edwardian Britain. Watch fireworks blaze in November over the majestic ruins of 12th-century Augustarian monastery, Gisborough Priory or enjoy an evening of live music in this dramatic, historical setting.

Food & drink

Fancy a bite to eat or a relaxing drink? Here's a selection of food and drink venues to get you started. For lots more ideas go online at **enjoyengland.com/taste**.

Restaurants

Brewhouse Bistro – Pinchinthorpe Hall
Fine dining
Pinchinthorpe, Guisborough
TS14 8HG
t (01287) 630200
w pinchinthorpehall.co.uk

Crathorne Hall
Fine dining
Crathorne, Yarm TS15 0AR
t (01642) 700398
w handpicked.co.uk/crathornehall

D P Chadwicks
Global
104b High Street, Yarm TS15 9AU
t (01642) 788558

Kirklevington Hall
English
Kirklevington, Yarm TS15 9LW
t (01642) 789000
w judgeshotel.co.uk

Krimo's
Algerian
The Marina, Hartlepool TS24 0YB
t (01429) 266120
w krimos.co.uk

La Terrasse – The Highfield Hotel
French
Marton Road, Middlesbrough
TS4 2PA
t (01642) 817638
w la-terrasse.co.uk

Lotus Garden
Eastern
Unit 1, Navigation Point,
Hartlepool Marina, Hartlepool
TS24 0UG
t (01429) 275527
w lotus-garden.co.uk

Maxine's
Fine dining
Hotel Bannatyne, Southend
Avenue, Darlington DL3 7HZ
t (01325) 365858
w hotelbannatyne.com

Reeds @ 636, Parkmore Hotel
English
636 Yarm Road, Eaglescliffe
TS16 0DH
t (01642) 786815
w parkmorehotel.co.uk

Portofino
European
The Historic Quay, Hartlepool
TS24 0XZ
t (01429) 266166
w portofino.co.uk

Raffles at the Croft
Global
The Croft Hotel, Croft-on-Tees,
Darlington DL2 2ST
t (01325) 720319
w rafflesuk.com

Thai Harbour
Thai
Navigation Point, Hartlepool
Marina, Hartlepool TS24 0UG
t (01429) 866789
w thaiharbour.co.uk

Tocketts Restaurant – Gisborough Hall Hotel
Fine dining
Whitby Lane, Guisborough
TS14 6PT
t 0870 400 8191
w macdonaldshotels.co.uk/gisborough

The Waiting Room
Vegetarian
9 Station Road, Eaglescliffe,
Stockton-on-Tees TS16 0BU
t (01642) 780465
w the-waiting-room.co.uk

Pubs

The Circus Bar and Brasserie
3-4 Bakehouse, Darlington
DL1 5QA
t (01325) 366367

The Smiths
Carlton Village, Stockton-on-Tees
TS21 1EA
t (01740) 630471
w thesmithscarlton.co.uk

Tearooms, coffee shops and cafes

Angel Tea Room
22 High Street, Stokesley,
Middlesbrough TS9 5DQ
t (01642) 713622

Goodbody's
58 Albert Road, Middlesbrough
TS1 1QD
t (01642) 253503

Mrs Bridge's Coffee Shop
2 Craigton House, Queen Street,
Redcar TS10 1DL
t (01642) 489818

Piercebridge Organic Farm
Piercebridge, Darlington DL2 3SE
t (01325) 374251

Priory Coffee House
2 Chaloner Mews, Guisborough
TS14 6QD
t (01287) 635284

Signals Coffee Shop
Station Square, Saltburn-by-Sea
TS12 1AG
t (01287) 622982

Tastebud
45 Station Road, Billingham,
Cleveland TS23 18S
t (01642) 360605

Virgos
7 Dundas Street,
Saltburn-by-the-Sea TS12 1AH
t (01287) 624031

Windlebridge Tea Room
Old Middlesbrough Road,
Guisborough TS14 6QS
t (01287) 635642

where to stay in
Tees Valley

Maps
All place names in the blue bands are shown on the maps at the front of this guide.

Accommodation symbols
Symbols give useful information about services and facilities. Inside the back-cover flap you can find a key to these symbols. Keep it open for easy reference.

DARLINGTON, Tees Valley Map ref 1C3 — **GUEST ACCOMMODATION**

★★★
INN

B&B per room per night
s £30.00–£35.00
d £45.00–£50.00

Boot & Shoe

Church Row, Darlington DL1 5QD **t** (01325) 287501 **f** (01325) 287501
e enquiries@bootandshoe.com **w** bootandshoe.com

A Grade II Listed building situated on Darlington's busy marketplace, fully refurbished in 2000. Only minutes away from train and bus station, and A1

open All year
bedrooms 5 double, 2 twin, 2 family
bathrooms 7 en suite
payment Credit/debit cards, cash/cheques

Room General

DARLINGTON, Tees Valley Map ref 1C3 — **SELF CATERING**

★★
SELF CATERING

Units 1
Sleeps 2
Low season per wk
£270.00–£280.00
High season per wk
£280.00–£310.00

63 Cumberland Street, Darlington

contact Mrs Kathleen Reeve, 130 St Margarets Avenue, Rushden NN10 9PW
t (01933) 387945 **f** (01933) 350203 **e** barry.reeve1@ntlworld.com

open All year
payment Cash/cheques

Pleasant terraced property, 20-minutes walk to centre of town and train station. Fully equipped kitchen, bedding and towels supplied. Ideally located for many attractions such as Durham, Newcastle, the city of York and the tranquillity of the North York Moors. Three double bedrooms, two double futons on ground floor. Teesside Airport eight miles.

A1 jct 59, follow signs to Darlington onto A167. Straight on at roundabout. Straight on at traffic lights. Cumberland street is 6th road on right.

Unit
General

MIDDLESBROUGH, Tees Valley Map ref 1C3 — **GUEST ACCOMMODATION**

★★
GUEST HOUSE

B&B per room per night
s £25.00
d £40.00–£45.00

The Chadwick

Clairville Road, Middlesbrough TS4 2HN **t** (01642) 287235 **e** chadwickguesthouse@hotmail.com
w chadwickguesthouse.com

Elegant, recently refurbished, family-run guesthouse close to town and all amenities. Long lets available by negotiation. Bilingual staff. Credit cards welcome. For information, visit our website. Online bookings taken.

open All year
bedrooms 2 double, 3 single, 1 family
bathrooms 1 private
payment Credit/debit cards, cash/cheques

Room General

SALTBURN-BY-THE-SEA, Tees Valley Map ref 1C3 — **GUEST ACCOMMODATION**

★★★★
GUEST HOUSE

B&B per room per night
s £35.00–£40.00
d £60.00–£80.00

The Arches

Low Farm, Ings Lane, Brotton, Saltburn-by-the-Sea TS12 2QX **t** (01287) 677512 **f** (01287) 677150
e hotel@gorallyschool.co.uk **w** gorallyschool.co.uk

open All year
bedrooms 4 double, 3 twin, 4 family
bathrooms All en suite
payment Credit/debit cards, cash/cheques, euros

The Arches offers a relaxing environment and overlooks spectacular views of cliffs and golf course. All the rooms are individually furnished with en suite bathrooms.

Room General Leisure

STOCKTON-ON-TEES, Tees Valley Map ref 1C3 — **CAMPING & CARAVANNING**

★★★★★
TOURING PARK
(115) £9.50–£21.40
(115) £9.50–£21.40
115 touring pitches

See Ad on inside front cover

White Water Caravan Club Park

Tees Barrage, Stockton-on-Tees TS18 2QW **t** (01642) 634880 **w** caravanclub.co.uk

open All year
payment Credit/debit cards, cash/cheques

Pleasantly landscaped site, part of the largest white-water canoeing and rafting course built to an international standard in Britain. Nearby Teesside Park for shopping, restaurants etc.

Come off the A66 Teesside Park. Follow Teesdale sign, go over Tees Barrage Bridge, turn right. Site 200yds on the left.

Special member rates mean you can save your membership subscription in less than a week. Visit our website to find out more.

General Leisure

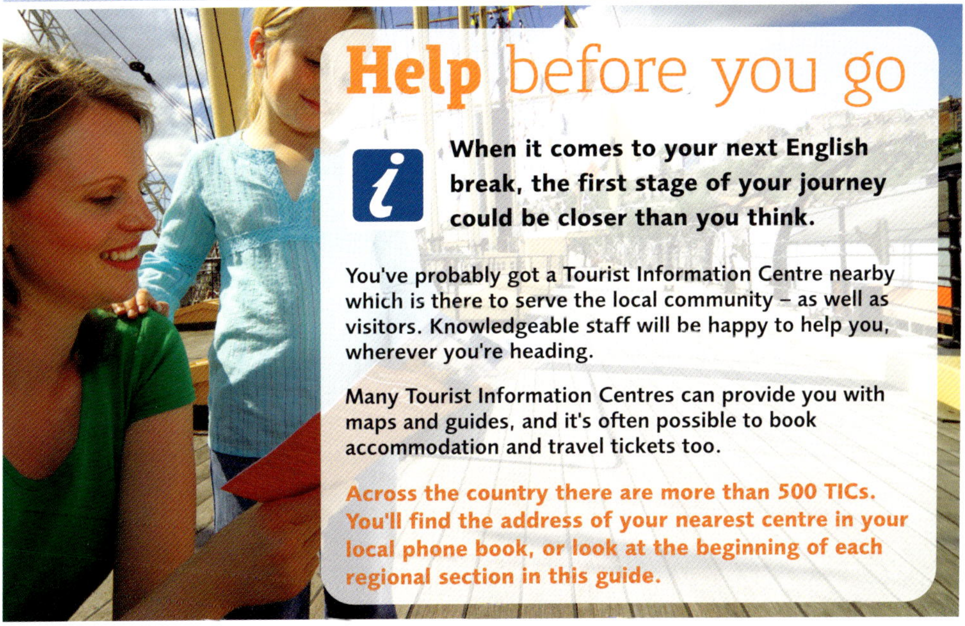

Help before you go

When it comes to your next English break, the first stage of your journey could be closer than you think.

You've probably got a Tourist Information Centre nearby which is there to serve the local community – as well as visitors. Knowledgeable staff will be happy to help you, wherever you're heading.

Many Tourist Information Centres can provide you with maps and guides, and it's often possible to book accommodation and travel tickets too.

Across the country there are more than 500 TICs. You'll find the address of your nearest centre in your local phone book, or look at the beginning of each regional section in this guide.

Capturing the moment by the Millennium Bridge in NewcastleGateshead

Find fascinating art, intriguing nature and entertainment in abundance. Discover cafe culture and a shoppers' paradise in the cities, give the kids a treat and explore **rich history in every hidden corner.**

Explore Tyne and Wear

Fully entertained

Treat yourself to some retail therapy in NewcastleGateshead: browse Europe's largest indoor shopping complex, the MetroCentre, wander down Grey Street in Grainger Town and admire the superb Regency architecture or seek out something individual in the boutiques and markets. Relax in one of the numerous pavement cafes – cappuccino in hand – and take your pick from dishes spanning the globe.

Take in a play at The Sage Gateshead, a truly magnificent building staging outstanding theatrical performances and live music. Explore the constantly changing exhibitions in the Baltic Centre for Contemporary Art and listen intently to talks given by the featured artists. Then stride over the awesome Millennium Bridge to NewcastleGateshead Quayside to see even more spectacular architecture and party the night away in one of the many nightclubs.

History in the making at Bede's World, Jarrow

Step back in time at Segedunum Roman Fort

Out and about

Take a break and head to 'city by the sea' Sunderland and relax on one of its award-winning beaches. Admire works of art carved in stone along St Peter's Riverside Sculpture Trail or take a deep breath and step out along the treetop walkway at the inspiring Winter Gardens.

For art leaning towards the classics, take a trip to the Laing Art Gallery in NewcastleGateshead and find spectacular exhibits ranging from British oil paintings and watercolours to ceramics and glassware, then speed off on an interactive Art Adventure at the South Shields Museum and Art Gallery.

Hear recreated tales from Roman soldiers at Segedunum Roman Fort, Baths and Museum and walk through echoes of the past as you stroll through this superbly preserved gateway to Hadrian's Wall. Find true examples of great historical importance at Bede's World: gaze, awe-struck, at the excavations of the 7th-century St Paul's Monastery and discover the creation of early Anglo-Saxon kingdoms at the exhibition.

Watch tales come to life at Seven Stories, the Centre for Children's Books, NewcastleGateshead

Time with the kids

Come face to face with predators of the deep at the Blue Reef Aquarium. Find yourself mesmerised by the giant octopus who can unscrew jam jars to obtain food and be grateful for the glass that separates you from the giant spider crab! Have a splash yourself at Wet N' Wild and let the kids plummet down the water chutes while you relax in the bubbling jacuzzi.

Back in NewcastleGateshead children will be enthralled at Seven Stories, the Centre for Children's Books, where interactive activities reveal the magic of books. Allow them to get their hands on the exhibits at The Centre for Life where science and life are explored in tandem. Or head to the Discovery Museum to learn all there is to know about this fascinating region.

In the wings

Spot diving kingfishers and foraging red squirrels as you walk the grounds of Gibside – the ancestral estate of the Queen Mother near Rowlands Gill. Traverse the forest garden of this stunning National Trust property and admire spectacular views over Derwent Valley. Perch atop a hillside and feel dwarfed by the mighty Angel of the North, ready and waiting to greet you as you enter NewcastleGateshead.

You can find English country flowers throughout the beautiful meadow grounds of Washington Old Hall. Explore the manor-house in which the first American president's ancestors resided and take a moment to study mementoes from the War of Independence. Let the kids pick their way through the fresh grasslands of the Wildfowl and Wetlands Trust, Washington, to examine insects, and try to sight the rare and extremely elegant avocets – once declared extinct!

Food & drink

Fancy a bite to eat or a relaxing drink? Here's a selection of food and drink venues to get you started. For lots more ideas go online at **enjoyengland.com/taste**.

Restaurants

Azzuri
Italian
Foster Street, Quayside, Newcastle upon Tyne NE1 2NH
t (0191) 222 1110
w azzuriuk.com

Beamish Park Hotel
English
Beamish Burn Road, Marley Hill, Stanley NE16 5EG
t (01207) 230666
w beamish-park-hotel.co.uk

Cafe Spice
Indian
6-7 Douro Terrace, Ashbrooke, Sunderland SR2 7DX
t (0191) 510 2002

Close House Country Club
Fine dining
Heddon-on-the-Wall, Newcastle upon Tyne NE15 0HT
t (01661) 852255
w closehouse.co.uk

Grainger Rooms
English
7 Higham Place, Newcastle upon Tyne NE1 8AF
t (0191) 232 4949
w graingerrooms.co.uk

Il Forno
Italian
Station Buildings, Tynemouth Metro Station NE30 4RE
t (0191) 258 3200

Kisii
Global
Whitley Bay Metro Station, Station Road, Whitley Bay NE26 2QY
t (0191) 253 7077

La Riviera
European
Pipewellgate, Gateshead Quayside NE8 2BJ
t (0191) 477 7070
w lariviera.co.uk

Le Rivage Copthorne Hotel
Fine dining
The Close, Quayside, Newcastle upon Tyne NE1 3RT
t (0191) 222 0333
w millenniumhotels.com

Louis'
French
71 Osborne Road, Jesmond NE2 2AN
t (0191) 281 5284
w louisrestaurant.co.uk

McCoys at the Baltic
Fine dining
Baltic Centre for Contemporary Art, Gateshead NE8 2BE
t (0191) 440 4949
w mccoysbaltic.com

Bella Sicilia
Italian
235 High Street, Gosforth NE3 1HQ
t (0191) 284 9900
w bellasicilia.co.uk

Poon's Gosforth Palace Chinese Restaurant
Chinese
6a Salters Road, Gosforth NE3 1DJ
t (0191) 285 2288
w poons.com

Prickly Pear
Fine dining
4 Esplanade Mews, Sunderland SR2 7BQ
t (0191) 564 0982

Royal Circle
Cantonese
16-18 Stowell Street, Newcastle upon Tyne NE1 4XQ
t (0191) 261 2300

Treasure of the Orient
Chinese
26 Stowell Street, Newcastle upon Tyne NE1 4XQ
t (0191) 230 4008

Pubs

Black Horse Inn
The Black Horse, Rectory Bank, West Boldon NE36 0QQ
t (0191) 536 1814

Magnesia Bank
1 Camden Street, North Shields NE30 1NH
t (0191) 257 4831
w magnesiabank.com

Tearooms, coffee shops and cafes

Bruges!
46 Brentwood Avenue, Jesmond NA2 3DH
t (0191) 281 8081

Cafe 21
21 Queens Street, Quayside, Newcastle upon Tyne NE21 3UG
t (0191) 222 0755

Charlotte's Tea Rooms
172 Park View, Whitley Bay NE26 3QW
t (0191) 280 2607

Gibside Tea Room
Gibside Estate, Burnopfield, Newcastle upon Tyne NE16 6BG
t (01207) 541828
w nationaltrust.org.uk

Paprika Cafe
46 Frederick Street, Sunderland SR1 1NF
t (0191) 564 0606

Souter Lighthouse Tea Room
Coast Road, Whitburn, Sunderland SR6 7NH
t (0191) 529 3161
w nationaltrust.org.uk

Waterside Cafe
Wildfowl and Wetands Trust, District 15, Washington NE38 8LE
t (0191) 416 5454
w wwt.org.uk/washington

where to stay in

Tyne and Wear

Maps

All place names in the blue bands are shown on the maps at the front of this guide.

Accommodation symbols

Symbols give useful information about services and facilities. Inside the back-cover flap you can find a key to these symbols. Keep it open for easy reference.

GATESHEAD, Tyne and Wear Map ref 1C2 — **GUEST ACCOMMODATION**

★★★
GUEST HOUSE

B&B per room per night
s £30.00–£40.00
d £46.00–£60.00

Shaftesbury Guest House

245 Prince Consort Road, Gateshead NE8 4DT **t** (0191) 478 2544 **f** (0191) 478 2544
e shaftesbury.hotel@hotmail.com

Charming family business. Close to leisure and civic centre, athletics stadium, Team Valley, MetroCentre, Newcastle, Beamish Museum, Newcastle Arena, beaches and excellent nightlife.

open All year
bedrooms 6 twin, 2 single, 2 family
bathrooms 2 en suite
payment Cash/cheques, euros

Room General

NEWCASTLE UPON TYNE, Tyne and Wear Map ref 1C2 — **HOTEL**

★★★
HOTEL

B&B per room per night
s £59.00–£105.00
d £65.00–£120.00

Britannia Hotel Newcastle Airport

Newcastle International Airport, Newcastle upon Tyne NE13 8DJ **t** (0191) 401 9988
f (01661) 860157 **e** res716@britanniahotels.com **w** britanniahotels.com

open All year
bedrooms 48 double, 44 twin, 6 family, 1 suite
bathrooms All en suite
payment Credit/debit cards, cash/cheques, euros

The Britannia Hotel is only 350yds from the airport terminal and five minutes from the A1, with a direct Metro link straight into the city. The hotel boasts 99 refurbished bedrooms. The Rangoon Restaurant and cocktail bar provide you with the perfect opportunity to sit back, relax and enjoy the homely atmosphere.

From the A1 follow signs for Newcastle International Airport. The hotel is located within the airport grounds opposite the main terminal.

See website for availability and prices.

Room General Leisure

Check it out

Information on accommodation listed in this guide has been supplied by proprietors. As changes may occur you should remember to check all relevant details at the time of booking.

NEWCASTLE UPON TYNE, Tyne and Wear Map ref 1C2 — **GUEST ACCOMMODATION**

★★★
BED & BREAKFAST

B&B per room per night
s £35.00–£38.00
d £46.00–£52.00
Evening meal per person
£10.00–£12.00

Greenholme

40 South View, East Denton, Newcastle upon Tyne NE5 2BP **t** (0191) 267 4828 & 07910 529089
e info@greenholmeguesthouse.co.uk **w** greenholmeguesthouse.co.uk

Greenholme is a family-run bed and breakfast specifically targeted at travellers who do not wish to stay at large impersonal hotels and who like to be pampered.

open All year except Christmas and New Year
bedrooms 1 twin, 1 family
bathrooms 1 en suite
payment Cash/cheques

Room General Leisure

NEWCASTLE UPON TYNE, Tyne and Wear Map ref 1C2 — **GUEST ACCOMMODATION**

♦♦♦♦
GUEST ACCOMMODATION

B&B per room per night
s £45.50
d £65.00
Evening meal per person
£7.50–£15.00

The Keelman's Lodge

Grange Road, Newcastle upon Tyne NE15 8NL **t** (0191) 267 1689 & (0191) 414 0156
f (0191) 267 7387 **e** admin@biglampbrewers.co.uk **w** keelmanslodge.co.uk

open All year
bedrooms 8 double, 5 twin, 1 family
bathrooms All en suite
payment Credit/debit cards, cash/cheques

The Keelman's Lodge is a purpose-built accommodation lodge which stands in its own grounds on the edge of the Tyne Riverside Country Park. Sharing its grounds are the Big Lamp Brewery (listed building) and the very popular Keelman pub, selling good food and real ale on tap.

Follow signs to Newburn. Once in Newburn, head towards the leisure centre. The Keelman's Lodge is 50yds further up the road.

Free child places (under 3s).

Room General Leisure

WHICKHAM, Tyne and Wear Map ref 1C2 — **GUEST ACCOMMODATION**

★★★★
GUEST HOUSE

B&B per room per night
s £40.00–£50.00
d £58.00–£65.00

East Byermoor Guest House

Fellside Road, Whickham, Newcastle upon Tyne NE16 5BD **t** (01207) 272687
e stay@eastbyermoor.co.uk **w** eastbyermoor.co.uk

17thC stone farmhouse in open countryside. Ideally placed for visiting Hadrian's Wall, Durham Cathedral, Beamish Museum and the Northumberland coastline as well as the MetroCentre and Newcastle city centre.

open All year except Christmas
bedrooms 2 double, 2 twin
bathrooms All en suite
payment Credit/debit cards, cash/cheques

Room General Leisure

WHITLEY BAY, Tyne and Wear Map ref 1C2 — **GUEST ACCOMMODATION**

★★★★
GUEST ACCOMMODATION

B&B per room per night
s £40.00–£50.00
d £55.00–£65.00

York House Hotel

106-110 Park Avenue, Whitley Bay NE26 1DN **t** (0191) 252 8313 **f** (0191) 251 3953
e reservations@yorkhousehotel.com **w** yorkhousehotel.com

open All year
bedrooms 6 double, 3 twin, 1 single, 4 family
bathrooms All en suite
payment Credit/debit cards, cash/cheques

Delightfully decorated en suite bedrooms, all spacious and well equipped. Rooms overlooking the park. Ground-floor rooms and suites available. WI-FI access. Close to restaurants and shops. On-site car parking. New online direct booking facility.

Location maps and directions can be found on the website.

Room General Leisure

WHITLEY BAY, Tyne and Wear Map ref 1C2 **SELF CATERING**

★★★★
SELF CATERING

Units **3**
Sleeps **4–6**
Low season per wk
£250.00–£350.00
High season per wk
£495.00–£595.00

Southcliff Apartments, Whitley Bay

contact Mr Alan Heslington, Southcliff Apartments, 4 Southcliff, Whitley Bay NE26 2PB
t (0191) 251 3121 **e** southcliffapartments@theseaside.co.uk **w** southcliffapartments.co.uk

open All year
payment Cash/cheques, euros

'Far from the madding crowd', yet only five minutes from Cullercoats Metro. Only a pedestrian walkway between you and the sea – the views are breathtaking. Private lounge, fully equipped kitchen, bathroom (bath and shower), linen, towels, utilities included in price.

From A1 follow signs for Tyne Tunnel. Take A1058 east to coast. Left towards Whitley Bay, through Cullercoats. Southcliff Apartments on right overlooking Brown's Bay.

Jan-Mar 4 days for the price of 3, excl Friday and Saturday nights.

Unit
General P Leisure Shop < 0.5 miles Pub < 0.5 miles

What makes the **perfect break?**

Big city buzz or peaceful country panoramas? Take a fresh look at England and you may be surprised at what's on your own doorstep.

experience... paddling on sandy beaches, playing Poohsticks in the forest, picnics at open-air concerts, tearooms offering home-made cakes... **discover...** make your own journey of discovery through England's cultural delights: surprising contrasts between old and new, traditional and trendsetting, time-honoured and contemporary... **explore...** drink in lungfuls of fresh air on a hillside with heart-stopping views, wander through the maze in the garden of a stately home or tug on the sails of a boat skimming across a lake... **relax...** no rush to do anything or be anywhere, take time to immerse yourself in your favourite book by a roaring log fire or glide from a soothing massage to a refreshing facial, ease away the tension...

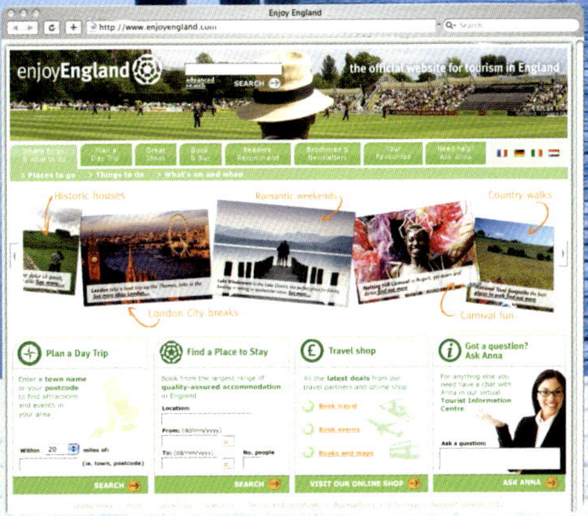

To help you make up your mind go online at

enjoy**England**.com

Rest awhile on the Cleveland Way National Trail at Sutton Bank, North Yorkshire

proud heritage, big attractions, lush dales

With its rolling hills and dramatic, lush green landscapes, Yorkshire boasts some of the most picturesque pockets to be found in the country. Along with lively cities and ancient, ruined abbeys, this region is **rich in both history and culture.**

Explore Yorkshire

Investigate the mysteries of The Deep, Hull

A sea of green

Experience the spine-tingling desolation of the Yorkshire Moors as they sweep you into the world of Emily Brontë's *Wuthering Heights*. Coupled with a visit to the Brontë Parsonage and museum, where the works of the remarkable sisters came to life, Brontë Country is truly inspiring.

Lose yourself in 30,000 acres of stunning countryside encompassing the Bolton Abbey estate, traverse woodland and riverside paths and soak up the incredible vistas. Head to the vibrant coastal town of Scarborough – the country's first seaside resort – and immerse yourself in marine life at the Sea Life Centre. Or explore ocean life further at The Deep in Hull.

Eye it up

Allow the innovative space at Sheffield's Millennium Galleries to guide you on a journey of art throughout the ages. Or take a trip to Bradford and experience art of a different nature at the National Museum of Photography, Film & Television, the country's most visited museum outside the capital. Be amazed by the new interactive exhibition, Experience TV, and discover the ins and outs of television.

At the Yorkshire Sculpture Park in West Bretton, you will find that no two visits are ever the same. Changing weather and seasons will alter your perception of this unique park where art is integrated into the landscape in a complementary fashion.

Take time to soak up some of the rich heritage that Yorkshire has to offer. Pay the 11th-century Middleham Castle a visit and discover the childhood home of Richard III, or hunt for ghosts in the ruins of the majestic Rievaulx Abbey and admire its graceful arches and elegant structure.

Discover the history behind your TV at the National Museum of Photography, Film & Television, Bradford

A helping hand on the limestone pavement at Malham Cove, North Yorkshire

Put your boots on

Pull on your hiking boots and explore the 1,000 square miles of National Parks (the Yorkshire Dales, the North York Moors and the Peak District). Stride out along the Pennine or Dales Way or take a leisurely stroll along one of the many trails across this vast expanse of beautiful countryside.

Gaze in awe at mighty Malham Cove – a curved crag of limestone formed after the last ice age – and attempt to understand this truly magnificent spectacle. Pick your way across the dissected limestone pavement running across the surface of the cove – a result of chemical weathering – and admire the simplistic beauty of the eroded channels.

The charming fishing village of Robin Hood's Bay near Whitby is the perfect place to relax and dip into the rock pools dotted about the delightful sandy beaches. Or take your binoculars up the 400 feet chalk cliffs of the Flamborough Headland Heritage Coast and spot the intriguing selection of wildlife.

But above all, don't forget about the wonderful tastes the region has to offer. Sup a true pint of Yorkshire bitter and nibble on a chunk of Wensleydale, or warm your cockles with a selection of traditional pies and Yorkshire pudding. And for that sweet tooth, there's always Bakewell tart for dessert.

Food & drink

Fancy a bite to eat, a relaxing drink or some fresh local produce? Here's a selection of food and drink venues to get you started. For lots more ideas go online at **enjoyengland.com/taste**.

Restaurants

Est Est Est – Cookridge
Italian
151 Otley, Old Road, Leeds
LE16 6HN
t 0870 401 2105
w estestest.co.uk

Georgetown
Indian
Dysons Clock Building,
24-26 Briggate, Leeds LS1 6EP
t (0113) 245 6655
w georgetownrestaurants.co.uk

Kings Ramson
Indian
12a King Street, York YO1 1SP
t (01904) 630420
w kings-ramson.co.uk

Lanterna Restaurant
Italian
33 Queen Street, Scarborough
YO11 1HQ
t (01723) 363616
w lanterna-ristorante.co.uk

Luciano's
Italian
2 Ferriby Road, Hessle, Hull
HU13 0PG
t (01482) 641109

The Magpie Cafe
Seafood
14 Pier Road, Whitby YO21 3PU
t (01947) 602058
w magpiecafe.co.uk

The Old Vicarage
Fine dining
Ridgeway Moor, Ridgeway
Villiage, Sheffield S12 3XW
t (0114) 247 5814
w theoldvicarage.co.uk

Olive Tree Greek Rest
Greek
55 Rodley Lane, Oakland, Leeds
LS13 1NG
t (0113) 256 9283
w theolivetreerestaurant.co.uk

Pubs

The Black Sheep Brewery
Wellgarth, Masham, Ripon
HG4 4EN
t (01765) 689227
w blacksheepbrewery.com

Dog & Gun Inn
Colne Road, Glusburn, Keighley
BD20 8DS
t (01535) 633855

Fleece
154 Main Street, Addingham,
Ilkley LS29 0LY
t (01943) 830491

Oscars Wine Bar & Bistro
English
8 Little Stonegate, York YO1 2AZ
t (01904) 652002

Sandpiper Inn
Market Place, Leyburn DL8 5AT
t (01969) 622206
w sandpiperinn.co.uk

Woolly Sheep Inn
Sheep Street, Skipton BD23 1HY
t (01756) 700966
w timothytaylor.co.uk/woollysheep

Tearooms, coffee shops and cafes

Bettys Cafe Tea Rooms
1 Parliament Street, Harrogate
HG1 2QU
t (01423) 502746
w bettys.co.uk

The Georgian Tea Rooms
56 High Street, Old Town,
Bridlington YO16 4QA
t (01262) 608600
w thegeorgianroomsbridlington.webeden.co.uk

Little Bettys
46 Stonegate, York YO1 8AS
t (01904) 622865
w bettysandtaylors.co.uk

Thyme Cafe
490-492 Glossop Road, Broomhill,
Sheffield S10 2QA
t (0114) 267 0735
w thymeforfood.co.uk

Delis

Leventhorpe Vineyard
Bullerthorpe Lane, Woodlesford,
Leeds LS26 8AF
t (0113) 288 9088
w englishwineproducers.com

Longley's Dairy Shop
33a Huddersfield Road, Holmfirth,
Huddersfield HD7 1RS
t (01484) 681252

Roberts & Speight
40 Norwood, Beverley HU17 9EY
t (01482) 870717
w hamperbox.co.uk

Farm shops and local produce

Blacker Hall Farm Shop
Branch Road, Calder Grove,
Wakefield WF4 3DN
t (01924) 267202
w blackerhall.com

Cannon Hall Farm
Bark House Lane, Cawthorne,
Barnsley S75 4AT
t (01226) 790427
w cannonhallfarm.co.uk

Langthorne Buffalo Products
Farm, Brompton, Northallerton
DL6 2PD
t (01609) 776937

Round Green Deer Farm
Worsbrough, Barnsley S75 3DR
t (01226) 205577
w roundgreenfarm.co.uk

where to stay in Yorkshire

Maps

All place names in the blue bands are shown on the maps at the front of this guide.

Accommodation symbols

Symbols give useful information about services and facilities. Inside the back-cover flap you can find a key to these symbols. Keep it open for easy reference.

AIRTON, North Yorkshire Map ref 2B1 — **GUEST ACCOMMODATION**

★★★
BED & BREAKFAST

B&B per room per night
d £50.00–£59.00

Lindon House

Malham Road, Airton, Skipton BD23 4BE **t** (01729) 830418
w yorkshirenet.co.uk/stayat/lindonguesthouse

Friendly family-run converted dales barn. Beautiful views of Malhamdale. Noted for good food. Established 29 years ago by the Robinson family. A warm welcome awaits you.

open All year except Christmas
bedrooms 2 double, 1 twin
bathrooms All en suite
payment Cash/cheques

Room General P Leisure

ALDBROUGH, East Riding of Yorkshire Map ref 2D1 — **SELF CATERING**

★★★★
SELF CATERING

Units 1
Sleeps 4
Low season per wk
£180.00–£250.00
High season per wk
£250.00–£325.00

Lilac Cottage, Aldbrough, Nr Hull

contact Helen Stubbs, Lilac Cottage, 19 Seaside Road, Aldbrough HU11 4RX
t (01964) 527645 & 07967 566848 **e** helen@seasideroad.freeserve.co.uk **w** lilac-cottage.net

Cosy, comfortable and extremely well-equipped cottage with TV, video, CD player etc. Two bedrooms sleep up to four adults plus cot – one double room, one twin. Private garden.

open All year
payment Cash/cheques

Unit
General P Leisure Shop < 0.5 miles Pub < 0.5 miles

ALLERSTON, North Yorkshire Map ref 1D3 — **CAMPING & CARAVANNING**

★★★★★
TOURING & CAMPING PARK

£11.00–£16.50
£11.00–£16.50
£9.00–£14.50
120 touring pitches

Vale of Pickering Caravan Park

Pickering YO18 7PQ **t** (01723) 859280 **f** (01723) 850060 **e** tony@valeofpickering.co.uk
w valeofpickering.co.uk

Family-owned park in Allerston offering a high standard of service and superb facilities. Peacefully located in open countryside offering panoramic views. The park offers a well-stocked shop. Closed 7 January to 3 March.

payment Credit/debit cards, cash/cheques

General P Leisure

Key to symbols

Open the back flap for a key to symbols.

BISHOP THORNTON, North Yorkshire Map ref 1C3 — **HOTEL**

★
HOTEL

B&B per room per night
s Max £45.00
d Max £55.00
HB per person per night
Max £35.00

Chequers Inn Country Hotel & Restaurant

Harrogate HG3 3JN **t** (01423) 770173 **f** (01423) 770049 **w** chequers-inn-hotel.co.uk

A country inn with great charm and character, situated halfway between John O' Groats and Lands End. The property is only six miles from the floral town of Harrogate. Adults only.

open All year
bedrooms 7 double, 7 twin
bathrooms All en suite
payment Credit/debit cards, cash/cheques, euros

Room General Leisure

BISHOP THORNTON, North Yorkshire Map ref 1C3 — **GUEST ACCOMMODATION**

★★★★
GUEST ACCOMMODATION

B&B per room per night
s £50.00–£55.00
d £70.00–£75.00

Dukes Place

Harrogate HG3 3JY **t** (01765) 620229 **f** (01765) 620454 **e** enquiries@dukesplace-courtyard.co.uk

open All year except Christmas and New Year
bedrooms 1 double, 2 twin
bathrooms All en suite
payment Credit/debit cards, cash/cheques, euros

A Georgian country house close to Fountains Abbey and Ripley castle. Five miles from Harrogate. All bedrooms have en suite shower rooms, one with jacuzzi bath. Breakfast is served in a dining room full of Georgian charm and Paul and Jaki source produce within Yorkshire for their varied menu.

From Harrogate, A61 Ripon. At 2nd Ripley roundabout take B6165 Pateley Bridge. Half a mile turn right. Two and a half miles on left after Chequers Inn.

Special rates for Senior Citizens. Please phone.

Room General P Leisure

BISHOP THORNTON, North Yorkshire Map ref 1C3 — **SELF CATERING**

★★★★
SELF CATERING

Units **6**
Sleeps **2–6**
Low season per wk
£235.00–£300.00
High season per wk
£315.00–£455.00

The Courtyard at 'Dukes Place', Harrogate

contact Jaki Moorhouse, The Courtyard at 'Dukes Place', Bishop Thornton HG3 3JY
t (01765) 620229 **f** (01765) 620454 **e** enquiries@dukesplace-courtyard.co.uk

open All year
payment Credit/debit cards, cash/cheques, euros

Situated in glorious Nidderdale, six well-appointed, discrete cottages in the converted stables and granaries of this Georgian farmhouse. Close to Fountains Abbey and Ripley Castle. The spa town of Harrogate, York and Herriot Country are within easy reach.

From Harrogate A61 Ripon. At 2nd Ripley roundabout, take B6165 Pateley Bridge. After 0.5 miles turn right. 2.5 miles on left after Chequers Inn.

Nov-Mar 3-night break £125 for 1-bedroom cottage and £150 for 2 bedroom cottage (extra night free subject to availability).

Unit
General P Leisure Shop 2 miles Pub 0.5 miles

Check it out

Information on accommodation listed in this guide has been supplied by proprietors. As changes may occur you should remember to check all relevant details at the time of booking.

BISHOP WILTON, East Riding of Yorkshire Map ref 2C1 — **SELF CATERING**

★★★
SELF CATERING

Units 2
Sleeps 2–4
Low season per wk
£150.00–£220.00
High season per wk
£250.00–£350.00

Grange Farm Holiday Cottages, Bishop Wilton

contact Mr Richard & Mrs Judith Davy, Grange Farm Holiday Cottages, The Grange, Bishop Wilton YO42 1SA
t (01759) 369500 **e** richarddavy@supanet.com **w** thegrangefarm.com

Well-equipped, comfortable cottages on working farm. One double bed and one zip-linked twin bed. Peaceful, with panoramic views. Easy reach of York, coast and moors. Open all year. Pets and children welcome.

open All year
payment Cash/cheques

Unit
General Leisure Shop 1 mile Pub 1 mile

BLACKSHAW HEAD, West Yorkshire Map ref 2B1 — **SELF CATERING**

★★★
SELF CATERING

Units 1
Sleeps 1–2
Low season per wk
£200.00–£250.00
High season per wk
£300.00–£350.00

The Garden House, Hebden Bridge

contact Mr Martin Robinson, The Garden House, Manor House, Blackshawhead, Hebden Bridge HX7 7JR
t (01422) 842794 **e** manorhousestudio@talktalk.net **w** manorhousestudio.co.uk

open All year except Christmas and New Year
payment Cash/cheques

Twenty-first-century extension to 16thC hall house, set in large tranquil landscaped garden. Upstairs is a galleried bedroom with twin beds. Downstairs is a well-appointed living room with fully fitted kitchen area and luxurious shower room. Full-height windows lead on to terrace and overlook upper Calderdale.

⊕ *Will be sent at time of booking.*

Unit
General P Leisure Shop 1 mile Pub 1 mile

BOLTON ABBEY, North Yorkshire Map ref 2B1 — **SELF CATERING**

★★★★
SELF CATERING

Units 1
Sleeps 6
Low season per wk
£245.00–£420.00
High season per wk
£315.00–£525.00

The Beamsley Project, Skipton

contact John & Margaret Tomlinson, The Beamsley Project, Harrogate Road, Beamsley BD23 6JA
t (01756) 710255 **f** (01756) 710255 **e** info@beamsleyproject.org.uk **w** beamsleyproject.org.uk

Comfortable cottage with three twin bedrooms, fully equipped for people with disabilities: wheelchair lift, hoist, walk-in shower. Near Bolton Abbey with easy accessible footpaths for disabled.

open All year
payment Cash/cheques

Unit
General P Leisure Shop 4 miles Pub 2 miles

Our quality-rating schemes

For an explanation of the quality and facilities represented by the stars and diamonds please refer to the front of this guide. A more detailed explanation can be found in the information pages at the back.

BOLTON ABBEY, North Yorkshire Map ref 2B1 **SELF CATERING**

★★★★★
SELF CATERING

Units 1
Sleeps 7
Low season per wk
Max £700.00
High season per wk
Max £1,200.00

Low Laithe Barn, Langbar, Ilkley

contact Susan Gray, Low Laithe Barn, Langbar, Ilkley
t (01943) 609819 **f** (01943) 609819 **e** enquiries@beechhousebarns.co.uk **w** beechhousebarns.co.uk

open All year
payment Cash/cheques

A stylish well-equipped, detached 'field-barn' with absolute privacy and breathtaking, uninterrupted views. Midway between Ilkley and Bolton Abbey on the scenic back road. A unique place where old meets new and both win. Open-plan downstairs. Four bedrooms (three double and one single), three bathrooms (two en suite). All upstairs.

A69 from Harrogate. A65 from Leeds. Directions will be sent on receipt of balance.

Unit
General Leisure Shop 3 miles Pub 3 miles

BOYNTON, East Riding of Yorkshire Map ref 1D3 **SELF CATERING**

★★★★
SELF CATERING

Units 1
Sleeps 4
Low season per wk
£260.00–£300.00
High season per wk
£350.00–£470.00

No. 8 Boynton, Bridlington

contact Elizabeth Myhill, Glebe Farm, Rudston, Driffield YO25 4UG
t (01262) 420201 **e** liz.myhill@scarborough.gov.uk **w** no8boynton.co.uk

Delightful whitewashed country cottage. Original features, beautiful antique furniture. Fully equipped and centrally heated. Own garden and parking. Close to country houses, coastal resorts and RSPB reserve. Welcome refreshments provided.

open All year
payment Cash/cheques

Unit
General Leisure Shop 3 miles Pub 3 miles

BRADFIELD, South Yorkshire Map ref 2B2 **SELF CATERING**

★★★
SELF CATERING

Units 1
Sleeps 4
Low season per wk
£280.00
High season per wk
£375.00

Cricket View, Low Bradfield, Sheffield

contact Miss Shaz Thompson, Woodfall Lane, Bradfield, Sheffield S6 6LA
t (0114) 285 1235 **e** info@thepostcardcafe.com **w** thepostcardcafe.com

open All year
payment Cash/cheques, euros

Cricket View is a converted barn in the quintessentially English village of Low Bradfield within the Peak District. Ideally placed for the High Peak and Sheffield. Cricket View suites all types of holidaymakers. Tucked behind the post office in the centre of the village, a warm welcome awaits you.

Seven miles north-west of Sheffield city centre. Twenty minutes from M1 jct 36 or jct 35, 10 minutes from A57 Snake Pass.

Unit
General Shop < 0.5 miles Pub 0.5 miles

BRIDLINGTON, East Riding of Yorkshire Map ref 1D3 **HOTEL**

★★★
HOTEL

B&B per room per night
s £43.00–£70.00
d £82.00–£140.00
HB per person per night
£46.00–£90.00

Expanse Hotel

North Marine Drive, Bridlington YO15 2LS **t** (01262) 675347 **f** (01262) 604928
e reservations@expanse.co.uk **w** expanse.co.uk

Superbly positioned with panoramic views of the bay and Heritage Coast. This is an ideal place to relax or use as a touring base. The hotel, and each bedroom, is as individual as you.

open All year
bedrooms 14 double, 19 twin, 10 single, 2 family, 2 suites
bathrooms All en suite
payment Credit/debit cards, cash/cheques

Room General Leisure

BRIDLINGTON, East Riding of Yorkshire Map ref 1D3 **GUEST ACCOMMODATION**

★★★★
GUEST ACCOMMODATION

B&B per room per night
s £32.00–£46.00
d £64.00–£72.00

Balmoral House

21 Marshall Avenue, Bridlington YO15 2DT **t** (01262) 676678 **f** (01262) 424672
e brian@balmoral-house.com **w** balmoral-house.com

open All year
bedrooms 4 double, 1 twin, 2 single, 1 family
bathrooms All en suite
payment Credit/debit cards, euros

Centrally located in Bridlington, we offer quality accommodation, food and service in a no-smoking environment. En suite rooms, four-poster beds and all food prepared and cooked by a fully qualified Master Chef. Close to the town centre, shops, harbour and beaches. Ideal for overnight stays, short breaks and family holidays.

Directions can be found on our website.

Stay 4 nights (B&B for 2 people) pay for 3. Available Mon-Thu, Nov-Apr excl Bank Holidays.

Room General 8 Leisure

BRIDLINGTON, East Riding of Yorkshire Map ref 1D3 **GUEST ACCOMMODATION**

★★★
GUEST HOUSE

B&B per room per night
s £29.00–£31.00
d £50.00–£58.00
Evening meal per person
£10.00

Ivanhoe Guest House

63 Cardigan Road, Bridlington YO15 3JS **t** 0800 255 0789 & (01262) 675983 **f** (01262) 675983
e bookings@ivanhoeguesthouse.co.uk **w** ivanhoeguesthouse.co.uk

open All year
bedrooms 5 double, 3 twin
bathrooms All en suite
payment Credit/debit cards, cash/cheques

Family-run guesthouse located in a quiet residential area. Close to all amenities, Spa Theatre complex and the award-winning South Beach, only 250m away. Free off-street car parking available for guests. Small licensed guest bar. Fresh-cooked full-English or continental breakfast served every day.

From Hull A165 turn right after golf course, left at traffic lights. From M62/A614 past Morrisons, over railway bridge, right at traffic lights.

4 night mid-week mini-breaks from Sheffield postcode area, including door-to-door transport DB&B £150pp.

Room General P

BRIDLINGTON, East Riding of Yorkshire Map ref 1D3 **GUEST ACCOMMODATION**

♦♦♦♦
GUEST ACCOMMODATION

B&B per room per night
s £28.00–£37.00
d £56.00
Evening meal per person
£10.00–£15.00

Spinnaker House Hotel

19 Pembroke Terrace, Bridlington YO15 3BX **t** (01262) 678440 **f** (01262) 678440

open All year except Christmas
bedrooms 4 double, 3 twin, 3 single, 1 family
bathrooms All en suite
payment Credit/debit cards, cash/cheques, euros

A warm welcome to Spinnaker House Hotel. Seafront situation with spa complex, and harbour a very short walk away. Superb food is served in our well-appointed dining room, including a choice of five-course dinners. Ground-floor and sea-view rooms are available.

Room General 5 Leisure

BRIGHOUSE, West Yorkshire Map ref 2B1 — **HOTEL**

★★
HOTEL

B&B per room per night
s £34.95–£50.95
d £44.50–£90.00

Waterfront Lodge

Huddersfield Road, Brighouse HD6 1JZ **t** (01484) 715566 **f** (01484) 715588
e info@waterfrontlodge.co.uk **w** waterfrontlodge.co.uk

bedrooms 28 double, 9 twin, 21 single
bathrooms All en suite
payment Credit/debit cards, cash/cheques

Quality designer accommodation at realistic prices, situated on the banks of the picturesque Calder and Hebble canal in the heart of West Yorkshire Pennines. The Waterfront is ideally located off the M62, giving access to all of Yorkshire's attractions. Dine in our contemporary continental restaurant, 'Prego'.

From jct 25, M62 take A644 to Brighouse. Turn left at traffic lights. At roundabout go straight ahead into town centre on Bethel Street, taking 1st left.

Weekend breaks: double and twin rooms £40.

Room General

BRIGHOUSE, West Yorkshire Map ref 2B1 — **SELF CATERING**

★★★★
SELF CATERING

Units 4
Sleeps 4–6
Low season per wk
£400.00–£450.00
High season per wk
£400.00–£450.00

Beechwood Park Apartments, Brighouse

Nomorehotels Ltd, 153 Cavendish Road, London SW12 0BW
t 0870 850 8514 **f** (020) 8673 4078 **e** info@nomorehotels.co.uk **w** nomorehotels.co.uk

A modern block consisting of four apartments each with two double bedrooms. Just minutes away from the town centre and M62/A621 corridor. Fully furnished with all mod cons. Complimentary parking included.

open All year
payment Credit/debit cards, cash/cheques

Unit
General P

BURNSALL, North Yorkshire Map ref 1B3 — **HOTEL**

★★
HOTEL
SILVER AWARD

B&B per room per night
s £77.00–£133.25
d £129.00–£225.00
HB per person per night
£87.50–£140.00

The Devonshire Fell Hotel and Restaurant

Burnsall, Skipton BD23 6BT **t** (01756) 729000 **f** (01756) 729009 **e** res@devonshirehotels.co.uk
w devonshirehotels.co.uk

open All year
bedrooms 6 double, 4 twin, 2 family
bathrooms All en suite
payment Credit/debit cards, cash/cheques, euros

Unique city-chic hotel in the countryside with stunning views across the Yorkshire Dales. Bright, squishy sofas, vibrant decor, contemporary art, huge wood-burning stove, really well-equipped bedrooms and bathrooms, delicious, freshly prepared food with the best of local and estate produce – plus free access to The Devonshire Health Spa and Bolton Abbey Estate.

At the junction with the B6160 and the A59, travel north for 6 miles. Located on the left-hand side as you enter Burnsall.

Sun-night sleepover in a double room, including champagne, spa entry, Yorkshire breakfast and a delicious dinner, from £155 per couple.

Room General Leisure

Check it out

Please check prices, quality ratings and other details when you book.

CLAPHAM, North Yorkshire Map ref 1B3 — **SELF CATERING**

★★★★
SELF CATERING

Units 1
Sleeps 2–6
Low season per wk
£200.00–£300.00
High season per wk
£300.00–£500.00

Sherwood, Lancaster

contact Mr & Mrs Beresford, Beresmoor, Mill Lane, Long Preston BD23 4RY
t (01729) 840231 **f** (01729) 840769 **e** mrberesford@farming.co.uk

open All year
payment Cash/cheques

Luxury detached bungalow with panoramic views in the unspoilt, pretty village of Clapham, on the edge of the Yorkshire Dales and close to the Three Peaks. Skipton and the Lake District are within easy reach. Three bedrooms (one en suite), house bathroom, large lounge, dining/kitchen, large courtyard gardens with ample parking.

♥ *Short breaks available. Discounts for 2 people only.*

Unit
General Shop < 0.5 miles Pub < 0.5 miles

CLOUGHTON, North Yorkshire Map ref 1D3 — **GUEST ACCOMMODATION**

♦♦♦
GUEST ACCOMMODATION

B&B per room per night
s £26.00
d £44.00

Standingstones Rigg Farm

Whitby Road, Scarborough YO13 0DX **t** (01723) 870984

Eco-friendly farmhouse bed and breakfast. Wind-powered electricity, beautiful views of land and sea, lovely garden, very peaceful.

open All year
bedrooms 1 double, 1 family
payment Cash/cheques

Room General Leisure

CLOUGHTON, North Yorkshire Map ref 1D3 — **SELF CATERING**

★★★★
SELF CATERING

Units 1
Sleeps 6
Low season per wk
Max £450.00
High season per wk
Max £550.00

Station House, Scarborough

contact Mr & Mrs Steve & Barbara Hargreaves, Station Lane, Cloughton, Scarborough YO13 0AD
t (01723) 870896 **w** cloughtonstation.co.uk

open All year
payment Cash/cheques

Refurbished railway carriage situated in renovated railway station which is now a tea room and bed and breakfast establishment. Full air-conditioning/heating. Lovely walking area. Twenty minutes to the sea and Cleveland Way; 25 minutes' drive to Dalby Forest, Whitby, North York Moors Railway and 'Heartbeat' Country.

⊕ *Five miles north of Scarborough on A171 Scarborough to Whitby road. Station Lane is the 1st road on the right in Cloughton, heading north.*

♥ *3- and 4-night breaks available Nov-Easter.*

Unit
General Leisure Shop 0.5 miles Pub < 0.5 miles

DACRE, North Yorkshire Map ref 2B1 — SELF CATERING

★★
SELF CATERING

Units 1
Sleeps 4

Low season per wk
Min £245.00
High season per wk
Max £375.00

Burns Farm, Dacre

Burns Farm
t (01423) 780217

open All year
payment Cash/cheques

Burns Farm is a delightful, peaceful cottage in rural location with comfortable interior, well furnished and equipped. Two large bedrooms (both en suite). Set in Area of Outstanding Natural Beauty close to Pateley Bridge, the Nidderdale Way and Yorkshire Dales National Park with outstanding views.

Turn off A59, Stumps Cross Cavern. Stone House Inn on right, straight on. Turn next right 1 mile. 2nd farm on left.

Unit
General Leisure Shop 4 miles Pub 2 miles

DALBY, North Yorkshire Map ref 1D3 — GUEST ACCOMMODATION

♦♦♦
GUEST ACCOMMODATION

B&B per room per night
d £46.00–£56.00
Evening meal per person
£10.00–£20.00

South Moor Farm

Dalby Forest Drive, Scarborough YO13 0LW **t** (01751) 460285 **e** info@southmoorfarm.co.uk
w southmoorfarm.co.uk

open All year
bedrooms 1 double, 1 twin, 1 family
bathrooms 2 en suite, 1 private
payment Credit/debit cards, cash/cheques

Quiet rural location on Dalby Forest Drive between Pickering and Scarborough. An excellent base to explore Dalby Forest on foot, bike or horse after a full English breakfast. Packed lunches and evening meals by arrangement. Children's play area, orienteering courses, quad bikes, 4x4 driving and astronomy in Dalby Forest.

Follow Dalby Forest Drive (look for brown tourism signs). We are 10 miles from Thornton le Dale, 6 miles from Hackness. Grid Ref SE905905.

Reduced rates for children under 14 years. Discounts on stays of 5 nights or more.

Room General Leisure

DINNINGTON, South Yorkshire Map ref 2C2 — GUEST ACCOMMODATION

★★★★★
BED & BREAKFAST
GOLD AWARD

B&B per room per night
d £55.00–£85.00

Throapham House Bed + Breakfast

Throapham House, Oldcotes Road, Sheffield S25 2QS **t** (01909) 562208 **f** (01909) 567825
e enquiries@throapham-house.co.uk **w** throapham-house.co.uk

Family-run luxury en suite accommodation. Grade II Listed Georgian property. Rural location three miles from M1/M18/A57. Varied breakfast menu. Free broadband Internet all rooms. Off-road parking.

open All year except Christmas and New Year
bedrooms 2 double, 1 twin
bathrooms All en suite
payment Credit/debit cards, cash/cheques

Room General

Check the maps

Colour maps at the front pinpoint all places in which you will find accommodation entries in the regional sections. Pick your location and then refer to the place index at the back to find the page number.

DRIFFIELD, East Riding of Yorkshire Map ref 2C1 — **GUEST ACCOMMODATION**

★★★
GUEST HOUSE

B&B per room per night
s £35.00–£45.00
d £50.00–£60.00

Blacksmiths Cottage Country Guest House

Driffield Road, Driffield YO25 4SN **t** (01262) 420624 **e** maxatblacksmiths@ukonline.co.uk
w smoothhound.co.uk/hotels/blacksmithscottage.html

open All year except Christmas and New Year
bedrooms 2 double, 1 twin, 1 family
bathrooms All en suite
payment Cash/cheques

Blacksmiths Cottage Country Guest House is a beautiful 300-year-old cottage, located in Kilham. En suite, ground-floor bedrooms are in converted stables around a courtyard. Large garden with summerhouse for guests' use. Superb English breakfast taken by the inglenook fire. Family suite available. Private parking. Dogs by arrangement only.

⊕ *Off the 614 Bridlington to Driffield road.*

❤ *3-night break £69pp excl bank holidays. (£78pp bank holidays.)*

Room · General · Leisure

DUNSWELL, East Riding of Yorkshire Map ref 2C1 — **GUEST ACCOMMODATION**

★★★
INN

B&B per room per night
d £50.00–£60.00

The Ship's Quarters

Beverley High Road, Dunswell, Hull HU6 0AJ **t** (01482) 859160 **f** (01482) 859160
w theshipsquarters.co.uk

open All year
bedrooms 4 double, 1 twin
bathrooms All en suite
payment Credit/debit cards, cash/cheques

Ideally situated between Hull and Beverley, this newly opened, all-en suite accommodation nestles in the grounds of a 19thC ale house, with hand-pulled beers, open fires and wholesome food.

⊕ *The Ship's Quarters is located behind the Ship Inn at Dunswell, on the A1174 between Hull and Beverley.*

Room · General · Leisure

FILEY, North Yorkshire Map ref 1D3 — **SELF CATERING**

★★★
SELF CATERING

Units 1
Sleeps 2–5
Low season per wk
£200.00
High season per wk
£300.00–£315.00

Fisherman Cottage, Filey

contact Mrs Annette Cavell, Teathill Cottage, Sand Lane, Osgodby, Selby YO8 5HT
t (01757) 290020 & 07773 643917

A cosy two-bedroom former-fisherman's cottage located in the centre of Filey. Within walking distance of the beach.

open All year
payment Cash/cheques

Unit
General · Leisure

FILEY, North Yorkshire Map ref 1D3 — **SELF CATERING**

★★★
SELF CATERING

Units 1
Sleeps 1–6
Low season per wk
£270.00–£320.00
High season per wk
£420.00–£580.00

Langford Villa, Filey

contact Mr & Mrs D H Midgley, Langford Villa Holiday Flat, 44a The Crescent, Filey YO14 9JU
t (01723) 514813 **e** dhmidgley@ukonline.co.uk

open All year
payment Cash/cheques

Ground-floor apartment, with central heating. Sleeps six in three bedrooms (one double and two twins). Lounge with TV and DVD. Bathroom including bath with shower, washbasin and toilet. A cloakroom with toilet. Dining room with TV and video. Well-equipped kitchen. Parking space for one car on site.

⊕ *From centre of Filey proceed to Crescent, turn right along Crescent to White Lodge hotel. We are 2nd house on left past the hotel.*

Unit
General Shop 1 mile Pub < 0.5 miles

FLAMBOROUGH, East Riding of Yorkshire Map ref 1D3 — **SELF CATERING**

★★★
SELF CATERING

Units 2
Sleeps 1–8
Low season per wk
£250.00–£360.00
High season per wk
£450.00–£650.00

Flamborough Rock Cottages, Flamborough, Bridlington

contact Jannice Geraghty, Flamborough Rock Cottages, 11 High Holme, Flamborough YO15 1QL
t (01262) 850996 **f** (01723) 582375 **e** info@flamboroughrockcottages.co.uk
w flamboroughrockcottages.co.uk

open All year
payment Cash/cheques

Flamborough Rock Cottages are an ideal base to stay whilst exploring the scenic Yorkshire coast. The headland of Flamborough has impressive natural scenery. The chalk cliffs rise to 400ft and are home to nesting birds, including puffins. Private rear patio. Ground-floor, en suite bedroom in four-bedroom cottage.

⊕ *M62 east to jct 37 (Howden). Follow signs for Bridlington. B1255 to Flamborough. Turn into Dog and Duck Square opposite the Seabirds pub.*

♥ *Short breaks available Oct-Mar.*

Unit
General 1 Shop < 0.5 miles Pub < 0.5 miles

FOLLIFOOT, North Yorkshire Map ref 2B1 — **CAMPING & CARAVANNING**

★★★★
TOURING PARK

(71) £8.50–£19.60
(71) £8.50–£19.60
71 touring pitches

See Ad on inside front cover

Great Yorkshire Showground Caravan Club Site

Wetherby Road, Harrogate HG3 1TZ **t** (01423) 560470 **w** caravanclub.co.uk

payment Credit/debit cards, cash/cheques

A flat, pleasantly open site, very convenient to visit Harrogate, the floral capital of Yorkshire. Not only does the town have splendid examples of municipal gardens, but it also hosts two major flower shows. Open March to November.

⊕ *Turn left off A661 (Wetherby-Harrogate). Site on right in 400yds.*

♥ *Special member rates mean you can save your membership subscription in less than a week. Visit our website to find out more.*

General Leisure

Make it a date

Check out the events listing at the back of the guide, or for latest information go online at enjoyengland.com.

GIGGLESWICK, North Yorkshire Map ref 1B3 — **GUEST ACCOMMODATION**

★★★★
INN

B&B per room per night
s £38.00–£40.00
d £60.00–£80.00
Evening meal per person
£7.50–£11.50

The Black Horse

Church Street, Settle BD24 0BE **t** (01729) 822506 **f** (01729) 822506 **e** salbutt@tiscali.co.uk

A secluded, friendly inn, within easy reach of the Yorkshire Dales and the Lake District. Ideal for couples wishing to relax. Serving real ales and excellent food.

open All year except Christmas and New Year
bedrooms 2 double, 1 twin
bathrooms All en suite
payment Credit/debit cards, cash/cheques

Room General Leisure

GRANTLEY, North Yorkshire Map ref 1C3 — **GUEST ACCOMMODATION**

★★★★
GUEST ACCOMMODATION

B&B per room per night
s £40.00–£50.00
d £65.00–£75.00

St Georges Court

Old Home Farm, Ripon HG4 3PJ **t** (01765) 620618 **e** stgeorgescourt@bronco.co.uk
w stgeorges-court.co.uk

Farmhouse B&B with five en suite rooms, all on ground level, situated around a pretty courtyard.

open All year
bedrooms 3 double, 1 twin, 1 family
bathrooms All en suite
payment Credit/debit cards, cash/cheques

Room General Leisure

GRASSINGTON, North Yorkshire Map ref 1B3 — **SELF CATERING**

★★★
SELF CATERING

Units 1
Sleeps 1–4
Low season per wk
Min £250.00
High season per wk
Max £350.00

6a Garrs Lane, Skipton

contact Paul Borrill, 6 Garrs Lane, Grassington BD23 5AT
t (01756) 752436 & 07709 313716 **e** info@grassingtonapartment.co.uk
w grassingtonapartment.co.uk

open All year
payment Cash/cheques, euros

Our warm and comfortable first-floor apartment is just 50m from the cobbled village square. It has original oak beams and living flame gas fire in the spacious lounge. Two large bedrooms, one double and one twin, bed linen provided. Large, full kitchen. Bathroom has bath and separate shower. Brochure available.

M1 jct 47 to Grassington. Right fork from main square towards the Black Horse Hotel. Fish shop is located just behind, 6a Garrs Lane is above.

2/3-night stays available, Oct-Feb (excl Christmas and New Year).

Unit
General 8 Leisure

GREAT AYTON, North Yorkshire Map ref 1C3 **GUEST ACCOMMODATION**

★★★★
GUEST ACCOMMODATION
SILVER AWARD

B&B per room per night
s £55.00–£80.00
d £69.50–£95.00
Evening meal per person
£10.00–£40.00

Kings Head Hotel and Restaurant

The Green, Newton under Roseberry, Middlesbrough TS9 6QR **t** (01642) 722318 **f** (01642) 724750
e info@kingsheadhotel.co.uk **w** kingsheadhotel.co.uk

open All year except Christmas and New Year
bedrooms 5 double, 1 twin, 1 single, 1 family
bathrooms All en suite
payment Credit/debit cards, cash/cheques

Tourism NorthEast Bed and Breakfast of the Year 2005. A delightful family-owned hotel and restaurant, situated at the foot of Roseberry Topping. Our individually designed, luxurious en suite bedrooms are developed from two adjoining 18thC cottages oozing character and charm. The guest bedrooms are fitted with the latest facilities, and our restaurant serves a selection of freshly cooked dishes.

From A19 exit onto A174. 3rd exit onto A172/171. At roundabout take 2nd exit. Next roundabout take 3rd exit. Follow signs A173 Newton under Roseberry.

Business rates available. Winter offers available, from 1 Oct – 31 Mar inclusive.

Room General Leisure

GRINTON, North Yorkshire Map ref 1B3 **SELF CATERING**

★★★★
SELF CATERING

Units 3
Sleeps 2–13
Low season per wk
£305.00–£395.00
High season per wk
£415.00–£580.00

Feetham Holme, Richmond

contact Mr Ian Robinson, Plantation Business Services, Plantation House, Chipping Road, Clitheroe BB7 3LX
t (01254) 826546 **f** (01254) 826880 **e** plantation@talk21.com

open All year
payment Cash/cheques

Fully renovated cottages in the heart of the National Park, beautiful secluded location. Tastefully finished and fully equipped accommodation. Wood-burning stoves and original features make the cottages a delight to enjoy. Design award for renovation. Quote VB7 when booking.

Pass through Heelaugh, take 1st left (Askrigg), cross River Swale, right at T-junction. Feetham Holme is on right after approx 0.75 miles.

Weekend and mid-week breaks available. Discount for booking all units together.

Unit
General Shop 5 miles Pub 5 miles

GUISELEY, West Yorkshire Map ref 2B1 **GUEST ACCOMMODATION**

★★★
BED & BREAKFAST

B&B per room per night
s £28.00–£30.00
d £50.00–£55.00

Lyndhurst

Oxford Road, Leeds LS20 9AB **t** (01943) 879985 **w** guisley.co.uk/lyndhurst

Comfortable B&B two minutes from Guiseley rail station, and within easy walk of Otley Chevin and many leisure facilities. Free wireless Internet, DVD players in rooms.

open All year
bedrooms 1 double, 1 twin
bathrooms 1 en suite, 1 private
payment Cash/cheques

Room General Leisure

Place index

If you know where you want to stay the index at the back of the guide will give you the page number which lists accommodation in your chosen town, city or village. Check out the other useful indexes too.

HALIFAX, West Yorkshire Map ref 2B1 — **GUEST ACCOMMODATION**

★★★★
FARMHOUSE

B&B per room per night
s £31.00–£36.00
d £52.00–£62.00
Evening meal per person
£5.00–£10.00

Lane Ends Farm

Lane Ends, Wheatley, Halifax HX2 8TW **t** (01422) 348351 & 07974 764545
e enquiries@laneendsfarm.co.uk **w** laneendsfarm.co.uk

open All year
bedrooms 2 double, 1 twin/family
bathrooms All en suite
payment Cash/cheques

18thC smallholding in semi-rural location with large en suite, non-smoking rooms. One and a half miles from Halifax near the bridleway network. Linda and Douglas Whitehead extend an old-fashioned welcome to those visiting the area for business or pleasure. Stabling available during the summer when resident horses are out in the fields.

⊕ *From A58/A629 roundabout take A629 to Keighley. At traffic lights turn left (Mixenden/Wheatley). Take 2nd left, Hebble Lane. Continue forwards to Lane Ends, farm on left.*

♥ *Birthday and anniversary celebration-night package for four-poster en suite room, with flowers, chocolates and complimentary champagne etc £120 per couple.*

Room General Leisure

HARMBY, North Yorkshire Map ref 1B3 — **CAMPING & CARAVANNING**

★★★
TOURING & CAMPING PARK

(98) £9.50–£21.40
(98) £9.50–£21.40
98 touring pitches

See Ad on inside front cover

Lower Wensleydale Caravan Club Site

Harmby, Leyburn DL8 5NU **t** (01969) 623366 **w** caravanclub.co.uk

payment Credit/debit cards, cash/cheques

Set within the hollow of a disused quarry, now overrun with wild flowers and mosses. This site offers charming pitching areas. Many interesting attractions nearby and wonderful walking country. Open March to November.

⊕ *From east on A684, turn right 0.75 miles past railway bridge; turn immediately left and follow signs to site entrance.*

♥ *Special member rates mean you can save your membership subscription in less than a week. Visit our website to find out more.*

General Leisure

HARROGATE, North Yorkshire Map ref 2B1 — **HOTEL**

★★
HOTEL

B&B per room per night
s £60.00–£100.00
d £70.00–£110.00
HB per person per night
£60.00–£90.00

Balmoral Hotel & Villutoots Brasserie

Franklin Mount, Harrogate HG1 5EJ **t** (01423) 508208 **f** (01423) 530652 **e** info@balmoralhotel.co.uk
w balmoralhotel.co.uk

open All year
bedrooms 13 double, 3 twin, 2 single, 2 family, 3 suites
bathrooms All en suite
payment Credit/debit cards, cash/cheques

You are always assured of a Yorkshire welcome at this elegant Victorian building just five minutes' walk from the town centre. Individually decorated en suite bedrooms, many with four-poster beds, complemented by a unique restaurant serving modern English food. Free parking.

⊕ *Bottom of Parliament Street turn right. Kings Road. Keep conference centre on your left. The Balmoral Hotel is a few hundred yards on your right.*

♥ *Special luxury packages. Weekend breaks from £60pppn DB&B.*

Room General

HARROGATE, North Yorkshire Map ref 2B1 — GUEST ACCOMMODATION

♦♦♦♦
GUEST ACCOMMODATION

B&B per room per night
s £33.00–£38.00
d £65.00

Alamah Guest House

88 Kings Road, Harrogate HG1 5JX **t** (01423) 502187 **e** alamahguesthouse@btconnect.com

Comfortable rooms, personal attention, friendly atmosphere and full English breakfast. Conference centre 150m. A variety of restaurants, the Turkish baths and Valley Gardens are within a ten-minute walk.

open All year
bedrooms 2 double, 2 twin, 2 single, 1 family
bathrooms 6 en suite, 1 private
payment Credit/debit cards, cash/cheques

Room General 5

HARROGATE, North Yorkshire Map ref 2B1 — GUEST ACCOMMODATION

★★★★
GUEST HOUSE

B&B per room per night
s £45.00–£50.00
d £60.00–£70.00
Evening meal per person
Min £20.00

Coppice Guest House

9 Studley Road, Harrogate HG1 5JU **t** (01423) 569626 **f** (01423) 569005 **e** coppice@harrogate.com
w harrogate.com/coppice

open All year except Christmas and New Year
bedrooms 2 double, 1 twin, 1 single, 1 family
bathrooms All en suite
payment Credit/debit cards, cash/cheques, euros

Quietly located just five minutes' walk from the elegant shops and gardens of the town centre. This highly recommended Victorian guesthouse offers excellent food and a warm, friendly welcome. Ideal location to explore the beautiful Yorkshire Dales.

⊕ *Studley Road is off Kings Road. Kings Road is off Skipton Road (A59) at one end and off Ripon Road (A61) at the other end.*

Room General 5 Leisure

HARROGATE, North Yorkshire Map ref 2B1 — GUEST ACCOMMODATION

★★★
GUEST ACCOMMODATION

B&B per room per night
s £25.00–£30.00
d £50.00–£60.00

Glenayr

19 Franklin Mount, Harrogate HG1 5EJ **t** (01423) 504259 **f** (01423) 504259
e liz-glenayr@boltblue.com **w** glenayr.co.uk

Quietly situated, spacious Victorian house within five minutes' walk of all amenities. Great breakfast and a comfortable, relaxing atmosphere.

open All year except Christmas and New Year
bedrooms 2 double, 3 twin, 1 single
bathrooms 5 en suite
payment Credit/debit cards, cash/cheques

Room General

HARROGATE, North Yorkshire Map ref 2B1 — GUEST ACCOMMODATION

★★★
GUEST HOUSE

B&B per room per night
s £25.00–£30.00
d £55.00–£60.00

The Welford

27 Franklin Road, Harrogate HG1 5ED **t** (01423) 566041 **f** (01423) 566041
e judith.mudd@btopenworld.com **w** the-welford.co.uk

open All year
bedrooms 1 double, 2 twin, 3 single
bathrooms 4 en suite
payment Credit/debit cards, cash/cheques

Close to town and conference/exhibition centres. The Welford offers a warm welcome, immaculate accommodation and an excellent breakfast.

⊕ *Five minutes' walk from bus and railway stations. One minute's walk from conference centre.*

Room General

HARROGATE, North Yorkshire Map ref 2B1 — **SELF CATERING**

★★★★
SELF CATERING

Units 10
Sleeps 2–8
Low season per wk
£309.00–£449.00
High season per wk
£610.00–£892.00

Brimham Rocks Cottages, Harrogate

contact Jacqueline Martin, Brimham Rocks Cottages, High North Farm, Harrogate HG3 5EY
t (01765) 620284 **f** (01765) 620477 **e** brimhamrc@yahoo.co.uk **w** brimham.co.uk

open All year
payment Credit/debit cards, cash/cheques

Overlooking Brimham Rocks and with views of up to 60 miles, these individual cottages are ideally situated to explore both Dales and Moors, York, Ripon, Harrogate, Leeds and the east coast. Converted from old farm buildings, the cottages are warm, cosy, comfortable and decorated with flair and imagination. A warm welcome guaranteed.

From Harrogate A61 to Ripon. 2nd roundabout at Ripley left to Pateley Bridge. 1st right to Fountains Abbey. After 3.5 miles left. Proceed for 2.5 miles.

Short breaks at 70% of weekly rate.

Unit
General Leisure Shop 3 miles Pub 1.5 miles

HARWOOD DALE, North Yorkshire Map ref 1D3 — **SELF CATERING**

★★★★
SELF CATERING

Units 3
Sleeps 2–4
Low season per wk
£342.00–£522.00
High season per wk
£342.00–£522.00

Murk Head Holiday Cottages, Scarborough

contact Joanna Gray, Murk Head, Murk Head, Harwood Dale, Scarborough YO13 0LA
t (01723) 871686 **e** joannagray@aol.com

A brand new barn conversion of three two-bedroomed holiday cottages in the National Parks, all with en suite facilities. Scarborough eight miles, Whitby ten miles.

open All year
payment Cash/cheques

Unit
General Leisure Shop 4 miles Pub 0.5 miles

HAWORTH, West Yorkshire Map ref 2B1 — **HOTEL**

★★
HOTEL

B&B per room per night
s £52.50–£63.50
d £73.00–£83.00

Old White Lion Hotel

Main Street, Haworth, Keighley BD22 8DU **t** (01535) 642313 **f** (01535) 646222
e enquiries@oldwhitelionhotel.com **w** oldwhitelionhotel.com

open All year
bedrooms 8 double, 1 twin, 3 single, 2 family
bathrooms All en suite
payment Credit/debit cards, cash/cheques

Family-run, centuries-old coaching inn situated at the top of the charming cobbled Main Street. Most en suite rooms command spectacular views of surrounding countryside. Candlelit, a la carte restaurant, oak-beamed bars serving traditional ales and home-cooked food. As featured on BBC Holiday programme 2001.

Turn off Halifax-Keighley A629 at crossroads onto B6142. Hotel adjoining Tourist Information Centre at top of cobbled Main Street 0.5 miles past Haworth station.

Special bargain breaks available. Great value and good food in old-world surroundings.

Room General Leisure

Using map references

The map references refer to the colour maps at the front of this guide. The first figure is the map number; the letter and figure that follow indicate the grid reference on the map.

HAWORTH, West Yorkshire Map ref 2B1 — GUEST ACCOMMODATION

★★★★
GUEST HOUSE
SILVER AWARD

B&B per room per night
s £40.00–£50.00
d £65.00–£110.00

Ashmount Guest House

Mytholmes Lane, Keighley BD22 8EZ **t** (01535) 645726 **f** (01535) 645726
e info@ashmounthaworth.co.uk **w** ashmounthaworth.co.uk

open All year
bedrooms 3 double, 2 twin, 1 single, 2 family
bathrooms 7 en suite, 1 private
payment Credit/debit cards, cash/cheques, euros

Ashmount was the home of Charlotte Brontë's physician, Dr Amos Ingham. The house is steeped in history with wonderful original features, and is only a three-minute walk from the Parsonage. We have ample private parking and large gardens with wonderful views of the moors for you to enjoy and relax in.

Room General P

HAWORTH, West Yorkshire Map ref 2B1 — SELF CATERING

★★★
SELF CATERING

Units 3
Sleeps 3
Low season per wk
£325.00–£375.00
High season per wk
£325.00–£375.00

Haworth Cottages, Haworth, Keighley

contact Barbara Clayton, 30 Sun Street, Haworth BD22 8BP
t (01535) 646778 **e** info@haworthcottages.co.uk **w** haworthcottages.co.uk

Located in a quiet backwater in Haworth, you will find a choice of three old-world cottages, set within this old-fashioned Yorkshire village with most modern-day features.

open All year
payment Cash/cheques

Unit
General

HAWORTH, West Yorkshire Map ref 2B1 — SELF CATERING

★★★
SELF CATERING

Units 1
Sleeps 1–4
Low season per wk
£300.00–£325.00
High season per wk
£325.00–£350.00

Woolcombers Cottage, Haworth, Keighley

contact Ms Kay Doyle Johnson, 276 Broad Street, San Luis Obispo, California 93405, USA
t (01535) 646778 **e** woolcombers@clara.co.uk **w** bronte-country.com/accomm/woolcombers

Cosy, beautiful, charming, three-storey cottage in ultimate Brontë location. Situated in cobbled main street, yards from Parsonage. Built 1820, original beams, fully modernised. All our delighted guests come again!

open All year
payment Cash/cheques

Unit
General 6 S Shop < 0.5 miles Pub < 0.5 miles

HEBDEN, North Yorkshire Map ref 1B3 — GUEST ACCOMMODATION

★★★
BED & BREAKFAST

B&B per room per night
s £30.00–£35.00
d £25.00–£30.00

Court Croft

Church Lane, Hebden, Skipton BD23 5DX **t** (01756) 753406

500-acre livestock farm. Farmhouse in village location close to the Dales Way. Ideal for touring the Dales, Nidderdale and Ribblesdale.

open All year
bedrooms 2 twin, 1 suite
bathrooms 1 en suite
payment Cash/cheques

Room General P Leisure

WALKERS WELCOME WALKERS WELCOME

Best foot forward

Walkers feel at home in accommodation participating in our Walkers Welcome scheme. Look out for the symbol. Consider walking all or part of a long-distance route – go online at nationaltrail.co.uk.

HEBDEN BRIDGE, West Yorkshire Map ref 2B1 — **SELF CATERING**

★★★★
SELF CATERING

Units 1
Sleeps 4

Low season per wk
£200.00–£300.00
High season per wk
£300.00–£400.00

Old Town Hall Cottage

contact S Milner, Old Town Hall Cottage, 8 Old Town Hall Cottages, Old Town, Wadsworth HX7 8SP
t (01422) 846559 **e** oldtownhallcottage@yahoo.co.uk **w** cottageguide.co.uk/oldtownhallcottage

Old Town Hall Cottage is a comfortably appointed, early-17thC cottage in the historic hamlet of Old Town. One mile from Hebden Bridge. Accommodates four guests.

open All year
payment Cash/cheques, euros

Unit
General Leisure Shop < 0.5 miles Pub 0.5 miles

HEBDEN BRIDGE, West Yorkshire Map ref 2B1 — **CAMPING & CARAVANNING**

★★★★★
TOURING PARK
(45) £8.50–£19.60
(45) £8.50–£19.60
45 touring pitches

See Ad on inside front cover

Lower Clough Foot Caravan Club Site

Cragg Vale, Hebden Bridge HX7 5RU **t** (01422) 882531 **w** caravanclub.co.uk

payment Credit/debit cards, cash/cheques

Pretty site, set in a grassy enclave, well screened by mature trees and bordered by a stream. Good for walkers. Open March to November.

Turn off A646 onto B6138. Site on right in 1 mile.

Special member rates mean you can save your membership subscription in less than a week. Visit our website to find out more.

General Leisure

HELMSLEY, North Yorkshire Map ref 1C3 — **GUEST ACCOMMODATION**

★★★★
GUEST ACCOMMODATION
SILVER AWARD

B&B per room per night
s £37.50–£45.00
d £75.00–£90.00

Carlton Lodge

Bondgate, York YO62 5EY **t** (01439) 770557 **f** (01439) 770623 **e** enquiries@carlton-lodge.com
w carlton-lodge.com

open All year
bedrooms 5 double, 2 twin, 1 single
bathrooms 7 en suite, 1 private
payment Credit/debit cards, cash/cheques, euros

An exceptional guesthouse on the edge of the glorious North York Moors National Park. Operated under Sustainable Visitor Charter, the Carlton Lodge offers an ideal base from which to explore this unique heritage-rich area. Dinner is available to groups, minimum of eight guests.

On the A170 Thirsk to Scarborough road, 350m from the 12c Market Place on the east of town. Nearest rail stations, Malton and Thirsk.

Special 2- and 5-day breaks. Walking routes/maps, free lifts to start points on linear walks.

Room General Leisure

Friendly help and advice

Tourist Information Centres offer friendly help with accommodation and holiday ideas as well as suggestions of places to visit and things to do. You'll find contact details at the back of the guide.

HELMSLEY, North Yorkshire Map ref 1C3 — GUEST ACCOMMODATION

♦♦♦♦
GUEST ACCOMMODATION

B&B per room per night
s £37.00–£40.00
d £66.00–£80.00

Laskill Grange

Easterside, Hawnby, Nr Helmsley, York YO62 5NB **t** (01439) 798268 **f** (01439) 798498
e suesmith@laskillfarm.fsnet.co.uk **w** laskillgrange.co.uk

open All year except Christmas
bedrooms 1 double, 1 twin, 1 single
bathrooms 2 en suite, 1 private
payment Credit/debit cards, cash/cheques

Laskill Grange has earned its reputation from attention to detail and personal service. Peaceful, idyllic setting in North Yorkshire Moors. Luxury accommodation in beautiful grounds, with a lake, swans and ducks. Recommended on the BBC Holiday Programme. Own spring water.

WALKERS WELCOME

Room TV General P Leisure

HELMSLEY, North Yorkshire Map ref 1C3 — GUEST ACCOMMODATION

★★★★
GUEST ACCOMMODATION
GOLD AWARD

B&B per room per night
s £45.00
d £66.00–£72.00

West View Cottage

Pockley, York YO62 7TE **t** (01439) 770526 **e** westviewcottage@bedbreakfast.freeserve.co.uk
w s-h-systems.co.uk/hotels/westviewcottage

open All year
bedrooms 1 double, 1 twin
bathrooms 1 en suite, 1 private
payment Cash/cheques

Experience staying in our enchanting 17thC thatched Yorkshire longhouse where guests can enjoy the combination of high-quality accommodation with that touch of luxury; a special place to stay. West View Cottage is situated in a picturesque village on the edge of the North Yorkshire Moors National Park.

One mile east of Helmsley on A170 turn at crossroads, signed Pockley. Drive up lane 1 mile, turn right into walled entrance just before cottage.

Room TV General 12 Leisure

HELMSLEY, North Yorkshire Map ref 1C3 — SELF CATERING

★★★★
SELF CATERING

Units **1**
Sleeps **1–4**
Low season per wk
Min £190.00
High season per wk
£285.00–£350.00

Townend Cottage, Beadlam

contact Mrs Margaret Begg, Townend Farmhouse, High Lane, Beadlam, Nawton, York YO62 7SY
t (01439) 770103 **e** margaret.begg@ukgateway.net **w** visityorkshire.com

open All year
payment Cash/cheques

Originally part of an 18thC farmhouse, this is a very warm, comfortable, two-bedroomed stone cottage with oak beams. Situated off the main road in a village three miles from the charming market town of Helmsley. Ideal for walking or touring Moors, coast and York. Central heating and log fire included in price.

Enter Beadlam on the A170 from Helmsley. Take 1st left turning into High Lane and then 1st right turning into Townend Cottage Drive.

Unit TV
General P Leisure Shop 3 miles Pub < 0.5 miles

Look at the maps

Colour maps at the front pinpoint the location of all accommodation found in the regional sections.

HIGH BENTHAM, North Yorkshire Map ref 1B3 — **GUEST ACCOMMODATION**

★★★★
INN

B&B per room per night
s £35.00–£45.00
d £60.00

The Coach House

16 Main Street, High Bentham LA2 7HE **t** (01524) 262305 **e** info@coachhousebentham.co.uk
w coachhousebentham.co.uk

The Coach House is a beautifully refurbished 17thC inn at the heart of High Bentham community life. Set back from the main street by a cobbled forecourt, it has superb car parking facilities at the rear.

open All year
bedrooms 4 double
bathrooms All en suite
payment Credit/debit cards, cash/cheques

Room General P Leisure

HIGH BENTHAM, North Yorkshire Map ref 1B3 — **SELF CATERING**

★★★★
SELF CATERING

Units 1
Sleeps 1–4

High season per wk
£190.00–£270.00

Holmes Farm Cottage, Lancaster

contact Mrs Story, Holmes Farm Cottage, Holmes Farm, Lower Bentham, Lancaster LA2 7DE
t (015242) 61198 **e** lucy@clucy.demon.co.uk

open All year
payment Cash/cheques

Tastefully converted stone cottage with large, landscaped garden, surrounded by 127 acres of beautiful pastureland. Ideal base for visiting Lake District, Dales and coast.

Unit
General P Leisure Shop 1 mile Pub 0.5 miles

HOLMFIRTH, West Yorkshire Map ref 2B1 — **GUEST ACCOMMODATION**

★★★★★
GUEST ACCOMMODATION
SILVER AWARD

B&B per room per night
s £45.00–£60.00
d £60.00–£80.00

Sunnybank

78 Upperthong Lane, Huddersfield HD9 3BQ **t** (01484) 684065 **e** info@sunnybankguesthouse.co.uk
w sunnybankguesthouse.co.uk

open All year
bedrooms 2 double, 1 family
bathrooms All en suite
payment Cash/cheques, euros

An elegant Victorian house in two acres of beautiful wooded gardens. Peaceful, yet near the centre of Holmfirth in the glorious countryside of the Holme Valley, as seen on the BBC's 'Last of the Summer Wine'. Attractive, stylish and comfortable rooms each individually furnished to a very high standard.

In Holmfirth take A6024 towards Woodhead. Upperthong Lane is between Ashley Jackson's and Worthington's. Sunnybank is next to the church.

For 6 guests booking together at the weekend we offer a superb, real Italian 4-course meal. Phone for details.

Room General 8 P Leisure

CYCLISTS WELCOME

A holiday on two wheels

For a fabulous freewheeling break seek out accommodation participating in our Cyclists Welcome scheme. Look out for the symbol and plan your route online at nationalcyclenetwork.org.

HOLMFIRTH, West Yorkshire Map ref 2B1 — **SELF CATERING**

★★★–★★★★★
SELF CATERING

Units **3**
Sleeps **3–6**
Low season per wk
£210.00–£290.00
High season per wk
£280.00–£375.00

Sycamore Farm Cottages

Sycamore Farm Cottages, Sycamore Farm, Farnley Tyas, Huddersfield HD4 6UG
t (01484) 661458 **e** info@sycamorefarmcottages.co.uk **w** sycamorefarmcottages.co.uk

open All year
payment Cash/cheques

Sycamore Farm Cottages are oak-beamed, stone-built farm cottages, located in Farnley Tyas, a delightful village in the rural south Pennines. 2006 Yorkshire in Bloom Silver Award winner, the cottages feature a pretty courtyard with flowers and garden furniture where guests can sit out and admire the wonderful views.

Unit General Leisure Shop 2 miles Pub < 0.5 miles

HOLMFIRTH, West Yorkshire Map ref 2B1 — **CAMPING & CARAVANNING**

★★★★
TOURING & CAMPING PARK

(62) £10.00–£11.50
(62) £8.50–£10.00
(62) £7.00–£9.00
62 touring pitches

Holme Valley Camping and Caravan Park

Thongsbridge, Huddersfield HD9 7TD **t** (01484) 665819 **f** (01484) 663870
e enquiries@homevalleycamping.com **w** holmevalleycamping.com

open All year
payment Credit/debit cards, cash/cheques, euros

Picturesque, peaceful park in central 'Summer Wine' country. Grass, concrete and gravel pitches. Optional 16-amp hook-ups. Well-stocked food shop with off-licence. Fishing in small lake and river. Small children's play area. Five minutes' walk from village with pub food, post office, buses and trains. David Bellamy Gold Award.

The entrance to lane leading down to park is 1 mile north of Holmfirth, off A6024. Passing bottle banks, continue to valley's bottom.

Fourth night free for every 3 nights booked from 10 Jun-10 Jul 07 upon producing this advertisement when paying at reception.

General Leisure

HORNSEA, East Riding of Yorkshire Map ref 2D1 — **GUEST ACCOMMODATION**

★★★★
GUEST HOUSE

B&B per room per night
s £35.00–£50.00
d £59.00–£65.00
Evening meal per person
£7.50–£20.00

Wentworth House Hotel

12 Seaside Road, Aldbrough, Hull HU11 4RX **t** (01964) 527246 **f** (01964) 527246
e mteale@eduktion.co.uk **w** wentworthhousehotel.com

open All year except Christmas
bedrooms 4 double, 1 twin, 2 family, 1 suite
bathrooms 7 en suite, 1 private
payment Credit/debit cards, cash/cheques, euros

A family-run hotel set in spacious gardens, offering delightful accommodation in a friendly and homely atmosphere. It is ideally suited to those who are working and require first-class facilities in a peaceful environment. Close to many amenities, rural and city. Away from the crowd in a safe, secure and discreet environment.

Take the A165, then the B1238 from Hull to Hornsea. See website for further details.

Fishing, bird-watching and art-themed breaks. Stately-home tours and Murder Mystery evenings. Licensed for civil ceremonies.

Room General Leisure

HORNSEA, East Riding of Yorkshire Map ref 2D1 — **SELF CATERING**

★★★
SELF CATERING

Units **1**
Sleeps **3**
Low season per wk
Min £230.00
High season per wk
Max £350.00

Cobble Cottage

contact Nick Clare, 6 Willows Drive, Hornsea HU18 1DA
t (01964) 536300 & 07918 647686 **e** nj.clare@btinternet.com

open All year
payment Cash/cheques

Cobble Cottage is a charming 17thC, beamed, self-catering cottage. Grade II Listed. Situated in town centre but close to the sea and Hornsea Mere, with great country walks. Fully equipped and all linen included etc. Sleeps three in two bedrooms. Parking on the doorstep. Dogs welcome by prior arrangement.

Unit
General Leisure

HOVINGHAM, North Yorkshire Map ref 1C3 — **HOTEL**

★★★
SMALL HOTEL

B&B per room per night
s £85.00–£95.00
d £115.00–£165.00
HB per person per night
£82.50–£92.50

Worsley Arms Hotel

High Street, York YO62 4LA **t** (01653) 628234 **f** (01653) 628130 **e** worsleyarms@aol.com
w worsleyarms.com

An attractive stone-built Georgian spa hotel in the heart of Hovingham, overlooking the village green and set amid delightful gardens. Built in 1841 by the Baronet Sir William Worsley.

open All year
bedrooms 7 double, 10 twin, 1 single, 1 family
bathrooms All en suite
payment Credit/debit cards, cash/cheques

Room General Leisure

HUDDERSFIELD, West Yorkshire Map ref 2B1 — **GUEST ACCOMMODATION**

♦♦♦
GUEST ACCOMMODATION

B&B per room per night
s £35.00
d £45.00
Evening meal per person
£5.00

Cambridge Lodge

4 Clare Hill, Huddersfield HD1 5BS **t** (01484) 519892 **f** (01484) 534534
e cambridge.lodge.hudd@btconnect.com **w** cambridgelodge.co.uk

open All year
bedrooms 11 double, 7 twin, 12 single, 4 family
bathrooms All en suite
payment Credit/debit cards, cash/cheques, euros

All 34 rooms en suite with tea-/coffee-making facilities, telephone and colour TV. Ample free car parking and CCTV coverage. We are based less than 0.5 miles from Huddersfield train and bus station, on Clare Hill off St Johns Road. Easy to find – follow Cambridge Road Parking, off ring road.

Room General

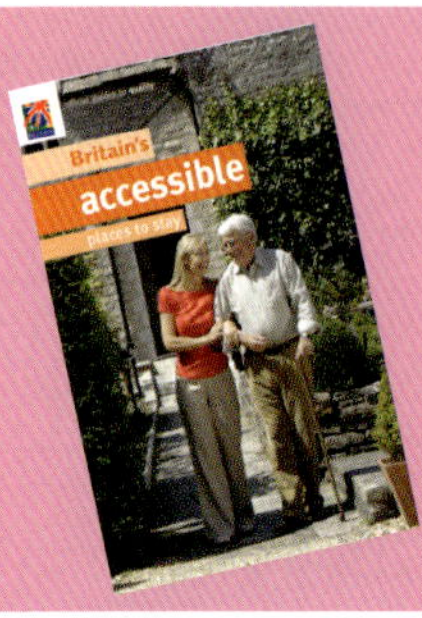

Accessible needs?

If you have special hearing, visual or mobility needs, there's an index of all National Accessible Scheme participants at the back of this guide. Or buy a copy of our informative guide – Britain's Accessible Places to Stay – available from good bookshops and online at visitbritaindirect.com.

HUDDERSFIELD, West Yorkshire Map ref 2B1 — **SELF CATERING**

★★★★
SELF CATERING

Units 1
Sleeps 6

Low season per wk
£293.00–£373.00
High season per wk
£434.00–£795.00

Tyas Cottage, Huddersfield

Tyas Cottage, Merrydale, Slaithwaite, Huddersfield HD7 5UZ
t (01484) 841010 **f** (01484) 315578 **e** vicky.berryman@gmail.com **w** yorkshire-holiday.co.uk

open All year
payment Credit/debit cards, cash/cheques, euros

Grade II Listed stone cottage within a Special Landscape Area (also designated as a Site of Special Scientific Interest – for flora and fauna). Furnished mainly with antiques, including four-poster bed. In addition to private patio, has large shared garden that includes a mill pond, waterfall and stream. Broadband access.

Directions sent on receipt of booking. See location page on website.

Off-peak short breaks from £205.

Unit · General · Leisure · Shop 2 miles · Pub 0.5 miles

HULL, East Riding of Yorkshire Map ref 2C1 — **GUEST ACCOMMODATION**

★★★
BED & BREAKFAST

B&B per room per night
s £25.00–£27.00
d £40.00
Evening meal per person
£5.00

The Admiral Guest House

234 The Boulevard, Hull HU3 3ED **t** (01482) 329664 **f** (01482) 329664

The guesthouse is located in a conservation area. The building is a spacious, late-Victorian, former vicarage.

open All year except Christmas and New Year
bedrooms 1 double/twin/family, 1 twin, 2 single
bathrooms 1 en suite, 1 private
payment Cash/cheques

Room · General 1

INGLETON, North Yorkshire Map ref 1B3 — **GUEST ACCOMMODATION**

★★★★
GUEST HOUSE

B&B per room per night
d £50.00–£55.00

Ingleborough View Guest House

Main Street, Ingleton LA6 3HH **t** (01524) 241523 **e** geoff@ingleboroughview.com
w ingleboroughview.com

open All year except Christmas
bedrooms 2 double, 1 twin, 1 suite
bathrooms 3 en suite, 1 private
payment Cash/cheques

A non-smoking guesthouse with comfortable, well-equipped rooms in a stunning riverside location where you will find a cheerful welcome, friendly atmosphere and great breakfasts. Few minutes' walk to the shops, cafes and pubs. Ideal for walkers and cyclists or simply for exploring the Yorkshire Dales and Lake District.

Reductions for 3 or more nights from Oct to Mar (excl Bank Holidays). Phone or see website for details.

Room · General · Leisure

INGLETON, North Yorkshire Map ref 1B3 — **GUEST ACCOMMODATION**

★★★★
GUEST ACCOMMODATION

B&B per room per night
d £50.00–£60.00

Inglenook Guest House

20 Main Street, Ingleton LA6 3HJ **t** (01524) 241270 **e** inglenook20@hotmail.com
w inglenookguesthouse.com

Craven Accommodation Provider of the Year 2005 – Runner-up. Quality en suite rooms with attention to detail. Excellent food and hospitality. Picturesque riverside location with superb views. Attractive terrace garden.

open All year except Christmas and New Year
bedrooms 2 double, 2 twin, 1 family
bathrooms 4 en suite, 1 private
payment Credit/debit cards, cash/cheques

Room · General 5

KETTLEWELL, North Yorkshire Map ref 1B3 — GUEST ACCOMMODATION

♦♦♦
GUEST ACCOMMODATION

B&B per room per night
d £52.00–£55.00

Lynburn

Langcliffe Garth, Skipton BD23 5RF **t** (01756) 760803 **e** www.lorna@lthornborrow.fsnet.co.uk

Dales cottage with views from each window. All rooms furnished for your comfort. Excellent food provided. Ideal place to tour/walk the Dales. NFWI cookery judge. A warm welcome awaits you.

open All year except Christmas
bedrooms 1 double, 1 twin
payment Cash/cheques

Room General 14 P Leisure

KILBURN, North Yorkshire Map ref 1C3 — GUEST ACCOMMODATION

★★★
FARMHOUSE

B&B per room per night
s Max £24.00
d Max £48.00
Evening meal per person
Max £10.00

Church Farm

Kilburn, York YO61 4AH **t** (01347) 868318 **e** churchfarmkilburn@yahoo.co.uk

Church Farm is a dairy farm set in the peaceful village of Kilburn, providing clean, comfortable and welcoming accommodation. Children welcome, ample parking. Large garden.

open All year except Christmas and New Year
bedrooms 1 double, 1 family
bathrooms 1 en suite, 1 private
payment Cash/cheques

Room General P Leisure

KIRKBY MALZEARD, North Yorkshire Map ref 1C3 — SELF CATERING

★★★★
SELF CATERING

Units 1
Sleeps 6
Low season per wk
£270.00–£370.00
High season per wk
£380.00–£535.00

Alma Cottage, Kirkby Malzeard, Ripon

contact Janet Barclay, 12 St Stephen's Road, Cold Norton, Chelmsford CM3 6JE
t (01621) 828576 **e** janet@lbarclay.demon.co.uk **w** almacottage.co.uk

Comfortable three-bedroom period cottage in stone terrace of friendly Nidderdale village. Ideal for dales, moors, walking, cycling, riding, sightseeing and bird-watching. Walled garden, secure garage, one double, two twins.

open All year
payment Cash/cheques

Unit
General P Leisure Shop < 0.5 miles Pub < 0.5 miles

KIRKBYMOORSIDE, North Yorkshire Map ref 1C3 — GUEST ACCOMMODATION

♦♦♦♦
GUEST ACCOMMODATION
SILVER AWARD

B&B per room per night
d £70.00–£105.00
Evening meal per person
Min £30.00

The Cornmill

Kirby Mills, Kirkbymoorside, York YO62 6NP **t** (01751) 432000 **e** cornmill@kirbymills.demon.co.uk
w kirbymills.demon.co.uk

open All year
bedrooms 4 double, 1 twin
bathrooms All en suite
payment Credit/debit cards, cash/cheques

Converted 18thC watermill and Victorian farmhouse providing well-appointed bed and breakfast accommodation on the River Dove. Bedrooms (two with four-posters), lounge, wood-burning stove and bootroom are in the farmhouse. Sumptuous breakfasts and pre-booked group dinners are served in the mill, with viewing panel in the floor.

From Thirsk, A170 to Scarborough. 1km after Kirkbymoorside roundabout take left turn into Kirby Mills. Entrance to car park is 20m up on right.

Room General P Leisure

Out and about

For ideas on places to visit see the attractions section towards the back of the guide or go online at enjoyengland.com.

KNARESBOROUGH, North Yorkshire Map ref 2B1 — **GUEST ACCOMMODATION**

♦♦♦♦
GUEST ACCOMMODATION
GOLD AWARD

B&B per room per night
s Min £75.00
d Min £99.00
Evening meal per person
Min £25.00

Gallon House

47 Kirkgate, Knaresborough HG5 8BZ **t** (01423) 862102 **e** gallon-house@ntlworld.com
w gallon-house.co.uk

open All year except Christmas and New Year
bedrooms 2 double, 1 twin
bathrooms All en suite
payment Cash/cheques

Overlooking the beautiful Nidd Gorge, Gallon House offers award-winning accommodation and mouthwatering, locally sourced fresh food. Recognised as a unique, special hotel, Gallon House offers individual service in a breathtaking setting. A recent guest said: 'thank you for making your special place our special place too.'

⊕ *Follow A59 through Knaresborough, turning left into the marketplace. Follow the road, turning right into Kirkgate. Gallon House is at the bottom by the railway station.*

♥ *Discounts are available for stays of 3 or more nights. Special mid-week DB&B rates.*

Room General Leisure

LEALHOLM, North Yorkshire Map ref 1C3 — **SELF CATERING**

★★★
SELF CATERING

Units **3**
Sleeps **3–6**
Low season per wk
£220.00–£245.00
High season per wk
£385.00–£585.00

Greenhouses Farm Cottages, Whitby

contact Nick Eddleston, Greenhouses Farm Cottages, Greenhouses, Lealholm YO21 2AD
t (01947) 897486 **f** (01947) 897486 **e** n_eddleston@yahoo.com **w** greenhouses-farm-cottages.co.uk

open All year
payment Cash/cheques

Stone and pantile cottages converted from traditional farm buildings, providing well-equipped, comfortable, centrally heated accommodation. The lounges have solid fuel stoves and colour TVs. The kitchens are all equipped with electric cooker, microwave, washing machine and pleasant dining area. In beautiful moorland hamlet within North York Moors National Park, nine miles Whitby.

⊕ *A171, Guisborough to Whitby road. Turn off to Lealholm on the right, 13 miles from Guisborough. Follow road for approx 1 mile, signpost on right 'Greenhouses only'.*

Unit
General Leisure Shop 1.5 miles Pub 1.5 miles

LEYBURN, North Yorkshire Map ref 1B3 — **HOTEL**

★
HOTEL

B&B per room per night
s £28.00–£36.00
d £56.00–£72.00
HB per person per night
£44.00–£52.00

Golden Lion Hotel & Licensed Restaurant

Market Place, Leyburn DL8 5AS **t** (01969) 622161 **f** (01969) 623836 **e** annegoldenlion@aol.com
w thegoldenlion.co.uk

Small, family-run hotel in the marketplace of a busy Dales town. A good base for touring the surrounding countryside. Special diets. Children/pets welcome.

open All year except Christmas
bedrooms 3 double, 4 twin, 2 single, 6 family
bathrooms 14 en suite, 1 private
payment Credit/debit cards, cash/cheques

Room General Leisure

It's all quality-assessed accommodation

VisitBritain's commitment to quality involves wide-ranging accommodation assessment. Ratings and awards were correct at the time of going to press but may change following a new assessment. Please check at the time of booking.

LEYBURN, North Yorkshire Map ref 1B3 — **GUEST ACCOMMODATION**

Rating Applied For
GUEST HOUSE

B&B per room per night
s Min £45.00
d £58.00–£60.00
Evening meal per person
£16.00

Dales Haven

Market Place, Leyburn DL8 5BJ **t** (01969) 623814 **e** info@daleshaven.co.uk **w** daleshaven.co.uk

open All year
bedrooms 3 double, 1 twin, 2 family
bathrooms All en suite
payment Credit/debit cards, cash/cheques

Enjoy a warm welcome, super accommodation, lovely views and sumptuous breakfasts in our family run guesthouse in beautiful Wensleydale. Situated in the centre of the bustling market town of Leyburn, Dales Haven is an ideal base for walking and touring. Murder mystery breaks available. Groups may book exclusive use of the guesthouse.

⊕ *Easy to find on Leyburn Market Place in the heart of Wensleydale.*

♥ *Winter Warmer save 20%. Summer Sizzler save 10%.*

Room General P Leisure

LEYBURN, North Yorkshire Map ref 1B3 — **GUEST ACCOMMODATION**

★★★★
GUEST ACCOMMODATION

B&B per room per night
s £27.00–£30.00
d £48.00–£58.00

The Old Vicarage

West Witton, Leyburn DL8 4LX **t** (01969) 622108 **e** info@dalesbreaks.co.uk **w** dalesbreaks.co.uk

open All year except Christmas and New Year
bedrooms 1 double, 1 twin, 1 family
bathrooms All en suite
payment Cash/cheques, euros

Four-poster, family and double en suite rooms with all facilities provided. This charming Grade II Listed former Dales vicarage has wonderful views right across Wensleydale. Spacious private car parking. Centrally placed for visiting the Dales, Lake District, Whitby or York. Friends old and new most welcome.

⊕ *Follow the A684 from Leyburn in direction of Hawes for 3 miles. On entering West Witton the property is the 1st guesthouse on the left-hand side.*

♥ *Stay 4 nights for the price of 3, Sun-Thu, Sep-Mar inclusive (mention 'Where to Stay' guide offer).*

Room General P Leisure

LEYBURN, North Yorkshire Map ref 1B3 — **GUEST ACCOMMODATION**

★★★★★
GUEST ACCOMMODATION
GOLD AWARD

B&B per room per night
s £70.00–£85.00
d £90.00–£115.00
Evening meal per person
Min £31.00

Waterford House

19 Kirkgate, Leyburn DL8 4PG **t** (01969) 622090 **f** (01969) 624020
e info@waterfordhousehotel.co.uk **w** waterfordhousehotel.co.uk

open All year except Christmas and New Year
bedrooms 5 double
bathrooms All en suite
payment Credit/debit cards, cash/cheques

Overlooking the picturesque square with a delightful, relaxed Georgian country-house atmosphere. Sporting antiques, open fires, four-poster beds, using local produce with comprehensive wine list. Step out of the front door and enjoy the many racehorses, the fabulous walking in exceptional countryside, Middleham's medieval castle. Come and be pampered.

⊕ *Southbound from A1 at Scotch Corner via Richmond and Leyburn. Northbound from A1 on B6267 via Masham. House in northern corner of square.*

♥ *Discounts on 4 or more days excl weekends, Nov-Mar. Please telephone.*

WALKERS WELCOME CYCLISTS WELCOME

Room General 12 P Leisure

LEYBURN, North Yorkshire Map ref 1B3 — **GUEST ACCOMMODATION**

★★★★
GUEST ACCOMMODATION
SILVER AWARD

B&B per room per night
d £58.00–£64.00

West Close Farmhouse

Melmerby in Coverdale, Leyburn DL8 4TW **t** (01969) 640275 **f** (01969) 640275
e thompson@westclose.wanadoo.co.uk **w** westclosefarmhouse.co.uk

open All year
bedrooms 1 double, 1 twin, 1 family
bathrooms All en suite
payment Credit/debit cards, cash/cheques

A warm welcome awaits you in our newly converted granary farmhouse, in village hamlet with spectacular views. All bedrooms are en suite, located on the first floor with their own private entrance. Set in four acres with secure parking. Close to Forbidden Corner and the market towns of Leyburn and Middleham.

A684 from Leyburn, signposted Hawes. After 1.5 miles at Wensley village, turn left after bridge, signposted Carlton/Coverdale. Follow road for 3 miles.

Room General Leisure

MARKET WEIGHTON, East Riding of Yorkshire Map ref 2C1 — **GUEST ACCOMMODATION**

★★★
FARMHOUSE

B&B per room per night
s £27.00–£29.00
d £46.00–£50.00

Arras Farmhouse

Arras, York YO43 4RN **t** (01430) 872404 **f** (01430) 872404

open All year except Christmas
bedrooms 2 double, 1 twin
bathrooms 2 en suite
payment Cash/cheques

Large farmhouse and garden on working farm. Peaceful atmosphere and comfortable, spacious rooms. Beautiful old-world dining room with lounge area, TV and good food. Friendly family welcome. Robert has knowledge of local history and large family tree.

Arras is on the A1079 between Market Weighton and Beverley, 3 miles from Market Weighton at crossroads.

General P

MASHAM, North Yorkshire Map ref 1C3 — **HOTEL**

★★★★
HOTEL
GOLD AWARD

B&B per room per night
s £150.00–£350.00
d £150.00–£350.00
HB per person per night
£120.00–£218.00

Swinton Park

Ripon HG4 4JH **t** (01765) 680944 **f** (01765) 680901 **e** felicity@swintonpark.com
w swintonpark.com

A family home since the late 1800s, Swinton Park has played host to country-house parties of legendary style and grandeur. Mark and Felicity Cunliffe-Lister are proud to welcome you to join them to continue this tradition.

open All year
bedrooms 26 double, 4 suites
bathrooms All en suite
payment Credit/debit cards, cash/cheques, euros

Room General P Leisure

NAWTON, North Yorkshire Map ref 1C3 — **GUEST ACCOMMODATION**

★★★
FARMHOUSE

B&B per room per night
s £30.00–£35.00
d £27.50–£32.50

Little Manor Farm

Highfield Lane, Nawton, Helmsley, York YO62 7TU **t** (01439) 771672 **e** penny-avison@tiscali.co.uk

Extremely comfortable Yorkshire farmhouse, set in own grounds. Panoramic views. Close to Helmsley, Castle Howard, coast and York. Stabling available. Delicious breakfasts. Garden room for guests.

open All year except Christmas and New Year
bedrooms 2 double
bathrooms 1 private
payment Cash/cheques

Room General 5 Leisure

NEWTON-ON-RAWCLIFFE, North Yorkshire Map ref 1D3 — **GUEST ACCOMMODATION**

♦♦♦♦
GUEST ACCOMMODATION

B&B per room per night
s £30.00–£32.00
d £52.00–£60.00

Swan Cottage

Newton-on-Rawcliffe, Pickering YO18 8QA **t** (01751) 472502 **e** swancottagenewton@yahoo.co.uk

Homely terraced village cottage. Situated opposite the village green and duck pond. Open fire, en suite and varied breakfast menu.

open All year except Christmas and New Year
bedrooms 1 double, 1 family
bathrooms All en suite
payment Cash/cheques

Room General Leisure

NORTH DALTON, East Riding of Yorkshire Map ref 2C1 — **SELF CATERING**

★★★
SELF CATERING

Units 1
Sleeps 3–4
Low season per wk
£182.00–£310.00
High season per wk
£300.00–£410.00

Old Cobbler's Cottage, Driffield, North Dalton

t (01377) 217523 & (01377) 217662 **f** (01377) 217754 **e** chris@adastra-music.co.uk
w waterfrontcottages.co.uk

open All year
payment Credit/debit cards, cash/cheques

19thC, mid-terraced, oak-beamed cottage overlooking picturesque pond in a peaceful and friendly farming village, between York and Yorkshire's Heritage Coast. Ideally located for walking, visiting the coast, historic houses, races at York and Beverley or just relaxing. Excellent inn/restaurant adjacent, shops 1.5 miles. Pets welcome.

⊕ *On entering North Dalton, take narrow lane up the side of The Star pub car park. Old Cobbler's is a mid-terraced cottage in the row.*

♥ *Short breaks available, 2 nights (excl Christmas, New Year, Easter and Bank Holidays).*

Unit General Leisure Shop 1.5 miles Pub < 0.5 miles

NORTHALLERTON, North Yorkshire Map ref 1C3 — **SELF CATERING**

★★★★
SELF CATERING

Units 4
Sleeps 2–4
Low season per wk
£175.00–£280.00
High season per wk
£290.00–£440.00

Hill House Farm Cottages, Northallerton

contact Julie & James Griffith, Hill House Farm, Little Langton, Northallerton DL7 0PZ
t (01609) 770643 **e** info@hillhousefarmcottages.com **w** hillhousefarmcottages.com

open All year
payment Credit/debit cards, cash/cheques

These four well-equipped cottages, converted from former farm buildings, are set around a lawned courtyard garden, in a peaceful rural setting with magnificent views. Situated three miles from the market town of Northallerton they are ideal for exploring both the Yorkshire Dales and the North York Moors.

Unit General Leisure Shop 3 miles Pub 1.5 miles

OVER SILTON, North Yorkshire Map ref 1C3 — **GUEST ACCOMMODATION**

★★★★
FARMHOUSE

B&B per room per night
s £35.00–£40.00
d £55.00–£60.00

Greystone Farm

Over Silton, Thirsk YO7 2LH **t** (01609) 883468 **e** greystone@freenet.co.uk

Small farm in secluded location offering comfortable homely accommodation. Guest lounge with drinks tray and TV. Substantial breakfasts using locally sourced food. Easy access to numerous attractions.

open All year
bedrooms 2 twin
bathrooms 1 en suite, 1 private
payment Cash/cheques

General Leisure

OXENHOPE, West Yorkshire Map ref 2B1 — **SELF CATERING**

★★★
SELF CATERING

Units **1**
Sleeps **4**
Low season per wk
£170.00–£200.00
High season per wk
£190.00–£250.00

Hawksbridge Cottage, Oxenhope, Keighley

contact Hazel Holmes, Hawksbridge Cottage, 2 Hawksbridge Lane, Oxenhope BD22 9QU
t (01535) 642203 **e** hazel.holmes1@virgin.net **w** oxenhope-accommodation.co.uk

19thC country cottage with original features, beams, and panoramic views from every window. Comfortable and warm: central heating, living flame gas fire. Large lounge, dining/kitchen, two bedrooms, bathroom, patio, parking.

open All year except Christmas
payment Cash/cheques

Unit
General Shop 1 mile Pub 1 mile

OXENHOPE, West Yorkshire Map ref 2B1 — **SELF CATERING**

★★★
SELF CATERING

Units **1**
Sleeps **4**
Low season per wk
£165.00–£175.00
High season per wk
£175.00–£250.00

Old Cote Cottage, Oxenhope

contact Mrs Groves, Old Cote Cottage, Rag Clough Beck Stairs, Oxenhope, Keighley BD22 9QY
t (01535) 644180 **e** johngroves@homecall.co.uk **w** oldcotecottage.co.uk

17thC cottage surrounded by farmland. Owner maintained. Haworth two miles. Worth Valley Railway 1.5 miles. Walks from door, easy drive to Leeds, Bradford, Yorkshire Dales. Dogs welcome by arrangement.

open All year
payment Cash/cheques

Unit
General Leisure Shop 1.5 miles Pub 1.5 miles

PATELEY BRIDGE, North Yorkshire Map ref 1C3 — **SELF CATERING**

★★★★
SELF CATERING & SERVICED APARTMENTS

Units **4**
Sleeps **2–10**
Low season per wk
£195.00–£385.00
High season per wk
£335.00–£710.00

Helme Pasture, Old Spring Wood, Harrogate

contact Mrs Rosemary Helme, Hartwith Bank, Summerbridge, Harrogate HG3 4DR
t (01423) 780279 **f** (01423) 780994 **e** info@helmepasture.co.uk **w** helmepasture.co.uk

open All year
payment Credit/debit cards, cash/cheques, euros

Scandinavian lodges and converted Dales barn. Award-winning conservation woodland. Holiday in tranquil surroundings. Country walks. Close to a multitude of attractions including Fountains Abbey, castles, Yorkshire villages and floral towns – Harrogate, Skipton, Ripon, York. Traditional markets. Pet friendly, and a warm family welcome.

Harrogate, B6165 towards Pateley Bridge. At Summerbridge (Flying Dutchman pub), turn up Hartwith Bank. Helme Pasture is 0.3 miles on left.

Short breaks available.

Unit
General Leisure Shop < 0.5 miles Pub < 0.5 miles

PICKERING, North Yorkshire Map ref 1D3 — **GUEST ACCOMMODATION**

★★★★★
GUEST ACCOMMODATION GOLD AWARD

B&B per room per night
d £75.00–£110.00
Evening meal per person
£7.50–£25.00

WALKERS WELCOME

17 Burgate

Pickering YO18 7AU **t** (01751) 473463 **f** (01751) 473463 **e** info@17burgate.co.uk
w 17burgate.co.uk

Renovated townhouse between town centre and castle. Luxury for the stressed and weary. 17 Burgate is different, 17 Burgate is special – indulge yourselves, and make it part of your North Yorkshire experience.

open All year
bedrooms 4 double, 1 twin
bathrooms All en suite
payment Credit/debit cards, cash/cheques, euros

Room General 12 Leisure

To your credit

If you book by credit card it's advisable to check the proprietor's policy in case you have to cancel.

PICKERING, North Yorkshire Map ref 1D3 — **GUEST ACCOMMODATION**

★★★
BED & BREAKFAST

B&B per room per night
s £25.00–£30.00
d £48.00–£56.00

Kirkham Garth Bed and Breakfast

Kirkham Garth, Whitby Road, Pickering YO18 7AT **t** (01751) 474931 **e** kirkhamgarth@hotmail.co.uk **w** kirkhamgarth.co.uk

Quiet, private, homely residence. Ideal for York, forests, 'Heartbeat' Country, Moors, coast and steam train. Open all year. Private off-road parking. Stay and discover this beautiful area.

open All year except Christmas
bedrooms 1 double, 1 twin, 1 family
bathrooms 1 en suite
payment Cash/cheques

Room General 4 P Leisure

PICKERING, North Yorkshire Map ref 1D3 — **SELF CATERING**

★★★★–★★★★★
SELF CATERING

Units 8
Sleeps 2–10
Low season per wk
£255.00–£855.00
High season per wk
£495.00–£1,835.00

Beech Farm Cottages, Nr Pickering

contact Mrs Pat Massara, Beech Farm Cottages, Wrelton YO18 8PG
t (01751) 476612 **f** (01751) 475032 **e** holiday@beechfarm.com **w** beechfarm.com

open All year
payment Credit/debit cards, cash/cheques, euros

Award-winning, luxury stone cottages with heated indoor pool, sauna, children's play area, gardens and paddock. Horse, pony and llama in field. Delightful location in quiet village on edge of North York Moors National Park. Also convenient for coast and York. The cottages are in a courtyard setting backing onto fields. Brochure available or please phone.

The village of Wrelton is just off the A170, 3 miles west of Pickering.

4-times winner of Yorkshire Tourist Board's Self-Catering Holiday of the Year award.

Unit General P Leisure Shop 2 miles Pub < 0.5 miles

PICKERING, North Yorkshire Map ref 1D3 — **SELF CATERING**

★★★★
SELF CATERING

Units 1
Sleeps 4
Low season per wk
Min £250.00
High season per wk
Max £500.00

High Kingthorpe Lodges

contact John Tunnicliffe, High Kingthorpe Lodges, Riseborough Hagg Farm, Marton Road, Pickering YO18 8LR
t (01751) 476457 **e** info@kingthorpe.com **w** kingthorpe.com

open All year
payment Cash/cheques

High Kingthorpe Lodge is a stunning log cabin located in the North York Moors National Park. The lodge nestles on the edge of 400 acres of privately owned woodland with breathtaking views of the valley, where the Pickering to Grosmont steam railway winds its way to 'Heartbeat' country.

From Pickering follow the A169 north towards Whitby for approx 2 miles. High Kingthorpe Lodge is located on the left.

Unit General P Shop 2 miles Pub 1 mile

Key to symbols

Symbols at the end of each entry help you pick out the services and facilities which are most important for your stay. A key to the symbols can be found inside the back-cover flap. Keep this open for easy reference.

PICKERING, North Yorkshire Map ref 1D3 — **SELF CATERING**

★★★★
SELF CATERING

Units 1
Sleeps 5
Low season per wk
£275.00–£325.00
High season per wk
£375.00–£575.00

WALKERS WELCOME · CYCLISTS WELCOME

Kale Pot Cottage, Newtondale

contact Diane & Mike Steele, Kale Pot Cottage, Kale Pot Hole, Newtondale, Pickering YO18 8HU
t (01751) 476654 **e** mike@kalepothole.fsnet.co.uk **w** northyorkmoorscottage.co.uk

Comfortable, spacious, former 18thC farmhouse in beautiful Newtondale. Well equipped and completely restored, with stunning views. Ideal for walking, steam railway, York, moors and coast.

open All year
payment Cash/cheques, euros

Unit
General Leisure Shop 4 miles Pub 3 miles

PICKERING, North Yorkshire Map ref 1D3 — **SELF CATERING**

★★★
SELF CATERING

Units 1
Sleeps 2
Low season per wk
Min £290.00
High season per wk
Min £320.00

Pan Cottage

Pan Cottage, 27 Rosamund Avenue, Pickering YO18 7HF
t (01751) 473618 **e** pancottage@hotmail.co.uk **w** pancottage.co.uk

open All year
payment Cash/cheques, euros

A small but perfectly formed luxury, beamed cottage with south-facing patio. Situated in a village with shops and non-smoking pub on the edge of Pickering. Ideal location for the North York Moors, the heritage coast, the famous steam railway and historic York. A welcome pack with wine on arrival.

Situated on the south side of the A170 1 mile west of Pickering in the village of Middleton. Nearest train station Malton, 7 miles.

Special champagne and chocolate breaks. Also Christmas and New Year breaks with luxury hamper available.

Unit
General Leisure Shop < 0.5 miles Pub < 0.5 miles

REETH, North Yorkshire Map ref 1B3 — **SELF CATERING**

★★
SELF CATERING

Units 1
Sleeps 9
Low season per wk
£250.00–£350.00
High season per wk
£450.00–£550.00

Half Moon House, Reeth, Richmond

contact Ms Doris Reed, 3 Netherby Close, Yarm TS15 9RD
t (01642) 866628 **e** d-reed@ntlworld.com

Cottage in village centre close to all amenities. Three double bedrooms, and an attic with three single beds. Two bathrooms, storage heating and open fire. Secure private patio/garden. Dogs welcome.

open All year
payment Cash/cheques

Unit
General Leisure Shop < 0.5 miles Pub < 0.5 miles

RICHMOND, North Yorkshire Map ref 1C3 — **GUEST ACCOMMODATION**

★★★
GUEST ACCOMMODATION

B&B per room per night
s £25.00–£26.00
d £48.00–£50.00

27 Hurgill Road

Richmond DL10 4AR **t** (01748) 824092 **f** (01748) 824092

27 Hurgill Road is a bed and breakfast establishment located in Richmond. Ideal location for touring the Dales.

open All year except Christmas and New Year
bedrooms 1 double, 1 twin, 1 single
payment Cash/cheques

Room General Leisure

What's in a quality rating?

Information about ratings and awards can be found at the front of this guide.

RICHMOND, North Yorkshire Map ref 1C3 — GUEST ACCOMMODATION

★★★★
GUEST ACCOMMODATION

B&B per room per night
s £40.00–£56.00
d Min £56.00

Frenchgate Guest House

66 Frenchgate, Richmond DL10 7AG **t** (01748) 823421 & 07889 768696 **f** (01748) 823421
e info@66frenchgate.co.uk

Panoramic views overlooking the Swale Valley, Richmond Castle, Easby Abbey and rolling countryside over the Dales. The historic marketplace and castle are nearby.

open All year
bedrooms 5 double, 3 twin
bathrooms 4 en suite, 4 private
payment Cash/cheques, euros

Room General 8 Leisure

RICHMOND, North Yorkshire Map ref 1C3 — SELF CATERING

★★★★
SELF CATERING

Units 1
Sleeps 4–10

Low season per wk
£370.00–£480.00
High season per wk
£700.00–£800.00

Lions Leap

contact Clive Haddon, Lions Leap, 94 Old Birmingham Road, Bromsgrove B60 1DG
t (01527) 876330 **f** (01748) 850310 **e** clive_haddon@hotmail.com
w uk-holiday-cottages.co.uk/lionsleap

open All year
payment Credit/debit cards, cash/cheques

Set in a quiet residential area in the ancient market town of Richmond, Lions Leap is a detached dormer bungalow offering excellent accommodation. Spacious, well equipped and comfortably furnished with the added benefit of a sun lounge/breakfast room and games room. Stunning views across the golf course and beyond.

From A1, right onto A6136, left onto B6271, left onto A6108. Right on Gallowgate, right Cut Purse Lane, 2nd left, 1st left.

Special discounts for up to 4 people. Last-minute offers please check website for availability or email for details.

Unit
General P Leisure Shop < 0.5 miles Pub 0.5 miles

RIPON, North Yorkshire Map ref 1C3 — HOTEL

★★★
HOTEL

B&B per room per night
s £85.00–£95.00
d £110.00–£140.00

The Old Deanery Restaurant and Hotel

Minster Road, Ripon HG4 1QS **t** (01765) 600003 **f** (01765) 600027
e reception@theolddeanery.co.uk **w** theolddeanery.co.uk

A historic 16thC building offering a contemporary, fine dining, 60-cover restaurant, individually designed bedrooms and modern meeting-room facilities.

open All year except Christmas
bedrooms 11 double
bathrooms All en suite
payment Credit/debit cards, cash/cheques

Room General P Leisure

RIPON, North Yorkshire Map ref 1C3 — GUEST ACCOMMODATION

★★★★
BED & BREAKFAST

B&B per room per night
s £50.00
d £60.00–£70.00

Ravencroft B&B

Moorside Avenue, Ripon HG4 1TA **t** (01765) 602543 **e** guestmail@btopenworld.com
w ravencroftbandb.com

bedrooms 2 double, 1 family
bathrooms All en suite
payment Credit/debit cards, cash/cheques, euros

Well-established, high-quality personal service, including several complimentary services, in luxury en suite accommodation. An hospitable family home in quiet location one mile from cathedral, 3.5 miles from Fountains Abbey. See website for further information and recommendations. Open all year except May and June.

From A1(M) take Ripon bypass, A61 to south end. Right at final roundabout past Morrisons entrance. Moorside Avenue 1st left after traffic lights (see website).

Room General 8 P

RIPON, North Yorkshire Map ref 1C3 — **GUEST ACCOMMODATION**

★★★★★
GUEST HOUSE
SILVER AWARD

B&B per room per night
s £50.00–£60.00
d £65.00–£75.00
Evening meal per person
£16.50–£20.00

Sharow Cross House

Dishforth Road, Ripon HG4 5BQ **t** (01765) 609866 **e** sharowcrosshouse@btinternet.com
w sharowcrosshouse.com

open All year except Christmas and New Year
bedrooms 3 double
bathrooms All en suite
payment Cash/cheques, euros

Spoil yourself. Elegant 1850s country house, retaining many original features, offering high standard en suite accommodation. One mile from Ripon centre with scenic country views in quiet location with off-road parking. Ideally situated for Yorkshire Dales, North York Moors, York, Harrogate, Fountains Abbey. Speciality home-cooked evening dinner on request.

Room General 8 P Leisure

RIPON, North Yorkshire Map ref 1C3 — **GUEST ACCOMMODATION**

★★★
GUEST ACCOMMODATION

B&B per room per night
s £30.00–£40.00
d £50.00–£60.00

The White Horse

61 North Street, Ripon HG4 1EN **t** (01765) 603622 **f** (01765) 609040
e david.bate13@btopenworld.com

A friendly, family-run pub close to Ripon Market Square. Entertainment at weekends and various mid-week activities

open All year
bedrooms 3 double, 3 twin, 3 single, 3 family
bathrooms All en suite
payment Credit/debit cards

Room General P Leisure

RIPON, North Yorkshire Map ref 1C3 — **SELF CATERING**

★★★★
SELF CATERING

Units 1
Sleeps 8
Low season per wk
Min £300.00
High season per wk
Max £600.00

Intake, Ripon

contact Fiona McConnell, 3 Hippingstones Lane, Corbridge NE45 5JP
t (01434) 632812 **e** kfiona@tiscali.co.uk **w** intakefarmhouse.co.uk

Traditional stone farmhouse, newly renovated. Furnished to high standard. Log fire, Stanley cooker. Lovely view over fields – listen to curlews. Many diverse attractions within easy reach.

open All year except Christmas and New Year
payment Cash/cheques

Unit
General P Shop 0.75 miles Pub 0.75 miles

RIPPONDEN, West Yorkshire Map ref 2B1 — **GUEST ACCOMMODATION**

★★★★
GUEST ACCOMMODATION

B&B per room per night
s £35.00–£45.00
d Max £70.00
Evening meal per person
£18.00–£25.00

Thurst House Farm

Ripponden, Sowerby Bridge HX6 4NN **t** (01422) 822820 **e** thursthousefarm@bushinternet.com

open All year except Christmas and New Year
bedrooms 1 double, 1 family
bathrooms All en suite
payment Credit/debit cards, cash/cheques

A warm welcome and good food await you at this Grade II Listed former farmhouse which stands in Pennine scenery. It is a place to relax in front of an open fire after visiting Manchester, Leeds or Huddersfield, which is renowned for its choral society and contemporary music festival.

Approaching Ripponden from Sowerby Bridge, 100yds before traffic lights turn right up 20yd lane. Right at Beehive Inn. Straight on for 1 mile. Farm is on the right.

Room General 8 P

ROBIN HOOD'S BAY, North Yorkshire Map ref 1D3 — **SELF CATERING**

★★★–★★★★★
SELF CATERING

Units 5
Sleeps 3–5
Low season per wk
£180.00–£320.00
High season per wk
£395.00–£620.00

Farsyde Farm Cottages, Robin Hood's Bay, Whitby

contact Angela Green, Farsyde Farm Cottages, Robin Hood's Bay, Whitby YO22 4UG
t (01947) 880249 **f** (01947) 880877 **e** farsydestud@talk21.com **w** farsydefarmcottages.co.uk

open All year
payment Cash/cheques

Adjacent to Robin Hood's Bay village, beach and Boggle Hole via field/woodland paths, the stone and pantile cottages, permanently heated in cooler months, have attractive gardens and magnificent panoramic views. Mistal Cottage guests enjoy private swimming (chalet pool). Horses/mountain bikes. Farm animals. Parking. Whitby six miles. Scarborough 16 miles. York 50 miles.

Follow the signs to Fylingthorpe from the A171. At crossroads take Middlewood Lane, then left into Mark Lane to end at Farsyde House.

Short breaks in autumn, winter and spring. Minimum 2 nights. Oct-Jun: 3-night weekends for riders also offered.

Unit
General Leisure Shop 0.75 miles Pub 0.75 miles

ROOS, East Riding of Yorkshire Map ref 2D1 — **CAMPING & CARAVANNING**

★★★★
HOLIDAY & TOURING PARK
ROSE AWARD

(16) £10.00–£15.00
(2) £10.00–£15.00
(26) £135.00–£375.00
18 touring pitches

Sand-le-Mere Caravan & Leisure Park

Seaside Lane, Tunstall, Hull HU12 0JQ **t** (01964) 670403 **f** (01964) 671099
e info@sand-le-mere.co.uk **w** sand-le-mere.co.uk

A great place to stay, with its natural park and mere leading to a gentle slope to the beach. No cliffs to climb.

payment Credit/debit cards, cash/cheques, euros

General Leisure

SAWDON, North Yorkshire Map ref 1D3 — **GUEST ACCOMMODATION**

Rating Applied For
GUEST ACCOMMODATION

B&B per room per night
s £30.00–£35.00
d £28.00–£35.00

Sawdon Heights

Scarborough YO13 9EB **t** (01723) 859321 **f** (01723) 859321

A warm welcome awaits on our family farm adjacent to forest. Quiet location, stunning views. Cycle hire and storage, walks and pack-ups available. Ideal location for exploring east coast and moors.

open All year except Christmas
bedrooms 2 double, 1 twin
bathrooms All en suite
payment Cash/cheques

Room General Leisure

SCARBOROUGH, North Yorkshire Map ref 1D3 — **GUEST ACCOMMODATION**

★★★★
GUEST ACCOMMODATION
SILVER AWARD

B&B per room per night
s £30.00–£34.00
d £60.00–£68.00
Evening meal per person
£14.00–£18.00

The Alexander Hotel

33 Burniston Road, Scarborough YO12 6PG **t** (01723) 363178 **f** (01723) 354821
e enquiries@alexanderhotelscarborough.co.uk **w** alexanderhotelscarborough.co.uk

bedrooms 7 double, 2 twin, 1 single
bathrooms All en suite
payment Credit/debit cards, cash/cheques

We offer you a detached, friendly, adult-only hotel, specialising in comfort and quality. Conveniently situated for visiting Whitby, and only five minutes' walk from the main beach. Our food is excellent, prepared by our professional chef. All rooms are well furnished and we have ample off-road parking. Open March to October.

On entering Scarborough head for North Bay. At North Bay take roundabout at Peasholm Park, head up hill towards 'Kinderland'. Property is 300m on left from roundabout.

Special discount breaks for spring and autumn.

Room General Leisure

SCARBOROUGH, North Yorkshire Map ref 1D3 — GUEST ACCOMMODATION

★★★
GUEST ACCOMMODATION

B&B per room per night
s £21.50–£35.00
d £43.00–£58.00

Blands Cliff Lodge

Scarborough YO11 1NR **t** (01723) 351747 & (01723) 363653 **e** tonight@yorkshire-coast.co.uk
w yorkshire-coast.co.uk/blandscliff

open All year except Christmas and New Year
bedrooms 6 double, 3 twin, 3 single, 4 family
bathrooms 11 en suite
payment Credit/debit cards, cash/cheques

A friendly welcome awaits you at our family-run town-centre hotel. Offering room only or B&B. All within easy walking distance of shops, cafes, bars and seafront. On-street or discounted secure parking available nearby. Respectful families and small groups welcome. Family rooms have fridges.

From the seafront road – either direction, turn at the Lifeboat station traffic lights into Eastborough, 3rd left into Blands Cliff (opposite Argos).

10% discount for stays of 5 nights or more. Oct-Feb 3 nights for the price of 2.

Room General Leisure

SCARBOROUGH, North Yorkshire Map ref 1D3 — GUEST ACCOMMODATION

★★★★
GUEST HOUSE

B&B per room per night
s £23.00–£25.00
d £46.00–£50.00
Evening meal per person
Min £8.00

Gordon Hotel

Ryndleside, Scarborough YO12 6AD **t** (01723) 362177 **e** sales@gordonhotel.co.uk
w gordonhotel.co.uk

open All year
bedrooms 4 double, 2 twin, 1 single, 3 family
bathrooms All en suite
payment Credit/debit cards, cash/cheques

Friendly, family-run, licensed guesthouse overlooking Peasholm Park. Family rooms are available. Senior Citizen discount. TV, complimentary tray, hairdryer and clock-radio in all rooms.

Room General

SCARBOROUGH, North Yorkshire Map ref 1D3 — GUEST ACCOMMODATION

♦♦♦♦
GUEST ACCOMMODATION

B&B per room per night
s £46.00–£55.00
d £80.00–£96.00
Evening meal per person
£15.00

Mansion House Hotel

45 Esplanade, South Cliff, North Yorkshire YO11 2AY **t** (01723) 373930 **f** 0870 757 8468
e mansionhouse45@aol.com **w** mansionhousehotel.com

open All year
bedrooms 9 double, 3 twin, 2 single, 3 family
bathrooms All en suite
payment Credit/debit cards, cash/cheques

Beautifully restored, award-winning Regency hotel, superbly positioned on Scarborough's lovely Esplanade, with unrivalled panoramic sea views of the South Bay and harbour. Situated above the Spa and opposite the delightful Italian and Rose gardens, the hotel is within walking distance of the beach, cliff-lift and town.

Follow A171 from the north, A64 from the west or A163 from the south. In Scarborough, follow signs for South Bay. Hotel is on main esplanade.

Room General Leisure

SCARBOROUGH, North Yorkshire Map ref 1D3 — **GUEST ACCOMMODATION**

★★★
GUEST HOUSE

B&B per room per night
s £26.00–£28.00
d £42.00–£46.00

Marine View Guest House

Blenheim Terrace, Scarborough YO12 7HD **t** (01723) 361864 **e** info@marineview.co.uk

Friendly, family-run, non-smoking guesthouse overlooking beautiful North Bay. Close to town centre, both beaches and all attractions, including Scarborough's historic castle, cricket ground and Stephen Joseph Theatre.

open All year
bedrooms 3 double, 1 twin, 1 single, 1 family
bathrooms All en suite
payment Credit/debit cards, cash/cheques

Room General

SCARBOROUGH, North Yorkshire Map ref 1D3 — **GUEST ACCOMMODATION**

♦♦♦♦
GUEST ACCOMMODATION

B&B per room per night
s £30.00–£40.00
d £54.00–£56.00
Evening meal per person
£10.00

The Russell Hotel

22 Ryndleside, Scarborough YO12 6AD **t** (01723) 365453 **f** (01723) 369029 **e** info@russellhotel.net **w** russellhotel.net

open All year
bedrooms 3 double, 2 twin, 2 single, 3 family
bathrooms All en suite
payment Credit/debit cards, cash/cheques

The Russell Hotel is beautifully situated overlooking the Glen of Peasholm Park. Convenient for North Bay, town centre, indoor pool and bowls centre, all a few minutes' walk away. Visit Dalby Forest (free pass available), and North Yorkshire Moors and Railway, a short drive away. Lots of information and maps available.

⊕ *On reaching Scarborough, follow brown road signs marked 'North Bay and Leisure Parks'. These will bring you to Peasholm Park. We overlook the Glen.*

♥ *Low-season breaks from £69pppn for 3 nights. 3-night Christmas special.*

Room General Leisure

SCARBOROUGH, North Yorkshire Map ref 1D3 — **GUEST ACCOMMODATION**

★★
GUEST HOUSE

B&B per room per night
s £20.00–£25.00
d £40.00–£60.00
Evening meal per person
£7.00

The Wickets Guest House

138 North Marine Road, Scarborough YO12 7HZ **t** (01723) 373472 **e** thewickets@talktalk.net

The Wickets, a family-run bed and breakfast close to Peasholm Park, the castle, Sea Life Centre and many more attractions and beautiful walks. Overlooking the cricket grounds. Proprietors Pauline and Derrick.

open All year except Christmas
bedrooms 1 double, 1 twin, 1 single, 1 family, 2 suites
bathrooms 2 en suite
payment Cash/cheques

Room General Leisure

SCARBOROUGH, North Yorkshire Map ref 1D3 — **SELF CATERING**

★★★★
SELF CATERING

Units **1**
Sleeps **1–4**
Low season per wk
Min £250.00
High season per wk
Max £450.00

Lendal House, Scarborough

contact Petra Scott, Lendal House, 34 Trafalgar Square, Scarborough YO12 7PY
t (01723) 372178 **e** info@lendalhouse.co.uk **w** lendalhouse.co.uk

Luxury, self-contained ground-floor flat with four-poster bed. Near cricket ground; five minutes' walk to North Bay Beach and town centre. Also great for walks on the North York Moors.

open All year
payment Cash/cheques

Unit
General

Using map references

Map references refer to the colour maps at the front of this guide.

SCARBOROUGH, North Yorkshire Map ref 1D3 — **CAMPING & CARAVANNING**

★★★★★
HOLIDAY, TOURING & CAMPING PARK
ROSE AWARD

(220) £13.50–£18.50
(30) £13.50–£18.50
(50) £11.00–£18.50
(20) £190.00–£450.00
300 touring pitches

Flower of May Holiday Parks

Lebberston, Scarborough YO11 3NU **t** (01723) 584311 **f** (01723) 581361 **e** info@flowerofmay.com
w flowerofmay.com

payment Credit/debit cards, cash/cheques

Excellent facilities on family-run park. Luxury indoor pool, adventure playground, golf course. Ideal for coast and country. Prices based per pitch, per night for four people with car. Open April to October.

From A64 take the A165 Scarborough/Filey coast road. Well signposted at Lebberston.

Early-booking discount: £25 off full week's hire. 10% discount off full week's pitch fees, booked by post in advance.

General Leisure

SETTLE, North Yorkshire Map ref 1B3 — **GUEST ACCOMMODATION**

★★★
INN

B&B per room per night
s £20.00–£40.00
d £35.00–£65.00
Evening meal per person
£6.50–£10.50

Royal Oak Hotel

Market Place, Settle BD24 9ED **t** (01729) 822561 **f** (01729) 823102 **e** royaloaksettle@hotmail.co.uk

A 17thC coaching inn overlooking the bustling marketplace of Settle, yet ideally situated on the edge of the Yorkshire Dales.

open All year
bedrooms 4 double, 1 twin, 2 family
bathrooms All en suite
payment Credit/debit cards, cash/cheques

Room General Leisure

SETTLE, North Yorkshire Map ref 1B3 — **GUEST ACCOMMODATION**

♦♦♦♦
GUEST ACCOMMODATION

B&B per room per night
s Min £35.00
d Min £50.00

Scar Close Farm

Feizor, Austwick, Lancaster LA2 8DF **t** (01729) 823496 **f** (01729) 823496

open All year except Christmas and New Year
bedrooms 1 double, 1 twin, 1 family, 1 suite
bathrooms All en suite
payment Cash/cheques

High-standard, en suite accommodation and food. Farmhouse in picturesque hamlet in Yorkshire Dales. Popular for touring and walking. Double, twin, family rooms. Ground-floor room available.

Take A65, Settle bypass towards Kendal. After 3 miles (red markings) sharp right. After 0.25 miles 1st right, 0.5 miles to crossroads. Bed and breakfast on right.

Room General Leisure

SHEFFIELD, South Yorkshire Map ref 2B2 — **GUEST ACCOMMODATION**

♦♦♦
GUEST ACCOMMODATION

B&B per room per night
s £25.00–£35.00
d £40.00–£50.00

Beighton Bed & Breakfast

48-50 High Street, Beighton S20 1EA **t** (0114) 269 2004 **f** (0114) 269 2875
e Beightonbandb@aol.com **w** beightonbandb.co.uk

We are a family-run B&B, located eight miles south-east of Sheffield. Within easy reach of Meadowhall, Hallam FM Arena and Don Valley Stadium. Five minutes from M1 jct 31.

open All year
bedrooms 1 double, 3 twin, 4 single, 1 family
bathrooms All en suite
payment Cash/cheques, euros

Room General Leisure

SHEFFIELD, South Yorkshire Map ref 2B2 — **SELF CATERING**

★★★★
SELF CATERING

Units **1**
Sleeps **5**

Low season per wk
£250.00–£295.00
High season per wk
£350.00–£450.00

Coppice House Farm Cottage, Sheffield

contact Pamela Revitt, Coppice House Farm Cottage, Coppice House Farm, Rivelin Valley, Sheffield S6 5SG
t (0114) 230 1753

open All year
payment Cash/cheques

The cottage is situated on a working farm on the edge of the Peak District, within easy reach of Sheffield. It has a fully fitted kitchen, dining room, spacious lounge, downstairs toilet, bathroom with shower and bath and three bedrooms: single, double and twin. Wonderful views and fantastic walks. Farm shop.

⊕ *Situated on the A6101 off the A57 to Glossop. Easy access to M1 north and south. Three miles from Supertram system, with direct link to bus and train.*

❤ *Nov-Mar 3-night min booking £150 (excl Christmas and New Year).*

Unit
General 2 Leisure Shop 1.5 miles Pub 0.5 miles

SKIPTON, North Yorkshire Map ref 2B1 — **HOTEL**

★★★
HOTEL
SILVER AWARD

B&B per room per night
s £87.00–£137.00
d £99.00–£149.00
HB per person per night
£109.50–£159.00

The Coniston Hotel

Coniston Cold, Skipton BD23 4EB **t** (01756) 748080 **f** (01756) 749487
e info@theconistonhotel.com **w** theconistonhotel.com

open All year
bedrooms 38 double, 12 family
bathrooms All en suite
payment Credit/debit cards, cash/cheques

Set in 1,400 acres of country estate overlooking Coniston Hall lake – The Coniston Hotel is the perfect getaway. The hotel has luxury and standard bedrooms, many overlooking the lake. Great food in a superb setting with a warm welcome guaranteed. Try your hand at on-site outdoor activities such as clay-pigeon shooting, archery or falconry.

⊕ *Five miles north of Skipton on A65, right-hand side of the road.*

❤ *Leisure and weekend-break packages available.*

Room General Leisure

SKIPTON, North Yorkshire Map ref 2B1 — **GUEST ACCOMMODATION**

★★★★★
BED & BREAKFAST
SILVER AWARD

B&B per room per night
s £50.00
d £70.00–£80.00

Cononley Hall Bed & Breakfast

Main Street, Cononley, Skipton BD20 8LJ **t** (01535) 633923 **f** (01535) 630200
e cononleyhall@madasafish.com **w** cononleyhall.co.uk

open All year except Christmas and New Year
bedrooms 2 double, 1 twin
bathrooms All en suite
payment Credit/debit cards, cash/cheques

Grade II Listed Georgian house in unspoilt village, near to Skipton. Cononley Hall is ideally located for those wishing to explore the picturesque Yorkshire Dales or the Brontë countryside and attractions. All rooms are en suite and offer excellent facilities. Breakfast consists of local produce, including our own free-range eggs.

⊕ *From A629, follow sign for Cononley station. Across level crossing, up Main Street. New Inn on right. We are 25yds further up on left.*

❤ *Stays of 3 nights or more only £35pp (based on 2 people sharing). Children aged 3 and under – free.*

Room General Leisure

SKIPTON, North Yorkshire Map ref 2B1 — **SELF CATERING**

★★★-★★★★★
SELF CATERING

Units 7
Sleeps 1–4
Low season per wk
£150.00–£260.00
High season per wk
£230.00–£400.00

Cawder Hall Cottages, Skipton

contact Graham Pearson, Cawder Hall Cottages, Cawder Lane, Skipton BD23 2TD
t (01756) 791579 **f** (01756) 797036 **e** info@cawderhallcottages.co.uk **w** cawderhallcottages.co.uk

open All year
payment Credit/debit cards, cash/cheques

Peaceful, tastefully converted farm cottages in open countryside, one mile from castle and historic market town of Skipton. Suitable for disabled.

Follow Keighley Road from Skipton town centre. After 0.5 miles you will reach some 'keep left' bollards. Here turn left over canal bridge. Cawder Lane is 100yds on right.

Unit General Leisure Shop 1 mile Pub 0.5 miles

SLINGSBY, North Yorkshire Map ref 1C3 — **GUEST ACCOMMODATION**

★★★★
GUEST ACCOMMODATION

B&B per room per night
d £65.00–£75.00

Slingsby Hall

Slingsby YO62 4AL **t** (01653) 628375 **e** info@slingsbyhall.co.uk **w** slingsbyhall.co.uk

Elegant Georgian family house set in beautiful gardens, only three miles from Castle Howard. Tastefully decorated bedrooms offering very comfortable and spacious accommodation, with a welcoming and relaxed atmosphere.

open All year except Christmas and New Year
bedrooms 3 double, 1 twin
bathrooms All en suite
payment Cash/cheques

Room General Leisure

SNEATON, North Yorkshire Map ref 1D3 — **CAMPING & CARAVANNING**

★★★★
TOURING PARK

(93) £8.50–£19.60
(93) £8.50–£19.60
93 touring pitches

See Ad on inside front cover

Low Moor Caravan Club Site

Sneaton, Whitby YO22 5JE **t** (01947) 810505 **w** caravanclub.co.uk

payment Credit/debit cards, cash/cheques

Grassy, level, moorland site, sheltered by fir trees. Beautiful views over moorland. Ideal site for dog owners and a paradise for walkers. Open March to November.

Turn left off A171 (Scarborough-Whitby). In 13.5 miles turn onto B1416. In 1.75 miles turn left through red gates. Site on right.

Special member rates mean you can save your membership subscription in less than a week. Visit our website to find out more.

General

Don't forget www.

Web addresses throughout this guide are shown without the prefix www. Please include www. in the address line of your browser. If a web address does not follow this style it is shown in full.

SOUTH MILFORD, North Yorkshire Map ref 2C1 — **HOTEL**

HOTEL

B&B per room per night
d Min £82.00
HB per person per night
£59.00–£60.00

Best Western Milford Hotel

Great North Road, Peckfield, Leeds LS25 5LQ **t** (01977) 681800 **f** (01977) 681245
e enquiries@mlh.co.uk **w** mlh.co.uk

open All year
bedrooms 20 double, 16 twin, 10 family
bathrooms All en suite
payment Credit/debit cards, cash/cheques

Modern hotel, recently refurbished and fully air-conditioned, with excellent, award-winning cuisine in the Watermill Restaurant. Situated just off the A1, the hotel provides the ideal centre from which to explore the delights of Yorkshire. Whether it's the natural beauty of Yorkshire's moors and dales that interests you, the history of York, shopping in Leeds or Sheffield's Meadow Hall, you will be spoilt for choice.

On A63, 1.5 miles west of A1 jct 42, 5 miles east of M1 jct 46, 11 miles east of Leeds.

Special weekend leisure breaks from £59pppn including full choice from set-price rosette dinner menu.

Room General

STAITHES, North Yorkshire Map ref 1C3 — **GUEST ACCOMMODATION**

★★★★★
GUEST ACCOMMODATION GOLD AWARD

B&B per room per night
s £44.00–£54.00
d £72.00–£84.00
Evening meal per person
£20.00

Grinkle Lodge

Snipe Lane, Easington, Nr Staithes TS13 4UD **t** (01287) 644701 **e** grinklelodge@yahoo.co.uk
w grinklelodge.co.uk

open All year
bedrooms 2 double, 1 twin
bathrooms All en suite
payment Credit/debit cards, cash/cheques

A comfortable, peaceful, Victorian gothic house with large secluded garden in glorious countryside with distant sea view. Hand painted murals and antique furniture complement its age and character. Varied and generous breakfasts and imaginative, freshly prepared evening meals. Staithes four miles, Danby five miles.

A171 Whitby to Guisborough road travelling north, take right turn to Grinkle and Easington. After 2 miles take right turn after entrance to Grinkle Park Hotel.

Off-peak 2- and 3-night DB&B special offers (excl holiday times). Please enquire for details.

Room General Leisure

STAITHES, North Yorkshire Map ref 1C3 — **SELF CATERING**

★★★
SELF CATERING

Units 1
Sleeps 5
Low season per wk
£237.00–£325.00
High season per wk
£330.00–£595.00

Pennysteel Cottage, Staithes

contact Chris Wade, Waterfront Cottages, 2 Star Row, North Dalton, Driffield YO25 9UX
t (01377) 217662 & (01377) 217523 **f** (01377) 217754 **e** chris@adastra-music.co.uk
w waterfrontcottages.co.uk

open All year
payment Credit/debit cards, cash/cheques

Old fisherman's cottage of unique character with beamed ceilings, wood-panelled walls and wood-burning stove. All windows and terrace overlook the picturesque harbour of Staithes. Ideal for the coast and walking. Top-quality restaurant, pub serving food, cafes, art gallery and craft and local shops all within a few yards.

Go down hill into the old village. Bear right at the bottom. Take the 2nd passage on the left after the pub. Take left fork.

5% discount for repeat booking for 2007.

Unit
General Leisure Shop < 0.5 miles Pub < 0.5 miles

THIRSK, North Yorkshire Map ref 1C3 **HOTEL**

★★
HOTEL SILVER AWARD

B&B per room per night
s £55.00–£65.00
d £90.00–£125.00
HB per person per night
£55.00–£75.00

The Golden Fleece Hotel

42 Market Place, Thirsk YO7 1LL **t** (01845) 523108 **f** (01845) 523996
e reservations@goldenfleecehotel.com **w** goldenfleecehotel.com

open All year
bedrooms 19 double, 2 twin, 1 single, 1 family
bathrooms All en suite
payment Credit/debit cards, cash/cheques

Charming coaching inn set in the heart of Herriot Country. Delicious food and real ales. Conference and banqueting facilities. Pets and children welcome.

Turn off A168(M) at Thirsk turn-off. Good access to A19(M) north and A1(M) south.

Race goers welcome. Weekend offers. Pamper your partner.

Room General Leisure

THIRSK, North Yorkshire Map ref 1C3 **GUEST ACCOMMODATION**

★★★★
GUEST ACCOMMODATION SILVER AWARD

B&B per room per night
s £37.50–£60.00
d £66.00–£70.00
Evening meal per person
£20.00–£25.00

Borrowby Mill Bed and Breakfast

Borrowby, Nr Thirsk YO7 4AW **t** (01845) 537717 **e** mvpborrowby@compuserve.com
w borrowbymill.co.uk

open All year except Christmas and New Year
bedrooms 1 double, 2 twin
bathrooms All en suite
payment Credit/debit cards, cash/cheques

Tastefully converted 18thC flour mill in a secluded location between Thirsk and Northallerton. Convenient for touring North Yorkshire Moors and Dales. Cosy en suite rooms, excellent breakfasts and dinners prepared by chef/proprietor. Relax in our drawing room with library or explore our woodland gardens.

From A19 trunk road take turn for Borrowby. The mill is situated just before turning into the village.

In spring and autumn we run courses in all types of embroidery. Please ask for our brochure.

Room General Leisure

THIRSK, North Yorkshire Map ref 1C3 **SELF CATERING**

★★★
SELF CATERING

Units 1
Sleeps **2–10**
Low season per wk
£230.00–£310.00
High season per wk
£330.00–£410.00

80 St James Green

contact Joanna Todd, 79 St James Green YO7 1AJ
t (01845) 523522 **e** enquiries@80stjamesgreen.freeserve.co.uk

Four-bedroom terraced cottage. Comfortably furnished and well equipped, overlooking St James Green and only a few minutes' walk from town marketplace. Two twin rooms, one double, one family.

open All year
payment Cash/cheques

Unit
General Shop < 0.5 miles Pub < 0.5 miles

It's all in the detail

Please remember that all information in this guide has been supplied by the proprietors well in advance of publication. Since changes do sometimes occur it's a good idea to check details at the time of booking.

THIRSK, North Yorkshire Map ref 1C3 — **CAMPING & CARAVANNING**

★★
TOURING & CAMPING PARK

(60) £9.35–£19.60
(60) £9.35–£19.60
60 touring pitches

See Ad on inside front cover

Thirsk Racecourse Caravan Club Site

Station Road, Thirsk YO7 1QL **t** (01845) 525266 **w** caravanclub.co.uk

payment Credit/debit cards, cash/cheques

Pitches are within sight of the racecourse main stand, looking over the famous turf, surrounded by Herriot Country and the Dales. Open March to October.

Site on left of A61 (Thirsk-South Kilvington).

Special member rates mean you can save your membership subscription in less than a week. Visit our website to find out more.

General P Leisure

THORALBY, North Yorkshire Map ref 1B3 — **GUEST ACCOMMODATION**

★★★★
GUEST ACCOMMODATION
SILVER AWARD

B&B per room per night
d £58.00

The Old Barn

Thoralby, Leyburn DL8 3SZ **t** (01969) 663590 **e** sueandjohn@dalesbarn.co.uk **w** dalesbarn.co.uk

Relax and unwind in the serenity of Bishopdale, a little gem of a dale. Stylish accommodation, superb breakfasts, four excellent pubs for eating out close by. A warm, homely welcome awaits.

open All year except Christmas and New Year
bedrooms 1 double
bathrooms En suite
payment Cash/cheques, euros

Room General P Leisure

THORNE, South Yorkshire Map ref 2C1 — **CAMPING & CARAVANNING**

★★★★
TOURING PARK

(10) £10.00–£11.00
£10.00–£11.00
£5.00–£8.00
10 touring pitches

Elder House Touring Park

Elder House Farm, Crow Tree Bank, Doncaster DN8 5TD **t** (01405) 813173

Elder House Touring Park offers landscaped gardens in lovely surroundings and ample space for exercising your dog. Modern toilet block with showers and shaving points, also a disabled toilet and shower.

open All year except Christmas and New Year
payment Cash/cheques

General P Leisure

TODMORDEN, West Yorkshire Map ref 2B1 — **GUEST ACCOMMODATION**

★★★★
BED & BREAKFAST

B&B per room per night
s £24.00–£35.00
d £48.00

Cherry Tree Cottage

Woodhouse Road, Todmorden OL14 5RJ **t** (01706) 817492

Sympathetically restored, part-17thC country cottage, nestling amid the beautiful Pennine countryside, with modern amenities and lovely views. Easy access to the Pennine Way and the Calderdale Way. Friendly atmosphere.

open All year except Christmas and New Year
bedrooms 1 double, 2 twin
bathrooms All en suite
payment Cash/cheques

Room General

TRIANGLE, West Yorkshire Map ref 2B1 — **GUEST ACCOMMODATION**

♦♦♦♦
GUEST ACCOMMODATION

B&B per room per night
s £25.00
d £45.00
Evening meal per person
£10.00

The Dene

Triangle, Sowerby Bridge HX6 3EA **t** (01422) 823562 **e** knoble@uk2.net

A Grade II Listed building. A mill owner's house with interesting courtyard setting and walled garden. Built in 1828. Quiet location but easy access to M62 and local towns.

open All year except Christmas
bedrooms 1 double, 1 twin, 1 family
bathrooms All en suite
payment Cash/cheques

Room General P Leisure

WHITBY, North Yorkshire Map ref 1D3 — **GUEST ACCOMMODATION**

♦♦♦♦
GUEST ACCOMMODATION

B&B per room per night
s Min £29.00
d Min £58.00

Arches Guesthouse

8 Havelock Place, Hudson Street, Whitby YO21 3ER **t** (01947) 601880 & 0800 915 4256
e archeswhitby@freeola.com **w** whitbyguesthouses.co.uk

open All year
bedrooms 5 double, 2 single, 2 family
bathrooms 7 en suite, 2 private
payment Credit/debit cards, cash/cheques

The Arches prides itself on cleanliness, a warm welcome and large breakfasts. The ideal base for experiencing the old-world charms of this historic seaside town, whose tranquil and pleasant atmosphere guarantees rest and relaxation. Pets welcome. Ground-floor rooms. WHICH? Good B&B Guide.

⊕ *From York A64, take A169 at Malton towards Pickering. At Pickering continue on A169 towards Whitby. Join A171 and follow Whitby signs.*

❤ *Stay 7 nights for the price of 6 with our compliments.*

Room General Leisure

WHITBY, North Yorkshire Map ref 1D3 — **GUEST ACCOMMODATION**

♦♦♦♦
GUEST ACCOMMODATION SILVER AWARD

B&B per room per night
s £60.00–£120.00
d £75.00–£150.00

Cross Butts Stable Hotel and Restaurant

Guisborough Road, Whitby YO21 1TL **t** (01947) 820986 **w** cross-butts.co.uk

Dine in our stable restaurant, relax on the patio overlooking a large fish pond, enjoying open views, retreat to your courtyard room. We offer anniversary suites with whirlpool bath, to gallery-styled rooms.

open All year
bedrooms 7 double, 2 suites
bathrooms All en suite
payment Credit/debit cards, cash/cheques

Room General P Leisure

WHITBY, North Yorkshire Map ref 1D3 — **GUEST ACCOMMODATION**

★★★★
GUEST HOUSE

B&B per room per night
s £27.00
d £29.00
Evening meal per person
£14.00

Glendale Guest House

16 Crescent Avenue, Whitby YO21 3ED **t** (01947) 604242

bedrooms 3 double, 1 single, 2 family
bathrooms 5 en suite
payment Cash/cheques

Glendale is ideally situated on West Cliff, close to all amenities. It offers excellent home cooking to be enjoyed in a pleasant dining room. It also has a high standard of hygiene and cleanliness. Rooms are comfortable and attractively decorated with quality facilities. We provide private car parking. Pets welcome. Open March to November.

Room General P

A holiday for Fido?

Some proprietors welcome well-behaved pets. Look for the symbol in the accommodation listings. You can also buy a copy of our new guide – Pets Come Too! – available from good bookshops and online at enjoyenglanddirect.com.

WHITBY, North Yorkshire Map ref 1D3 **GUEST ACCOMMODATION**

★★★★
GUEST ACCOMMODATION
SILVER AWARD

B&B per room per night
s £30.00–£40.00
d £58.00–£64.00

Haven Crest

137 Upgang Lane, Whitby YO21 3JW **t** (01947) 605187 **f** (01947) 605189
e enquiries@havencrest.co.uk **w** havencrest.co.uk

open All year except Christmas and New Year
bedrooms 4 double
bathrooms All en suite
payment Credit/debit cards, cash/cheques, euros

Haven Crest, a guesthouse for the discerning guest, with warm, comfortable, double en suite rooms, TV and hospitality trays. A breakfast fit for a king offering a wide choice of cereals, fruits and yoghurts followed by a sizzling English breakfast, Whitby Kippers or even omelettes, but above all a warm welcome.

Room General P Leisure

WHITBY, North Yorkshire Map ref 1D3 **GUEST ACCOMMODATION**

★★★★
GUEST ACCOMMODATION

B&B per room per night
s £45.00–£87.90
d £59.00–£87.90
Evening meal per person
£15.00–£35.00

Seacliffe Hotel

12 North Promenade, Whitby YO21 3JX **t** (01947) 603139 **f** (01947) 600829
e stay@seacliffehotel.co.uk **w** seacliffehotel.co.uk

open All year except Christmas
bedrooms 10 double, 2 twin, 1 single, 2 family
bathrooms All en suite
payment Credit/debit cards, cash/cheques, euros

A very friendly and relaxing seafront hotel with magnificent sea views. En suite rooms with digital TV/DVD/CD, Internet, hairdryer, tea/coffee facilities. Delicious 'Heartbeat'-Country cooking. Traditional Aidensfield Arms licensed bar, with patio garden, serving meals and snacks. James Cook candlelit restaurant for superb wines and fine dining (booking advised). Golf course nearby.

From A171 follow signs for West Cliff and West Cliff car park. The establishment is on the seafront.

Captain Cook country break: 2 nights' DB&B £124pp. 'Heartbeat'-Country break: 3 nights' B&B for the price of 2 – autumn, winter and spring.

Room General P Leisure

WHITBY, North Yorkshire Map ref 1D3 **GUEST ACCOMMODATION**

★★★★
GUEST ACCOMMODATION

B&B per room per night
s £32.00–£42.00
d £64.00
Evening meal per person
£7.00

Sneaton Castle Centre

Sneaton Castle, Whitby YO21 3QN **t** (01947) 600051 **f** (01947) 603490 **e** sneaton@globalnet.co.uk
w sneatoncastle.co.uk

open All year except Christmas and New Year
bedrooms 11 twin, 1 family
bathrooms All en suite
payment Credit/debit cards, cash/cheques

St Francis House is set in the stunning grounds and gardens of Sneaton Castle, adjacent to St Hilda's Priory, on the outskirts of Whitby and the edge of the North York Moors. High-quality en suite accommodation. Excellent home-cooked breakfast. Ample free and safe parking.

Follow signs to Whitby then to Sandsend, leaving the A171 and joining the B1460 to Sneaton Castle. Do not go to Sneaton village!

Special 3 nights for the price of 2 offer, 1 Nov–31 Mar, subject to availability.

Room General P Leisure

WHITBY, North Yorkshire Map ref 1D3 — **SELF CATERING**

★★★★
SELF CATERING

Units 1
Sleeps 2–7
Low season per wk
£450.00–£600.00
High season per wk
£600.00–£780.00

Borough House, Whitby

contact Julie Besford
t (01430) 430963 **e** ibesford@lix.co.uk

17thC property in the centre of Whitby Old Town which will accommodate up to seven in comfort. Well-equipped kitchen, open fires and exposed beams on all four floors.

open All year
payment Cash/cheques

Unit
General Leisure Shop < 0.5 miles Pub < 0.5 miles

WHITBY, North Yorkshire Map ref 1D3 — **SELF CATERING**

SELF CATERING

Units 1
Sleeps 1–5
Low season per wk
£225.00–£340.00
High season per wk
£440.00–£540.00

Kingfisher Cottage, Whitby

contact Ingrid Flute, Holiday Accommodation Agency, 1 Hillcrest Avenue,, Scarborough YO12 6RQ
t (01723) 376777 **f** (01723) 376777 **e** info@ingridflute.co.uk **w** ingridflute.co.uk

Close to water's edge with unrivalled views on redevelopment of an old fishing wharf in Whitby. Within walking distance of all amenities. Ideal for all east coast and North Yorkshire Moors. Cottage ref: 2588.

open All year
payment Credit/debit cards, cash/cheques

Unit
General Leisure Shop < 0.5 miles Pub < 0.5 miles

WHITBY, North Yorkshire Map ref 1D3 — **SELF CATERING**

★★★
SELF CATERING

Units 1
Sleeps 4
Low season per wk
£260.00–£320.00
High season per wk
£320.00–£485.00

Raygill Cottage, Whitby

contact John Knell, Raygill Cottage, 25 Beckwith Crescent HG2 0BH
t (01423) 566280 **f** (01423) 566280

Spacious, single-storey accommodation located in a rural village close to Whitby, with private garden and off-road parking. An ideal base for visiting the North Yorkshire coast and moors.

open All year
payment Cash/cheques

Unit
General Shop 0.5 miles Pub < 0.5 miles

WHITBY, North Yorkshire Map ref 1D3 — **SELF CATERING**

★★★★
SELF CATERING

Units 1
Sleeps 4
Low season per wk
£240.00
High season per wk
£460.00

Stable Cottage

contact Martin & Chrissie Warner, Stable Cottage, Sandfield House Farm, Sandsend Road, Whitby YO21 3SR
t (01947) 602660 **e** info@sandfieldhousefarm.co.uk **w** sandfieldhousefarm.co.uk

A good-quality, stone-built cottage, located in beautiful countryside, 0.25 miles from long sandy beach. One mile from Whitby centre.

open All year except Christmas and New Year
payment Cash/cheques

Unit
General Leisure Shop 0.5 miles Pub 0.5 miles

Looking for a little luxury?

VisitBritain's unique Gold and Silver Awards are given to hotels and B&B guest accommodation achieving the highest levels of quality and service. There's more information at the front of the guide.

YORK, North Yorkshire Map ref 2C1 **HOTEL**

★★★
HOTEL

B&B per room per night
s £85.00–£120.00
d £115.00–£205.00
HB per person per night
£95.00–£123.00

Dean Court Hotel

Duncombe Place, York YO1 7EF **t** (01904) 625082 **f** (01904) 620305 **e** info@deancourt-york.co.uk
w deancourt-york.co.uk

open All year
bedrooms 24 double, 5 twin, 3 single, 4 family, 1 suite
bathrooms All en suite
payment Credit/debit cards, cash/cheques

Superbly appointed hotel opposite York Minster. All the historic attractions of York are within easy walking distance. All public areas have been tastefully refurbished (February 2004) along with the rosette-awarded restaurant, re-launched as DCH. The new decor is contemporary with magnificent design features. The Court Café-Bistro opened April 2006.

⊕ *A1 to A64 York, then city centre signs A19/A1237 Clifton direction to Bootham Bar, through archway, up one-way street or continue to lights and turn left. Hotel at end.*

❤ *2-night, mid-week literary breaks with top authors. 2-night, mid-week wine and food breaks with top wine producers.*

Room General Leisure

YORK, North Yorkshire Map ref 2C1 **HOTEL**

★★
HOTEL

B&B per room per night
s Min £46.00
d Min £70.00
HB per person per night
Min £50.00

Holgate Hill Hotel

124 Holgate Road, York YO24 4BB **t** (01904) 653786 **f** (01904) 643223
e info@holgate-hillhotel.co.uk **w** holgatehillhotel.co.uk

Family hotel where home cooking is a speciality. Close to the city centre, points of historic interest and the racecourse. Own car park.

open All year
bedrooms 9 double, 10 twin, 8 single, 3 family, 2 suites
bathrooms All en suite
payment Credit/debit cards, cash/cheques

Room General Leisure

YORK, North Yorkshire Map ref 2C1 **HOTEL**

HOTEL

B&B per room per night
s £70.00–£85.00
d £100.00–£160.00

Luxury Hotels by Marmadukes

St Peters Grove, Bootham, York YO30 6AQ **t** 0870 243 0765 **f** 0870 066 0159
e mail@marmadukesworld.com **w** marmadukesworld.com

open All year
bedrooms 18 double, 1 twin, 3 single
bathrooms All en suite
payment Credit/debit cards, cash/cheques

Marmadukes Luxury is one of York's finest small hotels, situated just a short walk from the minster and the ancient walls of this world-famous city. We have taken a classic Victorian gentleman's residence and created a beautifully designed, family-owned and operated hotel with an emphasis on comfort and friendliness.

⊕ *Marmadukes Luxury is 600m from Bootham Bar, opposite St Peter's School. We are on the Thirsk Road (A19) from the centre of York.*

Room General 12 Leisure

If you have access needs...
Look for the National Accessible Scheme symbols if you have special hearing, visual or mobility needs.

YORK, North Yorkshire Map ref 2C1 — **HOTEL**

★★
HOTEL

B&B per room per night
s £45.00–£65.00
d £85.00–£115.00
HB per person per night
£55.00–£65.00

Newington Hotel

147-157 Mount Vale, York YO24 1DJ **t** (01904) 625173 **f** (01904) 679937
e info@thenewington.co.uk **w** thenewington.co.uk

Hotel in a fine Georgian terrace, next to York's famous racecourse and within walking distance of city centre. Car park, indoor swimming pool, sauna.

open All year except Christmas
bedrooms 15 double, 11 twin, 6 single, 8 family, 4 suites
bathrooms All en suite
payment Credit/debit cards, cash/cheques

Room General Leisure

YORK, North Yorkshire Map ref 2C1 — **GUEST ACCOMMODATION**

★★★★★
BED & BREAKFAST
GOLD AWARD

B&B per room per night
d £65.00–£85.00

Alexander House

94 Bishopthorpe Road, York YO23 1JS **t** (01904) 625016 **e** info@alexanderhouseyork.co.uk
w alexanderhouseyork.co.uk

open All year except Christmas and New Year
bedrooms 3 double, 1 twin
bathrooms All en suite
payment Credit/debit cards, cash/cheques

Lovingly restored and completely renovated Victorian townhouse. Centrally situated only seven minutes' walk to city centre, historic attractions and York racecourse. Attractive bedrooms with refreshingly new, en suite facilities, fluffy bath sheets and luxury toiletries. Enjoy a delicious breakfast in our cosy Victorian dining room. Friendly and informal. Free parking.

A1, A64, A1036, head towards city centre. Approx 2 miles, turn right into Scarcroft Road, right again at the end of the road into Bishopthorpe Road.

Mid-week bargain breaks – see website for details.

Room General

YORK, North Yorkshire Map ref 2C1 — **GUEST ACCOMMODATION**

★★★
GUEST HOUSE

B&B per room per night
s Max £60.00
d Min £90.00

Ambleside Guest House

62 Bootham Crescent, Bootham YO30 7AH **t** (01904) 637165 **f** (01904) 637165
e ambles@globalnet.co.uk **w** ambleside-gh.co.uk

Tastefully furnished Victorian townhouse, a few minutes' walk to the city centre. Cleanliness and hospitality guaranteed at all times. Non-smoking establishment.

open All year except Christmas and New Year
bedrooms 6 double, 1 twin, 1 family
bathrooms 6 en suite
payment Credit/debit cards, cash/cheques

Room General 10

Country Code
Always follow the Country Code

- Be safe – plan ahead and follow any signs
- Leave gates and property as you find them
- Protect plants and animals, and take your litter home
- Keep dogs under close control
- Consider other people

YORK, North Yorkshire Map ref 2C1 **GUEST ACCOMMODATION**

♦♦♦♦ GUEST ACCOMMODATION SILVER AWARD

B&B per room per night
s £30.00–£65.00
d £60.00–£75.00

Ascot House

80 East Parade, York YO31 7YH **t** (01904) 426826 **f** (01904) 431077 **e** admin@ascothouseyork.com
w ascothouseyork.com

open All year except Christmas
bedrooms 8 double, 3 twin, 1 single, 3 family
bathrooms 12 en suite, 1 private
payment Credit/debit cards, cash/cheques

A family-run Victorian villa, built in 1869, with en suite rooms of character and many four-poster or canopy beds. Delicious English, continental and vegetarian breakfasts served. Fifteen minutes' walk to historic walled city centre, castle museum or York Minster. Residential license and residents' lounge, sauna and private, enclosed car park.

From A1/M1 take A64 then A1036 into York (also signed Heworth). About 100yds past 30mph signs, take 2nd exit off roundabout. Right at traffic lights into East Parade.

Room General

YORK, North Yorkshire Map ref 2C1 **GUEST ACCOMMODATION**

★★★★ GUEST ACCOMMODATION

B&B per room per night
s £30.00–£35.00
d £60.00–£70.00

Ascot Lodge

112 Acomb Road, York YO24 4EY **t** (01904) 798234 **f** (01904) 786742 **e** info@ascotlodge.com
w ascotlodge.com

open All year
bedrooms 1 twin, 4 single, 5 family
bathrooms 7 en suite
payment Cash/cheques

Receive a warm welcome at this beautiful mid-Victorian guesthouse on the west side of York. Peaceful, yet near to the city centre – 25 minutes' walk or 5-10 minutes by regular bus service. Luxurious, en suite double, family and single rooms. Non-smoking throughout. Secure, private car park. Vegetarians catered for.

We are situated on the B1224 just to the east of Acomb, a mile from the city centre. Take taxi or Blue Line No 1 bus from station.

Single-night price reduction for 2 or more nights' stay.

Room General Leisure

YORK, North Yorkshire Map ref 2C1 **GUEST ACCOMMODATION**

★★★★ GUEST ACCOMMODATION

B&B per room per night
s £35.00–£45.00
d £60.00–£80.00

Ashberry Hotel

103 The Mount, York YO24 1AX **t** (01904) 647339 **f** (01904) 647339 **e** ashbury@talk21.com
w ashburyhotel.co.uk

Ashberry Hotel is a double-fronted Victorian town house, only five minutes from the town centre, Minster, railway station and racecourse. Enjoy an award-winning breakfast.

open All year except Christmas
bedrooms 3 double, 2 twin, 1 family
bathrooms All en suite
payment Credit/debit cards, cash/cheques, euros

Room General

Take a break

Look out for special promotions and themed breaks. This could be your chance to indulge an interest, find a new one, or just relax and enjoy exceptional value! Offers are highlighted in colour (and are subject to availability).

YORK, North Yorkshire Map ref 2C1 — **GUEST ACCOMMODATION**

The Bar Convent

★★★
GUEST ACCOMMODATION

B&B per room per night
s £30.00–£43.00
d £57.00–£80.00

17 Blossom Street, York YO24 1AQ **t** (01904) 643238 **f** (01904) 631792 **e** info@bar-convent.org.uk
w bar-convent.org.uk

open All year except Christmas and New Year
bedrooms 3 double, 5 twin, 9 single, 1 family
bathrooms 3 en suite, 3 private
payment Credit/debit cards, cash/cheques

Grade 1 Listed Georgian convent. We provide self-catering facilities but have a superb in-house cafe providing home-cooked fayre. Coin-operated washing facilities for guests, two sitting rooms with TVs. Comfortable bedrooms. There is also a museum in the convent and several libraries to explore.

⊕ *From station turn right down hill to traffic lights. Convent is opposite. By car enter York via A1036. Turn right at Micklegate Bar.*

♥ *A 10% discount is available for charities and delegates using our conference facilities.*

Room General Leisure

YORK, North Yorkshire Map ref 2C1 — **GUEST ACCOMMODATION**

Bishops Hotel

★★★★★
GUEST ACCOMMODATION SILVER AWARD

B&B per room per night
s £40.00–£50.00
d £70.00–£120.00

135 Holgate Road, York YO24 4DF **t** (01904) 628000 **f** (01904) 628181
e enquiries@bishopshotel.co.uk **w** bishopshotel.co.uk

open All year except Christmas
bedrooms 2 double, 1 twin, 1 single, 3 family, 6 suites
bathrooms 11 en suite
payment Credit/debit cards, cash/cheques, euros

Elegant Victorian villa, peaceful yet near to the city centre. Spacious, comfortable interior with individually styled suites and bedrooms all en suite. Hearty breakfast using fresh, local produce. Non-smoking, fully licensed establishment with a friendly family atmosphere. Ideal base for exploring our beautiful Roman city and the Yorkshire countryside. 5% surcharge on credit cards.

⊕ *Take the A59 from the A1. This becomes Holgate Road where the establishment is situated. Or a 15-minute walk from the railway station.*

♥ *Celebration Package of flowers, chocolates and champagne. Business-traveller and off-peak, mid-week, short-break rates available Sun-Thu.*

Room General Leisure

YORK, North Yorkshire Map ref 2C1 — **GUEST ACCOMMODATION**

★★★
GUEST HOUSE

B&B per room per night
s £27.00–£29.00
d £42.00–£60.00

Bull Lodge Guest House

37 Bull Lane, Lawrence Street, York YO10 3EN **t** (01904) 415522 **f** (01904) 415522
e stay@bulllodge.co.uk **w** bulllodge.co.uk

open All year except Christmas and New Year
bedrooms 4 double, 1 twin, 1 single
bathrooms 3 en suite
payment Credit/debit cards, cash/cheques

Modern, detached property in quiet, tree-lined side-street location off A1079, 0.75 miles (1 km) to centre. Close to bus route, University of York, Business/Science Park, nature park/cycle way. En suites include ground-floor double ideal for mobility impaired guests. Dogs welcome by arrangement. Freshly cooked, full-choice breakfast. Private on-site parking, bicycle/motorbike garaging.

Bull Lane is off Lawrence Street (A1079 Hull Road), 2 miles A64, 500yds city walls at Walmgate Bar. Local bus (no 10) from rail station.

Quote advert for discount when booking, 5% on 3-/4-night stay, 10% on 5 or more nights (excludes Bank Holidays and special events).

Room General 4 P Leisure

YORK, North Yorkshire Map ref 2C1 — **GUEST ACCOMMODATION**

♦♦♦
GUEST ACCOMMODATION

B&B per room per night
s £27.00–£29.00
d £52.00–£60.00

Foss Bank Guest House

16 Huntington Road, York YO31 8RB **t** (01904) 635548 **w** fossbank.co.uk

open All year except Christmas and New Year
bedrooms 3 double, 1 twin, 1 single
bathrooms 3 en suite
payment Cash/cheques, euros

At the Foss Bank Guest House you will be assured of a friendly welcome, delicious breakfast and comfortable accommodation. Overlooking the River Foss, just a ten-minute stroll to the city centre. All rooms have showers or are fully en suite. Private car park. Non-smoking.

Follow inner ring road to the north east of the city centre and turn into Monkgate (A1036) near Monkbar Hotel. At roundabout bear left. Foss Bank is 200yds on the left.

Reduction for 3 nights or more, all year round.

Room General 6 P

YORK, North Yorkshire Map ref 2C1 — **GUEST ACCOMMODATION**

★★★★
GUEST ACCOMMODATION

B&B per room per night
s £70.00–£80.00
d £85.00–£120.00

The Guy Fawkes Hotel

25 High Petergate, York YO1 7HP **t** (01904) 671001 **f** (01904) 631315
e info@theguyfawkeshotel.com **w** theguyfawkeshotel.com

open All year except Christmas
bedrooms 10 double, 1 twin, 1 family
bathrooms All en suite
payment Credit/debit cards, cash/cheques

Chic town house with 12 individually designed bedrooms, some four-posters, located by York Minster within the city walls. Our restaurant, Guido's, offers fine food and wine in informal surroundings, with alfresco dining in our courtyard. Perfect for shopping, attractions and theatres.

York station 0.5 miles, 10 minutes' walk from Marygate and Gillygate parking.

Room General

YORK, North Yorkshire Map ref 2C1 — **GUEST ACCOMMODATION**

♦♦♦♦
GUEST ACCOMMODATION
SILVER AWARD

B&B per room per night
s £50.00–£95.00
d £80.00–£110.00

The Hazelwood

24-25 Portland Street, York YO31 7EH **t** (01904) 626548 **f** (01904) 628032
e Reservations@thehazelwoodyork.com **w** thehazelwoodyork.com

open All year
bedrooms 7 double, 3 twin, 1 single, 2 family
bathrooms All en suite
payment Credit/debit cards, cash/cheques

Situated in the very heart of York only 400yds from York Minster in an extremely quiet residential area. An elegant Victorian townhouse with private car park providing high-quality accommodation in individually designed en suite bedrooms. Extensive breakfast menu catering for all tastes including vegetarian. Completely non-smoking.

⊕ *Situated in city centre close to York Minster in side street off inner ring road (Gillygate). Best approached from the north on the A19.*

♥ *3 nights for the price of 2, Sun-Thu, 1 Nov-Easter (excl school holidays).*

Room General 8 P Leisure

YORK, North Yorkshire Map ref 2C1 — **GUEST ACCOMMODATION**

★★★
GUEST ACCOMMODATION

B&B per room per night
s £35.00–£60.00
d £50.00–£75.00

Holgate Bridge

106-108 Holgate Road, York YO24 4BB **t** (01904) 635971 **f** (01904) 670049
e info@holgatebridge.co.uk **w** holgatebridge.co.uk

The Holgate Bridge is the result of a tasteful conversion of two early Victorian town houses built in 1848. Ideally situated for sightseeing, the owners and staff will ensure your stay is enjoyable.

open All year except Christmas
bedrooms 7 double, 1 twin, 1 single, 4 family
bathrooms 10 en suite, 2 private
payment Credit/debit cards, cash

Room General P

YORK, North Yorkshire Map ref 2C1 — **GUEST ACCOMMODATION**

★★★★
INN

B&B per room per night
s £30.00–£40.00
d £50.00–£70.00

The Lighthorseman

124 Fulford Road, Fishergate YO10 4BE **t** (01904) 624818 **f** (01904) 624818
e janinerobinson03@aol.com **w** lighthorseman.co.uk

open All year except Christmas
bedrooms 5 double, 2 twin, 1 single
bathrooms All en suite
payment Credit/debit cards, cash/cheques

Local inn with eight letting bedrooms all en suite. Full breakfast, car parking. Short walk along river to town centre and racecourse. For more information visit our website.

Room General Leisure

Town, country or coast?

The entertainment, shopping and innovative attractions of the big cities, the magnificent vistas of the countryside or the relaxing and refreshing coast – this guide will help you find what you're looking for!

YORK, North Yorkshire Map ref 2C1 — **GUEST ACCOMMODATION**

★★★
GUEST HOUSE

B&B per room per night
s £30.00–£38.00
d £25.00–£30.00

Northolme Guest House

114 Shipton Road, York YO30 5RN **t** (01904) 639132 **e** g.liddle@tesco.net
w northolmeguesthouse.co.uk

open All year except Christmas and New Year
bedrooms 2 double, 1 twin, 1 single, 1 family
bathrooms 4 en suite
payment Cash/cheques

Family-run, 1930s detached house in a semi-rural residential area providing non-smoking, comfortable, stylish accommodation. All our tastefully decorated rooms have colour TV and a hostess tray. Our generous selection of full English or continental breakfast is highly complimented, and we also cater for special diets.

Situated on the A19 north of York, approx 1.5 miles from the city centre and approx 0.75 miles from the outer ring road.

Discounts on stays of 3 or more nights. Special winter-break prices. Please phone for details.

Room TV — General 2 P — Leisure

YORK, North Yorkshire Map ref 2C1 — **GUEST ACCOMMODATION**

★★★
GUEST ACCOMMODATION

B&B per room per night
s £30.00–£32.00
d £52.00–£64.00

Romley House

2 Millfield Road, York YO23 1NQ **t** (01904) 652822 **e** info@romleyhouse.co.uk
w romleyhouse.co.uk

open All year
bedrooms 2 double, 1 twin, 1 single, 2 family
bathrooms 2 en suite
payment Credit/debit cards, cash/cheques, euros

A family-run guesthouse, a few minutes' walk from the city centre and all attractions, offers a happy atmosphere, hearty breakfast and home comforts. All rooms are well appointed (en suite available) with colour TV, radio-alarm clock and tea-/coffee-making facilities.

Room TV — General P — Leisure

YORK, North Yorkshire Map ref 2C1 — **GUEST ACCOMMODATION**

★★★
GUEST ACCOMMODATION

B&B per room per night
s £40.00–£55.00
d £40.00–£55.00

Tyburn House

11 Albemarle Road, York YO23 1EN **t** (01904) 655069 **f** (01904) 655069
e york@tyburnhotel.freeserve.co.uk

Family-owned and -run guesthouse overlooking the racecourse. In a quiet and beautiful area, close to the city centre and railway station. Open Easter to November.

bedrooms 3 double, 1 twin, 1 single, 8 family
bathrooms All en suite
payment Cash/cheques

Room TV — General

To your credit

If you book by phone you may be asked for your credit card number. If so, it is advisable to check the proprietor's policy in case you have to cancel your reservation at a later date.

YORK, North Yorkshire Map ref 2C1 — **GUEST ACCOMMODATION**

★★★★
GUEST ACCOMMODATION

B&B per room per night
s £35.00–£80.00
d £65.00–£90.00
Evening meal per person
£14.95–£20.00

Warrens

30-32 Scarcroft Road, York YO23 1NF **t** (01904) 643139 **f** (01904) 658297
e info@warrenshotel.co.uk **w** warrenshotel.co.uk

open All year except Christmas
bedrooms 8 double/twin, 1 twin, 3 family
bathrooms All en suite
payment Credit/debit cards, cash/cheques

Excellent location in conservation area, 350m from city walls. Park your car in our private car park and walk into the city. All rooms are en suite and include hospitality tray, trouser-press, hairdryer, colour TV. Four-poster and king-size beds. Enjoy breakfast in our conservatory; vegetarian options available. WI-FI Internet and email access available.

Please visit our website for travel directions.

Reductions for 3 or more days Sun-Thu inclusive (excl Bank Holidays and race days). Enhance your stay with a champagne and chocolate package.

Room General P Leisure

YORK, North Yorkshire Map ref 2C1 — **GUEST ACCOMMODATION**

★★★★
GUEST ACCOMMODATION

B&B per room per night
s £45.00–£55.00
d £56.00–£80.00

The Willows B&B

Willow Close, nr Hessay, York YO26 8JU **t** (01904) 738206 **f** (01904) 738206 **e** cathgal2@aol.com
w thewillowsbb.co.uk

open All year
bedrooms 1 double, 1 twin
bathrooms All en suite
payment Cash/cheques

Set in the peace and quiet of the countryside with outstanding views across our lakes. We have luxurious, large, modern, en suite rooms and free private parking. If it is a quiet, relaxing break in the countryside you seek but on the doorstep of the City and York Racecourse – this is it.

Only 10 minutes from A1, A19 and A64. We are directly on A59 Harrogate Road near Hessay.

3 nights for the price of 2, 31 Oct-31 Mar. 2 nights minimum.

Room General 12 P Leisure

YORK, North Yorkshire Map ref 2C1 — **GUEST ACCOMMODATION**

★★★★
INN

B&B per room per night
s Min £47.50
d Min £69.95
Evening meal per person
Min £8.00

The Windmill

Hull Road, York YO19 5LP **t** (01904) 481898 **f** (01904) 488480 **e** j.saggers@btopenworld.com
w thewindmilldunnington.co.uk

open All year
bedrooms 5 double, 5 twin
bathrooms All en suite
payment Credit/debit cards, cash/cheques

Eat – drink – relax – sleep. At The Windmill a warm and friendly welcome awaits you. Home-made food is available daily; traditional Sunday lunches; a selection of ales and lagers. A function/meeting room is also available. Large car park. The Park and Ride for York city centre is only one mile away.

The Windmill is located on the A1079 1 mile from the A64-A1079-A166 interchange.

Room General P

YORK, North Yorkshire Map ref 2C1 — **GUEST ACCOMMODATION**

★★★★
GUEST ACCOMMODATION

B&B per room per night
s £27.50–£33.00
d £55.00–£66.00

York House

62 Heworth Green, York YO31 7TQ **t** (01904) 427070 **f** (01904) 427070
e yorkhouse.bandb@tiscali.co.uk **w** yorkhouseyork.com

open All year except Christmas and New Year
bedrooms 5 double, 1 twin, 1 single, 1 family
bathrooms 7 en suite, 1 private
payment Credit/debit cards, cash/cheques

Located a short stroll from the heart of one of Europe's most historic cities. York House is the perfect base for a visit to beautiful York or the surrounding area. A Georgian house with later additions, rooms feature all the modern conveniences you could possibly need for a relaxing, enjoyable stay.

⊕ *North east of York, A1036 signed city centre. Straight over roundabout and traffic lights, next mini-roundabout 3rd exit. York House is 300yds on left.*

❤ *Four-poster rooms £33.00-£38.00 ppn.*

Room · General P

YORK, North Yorkshire Map ref 2C1 — **SELF CATERING**

★★★★★
SELF CATERING

Units 1
Sleeps 1–2
Low season per wk
£399.00–£469.00
High season per wk
£469.00–£518.00

Bishopgate Pavilion – Bishops Wharf, York

contact John Graham, Bishopgate Pavilion-Bishops Wharf, 6 Dansie Close, Poole BH14 0LN
t 07973 857187 **e** john@johnkgraham.com **w** johnkgraham.com

open All year
payment Credit/debit cards, cash/cheques, euros

Situated in the heart of the historic city of York adjacent to Skeldergate Bridge. Private on-site parking. Large balcony over the river with spectacular city views. No fixed starting day or number of nights. Free wireless broadband. Strictly two adults. Non-smoking only. Proprietor with 30 years' luxury hotel and self-catering experience.

❤ *Short breaks all year.*

Unit TV
General P S Leisure Shop < 0.5 miles Pub < 0.5 miles

YORK, North Yorkshire Map ref 2C1 — **SELF CATERING**

★★★★
SELF CATERING

Units 4
Sleeps 1–4
Low season per wk
£700.00–£1,400.00
High season per wk
£700.00–£1,400.00

The Blue Rooms, York

contact Miss Kirsty Reid, The Blue Bicycle York Ltd, 34 Fossgate, York YO1 9TA
t (01904) 673990 **f** (01904) 677688 **e** blue-rooms@thebluebicycle.com **w** thebluebicycle.com

open All year
payment Credit/debit cards, cash/cheques

Overlooking the River Foss, The Blue Rooms occupy a secluded mews position and are equipped to the very highest standards. They offer luxury, convenience, privacy and comfort for that short romantic break or business trip. You will be welcomed on arrival with a bottle of champagne and fresh fruit basket, with our compliments.

⊕ *Please request directions at time of booking.*

Unit TV
General P S Leisure Shop < 0.5 miles Pub < 0.5 miles

Rest assured

All accommodation in this guide has been rated, or is awaiting assessment, by a professional assessor.

YORK, North Yorkshire Map ref 2C1 — **SELF CATERING**

★★★
SELF CATERING

Units 1
Sleeps 4
Low season per wk
Max £380.00
High season per wk
Max £420.00

Mayfield Cottage, York

contact Lorraine McDonald, No 3 The Brae, Bannockburn FK7 8LR
t (01786) 818994 **e** mayfield-cottage@hotmail.co.uk **w** mayfield-york.co.uk

open All year
payment Cash/cheques

Charming two-bedroom Victorian railway cottage situated in a quiet residential area close to York racecourse. Small cottage garden and rear courtyard with barbecue. Excellent local amenities and within easy walking distance of the city walls – ideally located for a perfect family holiday.

Turn off A64 at York West onto A1036 for city centre. Pass Tesco supermarket onto Tadcaster Road. Turn left at BP garage onto Mayfield Grove.

Short breaks available, min 3 nights, £210.

Unit
General Leisure Shop < 0.5 miles Pub < 0.5 miles

YORK, North Yorkshire Map ref 2C1 — **SELF CATERING**

★★★★
SELF CATERING

Units 1
Sleeps 4
Low season per wk
£375.00–£420.00
High season per wk
£430.00–£570.00

Merchants Gate, York

York City Apartments, Oaklands, Harewood Road, Collingham, Wetherby LS22 5B2
t (01937) 574836 **f** (01937) 574836 **e** enquiries@york-city-apartments.co.uk
w york-city-apartments.co.uk

open All year
payment Credit/debit cards, cash/cheques

York Tourism Bureau Self-Catering Accommodation of the Year Finalist. Two-bedroom, contemporary-styled apartment in recently built development. One double and one twin bedroom, kitchen/diner, separate living room with TV, DVD, video. Off-road courtyard parking. Ten minutes' walk to York city centre with its numerous attractions.

Flexible start dates and short breaks Nov-Apr.

Unit
General Leisure Shop < 0.5 miles Pub < 0.5 miles

YORK, North Yorkshire Map ref 2C1 — **SELF CATERING**

★★★
SELF CATERING

Units 1
Sleeps 2–6
Low season per wk
£350.00
High season per wk
£425.00–£500.00

Old Rectory, York

contact Mr & Mrs A W Morley, Old Rectory, 109-111 Hempland Lane, York YO31 1AT
t (01904) 423506 **e** oldrectoryyork@hotmail.co.uk **w** oldrectoryyork.co.uk

Extremely spacious self-contained flat within old Victorian rectory, comprising fitted kitchen, bathroom, living room, three bedrooms. Children welcome, cot and highchair available. Short stays, minimum three nights.

open All year
payment Cash/cheques

Unit
General Shop < 0.5 miles Pub < 0.5 miles

YORK, North Yorkshire Map ref 2C1 — **CAMPING & CARAVANNING**

★★★★★
TOURING & CAMPING PARK

£11.00–£12.50
£11.00–£12.50
40 touring pitches

Alders Caravan Park

Home Farm, Monk Green, Alne, York YO61 1RY **t** (01347) 838722 **f** (01347) 838722
e enquiries@homefarmalne.co.uk **w** alderscaravanpark.co.uk

On a working farm in historic parkland where visitors may enjoy peace and tranquillity. York (on bus route), moors, dales and coast nearby. Open March to October inclusive.

payment Cash/cheques

General Leisure

Quality visitor attractions

Enjoy England operates a Visitor Attraction Quality Assurance Service.

Participating attractions are visited annually by trained, impartial assessors who look at all aspects of the visit, from initial telephone enquiries to departure, customer service to catering, as well as all facilities and activities.

Only those attractions which have been assessed by Enjoy England and meet the standard receive the quality marque, your sign of a Quality Assured Visitor Attraction.

Look out for the quality marque and visit with confidence.

Places **to visit**

On the following pages you'll find an extensive selection of indoor and outdoor attractions in Northern England. Get to grips with nature, stroll around a museum, have an action-packed day with the kids and a whole lot more...

Attractions are ordered by county, and if you're looking for a specific kind of experience each county is divided into the following sections.

- **Family fun**
- **Nature and wildlife**
- **Historic England**
- **Outdoor activities**
- **Entertainment and culture**
- **Food and drink**
- **Relaxing and pampering**

Look out, too, for the Quality Assured Visitor Attraction sign. This indicates that the attraction is assessed annually and meets the standards required to receive the quality marque. So rest assured, you'll have a great time.

The index on page 294 will help you to locate specific attractions with ease. For more great ideas for places to visit contact a local Tourist Information Centre or log on to **enjoyengland.com**.

Please note, as changes often occur after press date, it is advisable to confirm opening times and admission prices before travelling.

KEY TO ATTRACTIONS

Cafe/restaurant .... ☕
Picnic area ....
No dogs except service dogs ....
Partial disabled access ....
Full disabled access .... ♿

Where prices aren't specified, use the following guide for an adult admission:

£	up to £5
££	between £5 and £10
£££	between £10 and £15
££££	more than £15

Fascinating facts and inventions at the Discovery Museum, Newcastle upon Tyne

Cheshire

FAMILY FUN

Cheshire Ice Cream Farm and Tea Rooms
Drumlan Hall, Newton Lane, Tattenhall CH3 9NE
t (01829) 770446 **w** cheshirefarmicecream.co.uk
open Apr-Oct, daily 1000-1730. Nov-Mar, daily 1030-1700.
admission Free
Over 30 award-winning flavours of ice cream, a picturesque location, country tearoom, rare breeds, under 6's play barn and much more.

Jodrell Bank Visitor Centre
Lower Withington SK11 9DL
t (01477) 571339 **w** jb.man.ac.uk/scicen
open Apr-Oct, daily 1030-1730. Nov-Mar, Tue-Fri 1030-1500, Sat-Sun 1100-1600.
admission £
Home of the Lovell radio telescope. 3D theatre, small exhibition, observational pathway and 35-acre arboretum. Shop, picnic areas and space cafe.

Oulton Park Race Circuit
Little Budworth CW6 9BW
t (01829) 760301 **w** brandshatchcircuits.co.uk
open All year, daily 0900-1730.
admission Free
Car and bike racing March to October. Spectacular racing rally and Early Drive Experiences. Corporate event days, conference and exhibition facilities and hospitality.

Roman Soldier Patrol
Chester Visitor Centre and Town Hall TIC, Chester CH1 1QX
t (01244) 351609 **w** romantoursuk.com
open Jun-Aug, Thu-Sun 1345-1500.
admission £
Patrol Fortress Deva with Caius Julius Quartus! In full battle gear, he takes you on patrol and evokes the exciting adventures of an imperial warrior.

NATURE AND WILDLIFE

Blue Planet Aquarium
Longlooms Road, Cheshire Oaks, Ellesmere Port CH65 9LF
t (0151) 357 8800
w blueplanetaquarium.com
open All year, Mon-Fri 1000-1700, Sat-Sun 1000-1800.
admission £££
The UK's largest aquarium. Experience an exhilarating journey through the waters of the world. Join the moving walkway and observe an underwater carnival.

Chester Zoo
Upton-by-Chester, Chester CH2 1LH
t (01244) 380280
w chesterzoo.org.uk
open Daily 1000-1600.
admission £££
One of Europe's leading conservation zoos, with over 7,000 animals in spacious and natural enclosures. Now featuring the 'Tsavo' African Black Rhino Experience.

Cholmondeley Castle Gardens
Cholmondeley Castle, Malpas SY14 8AH
t (01829) 720383
open Apr-Sep, Wed-Thu, Sun 1130-1700.
admission £
Ornamental gardens, lakeside picnic area, a variety of farm animals including llamas. Tearoom and attractive gift shop. Ancient private chapel in the park. Plants for sale.

Cotebrook Shire Horse Centre
Cotebrook, Tarporley CW6 9DS
t (01829) 760506
w cotebrookshirehorses.co.uk
open Daily 1000-1700.
admission ££
There are lots of things to see and do at the centre. As well as the magnificent heavy horses, there is also a variety of other animals and birds.

Marbury Country Park
Comberbach CW9 6AT
t (01606) 77741
w cheshire.gov.uk/countryside
open Daily.
admission Free
The parkland of Marbury Hall, which was demolished in 1968, with walks, picnicking and a bird hide overlooking the mere.

Admission is based on an adult price. Please check opening times and admission before travelling.

Ness Botanic Gardens
University of Liverpool, Ness, Neston CH64 4AY
t (0151) 353 0123
w nessgardens.org.uk
open Feb-Oct, daily 0930-1700. Nov-Jan, daily 0930-1600.
admission ££

The gardens contain a large collection of trees, shrubs, roses and heathers. Facilities include a visitor centre, tearoom, shop and plant nursery.

Tatton Park Gardens
Tatton Park, Knutsford WA16 6QN
t (01625) 534400
w tattonpark.org.uk
open Apr-Sep, daily 1000-1800. Oct-Mar, Tue-Sun 1100-1600.
admission £

Fifty acres of splendid gardens, including a Japanese garden, rated amongst the best in the country and representing over 200 years of design and history.

HISTORIC ENGLAND

Adlington Hall
Mill Lane, Macclesfield SK10 4LF
t (01625) 829206
w adlingtonhall.com
open Aug, Mon-Wed, Sun 1400-1700.
admission ££

The home of the Legh family since 1315, Adlington Hall combines a medieval Hall with Cheshire black-and-white and elegant Georgian additions.

Arley Hall and Gardens
Arley CW9 6NA
t (01565) 777353 **w** arleyhallandgardens.com
open Gardens: Apr-Sep, Tue-Sun, Bank Hols 1100-1700. Oct, Sat-Sun 1100-1700. Hall: Apr-Sep, Tue, Sun, Bank Hols 1200-1700.
admission £

Early Victorian country house set in 12 acres of magnificent gardens, with a 15thC Grade I tithe barn. Plant nursery, gift shop and restaurant. A plantsman's paradise!

Beeston Castle (English Heritage)
Chapel Lane, Beeston CW6 9TX
t (01829) 260464 **w** english-heritage.org.uk
open See website for details.
admission £

A ruined 13thC castle situated on top of the Peckforton Hills, with views of the surrounding countryside. Exhibitions are also held featuring the castle's history.

Capesthorne Hall
Siddington SK11 9JY
t (01625) 861221 **w** capesthorne.com
open Apr-Oct, Wed, Sun, Bank Hols 1330-1600.
admission £

Sculptures, paintings, furniture and family monuments. A Georgian chapel, tearooms, gardens, lakes, nature walks and a touring caravan park.

Chester Cathedral
St Werburgh Street, Chester CH1 2HU
t (01244) 324756 **w** chestercathedral.com
open All year, Mon-Sat 0900-1700, Sun 1300-1700.
admission £

A 14thC-15thC cathedral. The 12thC monastic building has a magnificent refectory, and the church has spectacular carved choir stalls. Each visitor receives an audio tour.

Chester Visitor Centre
Vicars Lane, Chester CH1 1QX
t (01244) 402111 **w** chestertourism.com
open All year, Mon-Fri 1000-1700.
admission Free

Probably the biggest visitor information centre in Britain, and the ideal starting point for exploring Chester. Activities, history displays, gift shop, tourist service and cafe.

Little Moreton Hall (National Trust)
Congleton CW12 4SD
t (01260) 272018 **w** nationaltrust.org.uk
open Mar, Wed-Sun 1130-1600. Apr-Oct, Wed-Sun, 1130-1700. Nov, Sat-Sun 1130-1600.
admission ££

A perfect example of a half-timbered moated manor house with Great Hall, Elizabethan long gallery and chapel. Elizabethan-style knot and herb garden.

Lyme Park (National Trust)
Disley SK12 2NX
t (01663) 762023 **w** nationaltrust.org.uk
open House: Apr-Oct, Mon-Tue, Fri-Sun 1300-1700. Park: Apr-Sep, daily 0800-2030. Oct-Feb, daily 0800-1800.
admission ££

A National Trust country estate set in 1,377 acres of moorland, woodland and park. The magnificent house has 17 acres of historic gardens.

Roman Amphitheatre – Chester
Vicars Lane, Chester CH1 2HS
t (01244) 402260
w chester.gov.uk/amphitheatre/index.html
open Daily.
admission Free

The largest stone-built amphitheatre in Britain, discovered in the 1930s. A long-running archaeological dig has helped to add to knowledge of Roman history.

Stanley Palace
Watergate Street, Chester CH1 2LF
t (01244) 325586 **w** stanleypalace.com
open All year, Tue-Fri 1000-1300, 1400-1600.
admission Free

A late-16thC town house with original beams and floors, 18thC panelling and a plaster ceiling. The house contains period furniture of historical interest.

Stretton Watermill
Mill Lane, Stretton SY14 7HS
t (01606) 41331 **w** strettonwatermill.org.uk
open Apr, Sat-Sun 1300-1700. May-Aug, daily 1300-1700. Sep, Sat-Sun 1300-1700.
admission £

A restored watermill with two wheels and two sets of machinery in working order. A separate stable block has displays of the mill and the miller's upstairs rooms.

Tabley House Stately Home
Tabley House, Tabley Lane, Knutsford WA16 0HB
t (01565) 750151 **w** tableyhouse.co.uk
open Apr-Oct, Thu-Sun, Bank Hols 1400-1700.
admission £

A fine Palladian house designed by John Carr in 1761, containing a collection of English paintings, period furniture and Leicester family memorabilia.

ENTERTAINMENT AND CULTURE

Boat Museum
South Pier Road, Ellesmere Port CH65 4FW
t (0151) 355 5017 **w** boatmuseum.org.uk
open Apr-Oct, daily 1000-1700. Nov-Mar, daily 1000-1600.
admission ££

Home to the UK's largest collection of inland waterway craft. Working forge, Power Hall, Pump House, seven exhibitions of industrial heritage and waterways objects. Gift shop and cafeteria.

CATALYST: Science Discovery Centre
Gossage Building, Mersey Road, Widnes WA8 0DF
t (0151) 420 1121 **w** catalyst.org.uk
open All year, Tue-Fri 1000-1700, Sat-Sun 1100-1700.
admission £

A unique, award-winning formula of interactive exhibits and historical displays. Hands-on exploration will allow you to discover the world of chemistry, its heritage and its effect on our lives.

Cheshire Military Museum
The Castle, Chester CH1 2DN
t (01244) 327617 **w** chester.ac.uk/militarymuseum
open All year, daily 1000-1600.
admission £

A registered museum with stunning displays and collections telling the story of Cheshire's military history through the use of tableaux and hands-on exhibits.

The Cycle Museum
Old Coach House, Walton Hall Gardens, Walton Lea Road, Walton WA4 6SN
t (01928) 711395
open Weekdays: by appointment. Sat-Sun 1000-1630.
admission Free

The museum is housed in the magnificent park and includes cycles from Holland, Germany, Sweden, China, America and France. Many machines are complemented with anecdotes of social history.

Admission is based on an adult price. Please check opening times and admission before travelling.

Grosvenor Museum
27 Grosvenor Street, Chester CH1 2DD
t (01244) 402008 **w** grosvenormuseum.co.uk
open All year, Mon-Sat 1030-1700, Sun 1300-1600.
admission Free

See Chester come to life, from Roman soldiers to a historic house through time. Exciting special exhibitions, events and activities throughout the year.

Hack Green Secret Nuclear Bunker
PO Box 127, Nantwich CW5 8AQ
t (01270) 629219 **w** hackgreen.co.uk
open Apr-Oct, daily 1030-1730. Nov, Jan-Mar, Sat-Sun 1100-1630.
admission ££

Semi-submerged nuclear bunker containing a decontamination dormitory, sick bay, early-warning systems, communications centre, radio room and BBC studio.

Macclesfield Silk Museum
The Heritage Centre, Roe Street, Macclesfield SK11 6UT
t (01625) 613210 **w** silk-macclesfield.org
open All year, Mon-Fri 1100-1600, Sat 1100-1700, Sun 1200-1600.
admission £

The museum is situated in a Grade II Listed former Sunday school and presents the story of silk in Macclesfield, told through an award-winning audiovisual programme.

Quarry Bank Mill (National Trust)
Styal SK9 4LA
t (01625) 527468 **w** quarrybankmill.org.uk
open Apr-Sep, daily 1100-1700. Oct-Feb, Wed-Sun 1100-1600.
admission ££

A Georgian water-powered cotton-spinning mill, with five floors of displays and demonstrations and 300 acres of parkland surroundings.

Salt Museum
162 London Road, Northwich CW9 8AB
t (01606) 41331 **w** saltmuseum.org.uk
open Apr-Jul, Tue-Fri 1000-1700, Sat-Sun 1400-1700. Aug, Mon, Bank Hols 1400-1700, Tue-Fri 1000-1700, Sat-Sun 1400-1700. Sep-Mar, Tue-Fri 1000-1700, Sat-Sun 1400-1700.
admission £

The museum deals with the history and development of salt making in Cheshire from early times to the present day.

Warrington Museum and Art Gallery
Museum Street, Warrington WA1 1JB
t (01925) 442733 **w** warrington.gov.uk/museum
open All year, Mon-Fri 0900-1700, Sat 0900-1600.
admission Free

A museum combining diverse collections, photographic archive, mainly 19thC British fine art, and one of the best temporary exhibition spaces in the North West.

West Park Museum and Art Gallery
Prestbury Road, Macclesfield SK10 3BJ
t (01625) 613210
w silk-macclesfield.org
open Apr-Oct, Tue-Sun 1330-1630. Nov-Mar, Tue-Sun 1300-1600.
admission Free

A collection of paintings by C F Tunnicliffe and other artists. Displays include Egyptian antiquities and items of local historical interest.

RELAXING AND PAMPERING

McArthur Glen Designer Outlet Cheshire Oaks
Kinsey Road, Ellesmere Port CH65 9JJ
t (0151) 348 5600
w mcarthurglen.com/cheshireoaks
open All year, Mon-Fri 1000-2000, Sat 1000-1900, Sun 1000-1700, Bank Hols 1000-1800.
admission Free

The UK's largest designer outlet with over 140 stores offering discounts of up to 50% – all day, every day.

County Durham

FAMILY FUN

Bowlees Picnic Area
Newbiggin, Barnard Castle DL12 0XF
t (01913) 833594
w durham.gov.uk
open Daily.
admission Free

The picnic area is in a sheltered side valley of Teesdale. There are four waterfalls within the site and more falls alongside a footpath to Gibsons Cave.

Castlegate Quay Watersports Centre
Moat Street, Stockton-on-Tees TS18 3AZ
t (01642) 528689 **w** teesactive.co.uk
open All Year, summer 0900-2100, winter 0900-1700.
admission Free

A purpose-built centre specialising in water sports such as sailing, kayaking, canoeing and power boating. Both children and adults welcome.

Causey Arch and Picnic Area
The Derwent Centre, Stanley DH8 5SD
t (01913) 833594 **w** durham.gov.uk
open Daily.
admission Free

The world's oldest-surviving railway bridge, built between 1725 and 1726, stands over a rocky gorge. Woodland walks and access to Tanfield Railway.

Diggerland
Riverside Industrial Estate, Langley Park, Durham DH7 9TT
t 0870 034 4437 **w** diggerland.com
open Apr-Nov, Sat-Sun 1000-1700. School Holidays, daily 1000-1700.
admission £££

An adventure park based on JCB diggers and dumpers. Huge variety of equipment. Rides available for children of all ages, and drives from five years and upwards.

Hall Hill Farm
Lanchester DH7 0TA
t (01388) 731333 **w** hallhillfarm.co.uk
open Apr-Sep, daily 1030-1700. Oct, Sat-Sun 1030-1700. Dec, Sat-Sun 1030-1600.
admission £

Family fun set in attractive countryside with an opportunity to see and touch the animals at close quarters. Farm trailer ride, gift shop, tearoom, picnic and play area.

Splash
Church Road, Stockton-on-Tees TS18 3AZ
t (01642) 527272 **w** teesactive.co.uk
open All Year, Mon-Fri 0730-2115, Sat 1045-1630, Sun 0900-1630.
admission £

This exciting leisure complex provides fun for all the family, with two flume slides, a spa pool, a learner pool and a cafeteria on site. One visit is never enough!

Top Gear Indoor Karting
13 Rennys Lane, Durham DH1 2RS
t (01913) 860999 **w** durhamkarting.co.uk
open All year, Mon-Fri 1300-2100, Sat 0900-1900, Sun 1000-1800.
admission ££££

Indoor karting for anyone over eight years old. Fast, safe and exciting fun for all the family. Minimum height 1.4m/4ft 7in.

Weardale Railway
Stanhope Station, Station Road, Bishop Auckland DL13 2YS
t 0845 600 1348
w weardale-railway.org.uk
open Please phone for timetable.
admission ££

A steam (subject to availability) railway running for 8 miles between Wolsingham and Stanhope in beautiful Weardale within the North Pennines Area of Outstanding Natural Beauty.

NATURE AND WILDLIFE

Billingham Beck Valley Country Park
Visitor Centre, Ecology Park, Billingham TS23 1RA
t (01642) 360376
w stockton.gov.uk
open Park: Daily. Visitor Centre: All year, Sun 1000-1600.
admission Free

Country park with wetlands, wildflower meadows, picnic site and a ten-acre ecology park with visitor centre. Also shop, car park, various events and guided walks.

Burn Valley Gardens
Hartlepool TS25 5QS
t (01429) 523421
open Daily dawn to dusk.
admission Free

Opened in 1898, the gardens provide the town's central green belt area. Children's playground and bowls. A walkway takes you through the family wood, on to Ward Jackson Park.

Butterfly World
Preston Park, Yarm Road, Stockton-on-Tees TS18 3RH
t (01642) 791414
open Mar-Oct, daily 1000-1630
admission £

An indoor tropical garden populated by exotic free-flying butterflies and complemented by a display of fascinating insects.

Castle Eden Dene National Nature Reserve
Oakside Dene Lodge, Stanhope Chase, Peterlee SR8 1NJ
t (01915) 860004
w naturalengland.org.uk
open Daily, 0830-dusk.
admission Free

Picturesque wooded valley. National Nature Reserve with 550 acres of natural woodland and 12 miles of footpaths. Wild flowers, woodland birds and red squirrels can be seen.

For key to symbols see page 211.

Crook Hall and Gardens
Sidegate, Durham DH1 5SZ
t (01913) 848028 **w** crookhallgardens.co.uk
open See website for details.
admission £
Medieval hall with Jacobean drawing room, turret and gallery, set in four acres of gardens. Two walled gardens, maze, silver and white garden and Shakespeare garden.

Eggleston Hall Gardens
Garden Cottage, Eggleston DL12 0AG
t (01833) 650115 **w** egglestonhallgardens.co.uk
open All year, Mon-Sun, Bank Hols 1000-1700.
admission £
Old established gardens growing many species of plants. Vegetable garden with organically grown vegetables for sale in season. Also trees, shrubs, hardy perennials and herbs.

Hardwick Country Park
Sedgefield TS21 2EH
t (01913) 833594 **w** durham.gov.uk
open All year, dawn-dusk.
admission Free
A former landscaped garden designed by James Paine in the 18th century. Contains the remains of several follies and the serpentine lake.

High Force Waterfall
Forest-in-Teesdale, Middleton-in-Teesdale, Barnard Castle DL12 0QG
t (01833) 640209 **w** rabycastle.com/high_force.htm
open Apr-Oct, Mon-Sun 1000-1630. Nov-Mar, Tue,Thu,Sat,Sun 1000-1500.
admission £
Take a woodland walk to see England's largest waterfall, and the most majestic on the River Tees. Gift shop, picnic area and parking.

Houghall College
East Durham and Houghall Community College, Houghall, Durham DH1 3SG
t (01913) 754700 **w** edhcc.ac.uk
open Daily 1000-1600.
admission Free
Extensive gardens used as a horticultural training resource by Houghall College. Features include glasshouses, woodland garden, general display gardens and the newly opened 'The World of Trees' arboretum.

Low Barns Nature Reserve and Visitor Centre
Durham Wildlife Trust, Witton-le-Wear DL14 0AG
t (01388) 488728 **w** durhamwildlifetrust.org.uk
open Daily 1000-1600.
admission Free
Forty-hectare nature reserve with nature trail, bird hides, bird feeding station, observatory, woodland, ponds, meadow, butterfly garden, lake, river, visitor centre and coffee shop.

Pow Hill Country Park
East Cote House Farm, Edmundbyers, Consett DH8 9ND
t (01913) 833594 **w** durham.gov.uk
open Daily.
admission Free
The Country Park is a mixed woodland and moorland site on the banks of the Derwent Reservoir, offering panoramic views towards Castleside and the Hownsgill Viaduct.

Teesside White Water Course
Tees Barrage Way, Stockton-on-Tees TS18 2QW
t (01642) 678000 **w** 4seasons.co.uk
open Apr-Oct, daily 0800-2000. Nov-Mar, please phone for details.
admission ££
Britain's finest purpose-built course is a world-class facility, fully adjustable for absolute beginners to world champions. Cafe and shop. Canoeing, kayaking and rafting.

University of Durham Botanic Garden
Hollingside Lane, Durham DH1 3TN
t (01913) 345521 **w** dur.ac.uk/botanic.garden/
open Apr-Oct, daily 1000-1700. Nov-Feb, daily 1100-1600.
admission £
A botanic garden set in countryside and mature woodland. There are plants from North America, Himalayas and China as well as rainforest and desert plants. Also a Mediterranean conservatory.

Whitworth Hall Country Park
Whitworth, Spennymoor DL16 7QX
t (01388) 811772 **w** whitworthhall.co.uk
open Daily.
admission Free
Historic parkland with resident deer, ornamental lake, Victorian walled garden, Britain's most northerly vineyard, children's playground and Grade II listed building.

HISTORIC ENGLAND

Auckland Castle
Bishop Auckland DL14 7NR
t (01388) 601627 **w** auckland-castle.co.uk
open Apr-Jun, Mon, Sun 1400-1700. Jul-Aug, Mon, Wed 1100-1700, Sun 1400-1700. Sept, Mon, Sun 1400-1700.
admission £
Principal country residence of the Prince Bishops since 1190, the castle is now home to the Bishop of Durham. Visit St Peter's Chapel, state rooms and deer park.

Barnard Castle
Barnard Castle DL12 8PR
t (01833) 638212 **w** english-heritage.org.uk
open Apr-Sep, daily 1000-1800. Oct, daily 1000-1600. Nov-Mar, Mon, Thu-Sun 1000-1600.
admission £

A ruined castle overlooking the River Tees. Remains include the 14thC great hall, the three-storey keep and the circular round tower which inspired Sir Walter Scott (Rokeby).

Bowes Castle
Bowes, Barnard Castle DL12 9HP
t (01833) 638212 **w** english-heritage.org.uk
open Daily.
admission Free

Three-storey-high stone keep, dating from 1170 and set within the earthworks of a Roman fort, guarding the strategic Stainmore pass over the Pennines

Croxdale Hall
Durham DH6 5JP
t (01913) 780911
open Please see website for details.
admission Free

Croxdale, home to the Salvin family since 1402, stands boldly over the River Wear. Mid-Georgian rooms with fine rococo ceilings, chapel, walled gardens and orangery.

Durham Castle
Palace Green, Durham DH1 3RW
t (01913) 344106 **w** durhamcastle.com
open Apr-Sep, daily 1000-1200, 1400-1630. Oct-Mar, Mon, Wed, Sat-Sun 1400-1600.
admission £

Castle founded in 1072. Norman chapel dating from 1080. Kitchens and great hall dating from 1499 and 1284 respectively. A fine example of a motte-and-bailey castle.

Durham Cathedral
The College, Durham DH1 3EH
t (01913) 864266 **w** durhamcathedral.co.uk
open Apr-Jul, Mon-Sat 0930-1800, Sun 0930-1730. Aug, daily 0930-2000. Sep-Mar, Mon-Sat 0930-1800, Sun 0930-1730.
admission Free

Durham Cathedral is thought by many to be the finest example of Norman church architecture in England. The cathedral contains the tombs of St Cuthbert and The Venerable Bede.

Durham Heritage Centre and Museum
St Mary-le-Bow, North Bailey, Durham DH1 3ET
t (01913) 845589
open Apr-May, Sat-Sun, Bank Hols 1400-1630. June, daily 1400-1630. Jul-Sep, daily 1100-1630. Oct, Sat-Sun, Bank Hols 1400-1630.
admission £

Museum of local history which tells the story of Durham from the 10th century to the present day using displays, models and artefacts. Brass rubbing and shop.

Egglestone Abbey
Barnard Castle DL12 9TN
t (01912) 691200 **w** english-heritage.org.uk
open All year, Mon-Sun, Bank Hols 1000-1800.
admission Free

Picturesque ruins of Premonstratensian abbey. Greater part of the nave and chancel still standing, with remains of cloistral buildings.

Finchale Priory
Brasside, Durham DH1 5SH
t (01913) 863828 **w** english-heritage.org.uk
open Please see website.
admission Free

A 13thC Benedictine priory by the River Wear, built around the tomb of St Godric who lived in hermitage until he was 105.

Hartlepool Historic Quay
Part of Hartlepool's Maritime Experience, Jackson's Dock, Hartlepool TS24 0XZ
t (01429) 860077
w hartlepoolsmaritimeexperience.com
open Daily 1000-1700.
admission ££

An authentic reconstruction of an 18thC seaport. Step back in time to a remarkable period in British history. A superb day out for all ages.

HM Bark Endeavour
Castlegate Quay, Riverside, Stockton-on-Tees TS18 1BZ
t (01642) 608038 **w** hmbarkendeavour.co.uk
open Pre-bookings only. Please phone for details.
admission Free

Heritage visitor attraction. Full-size replica of Captain James Cook's ship HM Bark Endeavour. Situated on the river with shop, picnic area and children's games area.

HMS Trincomalee
Part of Hartlepool's Maritime Experience, Jackson's Dock, Hartlepool TS24 0XZ
t (01429) 223193 **w** hms-trincomalee.co.uk
open Apr-Oct, daily 1000-1700. Nov-Mar, daily 1030-1600.
admission ££

HMS Trincomalee, built in 1817, is the oldest ship afloat in the UK. Come aboard for a unique experience of Navy life two centuries ago.

Raby Castle
Staindrop, Darlington DL2 3AH
t (01833) 660202 **w** rabycastle.com
open Castle: May-Jun, Sep, Wed, Sun 1300-1700. Jul-Aug, Mon-Fri, Sun 1300-1700. Bank Hols including Sat 1300-1700. Park & Gardens: May-Jun, Sept, Wed, Sun 1100-1730. Jul-Aug, Mon-Fri, Sun 1100-1730. Bank Hols including Sat 1100-1730.
admission ££

The medieval castle, home of Lord Barnard's family since 1626, includes a 200-acre deer park, walled gardens, carriage collection, adventure playground, shop and tearoom.

Rokeby Park
Rokeby, Barnard Castle DL12 9RZ
t (01833) 690100 **w** rokebypark.com
open May-Sep, Mon-Tue 1400-1700.
admission £

A beautiful Palladian-style country house which was the setting for Sir Walter Scott's ballad 'Rokeby', containing a unique collection of 18thC needlework and period furniture.

Summerhill Visitor Centre
Summerhill Lane, Hartlepool TS25 4LL
t (01429) 284584 **w** sunnysummerhill.com
open All year, Mon-Sun, Bank Hols 0900-1700.
admission Free

A 100-acre country park on the western edge of Hartlepool which has been transformed for conservation and outdoor sports.

OUTDOOR ACTIVITIES

Prince Bishop River Cruiser
Browns Boathouse Ltd, Elvet Bridge, Durham DH1 3AF
t (01913) 869525 **w** princebishoprc.co.uk
open Apr-Oct, daily, please phone for details.
admission £

Luxury cruiser (seats 150) which sails in all weather, all year round. Observation deck, lower deck saloon, bar, cafe and commentary. Also rowing boats for hire.

ENTERTAINMENT AND CULTURE

Beamish, The North of England Open Air Museum
Beamish DH9 0RG
t (01913) 704000 **w** beamish.org.uk
open Apr-Oct, daily 1000-1700, Nov-Mar, Tue-Thu, Sat-Sun 1000-1600.
admission ££

Visit the town, colliery village, working farm, Pockerley Manor and 1825 railway, recreating life in the North East in the early 1800s and 1900s.

The Bowes Museum
Barnard Castle DL12 8NP
t (01833) 690606 **w** thebowesmuseum.org.uk
open Daily 1100-1700.
admission ££

This fascinating museum houses a collection of outstanding European fine and decorative art and offers an exhibition programme alongside special events and children's activities.

Durham Light Infantry Museum and Durham Art Gallery
Aykley Heads, Durham DH1 5TU
t (01913) 842214 **w** durham.gov.uk/dli
open Apr-Oct, daily 1000-1700. Nov-Mar, daily 1000-1600.
admission £

The museum tells the 200-year-old story of Durham's famous regiment. The art gallery presents an exciting programme of exhibitions and events, including concerts, talks and workshops.

Killhope, The North of England Lead Mining Museum
Weardale, Cowshill DL13 1AR
t (01388) 537505 **w** durham.gov.uk/killhope
open Apr-Oct, daily 1030-1700, Bank Hols 1030-1730.
admission £

National-award-winning Quality Assured Visitor Attraction. The most complete lead mining site in Britain. See the North of England's largest working water wheel and dress up in Victorian-style clothes. Shops and cafe.

Locomotion: the National Railway Museum at Shildon
Shildon DL4 1PQ
t (01388) 777999 **w** locomotion.uk.com
open Apr-Sep, daily 1000-1700. Sep-Dec, Wed-Sun 1000-1600.
admission Free

The museum incorporates historic monuments and buildings with interactive displays. View approximately 60 vehicles. Play area, picnic area, modern-art monument, gift shop, cafe.

Museum of Hartlepool
Part of Hartlepool's Maritime Experience, Jackson's Dock, Hartlepool TS24 0XZ
t (01429) 860077
w hartlepoolsmaritimeexperience.com
open Daily 1000-1700.
admission Free

Hartlepool Museum, situated beside Hartlepool Historic Quay, includes local historical exhibits, PSS Wingfield Castle, exhibitions and the original lighthouse light.

Preston Hall Museum
Preston Park, Yarm Road, Stockton-on-Tees TS18 3RH
t (01642) 527375
w stockton.gov.uk/museums
open Apr-Sep, daily 1000-1645. Oct-Mar, Mon-Sat 10-1630, Sun 1400-1630.
admission £

A Georgian country house set in over 100 acres of parkland overlooking the River Tees. There is a museum of social history, picnic areas, tropical-bird aviary and children's play area.

RELAXING AND PAMPERING

Dalton Park
Murton SR7 9HU
t (01915) 266500 **w** dalton-park.co.uk
open All year, Mon-Wed, Fri 1000-1800, Thu 1000-2000, Sat 0900-1800, Sun 1030-1700, Bank Hols 1000-1700.
admission Free

Retail outlet centre with up to 50% off the best brands. Cafes, creche and children's play area, all within 55 acres of parkland.

Cumbria – The Lake District

FAMILY FUN

Aquarium of the Lakes
Lakeside, Newby Bridge LA12 8AS
t (01539) 530153 **w** aquariumofthelakes.co.uk
open Apr-Oct. daily 0900-1700. Nov-Mar, daily 0900-1700.
admission ££

The UK's largest collection of freshwater fish in naturally themed habitats. Discover an underwater tunnel featuring giant carp and diving ducks. Spot British sharks, otters, harvest mice and voles.

Greystoke Gill Pottery
Greystoke Gill, Penrith CA11 0UQ
t (01768) 483123 **w** greystokegillpottery.co.uk
open Apr-Oct, daily 1000-1700. Nov-Mar, Wed-Sun 1000-1700.
admission Free

Small studio pottery where visitors can see work in progress, and on certain days make their own pot. Handmade individual and domestic pottery and wood-fired stoneware, glazed with rich, multiple colours.

Lake District Coast Aquarium Maryport
South Quay, Maryport CA15 8AB
t (01900) 817760
w lakedistrict-coastaquarium.co.uk
open All year, daily 1000-1700.
admission £

An all-year, all-weather attraction. Gift shop, mini-golf, remote-control boats. Cafe with harbour view. Regular fish feeding and talks.

Lakeland Heavy Horse Centre
Craika Farm, Dearham, Maryport CA15 7EH
t (01900) 818023
w lakesheavyhorses.co.uk
open Apr-Sep, daily 1000-1600. Oct, Tue-Sun 1000-1600.
admission ££

Heavy-horse demonstrations, pets' corner, cafe and various visitor attractions on a working farm. The centre was only opened to the public in July 2006.

Lakeland Miniature Village
The Coach House, Winder Lane, Grange-over-Sands LA11 7LE
t (015395) 58500
w lakelandminiaturevillage.com
open All year, daily 1030-dusk.
admission £

A fascinating insight into the buildings of Lakeland's yesteryear. Over 120 buildings made from Coniston slate. Houses, farms, barns etc, all hand made.

Lakeside & Haverthwaite Railway
Haverthwaite Station, Ulverston LA12 8AL
t (01539) 531594
w lakesiderailway.co.uk
open See website for details.
admission £

Steam trains running a seasonal daily service from Haverthwaite to Lakeside via the Leven valley. Licensed restaurant, engine sheds, shop, picnic area.

Pots of Fun
Clifton Dykes, Penrith CA10 2DH
t (01768) 892733
open Apr-Oct, daily 1030-1730. Nov-Mar, daily 1000-1630.
admission Free

Throw your own pot, or paint a pot, figurine, mask, glass or vase. Make a mosaic and much more. Suitable for all ages and levels of expertise.

South Tynedale Railway
The Railway Station, Alston CA9 3JB
t (01434) 381696
w strps.org.uk
open See website for details.
admission £

Travel behind preserved steam and diesel engines, from Britain and abroad, through this Area of Outstanding Natural Beauty.

For key to symbols see page 211.

NATURE AND WILDLIFE

Acorn Bank Garden & Watermill
Temple Sowerby, Penrith CA10 1SP
t (01768) 361893 **w** nationaltrust.org.uk
open Mar-Oct, Wed-Sun 1000-1700.
admission £

Delightful sheltered garden, with a backdrop of a red sandstone 17thC house, renowned for its herbs and orchards growing old English fruit varieties. Over 200 culinary and medicinal herbs.

Eden Ostrich World
Langwathby Hall Farm, Langwathby, Penrith CA10 1LW
t (01768) 881771 **w** ostrich-world.com
open Mar-Oct, daily 1000-1700. Nov-Feb, daily 1000-1700.
admission £

Meet African black ostrich and other animals. Tearoom, Hayloft gallery selling arts and crafts, play areas, riverside walk, sheep-milking parlour, soft play area.

Fell Foot Country Park
Newby Bridge, Ulverston LA12 8NN
t (01539) 531273 **w** nationaltrust.org.uk
open All year, daily 0900-1700.
admission Free

Discover this lakeshore Victorian park – just the place for families to enjoy access to Windermere with picnic areas, boat hire and tearoom.

Graythwaite Hall Gardens
Graythwaite, Ulverston LA12 8BA
t (01539) 531333 **w** graythwaitehall.co.uk
open Apr-Aug, daily 1000-1800.
admission £

A fine example of Thomas Mawson's architecture comprising Dutch garden, rose garden, spring-flowering shrubs and rhododendrons.

Lakeland Sheep and Wool Centre
Egremont Road, Cockermouth CA13 0QX
t (01900) 822673 **w** sheep-woolcentre.co.uk
open All year, daily 0900-1730.
admission Free

Live farm show including cows, sheep, dogs and geese, all displaying their working qualities. Gift shop and licensed cafe/restaurant. An all-weather attraction.

Lakeland Wildlife Oasis
Hale, Milnthorpe LA7 7BW
t (01539) 563027 **w** wildlifeoasis.co.uk
open Apr-Jun, daily 1000-1600. Jul-Aug, daily 1000-1700. Sep-Mar, daily 1000-1600.
admission ££

Wildlife centre with a unique mix of exotic animals and educational interactive exhibitions. Includes tropical hall and butterfly house. Free parking.

Muncaster Gardens
Ravenglass CA18 1RQ
t (01229) 717614
w muncaster.co.uk
open Feb-Dec, daily 1030-1800.
admission ££

Plants from all over the world, especially the Sino-Himalayan region, nestle in the wild splendour of over 70 acres of gardens, with the dramatic backdrop of the glorious Lakeland fells.

Muncaster World Owl Centre
Ravenglass CA18 1RQ
w muncaster.co.uk
open Mar-Nov, daily 1030-1800.
admission ££

The centre cares for one of the finest and largest owl collections in the world with over 50 species, from the tiny Pygmy owl to the huge European Eagle owl.

South Lakes Wild Animal Park
Broughton Road, Dalton-in-Furness LA15 8JR
t (01229) 466086
w wildanimalpark.co.uk
open All year, daily 1000-1645.
admission £££

A unique concept in zoos, built to put animals first, and probably Britain's finest conservation park. Safari on foot amongst many animals wandering free.

Stagshaw Gardens
Stagshaw Lane, Ambleside LA22 0HE
t (015394) 46027
w nationaltrust.org.uk
open Apr-Jun, daily 1000-1830.
admission £

A woodland garden on a slope overlooking Lake Windermere. A superb collection of rhododendrons and azaleas blend perfectly under the hillside oaks.

Trotters World of Animals
Coalbeck Farm, Bassenthwaite CA12 4RD
t (01768) 776239
w trottersworld.com
open All year, daily 1000-1730.
admission ££

Wildlife park with collection of rare and interesting animals including primates, antelope, zebra and buffalo. Reptile house and bird of prey centre.

Winderwath Gardens
Winderwath, Temple Sowerby, Penrith CA10 2AG
t (01768) 88250
open Mar-Oct, Mon-Fri 1000-1600.
admission £

Mature gardens with herbaceous borders, alpines, pond with picnic area. Plants and second-hand garden tools for sale.

HISTORIC ENGLAND

Birdoswald Roman Fort
Gilsland, Brampton CA8 7DD
t (01697) 747602
w english-heritage.org.uk
open See website for details.
admission £

A Roman fort, turret and milecastle on an excellent stretch of Hadrian's Wall. Displaying the best-preserved defences of any wall fort, it was a base for some 1,000 Roman soldiers.

Blackwell, The Arts & Craft House
Bowness-on-Windermere, Windermere LA23 3JT
t (01539) 446139
w blackwell.org.uk
open Apr-Oct, daily 1030-1700. Nov-Dec, daily 1030-1600.
admission ££

Elegant arts and crafts house and gardens with spectacular views across Windermere. The restored interiors include many original features. Changing exhibitions of craft in upper galleries.

Carlisle Cathedral
The Abbey, Carlisle CA3 8TZ
t (01228) 548151
w carlislecathedral.org.uk
open All year, Mon-Sat 0730-1815, Sun 0730-1700.
admission Free

The cathedral dates from 1122 and has fine medieval stained glass, carved wood and stonework. Gift shop, restaurant, Treasury museum.

Conishead Priory House & Temple Tours
A5087 Coast Road, Ulverston LA12 9QQ
t (01229) 584029
w conisheadpriory.org
open Jun-Oct, Sat-Sun, Bank Hols 1400-1700. Nov-Mar, Sat-Sun 1400-1600.
admission £

A fascinating one-hour tour giving the history of the priory since 1160, together with an insight into the Buddhist way of life.

Dalemain Historic House & Gardens
Dalemain, Penrith CA11 0HB
t (01768) 486450
w dalemain.com
open Gardens: Apr-Oct, Mon-Thu, Sun 1030-1700. Nov-Mar, Mon-Thu, Sun 1100-1600. House: Apr-Oct, Mon-Thu, Sun 1115-1600.
admission ££

A medieval, Tudor and early-Georgian house. Guided tours available. Wonderful five-acre plantsman garden set against the splendour of the Lakeland Fells.

Dove Cottage and The Wordsworth Museum
Dove Cottage, Grasmere LA22 9SH
t (01539) 435544 **w** wordsworth.org.uk
open All year, daily 0930-1730.
admission ££

Wordsworth's home during his most creative period. Guided cottage tours, award-winning museum displaying manuscripts, portraits, paintings and memorabilia.

Furness Abbey
Abbey Approach, Barrow-in-Furness LA13 0PJ
t (01912) 691200 **w** english-heritage.org.uk
open See website for details.
admission £

A dramatic red sandstone abbey dating from 1123, so beloved by William Wordsworth. The exhibition explains the history of a powerful religious community.

Grizedale Forest Park and Visitor Centre
Grizedale, Hawkshead LA22 0QJ
w forestry.gov.uk/northwestengland
open All year, summer 1000-1700, winter 1000-1600.
admission Free

The park comprises 2,500 hectacres of Lakeland forest with walking and cycling trails. Scupltures in the forest, Go Ape, bike hire, visitor centre and cafe.

Hill Top
Nr Sawrey, Ambleside LA22 0LF
t (01539) 436269 **w** nationaltrust.org.uk
open Apr-May, Mon-Wed, Sat-Sun 1030-1630. Jun-Aug, Mon-Thu, Sat-Sun 1030-1630. Sep-Oct, Mon-Wed, Sat-Sun 1030-1630.
admission ££

Delightful, small 17thC house where Beatrix Potter wrote many of her famous children's stories. View her personal treasures.

Holker Hall and Gardens
Cark-in-Cartmel, Grange-over-Sands LA11 7PL
t (01539) 558328 **w** holker-hall.co.uk
open Gardens: Apr-Oct, Mon-Fri, Sun 1030-1730. Hall: Apr-Oct, Mon-Fri, Sun 1200-1600.
admission ££

Magnificent hall, award-winning gardens and museum – three attractions in one setting. There is also the Courtyard cafe, food hall and free parking.

Honister Slate Mine
Honister Pass, Borrowdale, Keswick CA12 5XN
t (01768) 777230 **w** honister.com
open All year, daily 1030-1530.
admission ££

The last working slate mine in England. Fully guided mine tours. Browse the visitor centre. Enjoy home-cooked fayre in the Yew Tree pub/restaurant.

Lanercost Priory
Lanercost, Brampton CA8 2HQ
t (01697) 73030 **w** english-heritage.org.uk
open See website for details.
admission £
Step back 800 years and explore this wonderful 12thC Augustinian priory which is situated near Hadrian's Wall.

Levens Hall & Gardens
Levens, Kendal LA8 0PD
t (01539) 560321 **w** levenshall.co.uk
open Gardens: Apr-Sep, Mon-Thu, Sun 1000-1700. House: Apr-Sep, Mon-Thu, Sun 1200-1600.
admission ££
Elizabethan mansion and world-famous topiary gardens designed by M Beaumont in 1694. Fountain garden and nuttery, licensed restaurant and gift shop.

Mirehouse Historic House and Gardens
Underskiddaw, Keswick CA12 4QE
t (01768) 772287 **w** mirehouse.com
open House: Apr-Oct, Sun, Wed 1400-1700. Gardens: Apr-Oct, daily 1000-1700.
admission £
Family-run historic house with strong literary connections in a spectacular location . Four playgrounds, beautiful gardens and tearoom.

Nenthead Mines Heritage Centre
Nenthead, Alston CA9 3PD
t (01434) 382726 **w** npht.com
open Apr-Oct, Wed-Sun 1030-1700. Apr-Oct, School Hols daily 1030-1700.
admission Free
Fantastic underground tour and interactive exhibits including working water wheels. Centuries of history interpreted in a unique environment.

Rydal Mount and Gardens
Rydal, Ambleside LA22 9LU
t (015394) 33002 **w** rydalmount.co.uk
open Apr-Oct, daily 0930-1700. Nov-Dec, Mon, Wed-Sun 0930-1700.
admission £
Wordsworth's best-loved home for 37 years. It was here that he wrote many of his poems. He became Poet Laureate to Queen Victoria at the age of 74.

St Mary & St Michael's Church
Church Road, Great Urswick, Ulverston LA12 0TA
t (01229) 582053
open Apr-Oct, daily 1000-1600. Nov-Mar, daily 1000-1500.
admission Free
A 10thC church, the oldest in Furness. Pre-Viking cross and Georgian gallery. Fine carvings by Alec Miller. Possible Celtic Roman connections.

Sizergh Castle and Garden
Sizergh, Kendal LA8 8AE
t (01539) 560951 **w** nationaltrust.org.uk
open Castle: Apr-Oct, Mon-Thu, Sun 1300-1700. Garden: Apr-Oct, Mon-Thu, Sun 1100-1700.
admission ££
Occupied by the Strickland family for over 760 years. View some of the finest Elizabethan carved overmantels, English and French furniture and Jacobite relics.

Stott Park Bobbin Mill
Low Stott Park, Ulverston LA12 8AX
t (01539) 531273 **w** english-heritage.org.uk
open See website for details.
admission £
See the industrial revolution come to life at this Victorian bobbin mill in an idyllic woodland setting at the south end of Lake Windermere.

Wordsworth House
Main Street, Cockermouth CA13 9RX
t (01900) 824805 **w** nationaltrust.org.uk
open Apr-Oct, Mon-Sat 1100-1630.
admission £
Meet the Wordsworth househould. Explore the garden. Enjoy the sights, sounds and smell of a working 18thC kitchen. Hands-on activities.

OUTDOOR ACTIVITIES

Coniston Launch
Coniston Boatlandings, Coniston LA21 8AJ
t (01539) 436216 **w** conistonlaunch.co.uk
open See website for details.
admission £
Cruise and ferry service calling at seven jetties including Brantwood. Special-interest cruises, eg Swallows & Amazons, Campbells on Coniston.

Steam Yacht Gondola
Pier Cottage, Coniston LA21 8AJ
t (015394) 41288 **w** nationaltrust.org.uk
open All year, daily 1100-1600. Weather permitting.
admission ££
The unrivalled cruising experience of the Lakes. View Coniston's spectacular scenery from a unique, rebuilt steam yacht sailing from Coniston pier.

Ullswater Steamers – Pooley Bridge
The Pier House, Glenridding, Ullswater CA11 0US
t (017684) 82229 **w** ullswater-steamers.co.uk
open See website for details.
admission £
Superb pier house offering tea and coffee overlooking the lake. Ticket sales and visitor information available.

Windermere Lake Cruises Bowness
Winander House, Glebe Road,
Bowness-on-Windermere, Windermere LA23 3HE
t (01539) 443360 **w** windermere-lakecruises.co.uk
open All year, please phone for details.
admission ££

Steamers and launches sail daily between Ambleside, Bowness and Lakeside. The steamers have saloons, promenade decks, teashops and licensed bars. Additional summer routes. Timetabled services.

ENTERTAINMENT AND CULTURE

Abbot Hall Art Gallery
Abbot Hall, Kendal LA9 5AL
t (01539) 722464 **w** abbothall.org.uk
open Mar-Nov, Mon-Sat 1030-1600. Dec-Feb, Mon-Sat 1030-1700.
admission £

The gallery's fine collection of 18thC, 19thC and 20thC art is set within an elegant Georgian villa. The permanent collection is complemented by a programme of critically acclaimed changing exhibitions.

Beatrix Potter Gallery
Main Street, Hawkshead LA22 0NS
t (01539) 436355 **w** nationaltrust.org.uk
open Apr-May, Mon-Wed, Sat-Sun 1030-1630. Jun-Aug, Mon-Thu, Sat-Sun 1030-1630. Sep-Oct, Mon-Wed, Sat-Sun 1030-1630.
admission £

Gallery showing original book illustrations by Beatrix Potter, once the office of her husband, William Heelis. An exhibition of sketches and watercolours painted for her children's stories changes annually.

Cars of the Stars Motor Museum
Standish Street, Keswick CA12 5LS
t (01768) 773757 **w** carsofthestars.com
open Apr-Nov, daily 1000-1700. Dec, Sat-Sun 1000-1700.
admission £

This motor museum features vehicles from TV and film: Chitty, Batmobiles, James Bond, Fab 1, the A Team van and many more.

Cumberland Pencil Museum
Southey Works, Keswick CA12 5NG
t (01768) 773626 **w** pencils.co.uk
open All year, daily 0930-1600.
admission £

Fascinating exhibits and film reveal 170 years of pencil heritage and how pencils are made today. Learn artists' techniques, and browse world-famous products in the gift shop.

The Dock Museum
North Road, Barrow-in-Furness LA14 2PW
t (01229) 876400 **w** dockmuseum.org.uk
open Apr-Oct, Tue-Fri 1000-1700, Sat-Sun 1100-1700. Nov-Mar, Wed-Fri 1030-1600, Sat-Sun 1100-1630.
admission Free

The museum explores the fascinating history of Barrow-in-Furness and how it grew from a tiny 19thC hamlet to a major shipbuilding force in just 40 years.

Gossipgate Gallery
The Butts, Alston CA9 3JU
t (01434) 381806 **w** gossipgate-gallery.co.uk
open Apr-Aug, Wed-Sat 1000-1700, Sun 1100-1700. Sep-Oct, Wed-Fri, Sun 1100-1630, Sat 1000-1700.
admission Free

The gallery has a reputation for quality art and craftwork from the north of England, with a continuous programme of exhibitions. Small coffee shop, tea terrace and wildflower garden.

Haig Colliery Mining Museum
Solway Road, Kells, Whitehaven CA28 9BG
t (01946) 599949 **w** haigpit.com
open All year, daily 0930-1630.
admission Free

The museum is situated on the former site of Haig Pit. Suitable for educational, group and corporate visits. Outreach talks, oral history and guided walks all available by booking.

Lake District Visitor Centre at Brockhole
Windermere LA23 1LJ
t (01539) 446601 **w** lake-district.gov.uk
open Gardens: daily 1000-1700. House: Apr-Oct, daily 1000-1700.
admission Free

Visitor centre with interactive exhibitions, thirty acres of Mawson gardens and grounds, adventure playground, shop and information centre. Lakeshore access for all.

Lakeland Motor Museum
Holker Hall and Gardens, Cark-in-Cartmel, Grange-over-Sands LA11 7PL
t (01539) 558328 **w** lakelandmotormuseum.co.uk
open Apr-Oct, daily 1030-1600.
admission ££

An award-winning visitor experience and a great educational resource. Over 30,000 motor-related exhibits including a 1930s garage recreation.

Lowes Court Gallery & Egremont TIC
12 Main Street, Egremont CA22 2DW
t (01946) 820693 **w** lowescourtgallery.co.uk
open Mar-Dec, Mon-Tue, Thu-Sat, 1000-1700, Wed 1000-1300.
admission Free

The gallery is housed in an 18thC listed building and is home to Egremont TIC and gift shop with 'Made in Cumbria' goods. The upper gallery has changing exhibitions.

For key to symbols see page 211.

Museum of Lakeland Life
Abbot Hall, Kendal LA9 5AL
t (01539) 722464 **w** lakelandmuseum.org.uk
open Apr-Oct, Mon-Sat 1030-1700. Nov, Feb-Mar, Mon-Sat 1030-1600.
admission £
The award-winning museum, housed in the stable block of the Georgian Abbot Hall Art Gallery, goes back in time to tell the story of the Lake District.

Ravenglass Railway Museum
Ravenglass CA18 1SW
t (01229) 717171 **w** ravenglass-railway.co.uk
open Apr-Oct, daily 0900-1700.
admission Free
The history of the Ravenglass and Eskdale railway told with relics, models, photographs and a 20-minute video.

The Rheged Centre
Redhills, Penrith CA11 0DQ
t (01768) 868000 **w** rheged.com
open Daily 1000-1730.
admission ££
International award-winning centre, and Europe's largest grass-covered building, home to a giant cinema screen showing epic movies daily. Regular events.

The Rum Story
27 Lowther Street, Whitehaven CA28 7DN
t (01946) 592933 **w** rumstory.co.uk
open All year, daily 1000-1630.
admission ££
The world's first exhibition depicting the story of the UK rum trade, including slavery, the effects of liquor on society, and the shipping and transport of rum.

Threlkeld Quarry & Mining Museum
Threlkeld Quarry, Threlkeld, Keswick CA12 4TT
t (01768) 779747 **w** threlkeldminingmuseum.co.uk
open Apr-Oct, daily 1000-1700.
admission £
Museum of mining, quarrying, geology and minerals. A large collection of excavators from the 20th century. Underground guided tours. Narrow-gauge railway.

Tullie House Museum & Art Gallery Museum
Castle Street, Carlisle CA3 8TP
t (01228) 534781 **w** tulliehouse.co.uk
open Apr-Jun, Mon-Sat 1000-1700, Sun 1200-1700. Jul-Aug, Mon-Sat 1000-1700, Sun 1100-1700. Sep-Oct, Mon-Sat 1000-1700, Sun 1200-1700. Nov-Mar, Mon-Sat 1000-1600, Sun 1200-1600.
admission ££
Travel through time at Tullie House and discover thousands of years of Carlisle and Border history, from prehistoric to recent times.

Greater Manchester

FAMILY FUN

East Lancashire Railway
Bolton Street Station, Bolton Street, Bury BL9 0EY
t (0161) 764 7790
w east-lancs-rly.co.uk
open All Year, 1000-1600.
admission £££
Beautifully restored, award-winning steam heritage railway. Passenger services run from Bury to Ramsbottom, Rawtenstall and Heywood as well as the villages of Summerseat and Irwell Vale.

Manchester City Experience (Museum and Tour)
Manchester City Football Club, Sportcity, Manchester M11 3FF
t 0870 062 1894
w mcfc.co.uk
open Museum: All year, Mon-Sat 0930-1630, Sun 1100-1500. Tour: Please phone for details.
admission ££
Tour Britain's stunning new stadium and experience the atmosphere of one of the country's most passionate clubs, Manchester City.

Reebok Stadium
Burnden Way, Lostock, Bolton BL6 6JW
t (01204) 673673
w bwfc.co.uk
open All year, Mon-Wed,Fri-Sat 0930-1730, Thu 0930-1900, Sun, Bank Hols 1000-1600.
admission £
Home of Bolton Wanderers Football Club and De Vere Whites Hotel, with a regional conference and exhibition centre. Stadium tours, sports hall and a merchandise store.

NATURE AND WILDLIFE

Etherow Country Park and Local Nature Reserve
George Street, Compstall SK6 5JD
t (0161) 427 6937
w marple-uk.com/community/etherow2.htm
open Daily, 1000-1600.
admission Free

The park covers approximately 92 hectares on the site of an old cotton mill and offers a variety of leisure pursuits with events and educational services.

Fletcher Moss Botanical Gardens
Millgate Lane, Didsbury, Manchester M20 2SW
t (0161) 434 1877
w manchester.gov.uk/leisure/parks/south/fletcher.htm
open Daily, dawn-dusk.
admission Free

The botanical gardens feature an interesting rock garden with many uncommon alpines, bulbs, screes and marginal plants. Also five grass tennis courts and five shale tennis courts.

Fletcher Moss Park
Millgate Lane, Didsbury M20 2RZ
t (0161) 434 1877
w manchester.gov.uk/leisure/parks/south/fletcher.htm
open Daily, dawn-dusk.
admission Free

The park has retained many of its original features such as the rock and heather gardens and the orchid houses situated in the Parsonage Gardens adjacent to Fletcher Moss.

Haigh Hall and Country Park
Haigh, Wigan WN2 1PE
t (01942) 832895 **w** haighhall.net
open Daily.
admission Free

Set in 350 acres of wood and parkland. Facilities include a model village, bouncy castle, play area, miniature railway, ladybird ride, mini-golf, craft gallery, information centre, gift shop and cafeteria.

HISTORIC ENGLAND

Bramall Hall
Bramall Park, Bramhall SK7 3NX
t (0161) 485 3708
w stockport.gov.uk/heritageattractions
open Apr-Sep, Mon-Thu, Sun 1300-1700, Fri-Sat 1300-1600. Oct-Dec, Tue-Sun 1300-1600. Jan-Mar, Sat-Sun 1300-1600. Bank Hols 1100-1700.
admission £

A Tudor manorhouse with 60 acres of landscaped grounds with lakes, woods and gardens. The house contains 16thC wall paintings. Tearoom and gift shop.

Dunham Massey Hall Park and Garden (National Trust)
Altrincham WA14 4SJ
t (0161) 941 1025 **w** thenationaltrust.org.uk
open House: Apr-Oct, Mon-Wed, Sat-Sun 1200-1700. Park: Apr-Oct, Daily 0900-1930. Nov-Feb, Daily 0900-1700.
admission ££

An 18thC mansion in a 250-acre wooded deer park with furniture, paintings and silver. Also, a 25-acre informal garden with mature trees and waterside plantings.

Hall i'th' Wood Museum
off Green Way, Crompton Way, Bolton BL1 8UA
t (01204) 332370 **w** boltonmuseums.org.uk
open Apr-Oct, Wed-Sun 1200-1700. Nov-Mar, Sat-Sun 1200-1700.
admission £

A 15thC furnished house with personal items belonging to Samuel Crompton, inventor of the Spinning Mule.

Manchester Cathedral
Cathedral Yard, Manchester M3 1SX
t (0161) 833 2220
open All year, Mon-Fri 0900-1730, Sat 0900-1530, Sun 0900-1830, Bank Hols 0900-1630.
admission Free

Dedicated to St Mary, St Denys and St George, this 15thC perpendicular church became a collegiate church in 1421 and was raised to cathedral status in 1847.

Admission is based on an adult price. Please check opening times and admission before travelling.

ENTERTAINMENT AND CULTURE

City of Manchester Stadium
Sport City, Manchester M11 3FF
t (0161) 224 5000
w mcfc.co.uk
open Please phone for details.
admission ££

Manchester City Football Club moved to City of Manchester Stadium in July 2003. Museum and stadium tour, plus City Social cafe & Reebok City superstore.

The Lowry
Pier 8, Salford Quays, Salford M50 3AZ
t (0161) 876 2000
w thelowry.com
open All year, Mon-Sat 1000-2000, Sun, Bank Hols 1000-1800.
admission Free

The Lowry is a spectacular home to the arts and entertainment with a wealth of activity all under one roof, including two theatres and an art gallery of international renown.

Manchester Art Gallery
Mosley Street, Manchester M2 3JL
t (0161) 235 8888
w manchestergalleries.org
open All year, Tue-Sun 1000-1700.
admission Free

The gallery houses one of the country's finest art collections in spectacular Victorian and contemporary surroundings. Exciting exhibitions programme and a wide range of events.

Manchester United Museum & Tour
Sir Matt Busby Way, Old Trafford, Manchester M16 0RA
t 0870 442 1994
w manutd.com
open Museum: All year, Mon-Sun 0930-1700.Tours: All year, Mon-Sun 0940-1630.
admission ££

The official museum and tour of Old Trafford offers every football fan a unique insight into Manchester United Football Club and a fantastic day out.

The Museum of Science and Industry
Liverpool Road, Castlefield, Manchester M3 4FP
t (0161) 832 2244
w msim.org.uk
open All year, Mon-Sun 1000-1700.
admission Free

The museum is based on the site of the oldest passenger railway station in the world. Five historic buildings packed with fascinating exhibitions, hands-on galleries, historic working machinery and special exhibitions.

Museum of Transport
Boyle Street, Cheetham, Manchester M8 8UW
t (0161) 205 2122 **w** gmts.co.uk
open Apr-Oct, Wed, Sat-Sun 1000-1700, Nov-Dec Wed, Sat-Sun 1000-1600.
admission £

The museum has one of the largest transport collections in the country, with 90 buses and a small number of other vehicles.

Touchstones Rochdale
Esplanade, Rochdale OL16 1AQ
t (01706) 924492 **w** rochdale.gov.uk/touchstones
open All Year, Mon-Sat 1000-1715, Sun, Bank Hols 1200-1600.
admission Free

The gallery features exhibitions of contemporary art and changing displays from collections of painting and sculpture. Local-history museum and local-studies centre. Cafe, bookshop and tourist information centre.

Urbis
Cathedral Gardens, Manchester M4 3BG
t (0161) 605 8200 **w** urbis.org.uk
open All year, Mon-Wed, Sun 1000-1800, Thu-Sat 1000-2000.
admission Free

Located at the heart of Manchester, Urbis is an exhibition centre of city life, featuring interactive exhibits and dynamic changing exhibitions.

The Whitworth Art Gallery
The University of Manchester, Oxford Road, Manchester M15 6ER
t (0161) 275 7450 **w** whitworth.man.ac.uk
open All year, Mon-Sat 1000-1700, Sun 1400-1700.
admission Free

The gallery has a light and spacious modern interior and is home to an internationally famous collection of British watercolours, sculptures, textiles and wallpapers.

Wigan Pier
Trencherfield Mill, Wigan WN3 4EF
t (01942) 323666 **w** wiganmbc.gov.uk
open All year, Mon-Thu 1000-1700, Sun 1100-1700.
admission ££

The pier combines interaction with displays and reconstructions and performances by the Wigan Pier Theatre Company. Facilities include shops, boats and a cafe.

Follow the Country Code!

- Be safe – plan ahead and follow any signs
- Leave gates and property as you find them
- Protect plants and animals, and take your litter home
- Keep dogs under close control
- Consider other people

Lancashire

FAMILY FUN

Adrenalin Zone
South Pier, Promenade, Blackpool FY4 1BB
t (01253) 298080 **w** adrenalinezone.co.uk
open Mar-Nov, daily 0900-1700.
admission ££
Thrill to the adrenalin rush of the SkyCoaster, a reverse bungee jump reaching 200kmph in two seconds, the Crazy Mouse Roller Coaster, Sky Screamer or the new Skad Tower.

Blackpool Model Village
East Park Drive, Blackpool FY3 9RB
t (01253) 763827 **w** blackpoolmodelvillage.com
open Apr-Nov, daily 1000-dusk.
admission £
An enchanting attraction set in 2.5 acres of landscaped gardens. Marvel at the hand-crafted models and figures that depict many scenes of life in miniature.

Blackpool Sandcastle Waterworld
South Promenade, Blackpool FY4 1BB
t (01253) 343602 **w** sandcastle-waterworld.co.uk
open See website for details.
admission £
A subtropical paradise. Brave the 'Typhoon Lagoon' wave pool; relax in the fun pool with fountains and kiddies' slides; ride the 300ft 'Gentle Giant' waterslide or race down the 'Barracuda'.

Blackpool's Piers
North Pier, The Promenade, Blackpool FY1 1NE
t (01253) 621452 **w** blackpoollive.com
open Mar-Oct, daily 0900-2300. Nov-Feb, daily 0900-1800.
admission £
On foot or by tram, enjoy the golden sands and the bustle of Blackpool's Golden Mile. From late August until early November the illuminations make it a magical night experience.

Botany Bay Villages and Puddletown Pirates
Canal Mill, Botany Brow, Chorley PR6 9AF
t (01257) 261220
w botanybay.co.uk
open Botany Bay: All year, daily 1030-1730. Puddletown Pirates: All year, daily 1000-1800.
admission £
A shopping, leisure and heritage experience housed within a converted Victorian spinning mill. Includes Puddletown Pirates, the North West's largest indoor adventure play centre.

Camelot Theme Park
Charnock Richard, Chorley PR7 5LP
t (01257) 452100
w camelotthemepark.co.uk
open May-Jun Sat-Sun 1000-1600. Jul-Aug daily 1000-1630. Sep-Oct, Sat-Sun 1000-1600.
admission ££££
This is a land of great knights and amazing days where you can meet Merlin and King Arthur and his brave Knights of the Round Table.

Louis Tussaud's Waxworks
97-89 Promenade, Blackpool FY1 1HW
t (01253) 625953
w louistussaudswaxworks.co.uk
open Please see website for details.
admission ££
Experience CelebCity. Once you've walked the red carpet, you'll be immersed in a world of celebrity, rubbing shoulders with Hollywood's A List and the tabloid's favourites.

NATURE AND WILDLIFE

Beacon Country Park
Beacon Lane, Upholland WN8 7RU
t (01695) 622794
w westlancsdc.gov.uk/tourist_information/beacon_park.html
open Daily.
admission Free
Three hundred acres of open countryside, staging events and activities throughout the year. Golf course and driving range, visitor centre, cafe and bar, nature trails, orienteering course, heritage trail.

Blackpool Zoo Park
East Park Drive, Blackpool FY3 8PP
t (01253) 830830 **w** blackpoolzoo.org.uk
open All year, daily 1000-1545.
admission £££
In 32 acres of maturing parkland and lakes, this award-winning zoo is home to over 1,500 beautiful, rare and exotic animals from all around the world. Play areas, crafts, miniature railway, shops and picnic areas.

For key to symbols see page 211.

Bowland Wild Boar Park
Leagram,
Chipping PR3 2QS
t (01995) 61554
w wildboarpark.co.uk
open Daily 1100-1600.
admission £

Ideal for young families and grandparents with grandchildren. View wild boar, cattle, llama, wallabies, red squirrels and pet lambs – some of the animals can be fed. Beautiful woodland walks.

Marshside RSPB Nature Reserve
c/o 24 Hoghton Street,
Southport PR9 0PA
t (01704) 536378
w rspb.org.uk
open All year, daily 0830-1700.
admission Free

A nature reserve with coastal grasslands, lagoons and hides by the estuary. Thousands of ducks and geese, as well as large flocks of wading birds, gather from autumn to spring.

RSPB Leighton Moss
Myers Farm,
Silverdale LA5 0SW
t (01524) 701601
w rspb.org.uk
open All year, daily 0900-dusk.
admission £

An attractive wooded valley below limestone hills, the only place in the North West with breeding bitterns, bearded tits and marsh harriers. Reception centre, RSPB shop and tearoom.

Wildfowl & Wetland Trust Martin Mere
Fish Lane, Burscough,
Nr Ormskirk L40 0TA
t (01704) 895181
w wwt.org.uk
open Apr-Oct, daily 0930-1730. Nov-Mar, daily 0930-1700.
admission ££

The centre is home to over 1,600 ducks, geese and swans. Special events and exhibitions, visitor centre and gift shop.

Williamson Park
Lancaster LA1 1UX
t (01524) 33318
w williamsonpark.com
open All year, daily dawn-dusk.
admission £

Facilities include the Ashton Memorial, viewing and art gallery, tropical butterfly house, mini-beast cave, free-flying bird enclosure and small-mammal enclosure.

Witton Country Park
Preston Old Road, Blackburn BB2 2TP
t (01254) 55423
w blackburn.gov.uk
open Park: Daily. Visitor Centre: Apr-Sep, Mon-Sat 1300-1630, Sun, Bank Hols 1100-1600. Oct-Mar, Thu-Sat 1300-1630, Sun 1100-1600.
admission Free

The park covers 480 acres of countryside and is peppered with pretty picnic spots, walks, nature trails, a small animal reserve and a visitor centre.

Worden Park
Worden Lane, Leyland PR25 3EL
t (01772) 625400
w southribble.gov.uk/visitors
open Daily 0800-1730.
admission Free

The park is over 150 acres in size. It includes the formal gardens, overlooked by a magnificent conservatory originally built in 1892. Alongside is the famous maze or puzzle garden.

HISTORIC ENGLAND

Blackburn Cathedral
Cathedral Offices, Cathedral Close, Blackburn BB1 5AA
t (01254) 51491
w blackburn.anglican.org/cathedral
open All year, Mon-Sat 0800-1700.
admission Free

Blackburn Cathedral has a Georgian nave with 20thC extensions, featuring sculptures by John Hayward and Josephina De Vasconcellos, and Burne-Jones windows.

Blackpool Tower & Circus
Promenade, Blackpool FY1 4BJ
t (01253) 622242 **w** blackpooltower.co.uk
open See website for details.
admission £££

There's entertainment for all ages, night and day at the world-famous Blackpool Tower. Don't miss the Tower Circus, the magnificent Tower Ballroom and Jungle Jim's Adventure Playground.

Gawthorpe Hall and Estate Block (National Trust)
Burnley Road, Padiham, Burnley BB12 8UA
t (01282) 771004 **w** lancsmuseums.gov.uk
open Apr-Oct, Tue-Thu, Sat-Sun 1300-1700.
admission £

The house was built in 1600 and restored by Sir Charles Barry in the 1850s. A loan from the National Portrait Gallery adds to the notable paintings already displayed.

Hoghton Tower
Hoghton, Preston PR5 0SH
t (01254) 852986 **w** hoghtontower.co.uk
open Jul-Sep, Mon-Thu, Bank Hols 1100-1600, Sun 1300-1700.
admission ££

A historic house with magnificent state apartments, banqueting hall, ballroom, grounds and dolls' houses on display. Underground passages and dungeons.

Lancaster Castle
Shire Hall, Castle Parade, Lancaster LA1 1YJ
t (01524) 64998 **w** lancastercastle.com
open All year, daily 1000-1700.
admission £

Shire Hall has a collection of coats of arms, a crown court, a grand jury room, a 'drop room' and dungeons. There is also an external tour of the castle.

Lancaster Priory Church
Castle Hill, Lancaster LA1 1YZ
t (01524) 65338 **w** priory.lancaster.ac.uk
open All year, daily 1000-1630.
admission Free

This 15thC church stands on the site of a priory founded in 1094 and contains magnificent oak-canopied choir stalls. There are also modern embroideries on display.

Leighton Hall
Carnforth LA5 9ST
t (01524) 734474
w leightonhall.co.uk
open May-Jul, Tue-Fri, Bank Hols 1400-1700. Aug, Tue-Fri, Sun 1230-1700. Sep, Tue-Fri, Bank Hols 1400-1700.
admission ££

The award-winning hall is the lived-in house of the famous furniture-making Gillow dynasty. Here, visitors can unravel the fascinating past of this ancient Lancashire family.

Rufford Old Hall
200 Liverpool Road, Rufford, Ormskirk L40 1SG
t (01704) 821254
w nationaltrust.org.uk
open Apr-Oct, Mon-Wed, Sat-Sun 1300-1700.
admission £

One of the finest 16thC buildings in Lancashire. The magnificent timber-framed Tudor hall, with impressive wood carvings, is believed to have hosted the young William Shakespeare.

Samlesbury Hall
Preston New Road, Samlesbury,
Preston PR5 0UP
t (01254) 812229
w samlesburyhall.co.uk
open All year, Mon-Fri, Sun 1100-1630.
admission £

A black and white, oak-timbered medieval manor house dating from 1325. The hall is home to displays, craft exhibitions and antique sales.

Turton Tower
Chapeltown Road, Turton BL7 0HG
t (01204) 852203
w lancashire.com/lcc/museums
open Apr-May, Mon-Wed, Sat-Sun 1200-1600. Jun-Sep, Mon-Thu, Sat-Sun 1200-1700. Oct-Mar, Mon-Wed, Sat-Sun 1200-1600.
admission £

A medieval tower and Tudor country house, with 16thC Stuart and Victorian period rooms. The house features a collection of furniture from the Victoria and Albert Museum.

Admission is based on an adult price. Please check opening times and admission before travelling.

Whalley Abbey

Whalley, Clitheroe BB7 9SS
t (01254) 828400 **w** whalleyabbey.co.uk
open Daily 1000-Dusk.
admission £

Fourteenth-century Cistercian abbey ruins set in beautiful countryside beside the River Calder, with mini woodland trail, riverside path, exhibition centre, gift shop and coffee shop.

OUTDOOR ACTIVITIES

Wyre Estuary Country Park

River Road, Stanah,
Thornton Cleveleys FY5 5LR
t (01253) 857890 **w** wyrebc.gov.uk
open All year, daily.
admission Free

The park and visitor centre offer year-round activities and events for all the family, including ranger-led walks, natural-environment activities and workshops. Visit our gift shop, take refreshments or walk the network of footpaths on the river estuary. Tours by arrangement.

ENTERTAINMENT AND CULTURE

British Commercial Vehicle Museum

King Street, Leyland PR25 2LE
t (01772) 451011 **w** thevehicleworks.com
open Apr-Sep, Tue-Thu, Sun 1000-1700. Oct, Sun 1000-1700.
admission £

The museum contains the finest collection of historic and commercial vehicles in Europe, including the world-famous Popemobile, horse-drawn and steam vehicles and fire engines.

Carnforth Station and Heritage Centre

Warton Road, Carnforth LA5 9TR
t (01524) 735165 **w** carnforthstation.co.uk
open Apr-Sep, daily 1000-1600. Oct-Mar, Tue-Sun 1000-1600.
admission Free

Made famous as the setting for David Lean's Brief Encounter, this once-significant railway station has been restored and conserved as a 1940s working railway station, heritage centre and conference venue.

Clitheroe Castle Museum

Castle Hill, Castle Gate, Clitheroe BB7 1BA
t (01200) 424635 **w** visitlancashire.com
open Apr-Oct, Mon-Sat, Bank Hols 1115-1630, Sun 1300-1630. Nov, Sat 1115-1630, Sun 1300-1630.
admission £

The museum's displays cover a wide variety of topics including reconstructions of a Victorian kitchen, a printer's shop and a clogger's shop, birds of the Ribble Valley and local geology.

Doctor Who Museum

Central Promenade, Blackpool FY1 5AA
t (01253) 299982 **w** doctorwhoexhibitions.co.uk
open Apr-Oct, daily 1030-1730.
admission ££

The museum boasts the most extensive collection of Doctor Who exhibits ever, charting four decades of the memorable BBC science-fiction series.

Lancaster Maritime Museum

Custom House, St George's Quay, Lancaster LA1 1RB
t (01524) 64637 **w** lancsmuseums.gov.uk
open Apr-Oct, daily 1100-1700. Nov-Mar, daily 1230-1800.
admission £

The museum covers the maritime trade of Lancaster, the history of the port, the Lancaster canal and the fishing industry of the Lune Estuary and Morecambe Bay.

The National Football Museum

Sir Tom Finney Way, Deepdale, Preston PR1 6RU
t (01772) 908442 **w** nationalfootballmuseum.com
open All year, Tue-Sat 1000-1700, Sat 1000-1500, Sun 1100-1700.
admission Free

The museum offers a unique experience by bringing alive the fascinating story of football through a number of interactive and hands-on elements.

Ribchester Roman Museum

Riverside, Ribchester, Preston PR3 3XS
t (01254) 878261 **w** ribchestermuseum.org
open All year, Mon-Fri 1000-1700, Sat-Sun 1200-1700.
admission £

Located on the north bank of the beautiful River Ribble, the museum has recently reopened after major development of its facilities. Roman Ribchester is brought to life by dramatic displays.

RELAXING AND PAMPERING

Barden Mill Shop

Barden Lane, Burnley BB12 0DX
t (01282) 420333 **w** bardenmillshop.co.uk
open All year, Mon-Fri 0930-1730, Sat 0930-1800, Sun 1030-1700.
admission Free

Over 50 departments in one mill store – serious bargain hunting in the unique surroundings of a converted weaving mill. Plenty of free parking.

Freeport Fleetwood Outlet Village
Anchorage Road, Fleetwood FY7 6AE
t (01253) 877377
w freeport-fleetwood.com
open All year, Mon-Wed, Fri-Sun 1000-1800, Thur 1000-2000.
admission Free

A shopping and leisure village with over 40 retail outlets, selling at discounts of up to 50%. Children's adventure playground and indoor play area.

Sherry's Lancashire Mill Shop
Stockbridge Mill, Stockbridge Road, Burnley BB12 7HA
t (01282) 778416
w sherrytex.co.uk
open All year, Mon-Sat 0930-1730, Sun 1000-1630.
admission Free

Large mill shop attached to an existing traditional Lancashire weaving mill. 6,000 sq ft of bargains and gifts with 30-seater coffee shop serving drinks and snacks.

Winfield's
Hazel Mill, Blackburn Road, Haslingden BB4 5DD
t (01706) 831952
w winfieldsoutdoor.co.uk
open All year, Mon-Wed, Fri 1000-1730, Thu 1000-2000, Sat 0900-1730, Sun 1100-1700.
admission Free

Footwear, sports and designer wear, fashion, homeware, luggage. Winfield's has the answer, and all at discount prices you won't believe.

Merseyside

FAMILY FUN

The Cavern Quarter
Liverpool L2 6RE
t (0151) 227 1963 **w** beatles64.co.uk
open See website for details.
admission Free

The cultural birthplace of the Beatles is the home of many tourism landmarks, including the Cavern Club.

Liverpool Football Club Museum and Stadium Tour
Anfield Road, Liverpool L4 0TH
t (0151) 260 6677 **w** liverpoolfc.tv
open Daily 1000-1700. Match days, last admission one hour before kick-off.
admission ££

You'll never walk alone on the tour of Liverpool Football Club. The tour includes dressing rooms, players' tunnel, coaches' seating area and grandstand.

Model Railway Village
Lower Promenade, Kings Gardens, Southport PR8 1RB
t (01704) 214266 **w** southportmodelrailwayvillage.co.uk
open Daily 1000-1700.
admission £

One and a half acres of sheltered gardens comprising over 200 1:18 scale models and extensive 500m-long garden gauge railway.

National Wildflower Centre
Court Hey Park, Knowsley L16 3NA
t (0151) 738 1913 **w** nwc.org.uk
open 1 Mar-1 Sep 1000-1700, last entry 1600.
admission Adult: £3

A peaceful haven in an otherwise busy world. Full events programme, including Wildflower Heroes events and workshops – all ages and abilities welcome. Pre-booked groups welcome. Seasonal wildflower displays, children's play area (visitor centre charge applies). Award-winning Cornflower Cafe and gift shop on site (cafe open weekdays in winter).

V voucher offer – see back section

For key to symbols see page 211.

Spaceport
Victoria Place,
Wallasey CH44 6QY
t (0151) 330 1333
w spaceport.org.uk
open All year, Tue-Sun 1030-1730.
admission ££

Blast off on a virtual journey through space, from Earth to the farthest reaches of the known universe. Expand your mind at the amazing new £10million Spaceport in Merseyside.

NATURE AND WILDLIFE

Formby Red Squirrel Reserve (National Trust) (Formby Point)
Victoria Road, Freshfield,
Formby L37 1LJ
t (01704) 878591
w nationaltrust.org.uk
open Daily.
admission Free

This National Trust property is the home of red squirrels, which are the main attraction at this superb nature reserve.

Knowsley Safari Park
Prescot L34 4AN
t (0151) 430 9009
w knowsley.com
open Mar-Oct, daily 1000-1600. Nov-Feb, daily 1030-1500.
admission ££

A five-mile safari through 500 acres of rolling countryside and the world's wildest animals roaming free – that's the wonderful world of freedom you'll find at the park.

National Wildflower Centre

Court Hey Park, Knowsley L16 3NA
t (0151) 738 1913 **w** nwc.org.uk
open 1 Mar-1 Sep 1000-1700, last entry 1600.
admission Adult: £3

A peaceful haven in an otherwise busy world. Full events programme, including Wildflower Heroes events and workshops – all ages and abilities welcome. Pre-booked groups welcome. Seasonal wildflower displays, children's play area (visitor centre charge applies). Award-winning Cornflower Cafe and gift shop on site (cafe open weekdays in winter).

V voucher offer – see back section

Help before you go

When it comes to your next English break, the first stage of your journey could be closer than you think.

You've probably got a tourist information centre nearby which is there to serve the local community – as well as visitors. Knowledgeable staff will be happy to help you, wherever you're heading.

Many tourist information centres can provide you with maps and guides, and it's often possible to book accommodation and travel tickets too.

HISTORIC ENGLAND

Albert Dock
The Colonnades, Liverpool L2 7SU
t (0151) 708 8854
w albertdock.com
open See website for details
admission Free

A truly stunning architectural triumph, this award-winning attraction houses cafe bars, restaurants, shops, The Beatles Story, Merseyside Maritime Museum, Museum of Liverpool Life and Tate Liverpool.

Croxteth Hall and Country Park
Croxteth Hall Lane, Muirhead Avenue, Liverpool L12 0HB
t (0151) 228 5311
w croxteth.co.uk
open See website for details.
admission Free

An Edwardian stately home set in 500 acres of countryside (woodlands and pasture), featuring a Victorian walled garden and animal collection.

Liverpool Anglican Cathedral
St James Mount, Liverpool L1 7AZ
t (0151) 709 6271
w liverpoolcathedral.org.uk
open Daily 0800-1800.
admission Free

The largest cathedral in Britain. A great neo-Gothic building, designed by Giles Gilbert Scott, started in 1904 and completed in 1978.

Metropolitan Cathedral of Christ the King
Mount Pleasant, Liverpool L3 5TQ
t (0151) 709 9222
w liverpoolmetrocathedral.org.uk
open Daily 0800-1800.
admission Free

A 20thC circular cathedral famous for its 290ft lantern tower, stained glass and modern works of art. Monumental crypt of an earlier incomplete project by Edwin Lutyens.

Port Sunlight Village Trust
95 Greendale Road, Port Sunlight CH62 4XE
t (0151) 644 4803
w portsunlightvillage.com
open See website for details.
admission Free

A picturesque Grade II Listed village built for Lever's 19thC soap works. The heritage centre tells the story of the village and community.

Speke Hall, Gardens and Woodland (National Trust)
The Walk, Liverpool L24 1XD
t (0151) 427 7231 **w** nationaltrust.org.uk
open See website for details
admission ££

A wonderful, rambling Tudor mansion with rich Victorian interiors, set in a wooded estate on the banks of the Mersey with views of Wirral and North Wales.

OUTDOOR ACTIVITIES

Mersey Ferries
Victoria Place, Seacombe, Wallasey CH44 6QY
t (0151) 330 1444 **w** merseyferries.co.uk
open See website for details.
admission £

Cruises offering visitors the opportunity to view the spectacular Liverpool waterfront which is now a UNESCO World Heritage Site.

The Yellow Duckmarine
Britannia Vaults, Albert Dock, Liverpool L3 4AD
t (0151) 708 7799 **w** theyellowduckmarine.co.uk
open Daily 1100-dusk.
admission ££

A one-hour amphibious sightseeing tour of Liverpool's historic city and award-winning waterfront and docks with live commentary throughout.

ENTERTAINMENT AND CULTURE

The Beatles Story
Britannia Vaults, Albert Dock, Liverpool L3 4AD
t (0151) 709 1963 **w** beatlesstory.com
open Daily 1000-1800.
admission ££

The multi-award-winning attraction dedicated to Liverpool's most-famous sons – John, Paul, George and Ringo. Living-history audio guide. A personal journey through the Fab Four's meteoric rise to fame.

Lady Lever Art Gallery
Port Sunlight Village, Higher Bebington CH62 5EQ
t (0151) 478 4136 **w** ladyleverartgallery.org.uk
open Daily 1000-1700.
admission Free

The 1st Lord Leverhulme's magnificent collection of British paintings dated 1750-1900, British furniture, Wedgwood pottery and oriental porcelain.

Admission is based on an adult price. Please check opening times and admission before travelling.

Liverpool Museum
William Brown Street, Liverpool L3 8EN
t (0151) 478 4393
w liverpoolmuseum.org.uk
open Daily 1000-1700.
admission Free

One of Britain's finest museums with collections from all over the world. Features include the planetarium, the space gallery and the hands-on Natural History Centre.

Mendips & 20 Forthlin Road (National Trust)
Speke Hall, The Walk, Speke Hall Avenue, Speke L24 1XD
t (0151) 427 7231
w nationaltrust.org.uk
open Mar-Oct, Wed-Sun, by tour only.
admission £££

Number 20 Forthlin Road is where the Beatles met, rehearsed and wrote many of their earliest songs. Displays include contemporary photographs by Mike McCartney and early Beatles memorabilia.

Merseyside Maritime Museum
Albert Dock, Liverpool L3 4AQ
t (0151) 478 4499
w merseysidemaritimemuseum.org.uk
open Daily 1000-1700.
admission Free

Liverpool's seafaring heritage brought to life in the historic Albert Dock. Visitors can inspect the mueum's collection and, during the summer, explore the adjacent ships and quaysides.

Tate Liverpool
Albert Dock, Liverpool L3 4BB
t (0151) 702 7400
w tate.org.uk/liverpool/
open All year, Tue-Sun 1000-1750.
admission Free

Part of the historic Albert Dock, and home to the National Collection of modern art, Tate Liverpool has four floors of art, free daily talks, shop and cafe.

The Walker
William Brown Street, Liverpool L3 8EL
t (0151) 478 4199 **w** thewalker.org.uk
open Daily 1000-1700.
admission Free

The national gallery of the North, the Walker is one of the finest galleries in Europe, housing outstanding collections of British and European art.

Williamson Art Gallery
Slatey Road, Birkenhead CH43 4UE
t (0151) 652 4177 **w** wirral.gov.uk
open All year, Tue-Sun 1000-1700.
admission Free

The gallery features English watercolours, Liverpool school pictures, important collections of Merseyside pottery and porcelain (Liverpool, Seacombe, Della Robbia) and local-history galleries.

World Museum Liverpool
William Brown Street, Liverpool L3 8EN
t (0151) 478 4393
w worldmuseumliverpool.org.uk
open Daily 1000-1700.
admission Free

One of Britain's finest museums, with extensive collections from the Amazonian rain forest to the mysteries of outer space. Special attractions include the award-winning hands-on Natural History Centre and the Planetarium.

RELAXING AND PAMPERING

The World of Glass
Chalon Way East, St Helens WA10 1BX
t 0870 011 4466 **w** worldofglass.com
open All year, Tue-Sun 1000-1700.
admission ££

England's best small visitor attraction features live glass blowing, multi-media shows, exhibitions, cafe, gift shop and tourist information centre. It is also a first-class conference and corporate hospitality venue.

Northumberland

FAMILY FUN

Alnwick Castle

Alnwick Castle Ventures,
Estates Office, Alnwick NE66 1NQ
t (01665) 510777 **w** alnwickcastle.com
open 2 Apr-28 Oct 1000-1800.
admission Adult: £9

Alnwick is one of Europe's finest medieval castles, featuring glorious state rooms, fine art and architecture, fascinating exhibitions, children's activities, special events and the unique Knights Quest interactive games area. Fine food and drink is served by The Sanctuary at The Castle – Restaurant and Wine Bar, and the Courtyard Cafe. Best Large Attraction 2006 – North East Tourism Awards.

voucher offer – see back section

Prudhoe Waterworld

Front Street, Prudhoe NE42 5DQ
t (01661) 833144 **w** leisuretynedale.co.uk
open All year, Mon-Thu 0715-2100, Fri 0715-1915, Sat 0800-1630, Sun 0800-1730.
admission £

Leisure pool incorporating wave machine, 40m aqua slide, spa pool and other water features, fitness gym, fitness studio, soft play area, creche and bowling green.

Whitehouse Farm Centre

North White House Farm, Morpeth NE61 6AW
t (01670) 789998 **w** whitehousefarmcentre.co.uk
open Feb-Oct, Dec, Tue-Sun, Bank Hols 1000-1700. Nov, Jan, Sat-Sun 1000-1700.
admission ££

An all-weather fun attraction with soft play area, licensed restaurant, craft workshops and outdoor play areas. Tractor and trailer rides and lots of animals.

NATURE AND WILDLIFE

The Alnwick Garden

Denwick Lane, Alnwick NE66 1YU
t (01665) 511350 **w** alnwickgarden.com
open Apr-May, daily 1000-1800. Jun-Sep,daily, 1000-1900. Oct, daily 1000-1800. Nov-Mar, daily 1000-1600.
admission ££

An exciting, contemporary garden with beautiful and unique gardens, features and structures, brought to life with water. Fantastic eating, drinking and shopping. Events throughout the year.

Bide-a-Wee Cottage Gardens and Nursery

Stanton, Morpeth NE65 8PR
t (01670) 772262 **w** bideawee.co.uk
open May-Aug, Wed, Sat 1330-1700.
admission £

Set within the picturesque Northumbrian countryside, a unique garden created from a sandstone quarry, planted with unusual perennials, many available from the nursery.

Carlisle Park and Castle Woods

Castle Square, Morpeth NE61 1YD
t (01670) 500777 **w** castlemorpeth.gov.uk
open Apr-Oct, daily 0730-dusk. Nov-Mar, daily 0730-1600.
admission Free

Formal park containing historic architectural remains, riverside and woodland walks, aviary, tennis courts, bowling greens, paddling pool, boats and play area.

For key to symbols see page 211.

Chesters Walled Garden
The Chesters, Humshaugh, Hexham NE46 4BQ
t (01434) 681483 **w** chesterswalledgarden.co.uk
open Apr-Oct, daily 1000-1700.
admission £

Beautiful two-acre walled garden containing a unique extensive herb collection, Roman garden, National Collection of thyme, large herbaceous borders, herbal gift shop and nursery.

Dilston Physic Garden
Dilston Mill House, Corbridge NE45 5QZ
t (01434) 673593 **w** dilstonphysicgarden.com
open Apr-Sep, Wed-Thu 1100-1600.
admission £

An unusual and inspiring garden containing over 500 species of medicinal plants, and a wonderful place in which to relax and learn about the healing power of medicinal herbs.

Druridge Bay Country Park
Red Row, Druridge Bay NE61 5BX
t (01670) 760968 **w** northumberland.gov.uk
open Daily, dawn-dusk.
admission Free

Lake with woods and meadows plus three miles of beach and sand dunes. Visitor centre, walks, water sports, picnic areas, natural history and birdwatching. Cafe and gift shop.

Ford Nursery
Berwick-upon-Tweed TD15 2PZ
t (01890) 820379 **w** fordnursery.co.uk
open Mar-Sep, daily 1000-1700. Oct-Jan, daily 1000-1600.
admission Free

Garden nursery situated in the grounds of a walled garden. Container-grown shrubs, perennials, alpines, ground-cover plants, trees, grasses and demonstration gardens.

The Garden Station
Langley, Hexham NE47 5LA
t (01434) 684391 **w** thegardenstation.co.uk
open May-Aug, Tue-Sun, Bank Hols 1000-1700.
admission Free

An attractive, restored Victorian railway station in a woodland garden. A unique, tranquil place with gardening and art courses, woodland walk, unusual plants and refreshments.

Herterton House Garden Nursery
Hartington, Cambo NE61 4BN
t (01670) 774278
open Apr-Sep, Mon, Wed, Fri-Sun, Bank Hols 1330-1730.
admission £

One acre of formal gardens inside stone walls around a 16thC farmhouse incorporating topiary, physic, flower and nursery gardens, and fancy garden with gazebo.

Howick Hall Gardens
Estate Office, Howick Hall, Alnwick NE66 3LB
t (01665) 577285 **w** howickhallgardens.org.uk
open Apr-Oct, daily 1200-1800. Nov-Mar, Sat-Sun 1200-1600.
admission £

Lovely flower, shrub and rhododendron gardens. Extensive grounds with a collection of shrubs in woodland garden, formal gardens around the house, a bog garden and new arboretum (2006).

Kielder Water Birds of Prey Centre
Leaplish Waterside Park, Falstone, Hexham NE48 1AX
t (01434) 250400 **w** kielderwaterbirdsofpreycentre.com
open Mar-Sep, daily 1030-1700. Oct-Feb, daily 1030-dusk.
admission £

Visit one of the largest and most fascinating collections of birds of prey in the North of England, located within the magnificent forest lakeside surrounding Kielder Water.

Kirkley Hall Gardens
Kirkley Hall, Ponteland NE20 0AQ
t (01670) 841200 **w** northland.ac.uk
open All year, Mon-Fri 0830-1700.
admission Free

Ornamental gardens and grounds with all plants labelled. Shrubs, ornamental borders, sunken garden and alpines. Wall-trained fruit trees and greenhouse plants.

Leaplish Waterside Park
Northumbrian Water Ltd, Hexham NE48 1BT
t 0870 240 3549 **w** nwl.co.uk/kielder
open Daily.
admission Free

Situated in the north Tyne Valley and close to the Scottish Borders, with breathtaking scenery around the 27-mile shoreline. Facilities and activities to suit all ages.

Longframlington Gardens
Swarland Road, Longframlington NE65 8BE
t (01665) 570382 **w** longframlingtongardens.co.uk
open Daily 0830-1700.
admission £

Twelve acres of garden and arboretum walks including a wild-flower meadow, rope art, garden design and nursery and plant centre, all in a peaceful countryside setting with fabulous views.

Queen Elizabeth II Jubilee Country Park, Local Nature Reserve
Woodhorn Road, Ashington NE63 9AS
t (01670) 843444
open Daily.
admission Free

Woodhorn Colliery is a heritage museum. The country park, once the site of a colliery spoil heap, features a wide variety of wildlife in its woodland and a 40-acre lake.

Tyne Green Country Park
Tyne Green, Hexham NE46 3SG
t 07811 129525 **w** tynedale.gov.uk
open Daily.
admission Free

Riverside park in a wooded setting with golf, fishing and canoeing on the river. Waymarked country trail, children's play area and picnic and barbecue area.

Tourist Information Centres
To find your nearest Tourist Information Centre text TIC LOCATE to 64118.

Aydon Castle
Corbridge NE45 5PJ
t (01434) 632450 **w** english-heritage.org.uk
open See website for details.
admission £

Fine example of a small castle built as a manor house in the late 13th century and fortified shortly after. It was converted to a farmhouse in the 17th century.

Bamburgh Castle
Bamburgh NE69 7DF
t (01668) 214515 **w** bamburghcastle.com
open Apr-Oct, daily 1000-1700.
admission ££

Magnificent coastal castle completely restored in 1900 housing collections of china, porcelain, furniture, paintings, arms and armour. The castle is home to the Armstrong family.

Barter Books
Alnwick Station, Alnwick NE66 2NP
t (01665) 604888 **w** barterbooks.co.uk
open Apr-Sep, daily 0900-1900. Oct-Mar, Mon-Wed, Fri-Sun 0900-1700, Thu 0900-1900.
admission Free

The bookshop, selling second-hand books, is one of the largest in Britain. Lots of seating, a children's room, light refreshments, free parking.

Belsay Hall, Castle and Gardens
Belsay NE20 0DX
t (01661) 881636 **w** english-heritage.org.uk
open See website for details.
admission ££

Home of the Middleton family for 600 years. Thirty acres of landscaped gardens and winter garden. Fourteenth-century castle, ruined 17thC manor house and neoclassical hall.

Berwick Castle
The Walls, Berwick-upon-Tweed TD15 1HP
t (01289) 304493 **w** english-heritage.org.uk
open See website for details.
admission £

West wall of 12thC castle with 16thC gun tower which survived as a boundary for the railway yard, and late 13thC curtain wall descending to the river.

Brinkburn Priory
Longframlington NE65 8AR
t (01665) 570628 **w** english-heritage.org.uk
open See website for details.
admission £

Founded in 1135, the priory was restored in the 19th century, and now survives in its entirety as Northumberland's finest example of early Gothic architecture.

Admission is based on an adult price. Please check opening times and admission before travelling.

Chesters Roman Fort (Cilurnum) Hadrian's Wall

Chollerford, Humshaugh NE46 4EU
t (01434) 681379 **w** english-heritage.org.uk
open Apr-Sep, daily 0930-1800. Oct-Mar, daily 1000-1600.
admission £

The best-preserved example of a Roman cavalry fort in Britain, including remains of the bath house. The Clayton Collection Museum houses a fascinating collection of Roman sculpture and inscriptions.

Chillingham Castle

Chillingham, Alnwick NE66 5NJ
t (01668) 215359 **w** chillingham-castle.com
open Castle: Apr-Sep, Mon-Fri, Sun 1300-1700. Grounds: Apr-Sep, Mon-Fri, Sun 1200-1700.
admission ££

Medieval fortress with Tudor additions. Torture chamber, shop, dungeon, tearoom, woodland walks, beautifully furnished rooms and Italian topiary garden with spectacular herbaceous borders.

Chipchase Castle

Wark, Chillingham NE48 3NT
t (01434) 230203
open Jun, daily 1400-1700.
admission £

One of the best examples of Jacobean architecture in the Borders. Chapel, 14thC pele tower, walled vegetable garden, wild garden with lake, nursery garden selling plants.

Corbridge Roman Site (Corstopitum) Hadrian's Wall

Corbridge NE45 5NT
t (01434) 632349 **w** english-heritage.org.uk
open See website for details.
admission £

Extensive remains include two large granaries, strong room, headquarters building, fountain house, aqueduct, 2 military compounds, Stanegate road and museum.

Cragside House, Gardens and Estate

Cragside, Rothbury, Morpeth NE65 7PX
t (01669) 620333 **w** nationaltrust.org.uk
open House: Apr-Sep, Tue-Sun 1300-1730. Oct, Tue-Sun 1300-1630. Gardens: Apr-Oct, Tue-Sun 1030-1730. Nov, Wed-Sun 1100-1600.
admission £££

The creation of Lord Armstrong, Cragside is a garden of breathtaking drama, whatever the season. This magnificent estate provides one of the last shelters for the endangered red squirrel.

Dunstanburgh Castle

Craster NE66 3TT
t (01665) 576231 **w** english-heritage.org.uk
open See website for details.
admission £

Romantic ruins of extensive 14thC castle in dramatic coastal situation on 100ft cliffs. Built by Thomas, Earl of Lancaster. Remains include gatehouse and curtain wall.

Edlingham Castle

Edlingham NE66 2BL
t (01289) 304493 **w** english-heritage.org.uk
open Daily, dawn-dusk.
admission Free

In a remote and picturesque valley, this complex ruined castle comprises a 13thC hall and house, a 14thC courtyard and a domestic tower added in the 15th century.

Etal Castle

Etal Village, Etal TD12 4TN
t (01890) 820332 **w** english-heritage.org.uk
open Apr-Oct, daily 1100-1600.
admission £

Typical compact 14thC border castle comprising four-storey keep, gatehouse, parts of curtain wall and corner tower. The 19thC chapel displays an award-winning exhibition.

Hexham Abbey

Beaumont Street, Hexham NE46 3NB
t (01434) 602031 **w** hexhamabbey.org.uk
open Daily 0930-1700.
admission £

Saxon crypt, 15thC paintings, misericords and Saxon chalice, 7thC Frith stool and Augustinian night stair. Most of the church is in the Early English style of architecture.

Housesteads Roman Fort (Vercovicium) Hadrian's Wall

Haydon Bridge NE47 6NN
t (01434) 344363 **w** english-heritage.org.uk
open Apr-Sep, daily 1000-1800. Oct-Mar, daily 1000-1600.
admission £

The best preserved and most impressive of the Roman forts, Vercovicium was a five-acre fort for an extensive 800-strong civil settlement and contains the only example of a Roman hospital in Britain.

Kielder Castle Forest Park Centre

Kielder Castle, Kielder, Hexham NE48 1ER
t (01434) 250209 **w** forestry.gov.uk
open Apr-Oct, daily 1000-1700. Nov-Dec, Sat-Sun 1100-1600.
admission Free

Kielder Castle is the visitor centre for Kielder Forest. Features include forest shop, information centre, tearoom and exhibitions about forestry and conservation.

National Park Centre Once Brewed

Military Road, Hadrian's Wall, Hexham NE47 7AN
t (01434) 344396
w northumberland-national-park.org.uk
open Apr-Oct, daily 0930-1700. Dec-Mar, Sat-Sun 1000-1500.
admission Free

National Park visitor centre with exhibitions, shop selling refreshments, maps, books, souvenirs and clothing, picnic area, toilets, car park and easy access onto Hadrian's Wall.

Norham Castle
Norham TD15 1DF
t (01289) 382329 **w** english-heritage.org.uk
open Apr-Sep, Sun, Bank Hols 1000-1700.
admission Free

One of the strongest of Border castles and one of the finest Norman keeps in England. The most famous siege in Sir Walter Scott's Marmion.

Otterburn Mills
Otterburn NE19 1JT
t (01830) 520225 **w** otterburnmill.co.uk
open Apr-Oct, Mon-Sat 0900-1700, Sun 1000-1630. Nov-Mar, daily 1000-1630.
admission Free

Retailers of high-quality woollen rugs, knitwear, jackets and outdoor leisurewear gifts. Fully licensed coffee shop and exhibition of textile machines and water turbine.

Preston Tower
Chathill NE67 5DH
t (01665) 589227
open Apr-Sep, daily 1000-dusk. Oct-Mar, daily 1000-1600.
admission £

The tower, built by Sir Robert Harbottle in 1392, is one of the few-surviving pele towers. The tunnel-vaulted rooms remain unaltered, and two are furnished in contemporary style.

Seaton Delaval Hall
Seaton Sluice, Whitley Bay NE26 4QR
t (01912) 371493
open Jun-Sep, Wed, Sun 1400-1800.
admission £

A splendid English baroque house comprising a centre block between two arcaded and pedimented wings. The east wing contains fine stables, and there are gardens with statues.

Wallington House, Walled Garden and Grounds
Wallington, Cambo, Morpeth NE61 4AR
t (01670) 773600 **w** nationaltrust.org.uk
open House: Apr-Aug, Mon, Wed-Sun 1300-1730. Sep-Oct, Mon, Wed-Sun 1300-1630. Walled Garden: Apr-Sep, daily 1000-1900. Oct, daily 1000-1800. Nov-Feb, daily 1000-1600. Grounds: Daily, dawn-dusk.
admission ££

The country home of the Trevelyan family sits in 100 acres of lawns, lakes and woodland. Visit the beautiful walled garden or enjoy a woodland or riverside walk.

Warkworth Castle
Warkworth NE65 0UJ
t (01665) 711423 **w** english-heritage.org.uk
open See website for details.
admission £

Dramatic ruins dating from the 12thC-14thC, owned by the Percy family for 600 years. Remains include the 15thC keep, chapel, great hall and lion tower with carved lion.

Warkworth Hermitage
Warkworth NE65 0UJ
t (01665) 711423 **w** english-heritage.org.uk
open See website for details.
admission £

The hermitage is cut into the rock of the river cliff, hidden away underneath the wooded bank, a short walk upstream from the castle.

OUTDOOR ACTIVITIES

Billy Shiel's Farne Island Boat Trips
Seahouses NE68 7YT
t (01665) 720308 **w** farne-islands.com
open Daily 1000-1600, weather permitting.
admission £££

Boat trips to the Farne Islands from Seahouses. Visit the grey-seal colonies whilst listening to the commentary. All-day birdwatching trips during the breeding season.

Kielder Water Cruises
Northumbrian Water Ltd, Hexham NE48 1AX
t 0870 240 3549 **w** nwl.co.uk/leisure
open Apr-Oct, daily 1015-1615, weather permitting.
admission ££

Cruise around Kielder Water in an 80-passenger cruiser with heated lounge, light refreshments, toilets and on-board commentary. Full safety equipment.

Puffin Cruises Dave Gray Boat Trips
21 Broomhill Street, Amble NE65 0AN
t (01665) 711975
open Please phone for details.
admission ££

Take a boat trip around Coquet Island to see the puffins, terns, ducks and seals. A lighthouse, built by monks, and ruins of a monastery window are visible.

ENTERTAINMENT AND CULTURE

Berwick-upon-Tweed Museum and Art Gallery
Ravensdowne Barracks,
Berwick-upon-Tweed TD15 1DG
t (01289) 301869 **w** english-heritage.org.uk
open Apr-Oct, daily 1000-1700.
admission £

The museum is housed in the historic Berwick Barracks and contains collections of fine and decorative art and local history displayed in innovative ways.

For key to symbols see page 211.

Cherryburn: Thomas Bewick Birthplace Museum
Cherryburn, Station Bank, Mickley,
Stocksfield NE43 7DD
t (01661) 843276 **w** nationaltrust.org.uk
open Apr-Oct, Mon-Tue, Thu-Sun 1100-1700.
admission £

The birthplace of Thomas Bewick. The 19thC farmhouse houses a small exhibition on his life and work. Farmyard animals including donkeys and lambs, garden with picnic lawn. Demonstrations most days.

Hexham Old Gaol
Hallgate, Hexham NE46 3NH
t (01434) 652349 **w** tynedaleheritage.org
open Mar-Oct, daily 1000-1630. Nov-Feb, Mon-Tue, Sat 1000-1630.
admission £

Tour the Old Gaol (1330AD) which has a glass lift down to the dungeon. Meet the gaoler, see a Reiver raid and try on costumes.

Lady Waterford Hall
Ford Village, Berwick-upon-Tweed TD15 2QA
t (01890) 820503 **w** ford-and-etal.co.uk
open Apr-Oct, daily 1030-1730.
admission £

A beautiful 19thC hall with watercolour paintings by Louisa Anne, Marchioness of Waterford, together with famous and unique 19thC murals and scenes from the Bible.

Morpeth Chantry Bagpipe Museum
The Chantry, Bridge Street, Morpeth NE61 1PD
t (01670) 500717 **w** castlemorpeth.gov.uk
open All year, Mon-Sat, Bank Hols 1000-1700.
admission Free

Set in a 13thC church building, this unusual museum specialises in the history and development of Northumbrian small pipes and their music.

Vindolanda (Chesterholm) Hadrian's Wall
Chesterholm Museum,
Bardon Mill NE47 7JN
t (01434) 344277
w vindolanda.com
open Apr-Sep, daily 1000-1800. Oct-Nov, daily 1000-1700.
admission £

Visitors may inspect the remains of the Roman fort and settlement and see its extraordinary finds in the superb museum. Full-scale replicas of Roman buildings.

Woodhorn
QEII Country Park, Ashington NE63 9YF
t (01670) 528080
w experiencewoodhorn.com
open Apr-Oct, Wed-Sun 1000-1700. Nov-Mar, Wed-Sun 1000-1600.
admission Free

A fascinating visitor attraction celebrating Northumberland. A stunning new building, inspired by monster coal-cutting machines that once worked underground, houses an emotive display about life in the local mining community.

Wylam Railway Museum
Falcon Centre, Falcon Terrace, Wylam NE41 8EE
t (01661) 852174
open Apr-Mar, Tue, Thu 1400-1930, Sat 0900-1200.
admission Free

This small museum shows the importance of Wylam in the history of railway development and the work of famous local railway pioneers George Stephenson, Timothy Hackworth and William Hedley.

Country ways

The Countryside Rights of Way Act gives people new rights to walk on areas of open countryside and registered common land.

To find out where you can go and what you can do, as well as information about taking your dog to the countryside, go online at countrysideaccess.gov.uk.

And when you're out and about...

Always follow the Country Code

- **Be safe – plan ahead and follow any signs**
- **Leave gates and property as you find them**
- **Protect plants and animals, and take your litter home**
- **Keep dogs under close control**
- **Consider other people**

Tees Valley

FAMILY FUN

Darlington Railway Centre and Museum

North Road Station, Darlington DL3 6ST
t (01325) 460532 **w** drcm.org.uk
open Daily 1000-1700 (excl 25 Dec, 1-2 Jan).
admission Adult: £2.50

Step back in time in one of the world's oldest railway stations – see, touch, feel and smell living railway heritage. More than just a museum, enjoy family-friendly events, too. There's always something to see and do, whatever the weather. Fun for everyone, from Grandma to the tiniest tot!

voucher offer – see back section

Nature's World

Ladgate Lane, Acklam, Middlesbrough TS5 7YN
t (01642) 594895
w naturesworld.org.uk
open Apr-Sep, daily 1000-1700. Oct-Mar, daily 1030-1530.
admission £

Demonstration gardens, wildlife pond, white garden, shop, tearoom and unique River Tees model. Futuristic Hydroponicum and Eco Centre now open, powered by renewable energy. Family trails and play areas.

NATURE AND WILDLIFE

Flatts Lane Woodland Country Park

Woodland Country Park, Visitor Centre, Flatts Lane, Middlesbrough TS6 0NN
t (01642) 459629
w redcar-cleveland.gov.uk/countryside
open All year, Mon-Fri 0830-1630, Sun 1000-1600.
admission Free

Country park comprising 100 acres of woodland and scrub. Visitor centre with exhibition showing the past, present and future landscape. Shop, picnic site and play area.

Gisborough Forest and Walkway Visitor Centre

Pinchinthorpe, Guisborough TS14 8HD
t (01287) 631132
w redcar-cleveland.gov.uk
open Summer: Mon-Fri, 0900-1630, Sat-Sun 1000-1700. Winter: Mon-Fri 0900-1600, Sat-Sun 1000-1630.
admission Free

Countryside visitor centre with self-guided trails, orienteering, walks and mountain biking. Situated on the edge of Guisborough Forest. Picnic areas with fantastic views of the Tees Valley.

HISTORIC ENGLAND

Guisborough Priory

Church Street, Guisborough TS14 6HG
t (01287) 633801
open All year, Wed-Sun 0900-1700.
admission £

An Augustinian priory founded by Robert the Bruce in 1119, the remains of which include the gatehouse and the east end of a 14thC church.

Tocketts Water Mill

Skelton Road, Guisborough TS14 6TC
t (01287) 634437
open Jul-Sep, Sun 1400-1600.
admission £

Fully restored water-driven corn mill and Grade II listed building. Flour-grinding and -grading machinery dating from the 18thC and 19thC. Wholemeal flour, stone-ground on some Sundays.*

Transporter Bridge and Visitor Centre

Ferry Road, Middlesbrough TS2 1PL
t (01642) 728162
w middlesbrough.gov.uk
open Bridge: All Year, Mon-Sat 0500-2300, Sun 1400-2300. Visitor Centre: All Year, Mon-Sat 0900-1700, Sun 1400-1700.
admission Free

A unique structure which can carry nine cars or 200 people on each crossing. Gantry system. Visitor information centre and shop.

ENTERTAINMENT AND CULTURE

Captain Cook Birthplace Museum

Stewart Park, Marton, Middlesbrough TS7 8AT
t (01642) 311211
w captcook-ne.co.uk
open Mar-Oct, Tue-Sun 1000-1730. Nov-Feb, Tue-Sun 0900-1600.
admission Free

Discover why Captain Cook is the world's most famous navigator and explorer. Find out about life below decks in the 18th century. Temporary exhibitions and permanent displays.

Cleveland Ironstone Mining Museum

Deepdale, Skinningrove,
Saltburn-by-the-Sea TS13 4AP
t (01287) 642877
w ironstonemuseum.co.uk
open Apr-Oct, daily 1300-1700.
admission £

Discover the special skills and customs of the miners that helped make Cleveland the most important ironstone-mining district in Victorian and Edwardian England.

Darlington Railway Centre and Museum

North Road Station, Darlington DL3 6ST
t (01325) 460532 **w** drcm.org.uk
open Daily 1000-1700 (excl 25 Dec, 1-2 Jan).
admission Adult: £2.50

Step back in time in one of the world's oldest railway stations – see, touch, feel and smell living railway heritage. More than just a museum, enjoy family-friendly events, too. There's always something to see and do, whatever the weather. Fun for everyone, from Grandma to the tiniest tot!

V voucher offer – see back section

MIMA, Middlesbrough Institute of Modern Art

Middlesbrough Central Square,
Middlesbrough TS1 2BG
t (01642) 803434 **w** mima.uk.com
open Apr-Mar, Mon-Sat 1000-1700, Sun 1200-1600, Bank Hols 1000-1700.
admission Free

MIMA is a new gallery of modern and contemporary art in central Middlesbrough. Admission is free. Exhibitions of fine art and craft change every three months.

Friendly help and advice

Tourist Information Centres offer suggestions of places to visit and things to do as well as friendly help with accommodation and holiday ideas. To find the one nearest to you text TIC LOCATE to 64118.

Tyne and Wear

FAMILY FUN

Karting North East
Warden Law Motorsport Centre, Sunderland SR3 2PR
t (01915) 214050 **w** kartingnortheast.com
open Daily, 0900-2000.
admission ££££

A 1,250m outdoor karting and off-road centre offering high standards of safety and professionalism. Clubhouse with showers, changing facilities and meeting room.

New Metroland
39 Garden Walk, MetroCentre, Gateshead NE11 9XY
t (01914) 932048 **w** metroland.uk.com
open School Hols: Mon-Sat 1000-2000, Sun 1100-1800. Term Time: Mon-Fri, 1200-2000, Sat 1000-2000, Sun 1100-1800.
admission £££

Europe's largest indoor funfair with twelve major attractions including the New Rollercoaster, Disco Dodgems, Whirling Waltzer and Children's Adventure Play Area.

Ocean Beach Pleasure Park
Sea Road, South Shields NE33 2ld
t (01914) 561617 **w** oceanbeach.co.uk
open Apr-Nov, daily. Please phone for times.
admission Free

This is the only funfair on the north east coast. Guaranteed new attractions every season. A great day out for all the family. See website for details.

Pier Amusements Centre
South Shields NE33 2JS
t (01914) 553885
open Daily 1000-2000.
admission £

The centre has all the latest in amusement equipment including Quasar, a futuristic game where each player is armed with a laser gun and shoots the opposition to win points.

Sunderland Wall
Doxford Works, Pallion Quay,
Sunderland SR4 6TQ
t (01915) 144234
w sunderlandwall.co.uk
open All year, Mon-Fri 1000-2200, Sat-Sun 1000-2000.
admission ££

The highest and largest indoor climbing centre in Europe, offering a bouldering wall as well as larger, top-roped and lead walls.

Wet 'N Wild
Rotary Way, Royal Quays,
North Shields NE29 6DA
t (01912) 961333
w wetnwild.co.uk
open Apr-Jun, Wed-Thu 1200-1930, Fri 1200-2000, Sat 1000-2000, Sun 1000-1900. July-Sep, Bank Hols, Mon-Sat 1000-2000, Sun 1000-1900. Oct-Mar, Wed-Thu 1200-1930, Fri 1200-2000, Sat 1000-2000, Sun 1000-1900.
admission ££

Tropical indoor water park. A fun water playground providing the wildest and wettest indoor rapid experience. Whirlpools, slides and meandering lazy river.

Whickham Thorns Outdoor Activity Centre
Market Lane,
Dunston NE11 9NX
t (01914) 335767
w gateshead.gov.uk
open Apr-Oct, Mon-Fri 0900-2000, Sat 1100-1830, Sun 1200-1500. Nov-Mar, Mon-Fri 1100-1000, Sat 1100-1830, Sun, 1200-1500.
admission Free

Multi-activity outdoor centre featuring skiing, snowboarding, indoor climbing, archery, assault course, orienteering, mountain biking and team challenges.

NATURE AND WILDLIFE

Blue Reef Aquarium
Grand Parade,
Tynemouth NE30 4JF
t (01912) 581031
w bluereefaquarium.co.uk
open Apr-Oct, Mon-Sat 1000-1730, Sun 1200-1730. Nov-Mar, Mon-Sat 1000-1630, Sun 1200-1630.
admission ££

More than 30 living displays exploring the drama of the North Sea and the dazzling beauty of a spectacular coral reef with its own underwater tunnel.

For key to symbols see page 211.

Birkheads Secret Gardens & Nursery

Birkheads Lane, nr Hedley Hall Woods, Sunniside, Newcastle upon Tyne NE16 5EL
t (01207) 232262 **w** birkheadsnursery.co.uk
open Mar-Oct, Tue-Sun 1000-1700.
admission Adult: £2.50

Discover Birkheads, a magical place. Follow winding paths into hidden, individually themed areas making up the three-acre country garden rich with colour, scent, ideas, inspirational plants and wildlife. Before browsing the nursery for unusual plants, enjoy panoramic views and freshly ground coffee on the terrace of the topiary garden.

V voucher offer – see back section

Derwent Walk Country Park

Rowlands Gill NE39 1AU
t (01207) 545212 **w** gateshead.gov.uk
open All Year, Mon-Fri 1200-1400, Sat-Sun, Bank Hols 1200-1700.
admission Free

Woodlands, riverside meadows and the Derwent Walk (a disused railway line). Served by Thornley Woodlands Visitor Centre and Swalwell Visitor Centre.

Gateshead Angel of the North

Durham Road, Low Eighton, Gateshead NE9 6AA
t (01914) 784222 **w** gateshead.gov.uk
open Daily.
admission Free

Britain's largest sculpture designed by Antony Gormley, standing 20m high with a wing span of 54m. The steel structure can withstand winds of more than 100 miles per hour.

Mowbray Park

Burdon Road, Sunderland SR1 1PP
t (01915) 532323
w sunderland.gov.uk
open All Year, Mon-Sat 1000-1700, Sun 1400-1700.
admission Free

The park recreates the heyday of Victorian leisure with features for young and old alike. Nearby, the Winter Gardens will fascinate and entertain – all for free!

Saltwell Park

Saltwell Road, Gateshead NE8 4SF
t (01914) 335900
w gateshead.gov.uk
open Daily, dawn-dusk.
admission Free

One of Britain's finest examples of a Victorian Park and offering bedding displays, rose garden, play areas, shrubbery, a lake with boating and bowls.

WWT Washington Wetland Centre

Pattinson, Washington NE38 8LE
t (01914) 165454
w wwt.org.uk
open Apr-Oct, daily 0930-1700. Nov-Mar, daily 0930-1600.
admission ££

Conservation site with 100 acres of wetland and woodland. Home to wildfowl, insects and flora. Lakeside hides, wild bird feeding, station, waterside cafe, picnic areas and playground.

HISTORIC ENGLAND

Gateshead Millennium Bridge

South Shore Road, Gateshead NE8 3AE
t (01914) 784222
w gateshead.gov.uk/bridge
open Daily.
admission Free

A stunning pedestrian and cycle bridge which operates like the giant lid of an eye slowly opening, forming an arch to allow the passage of river traffic.

Gibside

Burnopfield NE16 6BG
t (01207) 541820
w nationaltrust.org.uk
open Grounds: Apr-Oct, daily 1000-1800. Nov-Feb, daily 1000-1600. Chapel: Apr-Oct, daily 1100-1630. Stables: Apr-Oct, daily 1100-1630. Nov-Feb, daily 1100-1530.
admission ££

Sixteen miles of riverside and woodland walks beside the River Derwent. Also there is a beautiful 18thC Palladian chapel, Georgian stables and greenhouse to view.

National Glass Centre

Liberty Way, Sunderland SR6 0GL
t (01915) 155555 **w** nationalglasscentre.com
open Daily, 1000-1700.
admission Free

An inspirational visitor experience. Enjoy an ever-changing programme of exhibitons in glass, live glass blowing and a stunning restaurant overlooking the River Wear.

St Nicholas Cathedral

St Nicholas Church Yard, Newcastle upon Tyne NE1 1PF
t (01912) 321939
w newcastle-ang-cathedral-stnicholas.org.uk
open All Year, Mon-Fri 0700-1800, Sat 0830-1600, Sun 0700-1200 1600-1900, Bank Hols 0700-1200.
admission Free

Thirteenth and 14thC church, added to in the 18thC-20thC. Famous lantern tower, pre-reformation font and font cover and 15thC stained glass roundel in the side chapel.

Saint Pauls Monastery

Church Bank, Jarrow NE32 3DZ
t (01914) 897052
open All year, Mon-Sat 100-1600, Sun 1430-1600.
admission Free

Founded in 682, home of the Venerable Bede, re-founded in 1075. Remains of cloister buildings. Part of Bede's church survived as chancel of parish church.

Segedunum (Wallsend) Roman Fort, Baths and Museum

Buddle Street, Wallsend NE28 6HR
t (01912) 369347 **w** twmuseums.org.uk/segedunum
open Apr-Oct, daily 1000-1700. Nov-Mar, daily 1000-1500.
admission £

Discover life on Hadrian's Wall 1,800 years ago. Explore buildings and excavated ruins, and see original remains of the wall, fascinating displays and exciting computer interactives.

Seven Stories, The Centre for Children's Books

30 Lime Street, Ouseburn Valley, Newcastle upon Tyne NE1 2PQ
t 0845 271 0777 **w** sevenstories.org.uk
open All year, Mon-Sat 1000-1700, Sun 1100-1700.
admission £

Britain's first centre dedicated to children's literature, bringing together original manuscripts and artwork from some of the best-loved children's books. There is a changing programme of exhibitions.

Souter Lighthouse and The Leas

Coast Road, Whitburn, Sunderland SR6 7NH
t (01915) 293161 **w** nationaltrust.org.uk
open Apr-Oct, Mon-Thu, Sat-Sun 1100-1700.
admission £

A magnificent lighthouse located on a beautiful stretch of coastline. Explore the engine room, and climb the winding staircase to the top of the tower.

Tynemouth Castle and Priory

Tynemouth NE30 4BZ
t (01912) 571090
w english-heritage.org.uk
open See website for details.
admission £

Dating from the 7th century, the burial place of Northumbrian kings. The priory was destroyed by the Danes, later founded as a Benedictine Priory, and is now a picturesque ruin.

Washington Old Hall

The Avenue, Washington Village, Washington NE38 7LE
t (01914) 166879 **w** nationaltrust.org.uk
open House: Apr-Oct, Mon-Wed, Sun 1100-1700. Gardens: Apr-Oct, Mon-Wed, Sun 1000-1700.
admission £

A delightful stone-built manor house on the site of the home of the ancestors of George Washington. Displays, gardens and 17thC room recreations. A gem of a property!

ENTERTAINMENT AND CULTURE

BALTIC Centre for Contemporary Art

Gateshead Quays, South Shore Road, Gateshead NE8 3BA
t (01914) 781810 **w** balticmill.com
open Daily 1000-1800.
admission Free

Housed in a landmark industrial building on the River Tyne is the biggest gallery of its kind in the world presenting a dynamic, diverse and international programme of contemporary visual art.

Bede's World

Church Bank, Jarrow NE32 3DY
t (01914) 892106 **w** bedesworld.co.uk
open Apr-Oct, Mon-Sat 1000-1730, Sun 1200-1730. Nov-Mar, Mon-Sat 1000-1630, Sun 1200-1630.
admission £

Discover the exciting world of the Venerable Bede, early medieval Europe's greatest scholar. Church, monastic site, museum with exhibitions and recreated Anglo-Saxon farm.

Biscuit Factory

16 Stoddart Street, Newcastle upon Tyne NE2 1AN
t (01912) 611103 **w** thebiscuitfactory.com
open All year, Mon 1100-1700, Tues-Sat 1000-2000, Sun 1100-1700.
admission Free

A large commercial art space providing a vibrant, relaxed environment of the highest quality for a wide range of art and artists and for the public.

Childhood Memories Toy Museum

Palace Building, Grand Parade, Tynemouth NE30 4JH
t (01912) 591776 **w** tynemouthtoymuseum.co.uk
open Apr-May, Sat-Sun 1030-1700. Jun-Sep, Tue-Sun 1030-1700. Oct-Nov, Sat-Sun 1030-1700.
admission £

The museum has over 7,000 toys on display dating from 1890-1970. Childhood memorabilia, dolls, games, pedal cars, prams, cars, puzzles, clockwork and mechanical toys.

Discovery Museum

Blandford House, Blandford Square, Newcastle upon Tyne NE1 4JA
t (01912) 326789 **w** twmuseums.org.uk/discovery
open All year, Mon-Sat 1000-1700, Sun 1400-1700.
admission Free

The museum offers a wide variety of experiences for all the family to enjoy. Explore Newcastle Story, Live Wires, Science Maze and Fashion Works.

Laing Art Gallery

New Bridge Street, Newcastle upon Tyne NE1 8AJ
t (01912) 327734 **w** twmuseums.org.uk
open All Year, Mon-Sat 1000-1700, Sun 1400-1700.
admission Free

The gallery is home to an important collection of 18thC and 19thC paintings, which are shown alongside temporary exhibitions of historic and contemporary art.

Monkwearmouth Station Museum

North Bridge Street, Sunderland SR5 1AP
t (01915) 677075
w twmuseums.org.uk/monkwearmouth
open All year, Mon-Sat 1000-1700, Sun 1400-1700.
admission Free

Take a look inside a real Victorian railway station and visit the fascinating ticket office. Watch trains pass by and 'drive' a full-size bus cab. Re-opening in 2007, visitors will be able to enjoy a range of exciting new displays.

North East Aircraft Museum

Old Washington Road, Sunderland SR5 3HZ
t (01915) 190662
open Daily 1000-1700.
admission £

A collection of aircraft and aero engines. Museum buildings with World War II exhibits. Vulcan bomber and over 30 aircraft under cover.

The Sage Gateshead

St Mary's Square, Gatshead Quays, Gateshead NE8 2JR
t (01914) 434666 **w** thesagegateshead.org
open Daily, 0900-1100.
admission Free

The pioneering centre for music and musical discovery on the south bank of the River Tyne, presenting leading British and international artists in all kinds of music.

Shipley Art Gallery

Prince Consort Road, Gateshead NE8 4JB
t (01914) 771495 **w** twmuseums.org.uk/shipley
open All year, Mon-Sat 1000-1700, Sun, 1400-1700.
admission Free

The gallery is home to one of the largest collections of contemporary craft in northern England. Exhibits include jewellery, textiles, ceramics, furniture and glass.

Stephenson Railway Museum

Middle Engine Lane, North Shields NE29 8DX
t (01912) 007146 **w** twmuseums.org.uk/stephenson
open Apr-Oct, Sat-Sun 1100-1600.
admission Free

Museum covering steam, diesel and electric trains. Use interactive exhibits to discover how trains work, and enjoy our new multi-sensory display.

Sunderland Museum and Winter Gardens

Burdon Road, Sunderland SR1 1PP
t (01915) 532323 **w** twmuseums.org.uk/sunderland
open All year, Mon-Sat 1000-1700, Sun 1400-1700.
admission Free

Stunning winter gardens, with 1,500 of the world's most exotic flowers, plants and trees. Dramatic 'Museum Street', 11 galleries, tree-top walkway, shop, brasserie and lifts.

FOOD AND DRINK

Birkheads Secret Gardens & Nursery

Birkheads Lane, nr Hedley Hall Woods, Sunniside, Newcastle upon Tyne NE16 5EL
t (01207) 232262 **w** birkheadsnursery.co.uk
open Mar-Oct, Tue-Sun 1000-1700.
admission Adult: £2.50

Discover Birkheads, a magical place. Follow winding paths into hidden, individually themed areas making up the three-acre country garden rich with colour, scent, ideas, inspirational plants and wildlife. Before browsing the nursery for unusual plants, enjoy panoramic views and freshly ground coffee on the terrace of the topiary garden.

voucher offer – see back section

Yorkshire

FAMILY FUN

Aerial Extreme

Camp Hill, Kirklington DL8 2LS
t (01845) 567100 **w** aerialextreme.co.uk
open Feb-Nov, Sat-Sun 0900-1700.
admission ££££

Get high above the forest floor travelling from tree-to-tree encountering rope bridges, log walks, tightropes, scramble nets and zip slides.

Barnsley Metrodome Leisure Complex

Queens Ground, Queens Road, Barnsley S71 1AN
t (01226) 730060 **w** themetrodome.co.uk
open All year, see website for details.
admission £

The Space Adventure is Britain's most exciting and imaginative indoor water attraction featuring the Space Bullet, possibly the fastest water slide in the universe!

Bridlington Leisure World

The Promenade, Bridlington YO15 2QQ
t (01262) 606715 **w** bridlington.net/leisureworld
open Please phone for details.
admission £

One of the East Riding's premier leisure attractions boasts three pools, including a fun pool with waves, slides, rainstorm effect and water features, a 25m training pool and a learner pool.

Brockholes Farm Visitor Centre

Warnington Lane, Branton DN3 3NH
t (01302) 535450 **w** brockholesfarm.co.uk
open All year, daily 1030-1730.
admission ££

Visitor centre housing a selection of farm animals including a pedigree herd of Limousin cattle. Also small animals including rabbits, guinea pigs, hamsters etc. Woodland walk and exotic birds.

For key to symbols see page 211.

Cannon Hall Farm
Bark House Lane, Cawthorne, Barnsley S75 4AT
t (01226) 790427 **w** cannonhallfarm.co.uk
open Apr-Sep, daily 1030-1630. Oct-Mar, daily 1030-1600.
admission £

A multiple-award-winning farm open to visitors all year round. A large variety of animals including donkeys, cows, rabbits, guinea pigs, wallabies and pygmy goats.

Cruckley Animal Farm
Foston-on-the-Wolds YO25 8BS
t (01262) 488337 **w** cruckley.co.uk
open Apr-Sep, daily 1000-1730.
admission £

A working family farm with many kinds of modern and rare breeds of cows, sheep and pigs. See the hatchery, children's paddock, waterfowl lake and daily milking demonstrations.

The Dome Leisure Centre
Doncaster Leisure Park, Bawtry Road, Doncaster DN4 7PD
t (01302) 370777 **w** the-dome.co.uk
open See website for details.
admission Free

The largest leisure facility in the UK with all the facilities under one roof. Activities include bowling, swimming, skating, gym, aerobic studio, saunas, badminton and basketball.

Embsay & Bolton Abbey Steam Railway
Bolton Abbey Station, Bolton Abbey BD23 6AF
t (01756) 710614 **w** embsayboltonabbeyrailway.org.uk
open See website for details.
admission ££

The railway runs between Embsay Station, built in 1888, and the new, award-winning Bolton Abbey Station. The five-mile journey through the Yorkshire Dales passes Holywell Halt.

Fast Track Karting
Poorhouse Lane, Preston Road, Hull HU9 5DF
t (01482) 308740 **w** ukfasttrack.com/
open All year, Mon-Fri 1000-2100, Sat-Sun 1000-1600.
admission ££

A purpose-built circuit designed by professional racing drivers. Experience fast straights, chicanes and hairpin bends. Race commentary is provided throughout the day to give that extra special Grand Prix atmosphere.

Flamingo Land Theme Park and Zoo
Kirby Misperton YO17 6UX
t (01653) 668287 **w** flamingoland.co.uk
open Apr-Oct, Mon-Fri 1000-1700, Sat-Sun 1000-1800.
admission ££££

One price family adventure park with over 100 rides and attractions including the UK's only motorbike launch rollercoaster, the free-falling cliff hanger and Kamali, the suspended looping rollercoaster.

Fosse Hill Jet Ski Centre
Catwick Lane, Brandesburton YO25 8SB
t (01964) 542608 **w** fossehill.co.uk
open Daily 1000-dusk.
admission Free

Jet-skiing lake on site. Lakeside walk, bar, fast food, ice cream, adventure playground. Seventy-two seasonal pitches for touring caravans.

The Foundry Climbing Centre
45 Mowbray Street, Sheffield S3 8EN
t (0114) 279 6331 **w** foundryclimbing.com
open Summer, Mon-Fri 1000-2200, Sat-Sun 1000-1800. Winter, Mon-Fri 1000-2200, Sat-Sun 1000-2000.
admission ££

A dedicated indoor climbing centre offering walls up to 13m high and lead/top rope climbs with 150 routes and bouldering. On-site cafe and climbing shop.

Hazel Brow Visitor Centre
Low Row DL11 6NE
t (01748) 886224 **w** hazelbrow.co.uk
open Apr-Sep, Tue-Thu, Sat-Sun 1030-1630.
admission £

Award-winning 200-acre organic livestock farm in the heart of Swaledale. Crafts and skills demonstrations including spinning and quilting, stick and rug making, butter making and sheepdog training.

Herringthorpe Leisure Complex
Middle Lane South, Rotherham S65 2HR
t (01709) 388500
open All year, Mon-Fri 0900-2200, Sat 0900-1900, Sun 0900-2000.
admission £

The complex comprises a leisure pool with wave machine and aqua slide, multi-sports facilities including four squash courts and ten badminton courts, fitness suite and five-a-side football pitches.

Hull Arena
Kingston Street, Hull HU1 2DZ
t (01482) 325252 **w** hullcc.gov.uk
open Daily, please phone for details.
admission £

Olympic-sized ice arena with seating for 2,000. Cafe, bar. Group skating lessons, private lessons, hockey matches, discount for parties and facilities for disabled.

Keighley and Worth Valley Railway
Haworth Station, Keighley BD22 8NJ
t (01535) 645214 **w** kwvr.co.uk
open See website for details.
admission ££

Fully operational, preserved railway branch line, five miles long (Keighley to Oxenhope). Six award-winning stations including Oakworth, 'The Railway Children' station. The location for many film and television productions.

Kirklees Light Railway
Park Mill Way, Clayton West HD8 9XJ
t (01484) 865727 **w** kirkleeslightrailway.com
open See website for details.
admission ££

Steam along on Hawk, Owl, Badger or Fox, our four handbuilt steam engines. An enchanting 50-minute return trip on narrow gauge rail takes you through superb scenery.

Laser Quest
29 St Johns Road, Huddersfield HD1 5DX
t (01484) 307040 **w** darkfuture.co.uk
open All year, Mon-Fri 1200-2300, Sat-Sun 1000-2300.
admission £

Laser Quest combines the classic games of tag and hide-and-seek with a high-tech twist. Donning the most sophisticated laser tag equipment available, the game is played in a large, multi-level arena.

Lightwater Valley Theme Park
North Stainley HG4 3HT
t 0870 458 0040 **w** lightwatervalley.net
open See website for details.
admission ££££

Visit Lightwater Valley for the ultimate day out. Experience the fun and thrills of this family-sized theme park. Pay once and enjoy the fun all day long.

Magna Science Adventure Centre
Sheffield Road, Templeborough, Rotherham S60 1DX
t (01709) 723123 **w** magnatrust.org.uk
open Mar-Nov, daily 1000-1700. Dec-Feb, Tue-Sun 1000-1700.
admission ££

Magna is the UK's first science adventure centre, set in the vast Templeborough steelworks in Rotherham. Within this cavernous space are four pavilions, giving you the ultimate interactive experience.

The Moors National Park Centre
Lodge Lane, Danby, Whitby YO22 2NB
t (01439) 772737 **w** moors.uk.net
open Apr-Oct, daily 1000-1700. Nov-Feb, Sat-Sun 1100-1600. Mar, daily 1100-1600.
admission Free

see ad on p254

National Railway Museum
Leeman Road, York YO26 4XJ
t 0870 421 4001 **w** nrm.org.uk
open All year, daily 1000-1800.
admission Free

Explore the three giant halls at the world's largest railway museum with true railway legends such as the Flying Scotsman and Mallard. An unforgettable experience for all the family.

Newham Grange Leisure Farm
Wykeham Way, Coulby Newham, Middlesbrough TS8 0TG
t (01642) 300202
w middlesbrough.gov.uk
open Apr-Sep, daily 0930-1730. Oct-Mar, Sat-Sun 1000-1600.
admission £

A working farm that is recognised as a Rare Breeds Survival Trust Approved Conservation Centre with many breeds to see. A great day out, allowing visitors to interact with animals.

North Yorkshire Moors Railway
Pickering Station, Park Street, Pickering YO18 7AJ
t (01751) 473799
w northyorkshiremoorsrailway.com
open See website for details.
admission £££

The country's most popular heritage railway with an 18-mile line running through the beautiful North York Moors National Park, between the market town of Pickering and the village of Grosmont.

The Norwich Union Yorkshire Wheel
Leeman Road, York YO26 4XJ
t (01904) 621261
w nrm.org.uk
open All year, daily 1000-1800.
admission ££

York's new gigantic observation wheel offers unforgettable views of the beautiful city of York and the surrounding countryside as you have never seen it before.

Saltburn Miniature Railway
Valley Gardens, Saltburn-by-the-Sea
t (01642) 502863
w saltburn-miniature-railway.org.uk
open Apr-Sep, Sat-Sun, Bank Hols 1300-1700.
admission £

A 15''-gauge miniature railway running from the seafront to the Valley Gardens and Woodland Centre. First established in 1947 and operated solely by volunteers.

Settle-Carlisle Railway
Town Hall, Market Place, Settle BD24 9EJ
t 0800 980 0766
w settle-carlisle.co.uk
open See website for details.
admission £

The 72-mile spectacular railway journey takes you through the breathtaking Yorkshire Dales, into the Eden Valley and Appleby, and on to Cumbria's vibrant capital city – Carlisle.

Thackray Museum

Nr St James's Hospital, Beckett Street, Leeds LS9 7LN
t (0113) 244 4343 **w** thackraymuseum.org
open Daily 1000-1700 (excl 24-26, 31 Dec, 1 Jan), last entry 1500.
admission Adult: £5.50

The award-winning Thackray Museum has something for everyone. Experience life as a character in the Victorian slums of 1840, where you will be flabbergasted at the incredible lotions and potions once offered as cures, and have fun exploring the human body in the new interactive Life Zone!

V voucher offer – see back section

Trans Pennine Trail

Westgate Plaza One, Westgate, Barnsley S70 2DR
t (01226) 772574
w transpenninetrail.org.uk
open Daily.
admission Free

Walk, cycle or horse-ride on the TPT, from Southport to Hornsea, Leeds to Chesterfield, or York. Enjoy varied scenery and many places of interest along the way. Easy going, mainly traffic-free trails that are ideal for families with young children. Amazing Space winner – National Lottery Awards 2006.

Waterworld
Leisure Park, Monks Cross, Huntington YO32 9XX
t (01904) 642111 **w** courtneys.co.uk
open All year, Mon-Thu 0630-2200, Fri 0630-2100, Sat-Sun 0800-1700.
admission £

A fun pool where you can surf the waves, ride the slides and float on the 'Lazy River'. Also fitness pool, health suite, sauna, steam room and sunbeds.

Xscape Castleford
Colorado Way, Glasshoughton WF10 4TA
t 0871 200 3221 **w** xscape.co.uk
open All year, daily 0600-2300.
admission Free

The UK's ultimate family entertainment destination housing the largest indoor real-snow slope, 14-screen cinema complex, 20-lane bowling alley, urban-lifestyle shops, bars, restaurants and more.

York Dungeon
12 Clifford Street, York YO1 9RD
t (01904) 632599 **w** thedungeons.com
open Apr-Sep, daily 1030-1700. Oct, daily 1030-1630. Nov-Jan, daily 1100-1600. Feb-Mar, daily 1030-1630.
admission £££

Catch the plague at York Dungeon, take a spine-tingling tour round the plague-ravaged streets of 14thC York. The Black Death wiped out a third of the population in Europe.

York Maze
Grimston Bar Park & Ride Site, Hull Road, York YO19 5LA
t (01904) 415364 **w** yorkmaze.co.uk
open Jul-Sep, daily 1000-1800.
admission ££

One of Yorkshire's most popular summer attractions, the maze is carved out of an amazing 1.5 million growing maize plants! Activities include talking sculptures, farm animals and monster tractor rides.

NATURE AND WILDLIFE

Anglers Country Park
Haw Park Lane, Wintersett WF4 2EB
t (01924) 303982 **w** wakefield.gov.uk
open Apr-Oct, Tue-Sun 1100-1600. Nov-Mar, Tue-Sun 1030-1530.
admission Free

Country park near Wakefield with visitor centre, nature reserve, picnic area and excellent winter wildfowl site. Booster scooters available for loan from discovery centre.

The Arboretum at Castle Howard
York YO60 7DA
t (01653) 648650
w kewatch.co.uk
open Mar-Oct, daily 1000-1800. Nov, daily 1000-1600.
admission £

The Arboretum Trust, a registered charity, holds an amazing collection of rare trees and shrubs collected as seed worldwide. Gathered from Chile to China, from Afghanistan to Australia, all flourish in this quiet corner of North Yorkshire.

Bolton Abbey Estate
Estate Office, Bolton Abbey BD23 6EX
t (01756) 718009
w boltonabbey.com
open Apr, daily 0900-1900. May-Aug, daily 0900-2100. Sep-Oct, daily 0900-1900. Nov-Mar, daily 0900-1800.
admission ££

Ruins of 12thC priory in a park setting by the River Wharfe. Tearooms, catering, nature trails, fishing, walking and picturesque countryside.

Brimham Rocks (National Trust)
Summer Bridge HG3 4DW
t (01423) 780688
w nationaltrust.org.uk
open All year, daily 0800-dusk.
admission Free

At nearly 300m high, Brimham Rocks enjoys spectacular views. Set within the Nidderdale Area of Outstanding Natural Beauty, this fascinating moorland is filled with strange and fantastic rock formations.

BTCV Wildlife Garden
Hollybush Conservation Centre, Broad Lane, Kirkstall LS5 3BP
t (0113) 274 2335
w btcv.org.uk
open All year, Mon-Fri 1300-1600.
admission Free

The Hollybush Nature Garden has been created on a formerly derelict site and consists of many varied habitats, creating a haven for wildlife and an inspiration to visitors.

Burnby Hall Gardens and Museum Trust
The Balk, Pocklington YO42 2QE
t (01377) 288359
w burnbyhallgardens.co.uk
open Apr-Sep, daily 1000-1800.
admission £

Yorkshire in Bloom winner. The gardens are a glorious haven of beauty and tranquillity and include the two lakes that house the National Collection of hardy water lilies.

For key to symbols see page 211.

Chevin Forest Park
White House, Johnny Lane, off Birdcage Walk, Otley LS21 3JL
t (01943) 465023
open Daily.
admission **Free**

Chevin Forest Park is a wooded escarpment overlooking Otley, with fabulous views over the Wharfe valley. This local nature reserve comprises 700 acres of woodland and crags.

Constable Burton Hall Gardens
Constable Burton DL8 5LJ
t (01677) 450428
w constableburtongardens.co.uk
open Apr-Oct, daily 0900-1800.
admission **£**

A terraced woodland garden attached to a beautiful Palladian house (not open) designed by John Carr. Near the main entrance drive is a stream, bog garden and rockery.

The Forbidden Corner
Tupgill Park Estate, Coverham, Middleham DL8 4TJ
t (01969) 640638
w yorkshirenet.co.uk/theforbiddencorner
open Apr-Oct, Mon-Sat 1200-1800, Sun, Bank Hols 1000-1800.
admission **££**

A unique labyrinth of tunnels, chambers, follies and surprises created in a four-acre garden in the heart of the Yorkshire Dales to challenge and delight children of all ages.

Green Garden Herbs
13 West Bank, Carlton, Nr Selby DN14 9PZ
t (01405) 860708
w greengardenherbs.co.uk
open Mar-Sep, Mon, Wed-Sun, 1000-1700.
admission **Free**

Small, independent herb nursery, specialising in aromatic, culinary, medicinal and ornamental herb plants. Lavender a speciality. Groups welcome, especially coach trips.

Hartshill Hayes Country Park
Oldbury Road, Hartshill CV10 0TE
t (024) 7639 5141
w warwickshire.gov.uk
open Apr, daily 0900-1900. May, daily 0900-2000. Jun-Jul, daily 0900-2100. Aug, daily 0900-2000. Sep, daily 0900-1900. Oct, daily 0900-1800. Nov-Dec, daily 0900-1600.
admission **Free**

One hundred and thirty-six acres of woodland and open hillside, reported site of Queen Boudicca's defeat by the Romans. Three waymarked walks and adventure playground for children.

Helmsley Walled Garden
Cleveland Way, Helmsley YO62 5AH
t (01439) 771427 **w** helmsleywalledgarden.co.uk
open Apr-Oct, daily 1030-1700.
admission **£**

A five-acre walled garden within the grounds of Duncombe Park. Constructed in 1756, the garden was derelict for many years but is now being restored by staff and volunteers.

Hollies Botanical Garden
off Weetwood Lane, Leeds LS16 5NZ
t (0113) 232 3069
open All year, dawn-dusk.
admission **Free**

Twenty-two hectares of land comprising flowering rhododendrons and azaleas from early spring to summer, herbaceous borders, mature plants and large woodland walks on three different levels.

Ingleborough Show Cave
Clapham LA2 8EE
t (01524) 251242 **w** ingleboroughcave.co.uk
open Mar-Sep, daily 1000-1700. Oct-Nov, daily 1000-1600.
admission **££**

The cave is 1.2 miles from Clapham village at the end of the nature trail through Ingleborough estate grounds (for which there is a separate small charge).

Kirkleatham Owl Centre
Kirkleatham, Redcar TS10 5NW
t (01642) 480512 **w** jillsowls.co.uk
open Summer: Tue-Sun 1030-1630.
admission **£**

Bird of prey centre with one of the most significant collections of owls in the British Isles. Falcons, buzzards vultures, kites, caracaras, baby owls and flying displays.

Land Farm Garden
Colden HX7 7PJ
t (01422) 842260
open May-Aug, Sat-Sun, Bank Hols 1000-1700.
admission **£**

The five-acre gardens have been constructed entirely by the owner for ease of maintenance. The gardens are well known for their sculpture, meconopses, azaleas, rhododendrons and summer borders.

Malham Tarn
Settle BD24 9PT
t (01729) 830416 **w** nationaltrust.org.uk
open Daily.
admission **Free**

The estate extends to over 7,200 acres of moor and farmland. Malham Tarn and the adjacent areas of raised bog, fen and woodland are protected as a National Nature Reserve.

The Moors National Park Centre
Lodge Lane, Danby, Whitby YO22 2NB
t (01439) 772737 **w** moors.uk.net
open Apr-Oct, daily 1000-1700. Nov-Feb, Sat-Sun 1100-1600. Mar, daily 1100-1600.
admission Free

see ad below

Newmillerdam Country Park
Barnsley Road, Newmillerdam WF2 6QF
t (01924) 303982 **w** wakefield.gov.uk
open Daily.
admission Free

Ninety-five hectares of woodland and water. The country park was once part of the medieval 'Chevet' estate. Attractions include woodland walks, easy walks around the lake and permanent orienteering course.

Ogden Water Country Park
Ogden Lane, Keighley Road, Ogden HX2 8YA
t (01422) 249136 **w** ogdenwater.org.uk
open Apr, daily 0800-2000. May, daily 0800-2100. Jun-Jul, daily 0800-2200. Aug, daily 0800-2100. Sep, daily 0800-2000. Oct, daily 0800-1900. Nov, daily 0800-1700. Dec, daily 0800-1700.
admission Free

A Calderdale 'Countryside Gateway' site with 174 acres of mixed woodland affording excellent views over Halifax and Calderdale. Reservoir and woodland walks. Information centre with guide books, leaflets, hot drinks.

Old Moor Wetland Centre
Old Moor Lane, Off Manvers Way, Broomhill, Wombwell S73 0YF
t (01226) 751593 **w** rspb.org.uk
open Feb-Oct, daily 0930-1700. Nov-Jan, daily 0930-1600.
admission £

An RSPB nature reserve set in 250 acres, including a visitor centre in converted farm buildings with hands-on, interactive displays and a film show.

Paddock Farm Water Gardens
West Lane, Dalton-on-Tees DL2 2PT
t (01325) 378286 **w** paddock-farm.co.uk
open Apr-Oct, Mon-Sat 1000-1800, Sun 1100-1700. Mov-Mar, Tue-Sat 1000-1800, Sun 1100-1700.
admission Free

Nine unique, individually designed gardens, taking inspiration from the Mediterranean to the Orient. Bridge, waterfall, pond and pagoda. Garden centre with experienced, friendly staff. Tearoom overlooking the gardens.

Parcevall Hall Gardens
Parceval Hall, Skyreholme BD23 6DE
t (01756) 720311 **w** parcevallhallgardens.co.uk
open Apr-Oct, daily 1000-1800.
admission £

The 16 acres of formal and woodland gardens offer magnificent views, and contain many specimen trees and shrubs collected from Western China and the Himalayas.

Admission is based on an adult price. Please check opening times and admission before travelling.

Pugneys Country Park
Asdale Road, off Denby Dale Road, Wakefield WF2 7EQ
t (01924) 302360 **w** wakefield.gov.uk
open All year, daily 0900-dusk.
admission Free

A 250-acre site with two lakes, the smaller of which is a nature reserve, and the larger a watersports lake for canoeing, sailing and windsurfing.

RHS Garden Harlow Carr
Crag Lane, (off B6162 Otley Road), Harrogate HG3 1QB
t (01423) 565418 **w** rhs.org.uk
open Mar-Oct, daily 0930-1800. Nov-Feb, daily 0930-1600.
admission ££

Spectacular 58 acres offering interest for all seasons – from vegetables to wildflowers and alpines to woodland. Bettys Cafe tea rooms and shop offering delicious food and drinks.

Rievaulx Terrace & Temples (National Trust)
The National Trust, Rievaulx YO62 5LJ
t (01439) 798340 **w** nationaltrust.org.uk
open Apr-Sep, daily 1100-1800. Oct, daily 1100-1700.
admission £

An 18thC grass-covered terrace, landscaped from wooded hillside with views of Rievaulx Abbey. Two classical temples, one furnished and decorated as a dining room. National Trust shop.

Rother Valley Country Park
Mansfield Road, Wales Bar, Rotherham S26 5PQ
t (01709) 856353 **w** rothervalleycountrypark.co.uk
open All year, daily 0830-dusk.
admission Free

This 750-acre country park offers woods and parkland, a visitor centre, craft centre, cafe and shop. Watersports activities include public hire of sailing dinghies, sailboards, canoes and family rowing boats.

Roundhay Park
1 Park Cottages, Roundhay Park, Leeds LS8 1ER
t (0113) 266 1850 **w** leeds.gov.uk
open Daily.
admission Free

One of Europe's largest municipal parks, comprising over 700 acres of rolling parkland with lakes, woodland, the gorge and ravine and specialist gardens. It is also home to Tropical World.

RSPB Blacktoft Sands Nature Reserve
Hillcrest, High Street, Whitgift DN14 8HL
t (01405) 704665 **w** rspb.org.uk
open All year, daily 0900-dusk.
admission £

One of North East England's best nature reserves. Nestled between the Yorkshire and Lincolnshire Wolds, the reserve is set on the banks of the Humber Estuary.

Sea Life and Marine Sanctuary
Scalby Mills, Scarborough YO12 6RP
t (01723) 376125 **w** sealife.co.uk
open All year, daily 1000-1600.
admission £££

Here, you will meet creatures that live in the oceans of the British Isles, ranging from starfish and crabs to rays and seals. Marine sanctuary and seal-rescue hospital.

Sheffield Botanical Gardens
Clarkehouse Road, Sheffield S10 2LN
t (0114) 267 6496 **w** sbg.org.uk
open Winter: Mon-Fri 0800-1600, Sat-Sun, Bank Hols 1000-1600. Summer: Mon-Fri 0800-dusk, Sat-Sun, Bank Hols 1000-dusk.
admission Free

Extensive gardens with over 5,500 species of plants. The gardens, which are Grade II Listed by English Heritage, were landscaped by Robert Marnock, a famous 19thC landscape designer.

Sheffield Winter Gardens
Surrey Street, Sheffield S1 2HH
t (0114) 273 6681 **w** sheffield.gov.uk
open Daily 0800-1800.
admission Free

One of the largest temperate glasshouses to be recently built in the UK, the award-winning Winter Gardens offer a stunning green world in the heart of the city.

Spurn Point
East Riding, Spurn Head YO24 1GN
t (01964) 650533
open Daily, weather permitting.
admission Free

A unique natural landscape: a narrow headland stretching into the Humber estuary spanning only 50m wide in some places and three and a half miles long.

Sutton Bank Visitor Centre North York Moors
Sutton Bank YO7 2EH
t (01439) 770657 **w** visitthemoors.co.uk
open Apr-Oct, daily 1000-1700. Nov-Feb, Sat-Sun 1100-1600. Mar, daily 1100-1600.
admission Free

A modern visitor centre set above Whitestone Cliffe with stunning views across the Vale of York. Exhibitions, tearoom, shop, local walks, guide books, tourist information, crafts and souvenirs for sale.

Thorp Perrow Arboretum & Falconry Centre
Thorp Perrow DL8 2PR
t (01677) 425323 **w** thorpperrow.com
open Daily, dawn-dusk.
admission ££

One of the largest collections of trees and shrubs in the North of England, set in 85 acres of woodland. Four national collections: ash, lime, walnut and laburnum.

Tropical Butterfly House, Wildlife and Farm
Hungerhill Farm, Woodsetts Road,
North Anston S25 4EQ
t (01909) 569416 **w** butterflyhouse.co.uk
open Apr-Sep, Mon-Fri 1000-1630, Sat-Sun 1000-1730. Nov-Mar, Mon-Fri 1100-1630, Sat-Sun 1000-1700.
admission ££

Exotic butterflies, plants and animals in a natural jungle environment. Falconry Centre, farm animals and pets, Unique Native Fauna and Flora Nature Trail, picnic area, formal gardens, gift shop and cafe.

Tropical World
Canal Gardens, Roundhay Park, Leeds LS8 1ER
t (0113) 266 1850 **w** leeds.gov.uk
open Summer: daily 1000-1800. Winter: daily 1000-1600.
admission £

An unforgettable, fun adventure on a tropical island. Land on the sandy white beach before forging inland to the rainforest where you will find waterfalls tumbling into jungle pools.

The Walled Garden at Scampston
Scampston Hall, Malton YO17 8NG
t (01944) 758224 **w** scampston.co.uk
open Apr-Oct, daily 1000-1700.
admission £

An inspired contemporary garden designed by the internationally acclaimed Piet Oudolf, winner of Gold and Best in Show at Chelsea in 2000. Rare plants for sale, restaurant.

Wentworth Castle Gardens
Lowe Lane, Stainborough S75 3ET
t (01226) 776040 **w** wentworthcastle.org
open Apr-Sep, daily 1000-1700. Oct-Mar, daily 1000-1600.
admission £

Wentworth Castle Gardens provide a wonderful day out for all the family. A secret Yorkshire treasure awaits you, hidden away in green rolling hills near Barnsley.

White Scar Cave
Ingleton LA6 3AW
t (01524) 241244 **w** whitescarcave.co.uk
open All year, daily 1000-1700, weather permitting.
admission ££

The longest show cave in Britain. A spectacular natural cave in the Yorkshire Dales National Park. See underground streams and waterfalls, thousands of stalactites, and the massive 200,000-year-old Battlefield Cavern.

Wolds Way Lavender
Deer Park Farm, Sandy Lane,
Wintringham YO17 8HW
t (01944) 758641 **w** deerparkfarm.com
open Apr-May, daily 1000-1600. Jun-Aug, daily 1000-1700. Sep-Oct, daily 1000-1600.
admission Free

Surrounded by mature woodland, on the edge of the picturesque Yorkshire Wolds, the newly created lavender and herb farm is a wonderful and relaxing place to visit.

York Gate Garden
Back Church Lane, Adel LS16 8DW
t (0113) 267 8240 **w** perennial.org.uk
open Apr-Sep, Thu, Sun, Bank Hols 1400-1700.
admission £

A one-acre garden created by the Spencer family between 1951 and 1994. It is recognised as one of the most innovative small gardens in the world.

Yorkshire Dales Falconry Centre
Crows Nest, Giggleswick LA2 8AS
t (01729) 822832 **w** falconryandwildlife.com
open Daily 1000-dusk.
admission ££

Falconry centre with many species of birds of prey from around the world including vultures, eagles, hawks, falcons and owls. Flying displays, lecture room and aviaries.

Yorkshire Lavender
Terrington YO60 6PB
t (01653) 648008 **w** lavenderland.co.uk
open Apr-Oct, daily 1000-1700.
admission Free

The North of England's premier lavender attraction/herb nursery is set in a hillside farm of 60 acres within the Howardian Hills, an Area of Outstanding Natural Beauty.

Yorkshire Sculpture Park
West Bretton WF4 4LG
t (01924) 832515 **w** ysp.co.uk
open Apr-Oct, daily 1000-1800. Nov-Mar, daily 1000-1700.
admission Free

Set in the beautiful grounds of a 500-acre, 18thC country estate, the park is one of the world's leading open-air galleries and presents a changing programme of international sculpture exhibitions.

HISTORIC ENGLAND

Beningbrough Hall & Gardens (National Trust)
Beningbrough, York YO30 1DD
t (01904) 470666 **w** nationaltrust.org.uk
open House: Jun, Mon-Wed, Sat-Sun 1200-1700. Jul-Aug, Mon-Wed, Fri-Sun 1200-1700. Sep-Oct, Mon-Wed, Sat-Sun 1200-1700. Grounds: Mar-June, Sep-Oct, Mon-Wed, Sat-Sun 1100-1730. Jul-Aug, Mon-Wed, Fri-Sun 1100-1730. Nov, Jan-Feb Sat-Sun 1100-1530.
admission ££

Handsome Baroque house, built in 1716, housing 100 portraits from the National Portrait Gallery. The attraction also includes a Victorian laundry, potting shed and restored walled garden.

For key to symbols see page 211.

Bramham Park
The Estate Office, Bramham Park, Bramham LS23 6ND
t (01937) 846000
open Apr-Jul, Sep, daily 1130-1630.
admission £

Bramham Park has been the home of the Lane Fox family for 300 years. The house was built in 1698 by Robert Benson, 1st Lord Bingley, in the style of the great Tuscan villas he had seen on a grand tour of Europe.

Beverley Minster
38 Highgate, Beverley HU17 0DN
t (01482) 868540
open Apr-Jul, Mon-Sat 0900-1700, Sun 1200-1630. Aug, Mon-Sat 0900-1730, Sun 1200-1630. Sep-Oct, Mon-Sat 0900-1700, Sun 1200-1630. Nov-Mar, Mon-Sat, 0900-1600, Sun 1200-1630.
admission Free

A splendid example of medieval Gothic architecture, built 1220-1400. The church is well known for the Percy tomb, burial place of St John of Beverley, Saxon sanctuary chair and large collection of misericords.

Bolling Hall
Bowling Hall Road, Bradford BD4 7LP
t (01274) 723057 **w** bradford.gov.uk
open All year, Wed-Fri, Bank Hols 1100-1600, Sat 1000-1500, Sun 1200-1500.
admission Free

Period house, medieval tower to 18thC wing. Period furnishings and splendid oak furniture, central hall with early stained-glass windows.

Bolton Castle
Leyburn DL8 4ET
t (01969) 623981 **w** boltoncastle.co.uk
open Apr-Sep, daily 1000-1700. Oct-Mar, daily 1000-1600.
admission £

Fortress with nine-foot-thick walls which has dominated Wensleydale since 1379. Mary Queen of Scots was imprisoned here during 1568 and 1569 and the Royalists were besieged here during the Civil War.

Brontë Parsonage Museum
Church Street, Haworth BD22 8DR
t (01535) 642323 **w** bronte.info
open Oct-Mar 1100-1700, last entry 1630 (excl 24-27 Dec, 2-21 Jan). Apr-Sep 1000-1730, last entry 1700.
admission Adult: £5.50

Haworth Parsonage was the home of Charlotte, Emily and Anne Brontë; its moorland setting inspired their timeless stories. Come and experience the tragic, romantic and fascinating lives of three of the best-loved novelists in English literature.

Brodsworth Hall and Gardens
Brodsworth DN5 7XJ
t (01904) 601974 **w** english-heritage.org.uk
open See website for details.
admission ££

One of the most complete surviving examples of an English Victorian country house set in 15 acres of formal and informal gardens and woodland.

Byland Abbey (English Heritage)
Coxwold YO61 4BD
t (01904) 601974 **w** english-heritage.org.uk
open See website for details.
admission £

Once one of the great northern monasteries, Byland Abbey's design influenced many other religious buildings throughout Europe. The abbey contains a splendid collection of medieval floor tiles.

Cannon Hall Country Park
Cawthorne S75 4AT
t (01226) 790270
open Daily.
admission Free

An 18thC landscaped parkland and formal gardens with lakes. Educational visits, fishing, important collections in the walled garden including extensive and rare pear trees.

Castle Howard
York YO60 7DA
t (01653) 648444 **w** castlehoward.co.uk
open Grounds: daily 1000-dusk. House: Mar-Oct, daily 1100-1600.
admission ££

Home to the Howard family since 1699. Extensive collections, breathtaking parkland, outdoor tours, historical-character guides, archaeological dig, exhibition wing and events programme. Cafe, gift shop.

Clifford's Tower
Tower Street, York YO1 9SA
t (01904) 601974 **w** english-heritage.org.uk/yorkshire
open See website for details.
admission £

Once the central stronghold of York Castle, the tower was at the heart of William the Conqueror's fearsome Harrying of the North campaign after his 1066 invasion.

Dewsbury Minster
Rishworth Road, Dewsbury WF12 8DD
t (01924) 465491
open All year, Mon-Sat 0930-1530.
admission Free

Refectory serving food and drinks, Heritage Centre containing information on the long history of the minster as part of the Church of England since St Paulinus in AD 627.

DIG – An Archaeological Adventure

St Saviour's Church, St Saviourgate, York YO1 8NN
t (01904) 543403 **w** digyork.co.uk
open Daily 1000-1600 (excl 24-26 Dec).
admission Adult: £5.50

JORVIK Viking Centre's sister attraction, DIG – An Archaeological Adventure, is NOW open. Ever fancied getting your hands dirty and learning about York's rich past? DIG offers visitors the opportunity to take part in an excavation, discover genuine artefacts from ancient civilisations and also understand how archaeologists recreate the past.

V voucher offer – see back section

Drax Power Station

PO Box 3, Selby YO8 8PQ
t (01757) 612507 **w** draxpower.com
open All year, Mon-Fri 1000-1700.
admission Free

Visit the largest, cleanest and most efficient coal-fired power station in the UK, providing enough power to meet 7% of the UK's electricity need.

Duncombe Park

Helmsley YO62 5EB
t (01439) 770213 **w** duncombepark.com
open Gardens: May-Oct, Mon-Thu, Sun 1100-1730. House: May-Oct, Mon-Thu, Sun 1230-1530.
admission £

A magnificent family home, owned and restored by Lord and Lady Feversham. The original 18thC house was remodelled after a serious fire in the late 19th century.

East Riddlesden Hall (National Trust)

Bradford Road, Keighley BD20 5EL
t (01535) 607075
w nationaltrust.org.uk
open Apr-Jun, Tue-Wed, Sat-Sun 1200-1700. Jul-Aug, Mon-Wed, Sat-Sun 1200-1700. Sep-Oct, Tue-Wed, Sat-Sun 1200-1700.
admission £

A homely 17thC merchant's house with fine plaster ceilings and mullioned windows. The house contains beautiful embroideries, textiles and Yorkshire oak furniture. Delightful garden, shop and tearoom.

Fairfax House

Castlegate, York YO1 9RN
t (01904) 655543
w fairfaxhouse.co.uk
open All year, Mon-Thu, Sat 0900-1700, Sun 1330-1700.
admission £

Fairfax House is one of the finest 18thC townhouses in England, richly decorated within. Home to the famous Noel Terry collection of furniture and clocks.

Fountains Abbey and Studley Royal Water Garden

Ripon HG4 3DY
t (01765) 608888
w fountainsabbey.org.uk
open Mar-Oct, daily 1000-1700. Nov-Feb, daily 1000-1600.
admission ££

The largest monastic ruin in Britain, founded by Cistercian monks in 1132. Landscaped garden laid 1720-1740 with lake, formal water garden, temples and deer park.

Harewood House

Harewood LS17 9LG
t (0113) 218 1010
w harewood.org
open Mar-Oct, daily 1000-1600. Winter, phone for details.
admission £££

The home of the Earl of Harewood is renowned for its stunning architecture and exquisite Adam interiors, and contains a rich collection of Chippendale furniture, fine porcelain and art collections.

Helmsley Castle

Helmsley YO62 5AB
t (01904) 601974
w english-heritage.org.uk/yorkshire
open See website for details.
admission £

Helmsley Castle has been in existence for over 900 years. Originally a medieval castle, a Tudor mansion was added in the 1600s before Cromwell's men blew up the great keep.

JORVIK Viking Centre

Coppergate, York YO1 9WT
t (01904) 543402 **w** jorvik-viking-centre.co.uk
open Apr-Oct 1000-1700. Nov-Mar 1000-1600 (excl 24-26 Dec).
admission Adult: £7.75

Get face to face with the vikings of JORVIK. Explore York's viking history on the very site where archaeologists uncovered the remains of the viking-age city of 'Jorvik'. Journey through a reconstruction of the actual streets, which stood here 1,000 years ago, complete with sound and smells. See over 800 of the items discovered on site. Learn what life was really like in our Special Exhibitions.

V voucher offer – see back section

King's Manor

Exhibition Square, York YO1 7EP
t (01904) 433995 **w** york.ac.uk
open All year, Mon-Sat 0900-dusk.
admission Free

One of historic York's most attractive and unusual sites, enjoying a renaissance which is both physical and intellectual. Home to University of York staff and students.

Kiplin Hall

Nr Scorton, Richmond DL10 6AT
t (01748) 818178 **w** kiplinhall.co.uk
open Apr-Sep, Mon-Wed, Sun 1400-1700.
admission £

Kiplin Hall was built as a hunting lodge in 1620 for James I's Secretary of State, George Calvert, later 1st Lord Baltimore and founder of the State of Maryland, USA.

Kirkham Priory (English Heritage)

Whitwell-on-the-Hill YO60 7JS
t (01904) 601974 **w** english-heritage.org.uk
open See website for details.
admission £

The ruins of this Augustinian priory, set in the peaceful Derwent valley, include a magnificent carved gatehouse, declaring to the world the priory's association with the rich and powerful.

Kirkstall Abbey

Abbey Road, Kirkstall LS5 3EH
t (0113) 247 8391 **w** leeds.gov.uk
open All year, daily dawn-dusk.
admission Free

One of the best-preserved medieval Cistercian monasteries in the country. Constructed between 1152 and 1182, many of its buildings still survive virtually intact up to eaves level.

Maister House

160 High Street, Hull HU1 1NL
t (01482) 324114 **w** nationaltrust.org.uk
open All year, Mon-Fri 1000-1600.
admission Free

This Georgian merchant's house was rebuilt in 1743 in the Palladian manner, acting as an impressive symbol of Hull's 18thC heyday. Superb staircase and hall with ironwork by Bakewell.

Merchant Adventurers' Hall

Fossgate, York YO1 9XD
t (01904) 654818 **w** theyorkcompany.co.uk
open Apr-Sep, Mon-Thu 0900-1700, Fri-Sat 0900-1730, Sun 1200-1600. Oct-Mar, Mon-Sat 0900-1530.
admission £

The finest medieval guildhall in Britain, built 1357-1361 and basically unaltered, operates today as a museum. Merchants conducted business and feasted in the superb timbered Great Hall.

Middleham Castle (English Heritage)

Middleham DL8 4QR
t (01904) 601974 **w** english-heritage.org.uk
open See website for details.
admission £

The castle was the childhood and favourite home of Richard III. The massive keep, one of the largest in England, served as a defensive building and self-contained residence.

Mother Shipton's Cave and Petrifying Well

Prophecy Lodge, High Bridge, Knaresborough HG5 8DD
t (01423) 864600 **w** mothershipton.co.uk
open Apr-Oct, daily 1000-1730. Feb-Mar, Sat-Sun 1000-1730.
admission ££

Mother Shipton is England's most famous prophetess. She lived some 500 years ago in the reign of Henry VIII and Queen Elizabeth I and was born in a legendary cave.

Newburgh Priory
Coxwold YO61 4AS
t (01347) 868372 **w** newburghpriory.co.uk
open Apr-June, Wed, Sun 1430-1645.
admission £

Founded in 1145, and standing on the site of an Augustinian priory, this fine stately home occupies a superb setting with breathtaking views to the Kilburn White Horse.

Newby Hall & Gardens
Ripon HG4 5AE
t 0845 450 4068 **w** newbyhall.com
open House; Apr-Jun, Tue-Sun1200-1700. Jul-Aug, daily 1200-1700. Sep, Tue-Sun 1200-1700. Gardens; Apr-Jun, Tue-Sun 1100-1730. Jul-Aug, daily 1100-1730. Sep, Tue-Sun 1100-1730.
admission ££

One of England's renowned Adam houses, an exceptional example of 18thC interior decoration. Contents include unique Gobelins tapestry room, classical statuary and fine Chippendale furniture.

Nostell Priory (National Trust)
Doncaster Road, Nostell WF4 1QE
t (01924) 863892 **w** nationaltrust.org.uk
open Park: All year, daily 0900-1700. House: Apr-Oct. Wed-Sun, 1300-1700. Dec, daily 1200-1600.
admission ££

A Palladian house built in 1733 by James Paine, where Chippendale started his career. The house probably exhibits some of the cabinet maker's finest work.

Nunnington Hall
Nunnington YO62 5UY
t (01439) 798340 **w** nationaltrust.org.uk
open Apr-May, Tue-Sun 1200-1600. Jun-Aug, Tue-Sun 1200-1730. Sep-Oct, Tue-Sun 1200-1700.
admission ££

Large 17thC manor house situated on the banks of River Rye. Hall, bedrooms, nursery, maid's room (haunted), Carlisle collection of miniature rooms and National Trust shop.

Oakwell Hall & Country Park
Nutter Lane, Birstall WF17 9LG
t (01924) 326245 **w** oakwellhallcountrypark.co.uk
open All year, Mon-Fri 1100-1700, Sat-Sun 1200-1700.
admission £

This Elizabethan manor house has delighted visitors for centuries. Charlotte Brontë was a regular visitor, and Oakwell Hall featured as Fieldhead, the home of the heroine in Charlotte's novel, Shirley.

Ormesby Hall
Church Lane, Ormesby, Middlesbrough TS7 9AS
t (01642) 324188 **w** nationaltrust.org.uk
open Apr-Nov, Sat-Sun 1330-1700.
admission £

Beautiful 18thC mansion with park, gardens, tearoom, impressive contemporary plasterwork, magnificent stable block attributed to Carr of York and model railway exhibition and layout.

Pickering Castle (English Heritage)
Pickering YO18 7AX
t (01904) 601974
w english-heritage.org.uk
open See website for details.
admission £

Originally built by William the Conqueror to suppress the rebellious northerners, this castle was used by a succession of medieval kings as a hunting lodge, holiday home and stud farm.

Piece Hall
Halifax HX1 1RE
t (01422) 358087
w calderdale.gov.uk
open All year, Mon-Wed 0800-1800, Thu 0700-1800, Fri 0800-1800, Sat 0700-1800, Sun 0800-1800.
admission Free

Built in 1779 and restored in 1976, this Grade I Listed building forms a unique and striking monument to the wealth and importance of the wool trade before the industrial revolution.

Pontefract Castle
Castle Chain,
Pontefract WF8 1QH
t (01977) 723440
open Apr-Oct, Mon-Fri 0830-1700, Sat-Sun 0930-1815. Nov-Mar, Mon-Fri 0830-dusk, Sat-Sun 1000-1700.
admission Free

In the Middle Ages, Pontefract Castle was one of the most important fortresses in the country. It became a royal castle in 1399, upon the accession of Henry Bolinbroke to the throne.

Richmond Castle
Richmond DL10 4QW
t (01904) 601974
w english-heritage.org.uk
open See website for details.
admission £

Built shortly after the Battle of Hastings, this is the best-preserved castle of such scale and age in the country and alleged to be where the legendary King Arthur lies sleeping.

Rievaulx Abbey (English Heritage)
Rievaulx YO62 5LB
t (01904) 601974
w english-heritage.org.uk
open See website for details.
admission £

Experience the beauty of this impressive monastic site. It was the first Cistercian abbey to be founded in the North, and one of the most powerful abbeys in Europe.

For key to symbols see page 211.

Ripley Castle
Ripley HG3 3AY
t (01423) 770152
w ripleycastle.co.uk
open Castle: Apr-Oct, daily 1100-1500. Nov, Tue, Thu, Sat-Sun 1100-1500. Dec-Feb, Sat-Sun 1100-1500. Mar, Tue-Thu, Sat-Sun 1100-1500.
Gardens: Apr-Oct, daily 0900-1700. Nov-Feb 0900-1630.
admission ££

Ripley Castle, home to the Ingilby family for over 26 generations, is set in the heart of a delightful estate with Victorian walled gardens, deer park and pleasure grounds.

Roche Abbey
Maltby YO1 6WP
t (01904) 601974
w english-heritage.org.uk
open See website for details.
admission £

Cistercian abbey ruins, beautifully set in a valley landscaped by Capability Brown in the 18th century. It displays one of the most complete ground plans of any English Cistercian monastery.

Royal Pump Room Museum

Crown Place, Harrogate HG1 2RY
t (01423) 556188 **w** harrogate.gov.uk/museums
open Apr-Oct, Mon-Sat 1000-1700, Sun 1400-1700 (Aug, Sun 1200-1700). Nov-Mar, Mon-Sat 1000-1600, Sun 1400-1600.
admission Adult: £2.95

Discover Harrogate's history as a spa town and visit Europe's strongest sulphur well. There's costume and textiles on show until 18 February. From 3 March explore 'Victorian Life' to find out all about work, play, fashion and much more.

Saltburn's Inclined Tramway
Marine Parade,
Saltburn-by-the-Sea TS12 1DP
t (01287) 622528
open Apr-May, daily 1000-1700. Jun-mid Sep, daily 1000-1900. Mid Sep-Oct, daily 1000-1700. Oct, Sat-Sun 1000-1700.
admission £

The oldest remaining water-balanced cliff lift in Britain, recently refurbished, with stained glass windows. It links Saltburn's pier, one of the few left in the country, with the town.

Sandal Castle
Manygates Lane, Sandal WF2 7DS
t (01924) 249779
open Apr-Oct, daily 1100-1630. Nov-Mar, Sat-Sun, School Hols 1100-1600.
admission Free

Sandal Castle stands in a commanding position overlooking the River Calder. Remains of the 13thC stone castle and the fine motte and bailey can be seen on site.

Scarborough Castle (English Heritage)
Castle Road, Scarborough YO11 1HY
t (01904) 601974 **w** english-heritage.org.uk
open See website for details.
admission £

This 12thC castle is set high on the cliff tops and conceals over 2,500 years of turbulent history. It played a key role in national events up to the 20th century.

Selby Abbey
The Crescent, Selby YO8 4PU
t (01757) 703123 **w** selbyabbey.org.uk
open All year, daily 1000-1600.
admission Free

The abbey's foundations date back to 1069. It is probably the most outstanding example of a monastic abbey in the North of England. Architectural features include Norman arches.

Sewerby Hall and Gardens
Church Lane, Sewerby YO15 1EA
t (01262) 673769 **w** bridlington.net/sewerby
open Hall: Apr-Oct, daily 1000-1700. Gardens: Daily, dawn-dusk.
admission £

Situated in a dramatic cliff-top position, forming the gateway to the Flamborough Heritage Coast, Sewerby Hall and Gardens, set in 50 acres of early 19thC parkland, enjoys spectacular views over Bridlington.

Shandy Hall
Coxwold YO61 4AD
t (01347) 868465 **w** shandy-hall.org.uk
open House: May-Sep, Wed, Sun 1430-1630. Gardens: May-Sep, Mon-Fri, Sun 1100-1600.
admission £

Shandy Hall was the home of Laurence Sterne from 1760 until his death in 1768. Here he wrote 'The Life and Opinions of Tristram Shandy, Gentleman'.

Sheffield Cathedral
Church Street, Sheffield S1 1HA
t (0114) 275 3434 **w** sheffield-cathedral.org.uk
open Mon-Fri 0845-1830, Sat 1000-1500, Sun 0800-1930. School Hols, Mon-Fri 0845-1700, Sat 1000-1500, Sun 0800-1930.
admission Free

There has been a church on this site since Saxon times. Rebuilt and modified over the centuries, history is written in to its stones. Guided tours available.

Shibden Hall
Lister's Road, Halifax HX3 6XG
t (01422) 352246
w calderdale.gov.uk
open Mar-Nov, Mon-Sat 1000-1700, Sun 1200-1700. Dec-Feb, Mon-Sat 1000-1600, Sun 1200-1600.
admission £

Dating from c1420, the hall is a distinctive half-timbered building furnished in the styles of the17thC, 18thC and 19thC. An important 17thC aisled barn houses a collection of horse-drawn vehicles.

Sir William Turner Alms Houses
1 Sir William Turner's Court,
Kirkleatham TS10 4QT
t (01642) 482828
w communigate.co.uk/ne/swthospital
open Group bookings only, please phone for details.
admission £

Founded in 1676 as Almshouses for the poor. They have been lived in continuously to this day. Fine Georgian chapel containing various historical items.

Sledmere House
Sledmere YO25 3XG
t (01377) 236637
open May, Tue-Thu, Sun 1100-1700. Jun-Aug, Tue-Fri, Sun, Bank Hols 1100-1700. Sep, Tue-Thu, Sun 1100-1700.
admission ££

Georgian house containing Chippendale, Sheraton and French furnishing and many fine pictures. Magnificent plasterwork by Joseph Rose (Adam style). Capability Brown parkland, woodland walks, rose and knot gardens, chapel.

Standedge Visitor Centre
Tunnel End, Marsden HD7 6NQ
t (01484) 844298
w standedge.co.uk
open Apr-Oct, daily 1000-1700.
admission £

The longest, deepest and highest canal tunnel in the country, Standedge – on the Huddersfield Narrow Canal – is nearly three and a half miles long.

Sutton Park
Sutton-on-the-Forest YO61 1DP
t (01347) 810249
w statelyhome.co.uk
open Apr-Sep, daily 1100-1700.
admission £

Georgian stately home with fine furniture, magnificent plasterwork by Cortese and paintings from Buckingham House, now Buckingham Palace. Important collection of porcelain. Wonderful award-winning gardens.

Temple Newsam House and Farm
Temple Newsam,
Leeds LS15 0AD
t (0113) 264 5535
w leeds.gov.uk/templenewsam
open Farm: Winter, Tue-Sun 1000-1600. Summer, Tue-Sun 1000-1700. House: Winter, Tue-Sun 1030-1600, Summer, Tue-Sun 1030-1700.
admission ££

The farm has over 400 head of stock including cattle, pigs, sheep, goats and poultry. Piglets, hens and cats run free around the farmyard.

Treasurer's House (National Trust)
Minster Yard,
York YO1 7JL
t (01904) 624247
w nationaltrust.org.uk
open Apr-Oct, Mon-Thu, Sat-Sun 1100-1630. Nov, Mon-Thu, Sat-Sun 1100-1500.
admission £

Nestled behind the minster, this elegant house was carefully restored by wealthy local Victorian industrialist Frank Green, and contains 16thC-20thC decoration, furniture, china and glass.

Underground RAF Bunker Tours
RAF Holmpton, Rysome Lane,
Withernsea HU19 2QR
t (01964) 630208
w rafholmpton.co.uk
open See website for details.
admission £

The massive Command Bunker at Royal Air Force Holmpton (built in 1952 and rebuilt in 1985) extends almost 100ft below ground and covers nearly 30,000sq ft.

Wassand Hall, Gardens & Grounds
Seaton HU11 5RJ
t (01964) 534488
w wassand.co.uk
open See website for details.
admission £

A fine Regency house in beautiful tranquil surroundings, containing 18thC and 19thC paintings and a collection of English and European silver, furniture and porcelain from the same period.

Whitby Abbey
Whitby YO22 4JT
t (01904) 601974
w english-heritage.org.uk/yorkshire
open See website for details.
admission £

The moody and magnificent Whitby Abbey has drawn successive generations to this site of settlement, and has been responsible for religious devotion and even literary inspiration.

Admission is based on an adult price. Please check opening times and admission before travelling.

Wilberforce House

25 High Street, Hull HU1 1NQ
t (01482) 613902 **w** hullcc.gov.uk/museums
open All year, Mon-Sat 1000-1700, Sun 1330-1630.
admission Free

The birthplace of William Wilberforce, Hull MP and slavery abolitionist whose campaign made the establishment of Freetown (Sierra Leone) possible. Slavery exhibits, period rooms and furniture.

York Minster

Deangate, York YO1 7HH
t (01904) 557216 **w** yorkminster.org
open All year, Mon-Sat 0900-1700, Sun 1200-1545.
admission £

The largest medieval Gothic cathedral in northern Europe, and a treasure house of 800 years of stained glass. Experience York's finest viewpoint from the top of the central tower's 275 steps.

OUTDOOR ACTIVITIES

M/V Yorkshire Belle

28 Roundhay Road, Bridlington YO15 3JY
t (01262) 673582 **w** yorkshire-belle.co.uk
open Apr-Oct, phone for details.
admission £

One-hour, non-landing coastal cruises from Bridlington harbour to Flamborough Head, and longer (at least two hours), non-landing cruises to the Bempton Cliffs RSPB Reserve. Vessel also available for private charter.

Trans Pennine Trail

Westgate Plaza One, Westgate, Barnsley S70 2DR
t (01226) 772574
w transpenninetrail.org.uk
open Daily.
admission Free

Walk, cycle or horse-ride on the TPT, from Southport to Hornsea, Leeds to Chesterfield, or York. Enjoy varied scenery and many places of interest along the way. Easy going, mainly traffic-free trails that are ideal for families with young children. Amazing Space winner – National Lottery Awards 2006.

YorkBoat Guided River Trips
The Boatyard, Lendal Bridge, York YO1 7DP
t (01904) 628324
w yorkboat.co.uk/buytickets-online.html
open Feb-Dec, daily 1030-1510.
admission ££

Sit back and relax as the sights of York city and country sail by. Trips include floodlit evening cruises, ghost cruises, lunch cruises and the Summer Nights Afloat cruise.

ENTERTAINMENT AND CULTURE

1853 Gallery
Salts Mill, Victoria Road, Saltaire BD18 3LA
t (01274) 531185
w saltsmill.org.uk
open All year, Mon-Fri, Bank Hols 1000-1730, Sat-Sun 1000-1800.
admission Free

Four comprehensive art galleries featuring over 400 works by David Hockney. Grade II Listed historic mill building set in a picturesque village which was built for the mill workers in 1853. Salts Mill and Saltaire include various retail outlets.

Abbey House Museum
Kirkstall Road, Leeds LS5 3EH
t (0113) 247 8391
w leeds.gov.uk/abbeyhouse
open All year, Tue-Fri, Sun, Bank Hols 1000-1700, Sat 1200-1700.
admission £

Travel through time at Abbey House by walking through three Victorian streets of shops and homes. Visit the Sunday School or dress up in the haberdasher's. Explore nursery rhymes in the Childhood Gallery and visit the new Smelly History Exhibition.

Aeroventure South Yorks Aircraft Museum
Dakota way, Airbourne Road, Doncaster DN4 7PD
t (01302) 761616
w aeroventure.org.uk
open Apr-Oct, Wed-Sun 1000-1700. School Hols, Tue-Sun 1000-1700. Nov-Mar, Wed-Sun 1000-1600.
admission £

Housed at former RAF Doncaster, this museum has an interesting collection of 15 British jets and helicopters on display in the historic aircraft hangar built in 1940.

Arctic Corsair
River Hull, Museum Quarter, Hull HU1 1PS
t (01482) 613902
w hullcc.gov.uk/museums
open Apr-Oct, Wed, Sat 1030-1600, Sun 1330-1530.
admission Free

This motor trawler is the last remaining deep-sea side-fishing trawler of Hull's once proud distant-water fishing fleet.

Ashley Jackson Galleries
13-15 Huddersfield Road,
Holmfirth HD9 2JR
t (01484) 686460
w ashley-jackson.co.uk
open All year, Mon-Sat, Bank Hols 0930-1700.
admission Free

See the work of one of the country's leading and most successful landscape water colourists, Ashley Jackson.

Beverley Art Gallery
Champney Road,
Beverley HU17 9HE
t (01482) 392772
open All year, Mon, Wed, Fri 0930-1700, Tue, Thu 0930-2000, Sat 0900-1600.
admission Free

The gallery holds the largest public collection of paintings by Beverley-born artist Fred Elwell. An exciting programme of changing exhibitions.

Body Parts: New for Old!
Thackray Museum,
Near St James's Hospital, Beckett Street,
Leeds LS9 7LN
t (0113) 244 4343
w thackraymuseum.org
open All year, daily 1000-1700.
admission ££

Explore the world of false body implants and limbs and see how similar we have become to science fiction characters.

Bradford Industrial Museum & Horses at Work
Moorside Mills, Moorside Road,
Bradford BD2 3HP
t (01274) 435900
w bradford.gov.uk
open All year, Tue-Sat, Bank Hols 1000-1700, Sun 1200-1700.
admission Free

An original spinning mill is alive with magnificent machinery which once converted wool into the world's worsted cloth. The shire horses give rides and pull a horse tram.

Bridlington Harbour Heritage Museum
Harbour Road, Bridlington YO15 2NR
t (01262) 608346
w bscps.com
open Apr-Oct, daily 1000-1600.
admission £

Located on Bridlington's historic harbourside and operated by the Bridlington Sailing Coble Preservation Society (BSCPS).

For key to symbols see page 211.

Brontë Parsonage Museum

Church Street, Haworth BD22 8DR
t (01535) 642323 **w** bronte.info
open Oct-Mar 1100-1700, last entry 1630 (excl 24-27 Dec, 2-21 Jan). Apr-Sep 1000-1730, last entry 1700.
admission Adult: £5.50

Haworth Parsonage was the home of Charlotte, Emily and Anne Brontë; its moorland setting inspired their timeless stories. Come and experience the tragic, romantic and fascinating lives of three of the best-loved novelists in English literature.

Captain Cook Memorial Museum, Whitby

Grape Lane, Whitby YO22 4BA
t (01947) 601900 **w** cookmuseumwhitby.co.uk
open March, daily 1100-1500. Apr-Oct, daily 0945-1700.
admission £

This handsome 17thC harbourside house is where James Cook, the great explorer, served his apprenticeship in 1746. It belonged to Cook's master, the Quaker ship owner, Captain John Walker.

Cusworth Hall

Cusworth Lane, Doncaster DN5 7TU
t (01302) 782342 **w** doncaster.gov.uk
open Apr-Dec, Mon-Sat 1000-1700, Sun 1300-1700.
admission Free

Built in the 1740s, Cusworth Hall is set in 50 acres of parkland and contains displays illustrating everyday life in South Yorkshire over the last 200 years.

Dales Countryside Museum

Station Yard, Hawes DL8 3NT
t (01756) 752748
open All year, daily 1000-1700.
admission £

The perfect place to start your visit to the Yorkshire Dales. Unique exhibits from the Stone Age to Victorian times, demonstration of traditional crafts and free exhibitions.

Dewsbury Museum

Crow Nest Park, Heckmondwike Road, Dewsbury WF13 2SG
t (01924) 325100 **w** dewsburymuseum.co.uk
open All year, Mon-Fri 1100-1700, Sat-Sun 1200-1700.
admission Free

With a busy programme of temporary exhibitions and events and the new 'Toys will be Toys' gallery, Dewsbury Museum is for anyone who's ever been a child.

DIG – An Archaeological Adventure

St Saviour's Church, St Saviourgate, York YO1 8NN
t (01904) 543403 **w** digyork.co.uk
open Daily 1000-1600 (excl 24-26 Dec).
admission Adult: £5.50

JORVIK Viking Centre's sister attraction, DIG – An Archaeological Adventure, is NOW open. Ever fancied getting your hands dirty and learning about York's rich past? DIG offers visitors the opportunity to take part in an excavation, discover genuine artefacts from ancient civilisations and also understand how archaeologists recreate the past.

V voucher offer – see back section

Dinostar

28-29 Humber Street, Hull HU1 1TH
t (01482) 320424 **w** dinostar.co.uk
open All year, Wed-Sun 1100-1700.
admission £

Dinosaurs have long held a fascination for kids of all ages. At Dinostar, Hull's newest visitor attraction, you can learn about these fascinating creatures close up.

Doncaster Museum & Art Gallery

Chequer Road, Doncaster DN1 2AE
t (01302) 734293 **w** doncaster.gov.uk/museums
open All year, Mon-Sat 1000-1700, Sun 1400-1700.
admission Free

Regional collections of human and natural history, art, glass and ceramics. King's Own Yorkshire Light Infantry Regimental Gallery. New 'By River and Road' gallery telling the history of Doncaster.

Eden Camp Modern History Theme Museum
Malton YO17 6RT
t (01653) 697777 **w** edencamp.co.uk
open All year, daily 1000-1700.
admission £

A look at wartime Britain, depicted through a series of expertly recreated scenes, constructed in the huts of a genuine prisoner of war camp.

Eureka! The Museum for Children
Discovery Road, Halifax HX1 2NE
t (01422) 330069 **w** eureka.org.uk
open Daily 1000-1700.
admission ££

Britain's leading interactive museum for children, opening up a fascinating world of hands-on exploration. Over 400 exhibits invite children to unleash their imaginations and learn about the world around them.

Graves Art Gallery
Surrey Street, Sheffield S1 1XZ
t (0114) 278 2612 **w** sheffieldgalleries.org.uk
open All year, Mon-Sat 1000-1700.
admission Free

The gallery houses an outstanding collection of British and European modern art, including works by Matisse, Picasso and Cézanne, together with a range of first-class touring exhibitions.

The Henry Moore Institute
74 The Headrow, Leeds LS1 3AH
t (0113) 246 7467 **w** henry-moore-fdn.co.uk
open All year, Mon-Tue, Thu-Sun 1000-1730, Wed 1000-2100.
admission Free

The Henry Moore Institute, formerly a neglected group of early Victorian merchants' offices, has been transformed into a unique building devoted to the exhibition, study and promotion of sculpture.

Hornsea Museum
11 Newbegin, Hornsea HU18 1AB
t (01964) 533443 **w** hornseamuseum.com
open Apr-Sep, Tue-Sat, Bank Hols 1100-1700, Sun 1400-1700.
admission £

Folk museum (village life), housed in 18thC farmhouse and associated buildings. Period rooms of the 1880s, village crafts, local history, the farming year, all attractively presented. Occasional craft demonstrations.

Huddersfield Art Gallery
Princess Alexandra Walk, Huddersfield HD1 2SU
t (01484) 221962 **w** kirklees.gov.uk
open All year, Mon-Fri 1000-1700, Sat 1000-1600.
admission Free

The gallery has a changing permanent collection of British paintings, drawings, sculpture and graphics from the mid-19th century to date, as well as exhibitions featuring contemporary art and craft work.

JORVIK Viking Centre
Coppergate, York YO1 9WT
t (01904) 543402 **w** jorvik-viking-centre.co.uk
open Apr-Oct 1000-1700. Nov-Mar 1000-1600 (excl 24-26 Dec).
admission Adult: £7.75

Get face to face with the vikings of JORVIK. Explore York's viking history on the very site where archaeologists uncovered the remains of the viking-age city of 'Jorvik'. Journey through a reconstruction of the actual streets, which stood here 1,000 years ago, complete with sound and smells. See over 800 of the items discovered on site. Learn what life was really like in our Special Exhibitions.

V *voucher offer – see back section*

Last of the Summer Wine Exhibition
30 Huddersfield Road, Holmfirth HD9 2JS
t (01484) 681408
open Apr-Sep, daily 1100-1600. Oct-Mar, Sat-Sun 1100-1500.
admission £

A collection of photographs and memorabilia connected with the television series 'Last of the Summer Wine'. The exhibition is inside Compo's house next door to Nora Batty's.

Leeds City Art Gallery
The Headrow, Leeds LS1 3AA
t (0113) 247 8391 **w** leeds.gov.uk
open All year, Mon-Tue, Thur-Sat 1000-1700, Wed 1000-2000, Sun 1300-1700.
admission Free

Since opening in 1888, Leeds City Art Gallery has acquired a remarkable collection of British 20thC art, voted by The Times as 'probably the best outside London'.

Leeds Industrial Museum at Armley Mills
Canal Road, Leeds LS12 2QF
t (0113) 263 7861 **w** leeds.gov.uk
open All year, Tue-Sat, Bank Hols 1000-1700, Sun 1300-1700.
admission £

Formerly the largest woollen mill in the world, the building now houses Leeds Industrial Museum. Located beside the River Aire, the museum explores the city's rich industrial past.

Maritime Museum Hull
Queen Victoria Square, Hull HU1 3DX
t (01482) 613902 **w** hullcc.gov.uk/museums
open All year, Mon-Sat 1000-1700, Sun 1330-1630.
admission Free

Formerly the Town Docks offices, the impressive building of the Hull Maritime Museum now houses a fine collection of paintings, artefacts and models. Whaling, fishing and trawling exhibits.

Mercer Art Gallery
Swan Road, Harrogate HG1 2SA
t (01423) 556188
w harrogate.gov.uk/museums
open Tue-Sat, Bank Holiday Mon 1000-1700, Sun 1400-1700. (Excl 12-23 Mar, 16-20 Jul, 24-26 Dec, 1 Jan).
admission Free

See an exciting and diverse exhibition programme including local artists and shows from the permanent collection. Visit 2007's blockbuster exhibition 'William Powell Frith: Painting the Victorian Age' – the first exhibition in over 50 years of Harrogate's most famous artist.

Millennium Galleries
Arundel Gate, Sheffield S1 2PP
t (0114) 278 2612 **w** sheffieldgalleries.org.uk
open All year, Mon-Sat 0800-1700, Sun 1100-1700, Bank Hols 1000-1700.
admission Free

With four different galleries, there is something for everyone. Enjoy new blockbuster exhibitions drawn from the collections of Britain's national galleries and museums, including the Victoria and Albert Museum.

National Coal Mining Museum for England
Caphouse Colliery, New Road, Overton WF4 4RH
t (01924) 848806 **w** ncm.org.uk
open All year, daily 1000-1700.
admission Free

Exciting, award-winning museum of the English coalfields with a unique collection of buildings, displays and activities revealing the hidden world of mining through the centuries.

National Museum of Photography, Film and Television
Bradford BD1 1NQ
t 0870 701 0200 **w** nmpft.org.uk
open All year, Tue-Sun 1000-1800.
admission Free

The museum includes ten free interactive galleries where you can ride on a virtual magic carpet, read the news or look back at your TV favourites from yesteryear.

Old Penny Memories
2 Marlborough Terrace, Bridlington YO15 2PA
t (01262) 603341 **w** oldpennymemories.co.uk
open Apr-Oct, Sat-Sun, Bank Hols 1000-1600.
admission Free

One of the largest collections of antique slot machines in England. Visitors to the museum can actually play the slot machines, exchanging their money for old pennies.

Richard III Museum
Monk Bar, York YO1 7LQ
t (01904) 634191 **w** richardiiimuseum.co.uk
open Mar-Oct, daily 0900-1700. Nov-Feb, daily 0930-1600.
admission £

The museum reconstructs a modern-day trial, presenting the case for and against England's most notorious king, Richard III. Afterwards, the visitor is invited to pass sentence in the comments book.

Royal Armouries Museum
Armouries Drive, Leeds LS10 1LT
t (0113) 220 1916 **w** armouries.org.uk
open All year, daily 1000-1700.
admission Free

Spectacular displays, live interpretations, unique handling collections, jousting tournaments and thousands of breathtaking exhibitions from one of the world's most famous collections of arms and armour.

Friendly help and advice
Tourist Information Centres offer suggestions of places to visit and things to do as well as friendly help with accommodation and holiday ideas. To find the one nearest to you text TIC LOCATE to 64118.

Royal Pump Room Museum

Crown Place, Harrogate HG1 2RY
t (01423) 556188 **w** harrogate.gov.uk/museums
open Apr-Oct, Mon-Sat 1000-1700, Sun 1400-1700 (Aug, Sun 1200-1700). Nov-Mar, Mon-Sat 1000-1600, Sun 1400-1600.
admission Adult: £2.95

Discover Harrogate's history as a spa town and visit Europe's strongest sulphur well. There's costume and textiles on show until 18 February. From 3 March explore 'Victorian Life' to find out all about work, play, fashion and much more.

Scarborough Art Gallery

The Crescent, Scarborough YO11 2PW
t (01723) 367326
open All year, Tue-Sun 1000-1700.
admission £

This Italianate villa was built in the 1840s as part of The Crescent. It houses Scarborough's fine-art collection which features seascapes and views of Scarborough, including works by Grimshaw.

Sheffield City Museum

Weston Park, Sheffield S10 2TP
t (0114) 278 2612 **w** sheffieldgalleries.org.uk
open All year, Mon-Sat 1000-1700, Sun 1100-1700.
admission Free

See Sheffield's vast natural and social history, archaeology and decorative arts collections, together with a programme of fascinating temporary exhibitions.

Site Gallery (Media, Art, Photography)

1 Brown Street, Sheffield S1 2BS
t (0114) 281 2077 **w** sitegallery.org
open All year, Wed-Sat 1100-1730.
admission Free

An international centre for contemporary art, offering a changing exhibitions programme, backed up with regular publications and a comprehensive calendar of conferences, artists' talks and events.

Spurn Lightship

River Hull, Museum Quarter, Hull HU1 1PS
t (01482) 613902 **w** hullcc.gov.uk/museums
open Apr-Oct, Mon-Sat 1000-1700, Sun 1330-1630.
admission Free

Built in 1927, the Spurn served for almost 50 years as a navigational aid in the treacherous River Humber. See how the crew lived and worked.

'Streetlife' – Hull Museum of Transport

High Street, Hull HU1 1PS
t (01482) 613902 **w** hullcc.gov.uk/museums
open All year, Mon-Sat 1000-1700, Sun 1330-1630.
admission Free

Streetlife has some of the finest period displays on railways, horse-drawn carriages, cycles, cars and trams. Animated horses, a simulated carriage ride and costumed figures add to the visual display.

Thackray Museum

Nr St James's Hospital, Beckett Street, Leeds LS9 7LN
t (0113) 244 4343 **w** thackraymuseum.org
open Daily 1000-1700 (excl 24-26, 31 Dec, 1 Jan), last entry 1500.
admission Adult: £5.50

The award-winning Thackray Museum has something for everyone. Experience life as a character in the Victorian slums of 1840, where you will be flabbergasted at the incredible lotions and potions once offered as cures, and have fun exploring the human body in the new interactive Life Zone!

V voucher offer – see back section

University of Hull Art Collection

University of Hull, Cottingham Road, Hull HU6 7RX
t (01482) 465035 **w** hull.ac.uk/artcoll
open All year, Mon-Fri 1000-1600.
admission Free

The collection features British art, paintings, drawings and sculpture from 1890-1940, including works by Sickert, Steer, Lucien Pissarro, Augustus John, Stanley Spencer, Epstein and Moore.

For key to symbols see page 211.

Vintage Carriages Trust – Museum of Rail
Ingrow Railway Station, Ingrow, Keighley BD21 5AX
t (01535) 680425 **w** vintagecarriagestrust.org
open All year, daily 1100-1630.
admission £

The museum houses a collection of beautifully restored railway carriages which evoke memories of rail travel in the past, brought to life by the use of sound presentations called 'Travellers' Tales'.

Wakefield Art Gallery
Wentworth Terrace, Wakefield WF1 3QW
t (01924) 305900 **w** wakefield.gov.uk
open All year, Tue-Sat 1030-1630, Sun 1400-1630.
admission Free

The gallery is housed in an attractive late-Victorian townhouse near the city centre and contains a large collection of sculptures, drawings and paintings by Henry Moore and Barbara Hepworth.

Wakefield Museum
Wood Street, Wakefield WF1 2EW
t (01924) 305356 **w** wakefield.gov.uk
open All year, Mon-Sat 1030-1630, Sun 1400-1630.
admission Free

Explorer and early conservationist Charles Waterton collected rare species from South America. Follow his journey, and also discover how he founded the world's first nature reserve.

Waterways Museum
Dutch Riverside, Goole DN14 5TB
t (01405) 768730 **w** waterwaysmuseum.org.uk
open Apr-Sep, Mon-Fri 0930-1600, Sun, Bank Hols 1100-1600. Nov-Mar, Mon-Fri 0930-1600.
admission Free

The Waterways Museum collection tells the story of Goole's development as a canal terminus to the Aire and Calder Navigation and port connection to the North Sea.

Whitby Lifeboat Museum (RNLI)
Pier Road, Whitby YO21 3PU
t (01947) 602001 **w** rnli.org.uk
open Apr-Oct, daily 1000-1700. Nov-Mar 1000-1600, weather permitting.
admission Free

The museum has as its main exhibit the last pulling lifeboat to be in service with the Royal National Lifeboat Institution (RNLI), plus models of lifeboats and other types of vessel.

The World of James Herriot
23 Kirkgate, Thirsk YO7 1PL
t (01845) 524234 **w** worldofjamesherriot.org
open Apr-Oct, daily 1000-1700. Nov-Mar, daily 1100-1600.
admission £

1940s nostalgia, veterinary equipment, TV studios and interactive children's gallery combine to make a fun, interesting and memorable visit to the home and surgery of James Herriot.

York & Lancaster Regimental Museum
Arts Centre, Walker Place, Rotherham S65 1JH
t (01709) 823635 **w** rotherham.gov.uk
open All year, Mon-Sat 0930-1700.
admission Free

At the museum, the York and Lancaster Regiment's history is shown in chronological order through displays of uniforms, campaign relics and over 1,000 medals.

York Castle Museum
The Eye of York, York YO1 9RY
t (01904) 650321 **w** yorkcastlemuseum.org.uk
open Daily, 0930-1700.
admission ££

England's most popular museum of everyday life including reconstructed streets and period rooms, costume and jewellery, arms and armour and craft workshops. Special exhibition 'From Cradle to Grave'.

York City Art Gallery
Exhibition Square, York YO1 7EW
t (01904) 650321 **w** yorkmuseumstrust.org.uk
open Daily 1000-1700.
admission Free

The gallery shows 600 years of painting, from gold-ground panels of 14thC Italy to the art of the 20th century. The collection includes pictures by Parmigianino, Bellotto, Lely and Reynolds.

York Cold War Bunker
Acomb Road, Holgate, York YO24 4HT
t 0870 333 1181 **w** english-heritage.org.uk
open See website for details.
admission £

Royal Observer Corps 20 Group Headquarters is the formal description of the semi-submerged nuclear bunker which is now owned by English Heritage.

Yorkshire Air Museum
Halifax Way, Elvington YO41 4AU
t (01904) 608595 **w** yorkshireairmuseum.co.uk
open Mar-Oct, daily 1000-1700. Nov-Feb, daily 1000-1530.
admission £

The award-winning museum is based on the largest authentic former WWII Bomber Command Station. Experience the tremendous atmosphere as you admire fascinating displays and the extensive collection of 43 historic aircraft.

Yorkshire Motor Museum
Alexandra Mills, Alexandra Road, Batley WF17 6JA
t (01924) 444423
open All year, Mon-Sat 1000-1700, Sun 1100-1630.
admission Free

A magnificent and diverse collection of over 60 types of cars from 1885-1985, including the only-surviving Bramham. Live restorations seen in progress.

Yorkshire Museum
Museum Gardens, York YO1 7FR
t (01904) 650321
w yorkmuseumstrust.org.uk
open Daily 1000-1700.
admission £

The award-winning museum is set in ten acres of botanical gardens and displays some of the finest Roman, Anglo-Saxon, Viking and medieval treasures ever discovered in Britain.

Yorkshire Museum of Farming
Murton Park, Murton Lane, Murton YO19 5UF
t (01904) 489966
w murtonpark.co.uk
open Mar-Oct, daily 1000-1600. Nov-Feb, daily 1000-1600.
admission £

This ten-acre site displays tools and machinery of a bygone age, reconstructions of James Herriot's surgery, blacksmith's shop, chapel, hardware shop and Land Army display.

RELAXING AND PAMPERING

Bramley Baths
Broad Lane, Bramley LS13 3DH
t (0113) 214 6000
w leeds.gov.uk
open See website for details.
admission £

Built in 1904, historic Bramley Baths has undergone a major refurbishment to restore this beautiful building to its former Edwardian splendour. Russian steam baths.

Freeport Hornsea Outlet Village
Rolston Road, Hornsea HU18 1UT
t (01964) 534211
w freeporthornsea.info
open All year, daily 0930-1800.
admission Free

Set in 25 acres of landscaped gardens with over 40 quality high street names, all selling stock with discounts of up to 50%. Licensed restaurant. Leisure attractions.

Lakeside Village
White Rose Way, Doncaster DN4 5JH
t (01302) 366444 **w** lakeside-village.co.uk
open All year, Mon-Wed, Fri 1000-1800, Thur 1000-2000, Sat 0930-1800, Sun 1030-1700.
admission Free

Lakeside Village, previously The Yorkshire Outlet, has recently undergone a radical and impressive makeover, greatly improving the landscape, centre facilities and range of outlet shops.

McArthurGlen Designer Outlet
St Nicholas Avenue, Fulford YO19 4TA
t (01904) 682705 **w** mcarthurglen.com/york
open All year, Mon-Wed, Fri-Sat 1000-1800, Thu 1000-2000, Sun 1000-1700.
admission Free

This is the designer destination of the north, with over 115 designer and high street stores with discounts of up to 50% off recommended retail prices.

The Mill Batley, Factory Outlet Shopping
Bradford Road, Batley WF17 5LZ
t (01924) 423172 **w** yorkshiremillvillage.com
open All year, Mon-Sat 0930-1730, Sun 1100-1700.
admission Free

The Mill covers four massive floors and offers unbelievable savings on famous high street brands including Puma, Wedgwood, FCUK, Elle, Liz Claibourne and Yorkshire's favourite discount store, Readmans.

Titanic Spa
Low Westwood Lane, Linthwaite HD7 5UN
t (01484) 843544 **w** titanicspa.com
open All year, daily 0900-2100.
admission ££££

Set in a beautifully restored 1900s textile mill, the spa blends organically inspired design features and cutting-edge botanical therapies to provide a stylish sense of escapism.

Turkish Baths & Health Spa
Parliament Street, Harrogate HG1 2WH
t (01423) 556746 **w** harrogate.gov.uk/turkishbaths
open Health Spa: Mon-Fri, Sun 0930-2030, Sat 0930-1630. Turkish Baths: Please phone for details.
admission £££

Unique, traditional Turkish baths built in 1897, plus steam rooms and various beauty treatments and types of massage. Also available: facial, manicure, pedicure, eyelash/brow tint, leg waxing and reflexology.

Admission is based on an adult price. Please check opening times and admission before travelling.

Further **information**

Hadrian's Wall, Northumberland

Enjoy England **Quality Rose assessment schemes**

When you're looking for a place to stay, you need a rating system you can trust. Enjoy England ratings are your clear guide to what to expect, in an easy-to-understand form.

Enjoy England professional assessors pay unannounced visits to establishments that are new to the rating scheme and stay overnight where appropriate. Once in the scheme establishments receive an annual pre-arranged day visit, with an overnight stay generally every other year for hotel and B&B guest accommodation. On these occasions the assessors book in anonymously, and test all the facilities and services.

Based on internationally recognised star ratings, the system puts great emphasis on quality, and reflects exactly what consumers are looking for. Ratings are awarded from one to five stars – the more stars, the higher the quality and the greater the range of facilities and services provided – and are the sign of quality assurance, giving you the confidence to book the accommodation that meets your expectations.

Look out, too, for Enjoy England Gold and Silver Awards, which are awarded to hotels and guest accommodation achieving the highest levels of quality within their star rating. While the overall rating is based on a combination of facilities and quality, the Gold and Silver Awards are based solely on quality.

Hotels

All hotels that are awarded a star rating will meet the minimum standards – so you can be confident that you will find the basic services that you would expect, such as:

- All bedrooms with an en suite or private bathroom
- A designated reception facility and staff members who will be available during the day and evening (24hrs in case of an emergency)
- A licence to serve alcohol (unless a temperance hotel)
- Access to the hotel at all times for registered guests
- Dinner available at least five days a week (with the exception of a Town House Hotel or Metro Hotel)
- All statutory obligations will be met.

Hotels have to provide certain additional facilities and services at the higher star levels, some of which may be important to you:

TWO-STAR hotels must provide:

- Dinner seven nights a week.

THREE-STAR hotels must provide:

- All en suite bedrooms (ie no private bathrooms)
- Direct dial phones in all rooms
- Room service during core hours
- A permanently staffed reception.

FOUR-STAR hotels must provide:

- 24-hour room service
- 50% of all en suites with bath **and** shower.

FIVE-STAR hotels must provide:

- Some permanent suites
- Enhanced services, such as concierge.

Sometimes a hotel with a lower star rating has exceptional bedrooms and bathrooms and offers its guests a very special welcome, but cannot achieve a higher rating because, for example, it does not offer dinner every evening (two star), room service (three star) or does not have the minimum 50% of bathrooms with bath and shower (four star).

Quality

The availability of additional services alone is not enough for an establishment to achieve a higher star rating. Hotels have to meet exacting standards for quality in critical areas. Consumer research has shown the critical areas to be: cleanliness, bedrooms, bathrooms, hospitality and service, and food.

Guest accommodation

All guest accommodation that is awarded a star rating will meet the minimum standards – so you can be confident that you will find the basic services that you would expect, such as:

- A clear explanation of booking charges, services offered and cancellation terms
- A full cooked breakfast or substantial continental breakfast
- At least one bathroom or shower room for every six guests
- For a stay of more than one night, rooms cleaned and beds made daily
- Printed advice on how to summon emergency assistance at night
- All statutory obligations will be met.

TWO-STAR accommodation provides all of the above but the rating reflects a higher quality of services and facilities than one-star accommodation.

Proprietors of guest accommodation have to provide certain additional facilities and services at the higher star levels, some of which may be important to you:

THREE-STAR accommodation must provide:

- Private bathroom/shower room (cannot be shared with the owners)
- Bedrooms must have a washbasin if not en suite.

FOUR-STAR accommodation must provide:

- 50% of bedrooms en suite or with private bathroom.

FIVE-STAR accommodation must provide:

- All bedrooms with en suite or private bathroom.

Sometimes guest accommodation has exceptional bedrooms and bathrooms and offers visitors a very special welcome, but cannot achieve a higher star rating because, for example, there are no en suite bedrooms, or it is difficult to put washbasins in the bedrooms (three star). This is sometimes the case with period properties.

Quality

The availability of additional facilities alone is not enough for an establishment to achieve a higher star rating. Guest accommodation has to meet exacting standards for quality in critical areas. Consumer research has shown the critical areas to be: cleanliness, bedrooms, bathrooms, hospitality and food.

Self-catering accommodation

All self-catering accommodation that is awarded a star rating will meet the minimum standards – so you can be confident that you will find the basic services that you would expect, such as:

- Clear information prior to booking on all aspects of the accommodation including location, facilities, prices, deposit, policies on smoking, children etc
- No shared facilities, with the exception of a laundry room in multi-unit sites
- All appliances and furnishings will meet product safety standards for self-catering accommodation, particularly regarding fire safety
- At least one smoke alarm in the unit and a fire blanket in the kitchen
- Clear information on emergency procedures, including who to contact
- Contact details for the local doctor, dentist etc
- All statutory obligations will be met including an annual gas check and public liability insurance.

Certain additional facilities and services are required at the higher star levels, some of which may be important to you:

TWO-STAR accommodation must provide:

- Single beds of 3ft width and double beds of 4ft 6in.

THREE-STAR accommodation must provide:

- Bed linen (with or without additional charge).

FOUR-STAR accommodation must provide:

- All sleeping space in bedrooms, unless a studio (bed settees can not be advertised)
- Bed linen included in the hire charge.

FIVE-STAR accommodation must provide:

- At least two of the following items: tumble-dryer, telephone, Hi-Fi, video, DVD.

Some self-catering establishments offer a choice of accommodation units that may have different star ratings. In this case, the entry shows the range available.

Quality

The availability of additional facilities, such as a dishwasher or DVD, is not enough to achieve a higher star rating. Self-catering accommodation with a lower star rating may offer some or all of the above, but to achieve the higher star ratings, the overall quality score has to be reached and exacting standards have to be met in critical areas. Consumer research has shown these to be: cleanliness, bedrooms, bathrooms, kitchens and public areas.

The British Graded **Holiday Parks Scheme**

When you're looking for a place to stay, you need a rating system you can trust. The British Graded Holiday Parks Scheme, operated jointly by the national tourist boards for England, Scotland, Wales and Northern Ireland, was devised in association with the British Holiday and Home Parks Association and the National Caravan Council. It gives you a clear guide of what to expect in an easy-to-understand form.

The process to arrive at a star rating is very thorough to ensure that when you make a booking you can be confident it will meet your expectations. Professional assessors visit parks annually and take into account over 50 separate aspects, from landscaping and layout to maintenance, customer care and, most importantly, cleanliness.

Strict guidelines are in place to ensure that every park is assessed to the same criteria. A random check is made of a sample of accommodation provided for hire (caravans, chalets etc) but the quality of the accommodation itself is not included in the grading assessment.

In addition to The British Graded Holiday Parks Scheme, VisitBritain operates a rating scheme for Holiday Villages. The assessor stays on the site overnight and grades the overall quality of the visitor experience, including accommodation, facilities, cleanliness, service and food.

So you can rest assured that when you choose a star-rated park or holiday village you won't be disappointed.

Star ratings

Parks are required to meet progressively higher standards of quality as they move up the scale from one to five stars:

ONE STAR Acceptable

To achieve this grade, the park must be clean with good standards of maintenance and customer care.

TWO STAR Good

All the above points plus an improved level of landscaping, lighting, refuse disposal and maintenance. May be less expensive than more highly rated parks.

THREE STAR Very good

Most parks fall within this category; three stars represent the industry standard. The range of facilities provided may vary from park to park, but they will be of a very good standard and will be well maintained.

FOUR STAR Excellent

You can expect careful attention to detail in the provision of all services and facilities. Four-star parks rank among the industry's best.

FIVE STAR Exceptional

Highest levels of customer care will be provided. All facilities will be maintained in pristine condition in attractive surroundings.

Advice and information

Making a booking

When enquiring about accommodation, make sure you check prices, the quality rating and other important details. You will also need to state your requirements clearly and precisely, for example:

- Arrival and departure dates, with acceptable alternatives if appropriate
- The type of accommodation you need – for example, room with twin beds, en suite bathroom
- The terms you want – for example, room only, bed and breakfast
- The age of any children with you, whether you want them to share your room or be next door, and any other requirements, such as a cot
- Any particular requirements you may have, such as a special diet, ground-floor room.

Confirmation

Misunderstandings can easily happen over the telephone, so do request a written confirmation, together with details of any terms and conditions.

Deposits

If you make a hotel or guest accommodation reservation weeks or months in advance, you will probably be asked for a deposit, which will then be deducted from the final bill when you leave. The amount will vary from establishment to establishment and could be payment in full at peak times.

Proprietors of self-catering accommodation will normally ask you to pay a deposit immediately, and then to pay the full balance before your holiday date. This safeguards the proprietor in case you decide to cancel at a late stage or simply do not turn up. He or she may have turned down other bookings on the strength of yours and may find it hard to re-let if you cancel.

In the case of camping and caravan parks the full charge often has to be paid in advance. This may be in two instalments – a deposit at the time of booking and the balance by, say, two weeks before the start of the booked period.

Payment on arrival

Some establishments, especially large hotels in big towns, ask you to pay for your room on arrival if you have not booked it in advance. This is especially likely to happen if you arrive late and have little or no luggage.

If you are asked to pay on arrival, it is a good idea to see your room first, to make sure it meets your requirements.

Cancellations

Legal contract

When you accept accommodation that is offered to you, by telephone or in writing, you enter a legally binding contract with the proprietor. This means that if you cancel your booking, fail to take up the accommodation or leave early, the proprietor may be entitled to compensation if he or she cannot re-let for all or a good part of the booked period. You will probably forfeit any deposit you have paid, and may well be asked for an additional payment.

At the time of booking you should be advised of what charges would be made in the event of cancelling the accommodation or leaving early. If this is not mentioned you should ask so that future disputes can be avoided. The proprietor cannot make a claim until after the booked period, and during that time he or she should make every effort to re-let the accommodation. If there is a dispute it is sensible for both sides to seek legal advice on the matter. If you do have to change your travel plans, it is in your own interests to let the proprietor know in writing as soon as possible, to give them a chance to re-let your accommodation.

And remember, if you book by telephone and are asked for your credit card number, you should check whether the proprietor intends charging your credit card account should you later cancel your reservation. A proprietor should not be able to charge your credit card account with a cancellation fee unless he or she has made this clear at the time of your booking and you have agreed. However, to avoid later disputes, we suggest you check whether this is the intention.

Insurance

A travel or holiday insurance policy will safeguard you if you have to cancel or change your holiday plans. You can arrange a policy quite cheaply through your insurance company or travel agent. Some hotels also offer their own insurance schemes and many self-catering agencies insist their customers take out a policy when they book their holidays.

Arrival time

If you know you will be arriving late in the evening, it is a good idea to say so when you book. If you are delayed on your way, a telephone call to say that you will be late would be appreciated.

It is particularily important to liaise with the owner of self-catering accommodation about key collection as he or she will not necessarily be on site.

Service charges and tipping

These days many places levy service charges automatically. If they do, they must clearly say so in their offer of accommodation, at the time of booking. The service charge then becomes part of the legal contract when you accept the offer of accommodation.

If a service charge is levied automatically, there is no need to tip the staff, unless they provide some exceptional service. The usual tip for meals is 10% of the total bill.

Telephone charges

Establishments can set their own charges for telephone calls made through their switchboard or from direct-dial telephones in bedrooms. These charges are often much higher than telephone companies' standard charges (to defray the cost of providing the service).

Comparing costs

It is a condition of Enjoy England's Quality Rose assessment scheme that an establishment's unit charges are on display by the telephones or with the room information. It is not always easy to compare these charges with standard rates, so before using a telephone for long-distance calls, you may decide to ask how the charges compare.

Security of valuables

You can deposit your valuables with the proprietor or manager during your stay, and we recommend you do this as a sensible precaution. Make sure you obtain a receipt for them. Some places do not accept articles for safe custody, and in that case it is wisest to keep your valuables with you.

Disclaimer

Some proprietors put up a notice that disclaims liability for property brought on to their premises by a guest. In fact, they can only restrict their liability to a minimum laid down by law (The Hotel Proprietors Act 1956). Under that Act, a proprietor is liable for the value of the loss or damage to any property (except a car or its contents) of a guest who has engaged overnight accommodation, but if the proprietor has the notice on display as prescribed under that Act, liability is limited to £50 for one article and a total of £100 for any one guest. The notice must be prominently displayed in the reception area or main entrance. These limits do not apply to valuables you have deposited with the proprietor for safekeeping, or to property lost through the default, neglect or wilful act of the proprietor or his staff.

Bringing pets to England

Dogs, cats, ferrets and some other pet mammals can be brought into the UK from certain countries without having to undertake six months' quarantine on arrival provided they meet all the rules of the Pet Travel Scheme (PETS).

For full details, visit the PETS website at
w defra.gov.uk/animalh/quarantine/index.htm or contact the PETS Helpline
t +44 (0)870 241 1710
e quarantine@defra.gsi.gov.uk
Ask for fact sheets which cover dogs and cats, ferrets or domestic rabbits and rodents.

What to expect

Hotels, guest and self-catering accommodation, holiday villages

The proprietor/management is required to undertake the following:

- To maintain standards of guest care, cleanliness and service appropriate to the type of establishment;
- To describe accurately in any advertisement, brochure or other printed or electronic media, the facilities and services provided;
- To make clear to visitors exactly what is included in all prices quoted for accommodation, including taxes, and any other surcharges. Details of charges for additional services/facilities should also be made clear;
- To give a clear statement of the policy on cancellations to guests at the time of booking ie by telephone, fax, email, as well as information given in a printed format;
- To adhere to and not to exceed prices quoted at the time of booking for accommodation and other services;

- To advise visitors at the time of booking, and subsequently if any change, if the accommodation offered is in an unconnected annexe or similar and to indicate the location of such accommodation and any difference in comfort and/or amenities from accommodation in the establishment;
- To register all guests on arrival;
- To give each visitor on request details of payments due and a receipt, if required;
- To deal promptly and courteously with all enquiries, requests, bookings and correspondence from visitors;
- To ensure complaint handling procedures are in place and that complaints received are investigated promptly and courteously and that the outcome is communicated to the visitor;
- To give due consideration to the requirements of visitors with disabilities and visitors with special needs, and to make suitable provision where applicable;
- To provide public liability insurance or comparable arrangements and to comply with all applicable planning, safety and other statutory requirements;
- To allow an Enjoy England assessor reasonable access to the establishment on request, to confirm the VisitBritain Code of Conduct is being observed.

What to expect

Caravan and camping parks

In addition to fulfilling its statutory obligations, including having applied for a certificate under the Fire Precautions Act 1971 (if applicable) and holding public liability insurance, and ensuring that all caravan holiday homes/chalets for hire and the park and all buildings and facilities thereon, the fixtures, furnishings, fittings and decor are maintained in sound and clean condition and are fit for the purposes intended, the management is required to undertake the following:

- To ensure high standards of courtesy, cleanliness, catering and service appropriate to the type of park;
- To describe to all visitors and prospective visitors the amenities, facilities and services provided by the park and/or caravan holiday homes/chalets whether by advertisement, brochure, word of mouth or other means;
- To allow visitors to see the park or caravan holiday homes/chalets for hire, if requested, before booking;
- To present grading awards and/or any other national tourist board awards unambiguously;
- To make clear to visitors exactly what is included in prices quoted for the park or caravan holiday homes/chalets, meals and refreshments, including service charge, taxes and other surcharges. Details of charges, if any, for heating or for additional services or facilities available should also be made clear;
- To adhere to, and not to exceed, prices current at time of occupation for caravan holiday homes/chalets or other services;
- To advise visitors at the time of booking, and subsequently if any change, if the caravan holiday home/chalet or pitch offered is in a different location or on another park, and to indicate the location of this and any difference in comfort and amenities;
- To give each visitor, on request, details of payments due and a receipt if required;
- To advise visitors at the time of booking of the charges that might be incurred if the booking is subsequently cancelled;
- To register all guests on arrival;
- To deal promptly and courteously with all visitors and prospective visitors, including enquiries, requests, reservations, correspondence and complaints;
- To allow a national tourist board representative reasonable access to the park and/or caravan holiday homes/chalet whether by prior appointment or on an unannounced assessment, to confirm that the VisitBritain Code of Conduct is being observed and that the appropriate quality standard is being maintained;
- The operator must comply with the provision of the caravan industry Codes of Practice.

Comments and complaints

The law

Places that offer accommodation have legal and statutory responsibilities to their customers, such as providing information about prices, providing adequate fire precautions and safeguarding valuables. Like other businesses, they must also abide by the Trades Description Acts 1968 and 1972 when they describe their accommodation and facilities. All the places featured in this guide have declared that they do fulfil all applicable statutory obligations.

Information

The proprietors themselves supply the descriptions of their establishments and other information for the entries, (except Enjoy England ratings and awards). VisitBritain cannot guarantee the accuracy of information in this guide, and accepts no responsibility for any error or misrepresentation. All liability for loss, disappointment, negligence or other damage caused by reliance on the information contained in this guide, or in the event of bankruptcy or liquidation or cessation of trade of any company, individual or firm mentioned, is hereby excluded. We strongly recommend that you carefully check prices and other details when you book your accommodation.

Quality Rose signage

All establishments/parks displaying a Quality Rose sign have to hold current membership of an Enjoy England Quality Rose assessment scheme or The British Graded Holiday Parks Scheme. When an establishment is sold the existing rating cannot be automatically transferred to the new owner.

Problems

Of course, we hope you will not have cause for complaint, but problems do occur from time to time. If you are dissatisfied with anything, make your complaint to the management immediately. Then the management can take action at once to investigate the matter and put things right. The longer you leave a complaint, the harder it is to deal with it effectively.

In certain circumstances, VisitBritain may look into complaints. However, VisitBritain has no statutory control over establishments or their methods of operating. VisitBritain cannot become involved in legal or contractual matters, nor can they get involved in seeking financial recompense.

If you do have problems that have not been resolved by the proprietor and which you would like to bring to our attention, please write to: Quality in Tourism, Farncombe House, Broadway, Worcestershire WR12 7LJ.

About the guide entries

Entries

All the establishments/parks featured in this guide have been assessed or have applied for assessment under an Enjoy England's Quality Rose assessment scheme or The British Graded Holiday Parks Scheme. Guest accommodation showing a diamond rating is awaiting re-assessment under the new common standards star-rating scheme.

Proprietors have paid to have their establishment/park featured in either a standard entry (includes description, facilities and prices) or enhanced entry (photograph and extended details).

Locations

Places to stay are generally listed under the town, city or village where they are located. If a place is in a small village, you may find it listed under a nearby town (providing it is within a seven-mile radius).

Place names are listed alphabetically within each regional section of the guide, along with the ceremonial county they are in and their map reference.

Complete addresses for self-catering properties are not given and the town(s) listed may be a distance from the actual establishment. Please check the precise location at the time of booking.

Map references

These refer to the colour location maps at the front of the guide. The first figure shown is the map number, the following letter and figure indicate the grid reference on the map. Some entries were included just before the guide went to press, so they do not appear on the maps.

Addresses

County names, which appear in the place headings, are not repeated in the entries. When you are writing, you should of course make sure you use the full address and postcode.

Telephone numbers

Telephone numbers are listed below the accommodation address for each entry. Area codes are shown in brackets.

Prices

The prices shown are only a general guide; they were supplied to us by proprietors in summer 2006. Remember, changes may occur after the guide goes to press, so we strongly advise you to check prices when you book your accommodation.

Prices are shown in pounds sterling and include VAT where applicable. Some places also include a service charge in their standard tariff, so check this when you book.

Bed and breakfast: the prices shown are per room for overnight accommodation with breakfast. The double room price is for two people. (If a double room is occupied by one person there is sometimes a reduction in price.)

Half board: the prices shown are per person per night for room, evening meal and breakfast. These prices are usually based on two people sharing a room.

Evening meal: the prices shown are per person per night.

Some places only provide a continental breakfast in the set price, and you may have to pay extra if you want a full English breakfast.

According to the law, establishments with at least four bedrooms or eight beds must display their overnight accommodation charges in the reception area or entrance. In your own interests, do make sure you check prices and what they include.

Self catering: prices shown are per unit per week and include VAT.

Camping: Touring pitches are based on the minimum and maximum charges for one night for two persons, car and either caravan or tent. (Some parks may charge separately for car, caravan or tent, and for each person and there may be an extra charge for caravan awnings.) Minimum and maximum prices for caravan holiday homes are given per week.

Children's rates

You will find that many places charge a reduced rate for children, especially if they share a room with their parents. Some places charge the full rate, however, when a child occupies a room which might otherwise have been let to an adult. The upper age limit for reductions for children varies from one hotel to another, so check this when you book.

Seasonal packages and special promotions

Prices often vary through the year and may be significantly lower outside peak holiday weeks. Many places offer special package rates – fully inclusive weekend breaks, for example – in the autumn, winter and spring. A number of establishments taking an enhanced entry have included any special offers, themed breaks etc that are available.

You can get details of other bargain packages that may be available from the establishments themselves, regional tourism organisations or your local Tourist Information Centre (TIC). Your local travel agent may also have information and can help you make reservations.

Bathrooms (hotels and guest accommodation)

Each accommodation entry shows you the number of en suite and private bathrooms available. En suite bathroom means the bath or shower and wc are contained behind the main door of the bedroom. Private bathroom means a bath or shower and wc solely for the occupants of one bedroom, on the same floor, reasonably close and with a key provided. If the availability of a bath, rather than a shower, is important to you, remember to check when you book.

Meals (hotels and guest accommodation)

It is advisable to check availability of meals and set times when making your reservation. Some smaller places may ask you at breakfast whether you want an evening meal. The prices shown in each entry are for bed and breakfast or half board, but many places also offer lunch.

Chalets/villas for hire (camping and caravan parks)

Where a site has chalets or villas for hire this is indicated by this symbol 🛖. Please note that this type of accommodation is not necessarily included within the official quality rating for the park and it is advisable that you contact the proprietor directly if you require further information.

Opening period

If an entry does not indicate an opening period, please check directly with the establishment.

Symbols

The at-a-glance symbols included at the end of each entry show many of the services and facilities available at each establishment. You will find the key to these symbols on the back-cover flap – open it out and check the meanings as you go.

Smoking

Many places provide no-smoking areas – from no-smoking bedrooms and lounges to no-smoking sections of the restaurant. Some places prefer not to accommodate smokers, and in such cases the descriptions or symbols in each entry make this clear.

Alcoholic drinks

All hotels (except temperance hotels) hold an alcohol licence. Some guest accommodation may also be licensed, however, the licence may be restricted – to diners only, for example. If a bar is available this is shown by the 🍷 symbol.

Pets

Many places accept guests with dogs, but we do advise that you check this when you book, and ask if there are any extra charges or rules about exactly where your pet is allowed. The acceptance of dogs is not always extended to cats and it is strongly advised that pet owners contact the establishment well in advance. Some establishments do not accept pets at all. Pets are welcome by arrangement where you see this symbol 🐕.

The quarantine laws have changed in England, and dogs, cats and ferrets are able to come into Britain from over 50 countries. For details of the Pet Travel Scheme (PETS) please turn to page 276.

Payment accepted

The types of payment accepted by an establishment are listed in the payment accepted section. If you plan to pay by card, check that the establishment will take your particular card before you book. Some proprietors will charge you a higher rate if you pay by credit card rather than cash or cheque. The difference is to cover the percentage paid by the proprietor to the credit card company. When you book by telephone, you may be asked for your credit card number as confirmation. But remember, the proprietor may then charge your credit card account if you cancel your booking. See under Cancellations on page 275.

Awaiting confirmation of rating

At the time of going to press some establishments/parks featured in this guide had not yet been assessed for their rating for the year 2007 and so their new rating could not be included. Rating Applied For indicates this.

Getting to the North

England is a country of perfect proportions – big enough to find a new place to discover, yet small enough to guarantee it's within easy reach. Getting from A to B can be easier than you think...

Planning your journey

Make transportdirect.info your first portal of call! It's the ultimate journey-planning tool to help you find the best way from your home to your destination by car or public transport. Decide on the quickest way to travel by comparing end-to-end journey times and routes. You can even buy train and coach tickets and find out about flights from a selection of airports.

With so many low-cost domestic flights, flying really is an option. Just imagine, you could finish work in Bristol and be in Newcastle just over an hour later for a fun-packed weekend!

If you're travelling by car and want an idea of distances check out the mileage chart overleaf. Or let the train take the strain – the National Rail network is also shown overleaf.

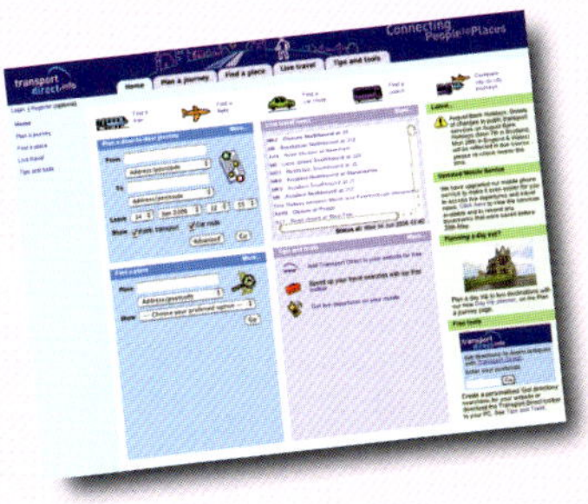

Think green

If you'd rather leave your car behind and travel by 'green transport' when visiting some of the attractions highlighted in this guide you'll be helping to reduce congestion and pollution as well as supporting conservation charities in their commitment to green travel.

The National Trust encourages visits made by non-car travellers. It offers admission discounts or a voucher for the tea room at a selection of its properties if you arrive on foot, cycle or public transport. (You'll need to produce a valid bus or train ticket if travelling by public transport.)

More information about The National Trust's work to encourage car-free days out can be found at nationaltrust.org.uk. Refer to the section entitled Information for Visitors.

To help you on your way you'll find a list of useful contacts at the end of this section.

By **car** and by **train**

Distance chart

The distances between towns on the chart below are given to the nearest mile, and are measured along routes based on the quickest travelling time, making maximum use of motorways or dual-carriageway roads. The chart is based upon information supplied by the Automobile Association.

To calculate the distance in kilometres multiply the mileage by 1.6

For example: Brighton to Dover
82 miles x 1.6 =131.2 kilometres

	Aberdeen	Aberystwyth	Barnstaple	Birmingham	Brighton	Bristol	Cambridge	Cardiff	Carlisle	Carmarthen	Dorchester	Dover	Edinburgh	Exeter	Fort William	Glasgow	Gloucester	Guildford	Hereford	Holyhead	Hull	Inverness	Kendal	Leeds	Lincoln	Liverpool	Maidstone	Manchester	Middlesbrough	Newcastle	Northampton	Norwich	Nottingham	Oxford	Penzance	Perth	Peterborough	Plymouth	Portsmouth	Preston	Salisbury	Sheffield	Shrewsbury	Southampton	Stoke-on-Trent	Stranraer	Taunton	Wick	York
Aberystwyth	472
Barnstaple	608	214
Birmingham	436	124	180
Brighton	613	288	210	171
Bristol	518	130	100	90	169
Cambridge	463	215	267	97	120	170
Cardiff	537	111	128	109	202	44	203
Carlisle	236	236	371	199	376	281	256	300
Carmarthen	520	48	190	172	264	107	266	68	284
Dorchester	600	206	94	172	119	62	184	120	364	182
Dover	587	326	272	208	82	205	124	239	381	301	200
Edinburgh	126	336	471	299	476	381	333	400	100	386	463	458
Exeter	593	198	44	165	178	84	259	113	356	175	57	248	455
Fort William	156	435	570	398	576	480	456	499	199	485	562	580	137	554
Glasgow	150	332	467	295	472	377	353	396	96	382	459	477	47	451	102
Gloucester	484	113	126	56	155	36	150	63	248	125	118	192	346	110	445	343
Guildford	571	224	175	128	44	106	96	139	335	201	97	97	433	150	532	430	99
Hereford	487	79	144	59	189	54	153	59	250	85	136	225	349	129	448	346	34	133
Holyhead	464	102	339	167	345	249	259	202	228	150	331	369	326	323	425	323	215	302	156
Hull	376	227	320	139	258	230	138	250	170	311	312	262	247	304	367	266	196	239	198	218
Inverness	106	496	631	459	637	541	517	561	260	546	623	641	157	616	66	176	507	595	510	488	430
Kendal	283	189	324	153	330	234	251	254	47	240	316	354	145	309	245	143	200	288	203	181	164	307
Leeds	329	173	301	120	262	211	146	230	123	224	293	271	200	285	321	219	177	220	179	165	59	383	110
Lincoln	388	199	275	98	216	185	95	205	182	267	246	220	258	260	379	277	151	173	154	204	44	441	176	74
Liverpool	362	110	272	101	278	182	193	202	126	158	264	302	224	257	324	222	148	236	151	102	128	386	79	74	139
Maidstone	545	284	234	166	50	167	82	200	339	262	161	41	416	209	537	435	153	58	186	327	220	599	313	231	178	261
Manchester	357	134	261	89	266	171	160	190	120	184	253	290	219	245	318	216	136	224	139	125	97	380	74	44	85	34	248
Middlesbrough	276	244	357	176	318	267	197	286	95	294	349	322	146	341	283	190	232	276	235	235	89	308	84	64	122	145	280	114
Newcastle	235	275	388	207	349	298	229	317	60	325	380	353	106	372	242	153	264	307	266	266	142	267	102	95	154	176	311	145	39
Northampton	486	174	212	56	133	115	56	162	249	224	159	155	348	196	447	345	79	90	111	217	152	509	203	136	94	151	113	139	189	220
Norwich	488	278	329	160	168	233	63	266	282	328	241	172	359	313	480	378	212	160	215	321	147	542	276	174	103	240	130	185	223	254	118
Nottingham	395	162	232	51	193	142	86	161	189	223	224	210	266	216	387	285	107	151	110	178	93	449	164	77	39	112	168	71	130	161	64	119
Oxford	510	160	170	68	109	73	82	107	274	169	115	146	373	154	472	370	48	67	81	242	190	534	228	174	132	176	107	164	227	258	44	146	102
Penzance	702	308	108	274	287	193	368	222	466	284	167	357	564	109	663	562	220	259	238	434	415	726	419	403	370	367	318	356	451	482	326	433	326	265
Perth	86	388	523	351	529	433	378	453	152	438	515	503	42	507	102	64	399	486	401	379	291	114	199	245	303	278	461	275	192	150	400	404	310	426	617
Peterborough	435	204	263	86	158	173	37	193	229	255	204	162	306	248	427	325	139	115	142	225	110	489	223	121	51	159	120	132	170	201	45	78	58	86	357	351
Plymouth	633	239	62	205	218	124	299	153	397	215	98	288	495	44	594	493	151	190	169	365	346	657	350	334	301	298	249	287	382	413	257	364	257	196	78	544	288
Portsmouth	596	244	162	154	53	125	137	158	360	220	73	141	458	132	558	456	118	45	152	328	276	620	314	260	215	262	102	250	313	344	130	204	188	85	241	508	157	172
Preston	326	146	281	110	287	191	209	211	89	197	273	311	188	266	287	185	157	245	160	138	122	349	43	69	134	36	269	35	103	139	159	235	121	184	375	237	180	306	270
Salisbury	549	184	118	121	90	52	145	98	313	160	39	160	411	93	511	409	72	62	105	281	261	573	267	244	202	215	121	203	298	329	115	212	173	70	203	461	165	134	44	223
Sheffield	397	166	272	91	233	182	122	201	161	263	264	247	236	256	359	257	148	191	150	157	66	421	115	38	47	79	205	39	100	131	104	148	45	142	366	309	93	297	228	73	212
Shrewsbury	417	75	220	48	226	130	140	111	181	110	212	250	279	205	379	277	96	184	52	105	162	441	135	119	124	65	208	71	190	221	98	203	87	123	314	329	129	245	209	92	161	88
Southampton	578	225	142	135	66	106	136	140	342	201	53	152	440	111	539	437	100	49	133	309	258	601	295	241	199	243	113	232	294	325	111	204	169	67	221	489	157	152	20	252	23	209	191
Stoke-on-Trent	392	112	220	48	226	130	140	150	156	211	212	250	254	205	353	251	96	184	99	123	129	415	109	93	91	57	208	46	164	195	98	172	54	123	314	303	99	245	209	66	161	50	38	191
Stranraer	235	342	477	305	482	387	363	406	106	392	469	487	132	461	181	86	352	440	355	333	276	261	153	229	288	232	445	229	201	163	354	388	295	380	571	149	333	502	466	195	418	267	287	447	261
Taunton	560	165	50	132	160	51	226	80	323	142	45	224	422	34	521	419	77	126	96	291	272	583	277	261	228	225	185	213	309	340	183	291	184	123	144	471	215	75	114	234	70	224	172	94	172	429
Wick	207	597	732	560	738	642	618	662	361	647	724	742	258	716	166	277	608	695	610	588	531	104	408	484	543	487	700	484	409	367	609	644	550	635	826	215	589	757	721	451	673	523	542	702	516	362	684
York	323	201	314	133	275	224	154	243	116	251	306	279	193	298	314	212	189	233	192	192	38	376	91	24	79	102	237	71	51	89	146	180	87	184	408	239	125	339	269	96	254	57	146	251	120	223	265	477
LONDON	550	239	216	121	54	120	59	153	314	215	125	78	413	200	512	410	102	31	136	282	186	574	268	201	143	216	39	204	254	285	68	118	129	56	310	462	86	241	75	225	85	169	163	77	161	420	167	675	211

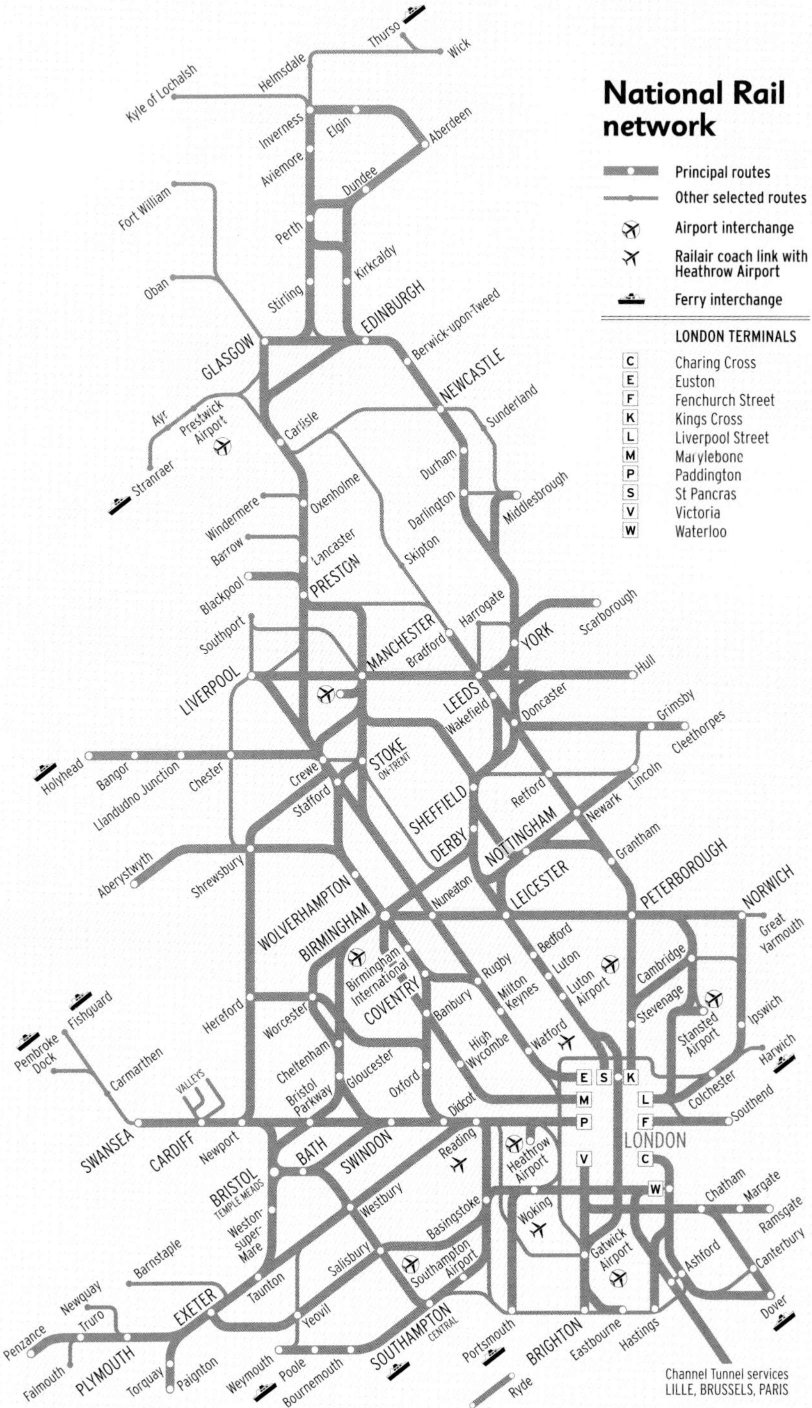

National Rail Enquiries
08457 48 49 50
www.nationalrail.co.uk

National Rail

06/NRE/1291

Travel information

General travel information

Streetmap	streetmap.co.uk	
Transport Direct	transportdirect.info	
Transport for London	tfl.gov.uk	(020) 7222 5600
Travel Services	departures-arrivals.com	
Traveline	traveline.org.uk	0870 608 2608

Bus & coach

Megabus	megabus.com	0901 331 0031
National Express	nationalexpress.com	0870 580 8080
WA Shearings	washearings.com	(01942) 824824

Car & car hire

AA	theaa.com	0870 600 0371
Green Flag	greenflag.co.uk	0845 246 1557
RAC	rac.co.uk	0870 572 2722
Alamo	alamo.co.uk	0870 400 4562
Avis	avis.co.uk	0870 010 0287
Budget	budget.co.uk	0844 581 2231
Easycar	easycar.com	0906 333 3333
Enterprise	enterprise.com	0870 350 3000*
Hertz	hertz.co.uk	0870 844 8844*
Holiday Autos	holidayautos.co.uk	
National	nationalcar.co.uk	0870 400 4581
Thrifty	thrifty.co.uk	(01494) 751500*

Air

Airport information	a2btravel.com/airports	0870 888 1710
Air Southwest	airsouthwest.com	0870 043 4553
Blue Islands (Channel Islands)	blueislands.com	(01481) 727567
BMI	flybmi.com	0870 607 0555
BMI Baby	bmibaby.com	0871 224 0224
BNWA (Isle of Man to Blackpool)	flybnwa.co.uk	0800 083 7783
British Airways	ba.com	0870 850 9850
British International (Isles of Scilly to Penzance)	islesofscillyhelicopter.com	(01736) 363871
Eastern Airways	easternairways.com	0870 366 9100
Easyjet	easyjet.com	0871 244 2366
Flybe	flybe.com	0871 700 0535
Jet2.com	jet2.com	0871 226 1737
Ryanair	ryanair.com	0871 246 0000
Skybus (Isles of Scilly)	islesofscilly-travel.com	0845 710 5555
VLM	flyvlm.com	0871 666 5050

Train

National Rail Enquiries	nationalrail.co.uk	0845 748 4950
The Trainline	trainline.co.uk	
UK train operating companies	rail.co.uk	
Arriva Trains	arriva.co.uk	0845 748 4950
c2c	c2c-online.co.uk	0845 601 4873*
Central Trains	centraltrains.co.uk	(0121) 634 2040
Chiltern Railways	chilternrailways.co.uk	0845 600 5165
First Capital Connect	firstcapitalconnect.co.uk	0845 748 4950
First Great Western	firstgreatwestern.co.uk	0845 700 0125*
Gatwick Express	gatwickexpress.co.uk	0845 850 1530
GNER	gner.co.uk	0845 722 5333
Heathrow Express	heathrowexpress.com	0845 600 1515
Hull Trains	hulltrains.co.uk	0845 071 0222
Island Line	island-line.co.uk	0845 748 4950
Merseyrail	merseyrail.org	0845 748 4950
Midland Mainline	midlandmainline.com	0845 712 5678
Northern Rail	northernrail.org	0845 748 4950
One Railway	onerailway.com	0845 600 7245
Silverlink	silverlink-trains.com	0845 601 4868
South Eastern Trains	southeasternrailway.co.uk	0845 748 4950
South West Trains	southwesttrains.co.uk	0845 600 0650
Southern	southernrailway.com	0845 127 2920
Stansted Express	stanstedexpress.com	0845 600 7245
Transpennine Express	tpexpress.co.uk	0845 748 4950
Virgin Trains	virgintrains.co.uk	0870 789 1234

Ferry

Ferry information	sailanddrive.com	
Condor Ferries (Channel Islands)	condorferries.co.uk	0870 243 5140*
Steam Packet Company (Isle of Man)	steam-packet.com	0870 552 3523
Isles of Scilly Travel	islesofscilly-travel.co.uk	0845 710 5555
Red Funnel (Isle of Wight)	redfunnel.co.uk	0870 444 8898
Wight Link (Isle of Wight)	wightlink.co.uk	0870 582 7744

Phone numbers listed are for general enquiries unless otherwise stated.

* Booking line only

A selection of **events for 2007**

This is a selection of the many cultural, sporting and other events that will be taking place throughout Northern England during 2007. For a more comprehensive list, visit **enjoyengland.com/events**.

Please note, as changes often occur after press date, it is advisable to confirm the date and location before travelling.

April

12 – 14 Apr
John Smith's Grand National
Aintree Racecourse, Liverpool, Merseyside
(0151) 522 2929
aintree.co.uk

21 Apr – 7 May
World Snooker Championships
The Crucible Theatre, Sheffield, South Yorkshire
(0114) 249 6000
worldsnooker.com

26 – 29 Apr
Harrogate Spring Flower Show
Great Yorkshire Showground, Harrogate, North Yorkshire
(01423) 561049
flowershow.org.uk

May

May–Oct
York Races
York Racecourse, North Yorkshire
(01904) 620911
yorkracecourse.co.uk

4 – 6 May
Moor and Coast Festival
Whitby, North Yorkshire
(01947) 820408
moorandcoast.co.uk

8 – 13 May
Pathways – Garstang Walking Festival
Garstang, Lancashire
(01995) 602125
wyrebc.gov.uk

9 – 11 May
May Festival
Chester Racecourse, Cheshire
(01244) 304600
chester-races.co.uk

19 May – 3 Jun
Northern Rocks 2007 – Festival of Geology and Landscape
Various venues throughout North Pennines
(01388) 528801
northpennines.org.uk

26 – 27 May
Arley Horse Trials & Country Fair
Arley Hall & Gardens, Northwich, Cheshire
(01565) 777353
arleyhallandgardens.com

28 May
The Northumberland County Show
Tynedale Park, Corbridge
(01434) 609533
northcountyshow.co.uk

June

1 – 3 Jun
The Holker Festival
Holker Hall & Gardens, Cumbria
(015395) 58838
holker-hall.co.uk

9 – 10 Jun
Durham Regatta
Durham, County Durham
durham-regatta.org

9 Jun
The Honley Show
Honley, nr Huddersfield, West Yorkshire
(01484) 661072
honleyshow.org.uk

14 – 16 Jun
Tynedale Beer Festival
Tynedale Park, Corbridge, Northumberland
(01434) 652220
tynedalebeerfestival.org.uk

15 – 17 Jun
Beverley Folk Festival
Various venues, Beverley, East Riding of Yorkshire
(01377) 217569
beverleyfestival.com

17 Jun*
Middlesbrough Music Live
Middlesbrough town centre, Tees Valley
(0114) 247755
middlesbroughmusiclive.co.uk

28 Jun – 15 Jul
Manchester International Festival
Various venues
(0161) 238 7300
manchesterinternationalfestival.com

30 Jun – 1 Jul
Sunderland International Kite Festival
Washington, Tyne and Wear
(0191) 553 2000
sunderland-kites.co.uk

July

2 – 15 Jul
Rotherham Walking Festival
Rotherham, South Yorkshire
(01709) 835904
visitrotherham.org

10 – 12 Jul
The Great Yorkshire Show
Harrogate, North Yorkshire
(01423) 541000
greatyorkshireshow.com

14 – 15 Jul
Mouth of the Tyne Festival
South Shields and Tynemouth, Tyne and Wear
(0191) 424 7985
visitsouthtyneside.co.uk

15 Jul
Middlesbrough Mela
Albert Park, Middlesbrough, Tees Valley
boromela.co.uk

18 – 22 Jul
RHS Flower Show at Tatton Park
Tatton Park, Knutsford, Cheshire
(020) 7649 1885
rhs.org.uk

19 Jul – 4 Aug
Harrogate International Festival
Harrogate, North Yorkshire
(01423) 562303
harrogate-festival.org.uk

20 – 22 Jul
Royal Lancashire Agricultural Show
Ribchester, Lancashire
(01254) 813769
rlas.co.uk

20 – 22 Jul
Scarborough Seafest
Scarborough, North Yorkshire
(01723) 383637
discoveryorkshirecoast.com

21 Jul
Doncaster Live 2007
Doncaster, South Yorkshire
(01302) 862480
visitdoncaster.co.uk

28 Jul – 4 Aug
Billingham International Folklore Festival
Billingham town centre and Forum Theatre, Tees Valley
(01642) 553220
billinghamfestival.co.uk

28 – 29 Jul
Sunderland International Airshow
Seaburn seafront, Sunderland, Tyne and Wear
(0191) 553 2000
sunderland-airshow.com

August

1 – 5 Aug
Stockton International Riverside Festival
Stockton Riverside, Tees Valley
(01642) 528130
sirf.co.uk

3 – 5 Aug
Lowther Horse Driving Trials
Penrith, Cumbria
(01931) 712577
lowther.co.uk

4 – 11 Aug
Alnwick International Music and Dance Festival
Alnwick, Northumberland
(01665) 510665
alnwickfestival.com

4 Aug
Georgian Fair
Beamish, The North of England Open Air Museum, County Durham
(0191) 370 4000
beamish.org.uk

11 – 13 Aug
Whitby Regatta
Whitby, North Yorkshire
(01723) 383636
whitbyregatta.co.uk

17 – 27 Aug
Manchester Pride
The Gay Village, city centre
(0161) 238 4548
machesterpride.com

22 – 28 Aug
International Beatle Week/ Mathew Street Festival
Various venues, Liverpool, Merseyside
(0151) 236 9091
caverncitytours.com

24 – 27 Aug
The Great British Rhythm & Blues Festival
Colne, Lancashire
(01282) 661234
bluesfestival.co.uk

25 – 26 Aug
Tractor Pulling Championships
Great Eccleston, Lancashire
(01253) 702930
tractorpulling.co.uk

31 Aug – 3 Sep
Pendle Walking Festival
Pendle, Lancashire
(01282) 661981
pendle.gov.uk

31 Aug – 2 Sep
Art in the Gardens
Botanical Gardens, Sheffield, South Yorkshire
(0114) 236 1398
sbg.org.uk

September

1 Sep – 5 Nov
Blackpool Illuminations
Blackpool, Lancashire
(01253) 478222
visitblackpool.com

1 – 2 Sep*
Rushbearing Festival
Sowerby Bridge, West Yorkshire
rushbearing.co.uk

12 – 15 Sep
St Leger Festival
Doncaster Racecourse, South Yorkshire
(01302) 304200
doncaster-racecourse.co.uk

13 Sep
Westmorland County Show
Kendal, Cumbria
(015395) 67804
westmorland-county-show.co.uk

14 – 16 Sep
Harrogate Autumn Flower Show
Great Yorkshire Showground, Harrogate, North Yorkshire
(01423) 561049
flowershow.org.uk

21 Sep – 7 Oct
Grin Up North Comedy Festival
Various venues, Sheffield, South Yorkshire
(0114) 221 1900
sheffieldcomedyfestival.com

28 – 30 Sep
Nantwich Food & Drink Festival
Mill Island, Nantwich, Cheshire
(01270) 610983
nantwichfoodfestival.co.uk

October

13 – 21 Oct
Haltwhistle Walking Festival
Haltwhistle, Northumberland
(01434) 321242
haltwhistle.org

November

23 Nov – 2 Dec
Huddersfield Contemporary Music Festival
Various venues, Huddersfield, West Yorkshire
(01484) 425082
hcmf.co.uk

December

Dec
Winter Festival
Various venues, NewcastleGateshead, Tyne and Wear
(0191) 243 8804
newcastlegateshead.com

Tourist Information Centres

When you arrive at your destination, visit a Tourist Information Centre for help with accommodation and information about local attractions and events, or email your request before you go.

Cheshire

Altrincham	20 Stamford New Road	(0161) 912 5931	tourist.information@trafford.gov.uk
Chester (Town Hall)	Northgate Street	(01244) 402111	tis@chestercc.gov.uk
Chester Visitor Centre	Vicars Lane	(01244) 402111	tis@chestercc.gov.uk
Congleton	High Street	(01260) 271095	tourism@congleton.gov.uk
Ellesmere Port	Kinsey Road	(0151) 356 7879	cheshireoaks-tic@hotmail.co.uk
Knutsford	Toft Road	(01565) 632611	ktic@macclesfield.gov.uk
Macclesfield	Town Hall	(01625) 504114	Informationcentre@macclesfield.gov.uk
Nantwich	Church Walk	(01270) 610983	touristi@crewe-nantwich.gov.uk
Northwich	1 The Arcade	(01606) 353534	tourism@valeroyal.gov.uk
Warrington	Academy Way	(01925) 632571	informationcentre@warrington.gov.uk
Wilmslow	Rectory Fields	(01625) 522275	i.hillaby@macclesfield.gov.uk

County Durham

Barnard Castle	Woodleigh Flatts Road	(01833) 690909	tourism@teesdale.gov.uk
Bishop Auckland	Market Place	(01388) 604922	bishopauckland.tourisminfo@durham.gov.uk
Durham	2 Millennium Place	(0191) 384 3720	touristinfo@durhamcity.gov.uk
Middleton-in-Teesdale	10 Market Place	(01833) 641001	middletonplus@compuserve.com
Peterlee	4 Upper Yoden Way	(0191) 586 4450	touristinfo@peterlee.gov.uk
Stanhope	Durham Dales Centre	(01388) 527650	durham.dales.centre@durham.gov.uk

Cumbria – The Lake District

Alston Moor	Front Street	(01434) 382244	alston.tic@eden.gov.uk
Ambleside	Market Cross	(015394) 32582	amblesidetic@southlakeland.gov.uk
Appleby-in-Westmorland	Boroughgate	(017683) 51177	tic@applebytown.org.uk
Barrow-in-Furness	Duke Street	(01229) 894784	touristinfo@barrowbc.gov.uk
Bowness	Glebe Road	(015394) 42895	bownesstic@lake-district.gov.uk
Brampton*	Market Place	(01697) 73433	tourism@carlisle-city.gov.uk
Broughton in Furness	The Square	(01229) 716115	email@broughton-tic.fsnet.co.uk
Carlisle	Greenmarket	(01228) 625600	tourism@carlisle-city.gov.uk
Cockermouth	Market Street	(01900) 822634	email@cockermouth-tic.fsnet.co.uk
Coniston	Ruskin Avenue	(015394) 41533	
Egremont	12 Main Street	(01946) 820693	email@egremont-tic.fsnet.co.uk

Grange-over-Sands	Main Street	(015395) 34026	grangetic@southlakeland.gov.uk
Kendal	Highgate	(01539) 725758	kendaltic@southlakeland.gov.uk
Keswick	Market Square	(017687) 72645	keswicktic@lake-district.gov.uk
Kirkby Lonsdale	24 Main Street	(01524) 271437	kltic@southlakeland.gov.uk
Kirkby Stephen	Market Street	(017683) 71199	ks.tic@eden.gov.uk
Maryport	Senhouse Street	(01900) 812101	maryporttic@allerdale.gov.uk
Millom*	Station Road	(01229) 774819	millomtic@copelandbc.gov.uk
Penrith	Middlegate	(01768) 867466	pen.tic@eden.gov.uk
Rheged		(01768) 860034	tic@rheged.com
Sedbergh	72 Main Street	(015396) 20125	tic@sedbergh.org.uk
Silloth-on-Solway	Liddell Street	(016973) 31944	sillothtic@allerdale.gov.uk
Southwaite	M6 Service Area	(016974) 73445	southwaitetic@visitscotland.com
Ullswater	Glenridding	(017684) 82414	ullswatertic@lake-district.gov.uk
Ulverston	County Square	(01229) 587120	ulverstontic@southlakeland.gov.uk
Whitehaven	Market Place	(01946) 852939	tic@copelandbc.gov.uk
Windermere	Victoria Street	(015394) 46499	windermeretic@southlakeland.gov.uk
Workington	21 Finkle Street	(01900) 606699	workingtontic@allerdale.gov.uk

Greater Manchester

Bolton	Le Mans Crescent	(01204) 334321	tourist.info@bolton.gov.uk
Bury	Market Street	(0161) 253 5111	touristinformation@bury.gov.uk
Manchester Visitor Information Centre	Lloyd Street	0871 222 8223	touristinformation@marketing-manchester.co.uk
Oldham	12 Albion Street	(0161) 627 1024	ecs.tourist@oldham.gov.uk
Saddleworth	High Street, Uppermill	(01457) 870336	ecs.tourist@oldham.gov.uk
Salford	Salford Quays	(0161) 848 8601	tic@salford.gov.uk
Stockport	30 Market Place	(0161) 474 4444	tourist.information@stockport.gov.uk
Wigan	Trencherfield Mill	(01942) 825677	tic@wlct.org

Lancashire

Accrington	Blackburn Road	(01254) 872595	leisure@hyndburnbc.gov.uk
Ashton-under-Lyne	Wellington Road	(0161) 343 4343	tourist.information@mail.tameside.gov.uk
Barnoldswick	Fernlea Avenue	(01282) 666704	tourist.info@pendle.gov.uk
Blackburn	50-54 Church Street	(01254) 53277	visit@blackburn.gov.uk
Blackpool	1 Clifton Street	(01253) 478222	tic@blackpool.gov.uk
Blackpool*	Central Promenade	(01253) 478222	tic@blackpool.gov.uk
Burnley	Croft Street	(01282) 664421	tic@burnley.gov.uk
Cleveleys	Victoria Square	(01253) 853378	cleveleystic@wyrebc.gov.uk
Clitheroe	12-14 Market Place	(01200) 425566	tourism@ribblevalley.gov.uk
Fleetwood	The Esplanade	(01253) 773953	fleetwoodtic@wyrebc.gov.uk
Garstang	High Street	(01995) 602125	garstangtic@wyrebc.gov.uk
Lancaster	29 Castle Hill	(01524) 32878	lancastertic@lancaster.gov.uk
Lytham St Annes	67 St Annes Road West	(01253) 725610	touristinformation@fylde.gov.uk

Morecambe	Marine Road Central	(01524) 582808	morecambetic@lancaster.gov.uk
Pendle Heritage Centre	Park Hill	(01282) 661701	heritage.centre@pendle.gov.uk
Preston	Lancaster Road	(01772) 253731	tourism@preston.gov.uk
Rochdale	The Esplanade	(01706) 864928	tic@rochdale.gov.uk

Merseyside

Birkenhead	Woodside Ferry Terminal, Wirral	(0151) 647 6780	touristinfo@wirral.gov.uk
Liverpool	John Lennon Airport	(0151) 907 1057	info@visitliverpool.com
Liverpool (Maritime Museum)	Albert Dock	(0151) 233 2008	info@visitliverpool.com
Liverpool 08 Place	Whitechapel	(0151) 233 2008	08place@liverpool.gov.uk
Southport	112 Lord Street	(01704) 533333	info@visitsouthport.com
St Helens	Chalon Way East	(01744) 755150	info@sthelenstic.com

Northumberland

Adderstone	Adderstone Garage	(01668) 213678	adderstone@hotmail.com
Alnwick	2 The Shambles	(01665) 510665	alnwicktic@alnwick.gov.uk
Amble*	Queen Street Car Park	(01665) 712313	ambletic@alnwick.gov.uk
Bellingham	Main Street	(01434) 220616	bellinghamtic@btconnect.com
Berwick-upon-Tweed	106 Marygate	(01289) 330733	tourism@berwick-upon-tweed.gov.uk
Corbridge*	Hill Street	(01434) 632815	corbridgetic@btconnect.com
Craster*	Craster Car Park	(01665) 576007	crastertic@alnwick.gov.uk
Haltwhistle	Station Road	(01434) 322002	haltwhistletic@btconnect.com
Hexham	Wentworth Car Park	(01434) 652220	hexham.tic@tynedale.gov.uk
Morpeth	Bridge Street	(01670) 500700	tourism@castlemorpeth.gov.uk
Once Brewed*	Military Road	(01434) 344396	tic.oncebrewed@nnpa.org.uk
Otterburn	Otterburn Mill	(01830) 520093	tic@otterburnmill.co.uk
Rothbury*	Church Street	(01669) 620887	tic.rothbury@nnpa.org.uk
Seahouses*	Seafield car park	(01665) 720884	seahousestic@berwick-upon-tweed.gov.uk
Wooler*	12 Padgepool Place	(01668) 282123	woolertic@berwick-upon-tweed.gov.uk

Tees Valley

Darlington	13 Horsemarket	(01325) 388666	tic@darlington.gov.uk
Guisborough	Church Street	(01287) 633801	guisborough_tic@redcar-cleveland.gov.uk
Hartlepool	Church Square	(01429) 869706	hpooltic@hartlepool.gov.uk
Middlesbrough	99-101 Albert Road	(01642) 729700	middlesbrough_tic@middlesbrough.gov.uk
Redcar	West Terrace	(01642) 471921	redcar_tic@redcar-cleveland.gov.uk
Saltburn-by-the-Sea	Station Square	(01287) 622422	saltburn_tic@redcar-cleveland.gov.uk
Stockton-on-Tees	Church Road	(01642) 528130	touristinformation@stockton.gov.uk

Tyne and Wear

Gateshead (Central Library)	Prince Consort Road	(0191) 433 8400	tic@gateshead.gov.uk

Gateshead (Visitor Centre, Quayside)	St Mary's Church	(0191) 478 4222	tourism@gateshead.gov.uk
Newcastle International Airport		(0191) 214 4422	niatic@hotmail.com
Newcastle upon Tyne (Grainger St)	132 Grainger Street	(0191) 277 8000	tourist.info@newcastle.gov.uk
Newcastle upon Tyne (Guildhall)	Quayside	(0191) 277 8000	tourist.info@newcastle.gov.uk
North Shields	Royal Quays Outlet Shopping	(0191) 200 5895	ticns@northtyneside.gov.uk
South Shields	Ocean Road	(0191) 454 6612	museum.tic@southtyneside.gov.uk
South Shields (Amphitheatre)*	Sea Road	(0191) 455 7411	foreshore.tic@southtyneside.gov.uk
Sunderland	50 Fawcett Street	(0191) 553 2000	tourist.info@sunderland.gov.uk
Whitley Bay	Park Road	(0191) 200 8535	ticwb@northtyneside.gov.uk

Yorkshire

Aysgarth Falls	Aysgarth Falls National Park Centre	(01969) 662910	aysgarth@ytbtic.co.uk
Barnsley	Central Library	(01226) 206757	barnsley@ytbtic.co.uk
Batley	Bradford Road	(01924) 426670	batley@ytbtic.co.uk
Beverley	34 Butcher Row	(01482) 867430	beverley.tic@eastriding.gov.uk
Bradford	City Hall	(01274) 739067	tourist.information@bradford.gov.uk
Bridlington	25 Prince Street	(01262) 673474	bridlington.tic@eastriding.gov.uk
Brigg	Market Place	(01652) 657053	brigg.tic@northlincs.gov.uk
Cleethorpes	42-43 Alexandra Road	(01472) 323111	cleethorpes@ytbtic04.freeserve.co.uk
Danby*	Lodge Lane	(01439) 772737	moorscentre@northyorkmoors-npa.gov.uk
Doncaster	38-40 High Street	(01302) 734309	tourist.information@doncaster.gov.uk
Filey*	John Street	(01723) 383637	fileytic@scarborough.gov.uk
Grassington	Hebden Road	(01756) 752774	grassington@ytbtic.co.uk
Guisborough	Church Street	(01287) 633801	guisborough_tic@redcar-cleveland.gov.uk
Halifax	Piece Hall	(01422) 368725	halifax@ytbtic.co.uk
Harrogate	Crescent Road	(01423) 537300	tic@harrogate.gov.uk
Hawes	Station Yard	(01969) 666210	hawes@ytbtic.co.uk
Haworth	2/4 West Lane	(01535) 642329	haworth@ytbtic.co.uk
Hebden Bridge	New Road	(01422) 843831	hebdenbridge@ytbtic.co.uk
Helmsley	Castlegate	(01439) 770173	helmsley@ytbtic.co.uk
Holmfirth	49-51 Huddersfield Road	(01484) 222444	holmfirth.tic@kirklees.gov.uk
Hornsea*	120 Newbegin	(01964) 536404	hornsea.tic@eastriding.gov.uk
Horton in Ribblesdale	Pen-y-ghent Cafe	(01729) 860333	horton@ytbtic.co.uk
Huddersfield	3 Albion Street	(01484) 223200	huddersfield.tic@kirklees.gov.uk
Hull	1 Paragon Street	(01482) 223559	tourist.information@hullcc.gov.uk
Humber Bridge	Ferriby Road	(01482) 640852	humberbridge.tic@eastriding.gov.uk
Ilkley	Station Road	(01943) 602319	ilkley@ytbtic.co.uk

Ingleton*	The Community Centre Car Park	(015242) 41049	ingleton@ytbtic.co.uk
Knaresborough	9 Castle Courtyard	08453 890177	kntic@harrogate.gov.uk
Leeds	The Arcade, City Station	(0113) 242 5242	tourinfo@leeds.gov.uk
Leeming Bar	The Great North Road	(01677) 424262	leeming@ytbtic.co.uk
Leyburn	4 Central Chambers	(01969) 623069	leyburn@ytbtic.co.uk
Malham		(01969) 652380	malham@ytbtic.co.uk
Malton	58 Market Place	(01653) 600048	maltontic@btconnect.com
Otley	Nelson Street	(01943) 462485	otleytic@leedslearning.net
Pateley Bridge*	18 High Street	08453 890179	pbtic@harrogate.gov.uk
Pickering	The Ropery	(01751) 473791	pickering@ytbtic.co.uk
Redcar	West Terrace	(01642) 471921	redcar_tic@redcar-cleveland.gov.uk
Reeth	The Green	(01748) 884059	reeth@ytbtic.co.uk
Richmond	Friary Gardens	(01748) 850252	richmond@ytbtic.co.uk
Ripon*	Minster Road	08453 890178	ripontic@harrogate.gov.uk
Rotherham Visitor Centre	40 Bridgegate	(01709) 835904	tic@rotherham.gov.uk
Saltburn-by-the-Sea	Station Square	(01287) 622422	saltburn_tic@redcar-cleveland.gov.uk
Scarborough	Brunswick Centre	(01723) 383636	tourismbureau@scarborough.gov.uk
Scarborough (Harbourside)	Sandside	(01723) 383636	harboursidetic@scarborough.gov.uk
Scunthorpe	Carlton Street	(01724) 297354	brigg.tic@northlincs.gov.uk
Selby	52 Micklegate	(01757) 212181	selby@ytbtic.co.uk
Settle	Cheapside	(01729) 825192	settle@ytbtic.co.uk
Sheffield	Winter Garden	(0114) 221 1900	visitor@sheffield.gov.uk
Skipton	35 Coach Street	(01756) 792809	skipton@ytbtic.co.uk
Sutton Bank	Sutton Bank	(01845) 597426	suttonbank@ytbtic.co.uk
Thirsk	49 Market Place	(01845) 522755	thirsktic@hambleton.gov.uk
Todmorden	15 Burnley Road	(01706) 818181	todmorden@ytbtic.co.uk
Wakefield	9 The Bull Ring	0845 601 8353	tic@wakefield.gov.uk
Wetherby	17 Westgate	(01937) 582151	wetherbytic@leedslearning.net
Whitby	Langborne Road	(01723) 383637	whitbytic@scarborough.gov.uk
Withernsea*	131 Queen Street	(01964) 615683	withernsea.tic@eastriding.gov.uk
York (De Grey Rooms)	Exhibition Square	(01904) 621756	tic@york-tourism.co.uk
York (Railway Station)	Station Road	(01904) 621756	kg@ytbyork.swiftserve.net

* *seasonal opening*

Alternatively, you can text **TIC LOCATE** to **64118** to find your nearest Tourist Information Centre

Places to visit index by **attraction name**

All places to visit featured in this guide are listed below. Places in colour have a detailed entry.

a

b

b continued — page

c — page

d — page

d continued

page

e

page

f

page

g

page

h

page

i

page

j

page

k

page

Places to visit in colour have a detailed entry in this guide.

Places to visit in colour have a detailed entry in this guide.

s continued

t

u

v

w

Quality visitor attractions

enjoyEngland.com QUALITY ASSURED VISITOR ATTRACTION

Enjoy England operates a Visitor Attraction Quality Assurance Service.

Participating attractions are visited annually by trained, impartial assessors who look at all aspects of the visit, from initial telephone enquiries to departure, customer service to catering, as well as all facilities and activities.

Only those attractions which have been assessed by Enjoy England and meet the standard receive the quality marque, your sign of a Quality Assured Visitor Attraction.

Look out for the quality marque and visit with confidence.

Accommodation index by **property name**

All accommodation featured in this guide is listed below.

e page

f page

g page

h page

i page

k page

l page

m page

Establishments listed here have a detailed entry in this guide.

Accommodation index by **place name**

The following places all have accommodation in this guide. If the place where you wish to stay is not shown, the location maps (starting on page 22) will help you to find somewhere to stay in the area.

Turn to the pages indicated for detailed accommodation entries in these places.

enjoyEngland™

Published by: VisitBritain, Thames Tower, Blacks Road, London W6 9EL
enjoyengland.com
Publishing Manager: Tess Lugos
Production Manager: Iris Buckley
Compilation, design, copywriting, production and advertisement sales:
Jackson Lowe, 3 St Andrews Place, Southover Road, Lewes, East Sussex
BN7 1UP
t (01273) 487487 jacksonlowe.com
Typesetting: Marlinzo Services, Somerset and Jackson Lowe
Maps: Based on digital map data © ESR Cartography, 2006
Printing and binding: Emirates Printing Press, Dubai, United Arab Emirates
Cover design: Jackson Lowe

Front cover: Waterhead, Windermere, Cumbria
(cumbriaphoto.co.uk/Ben Barden/Cumbria Tourism)

Photography credits: The Alnwick Garden; Bede's World; The Bowes Museum; britainonview.com/Daniel Bosworth/ Martin Brent/Rod Edwards/Adrian Houston/Pawel Libera/ James McCormick/McCormick-McAdam/Visit Chester & Cheshire; The Caravan Club; The Chester Grosvenor and Spa; Cumbria Tourism/Ben Barden; The Deep; England's Northwest; Imperial War Museum North; Killhope: The North of England Lead Mining Museum; Langley Castle Hotel; Malmaison, Leeds; Malmaison, NewcastleGateshead; National Museum of Photography, Film & Television; Nature's World; One NorthEast Tourism; Seven Stories, the Centre for Children's Books, Tyne & Wear Museums; Visit Southport/ Chris Horan; WWT

ISBN 978-0-7095-8335-6

A VisitBritain Publishing guide

SPECIAL OFFER VOUCHER

One child free with a full paying adult

Alnwick Castle
Alnwick NE66 1NQ

SPECIAL OFFER VOUCHER

Two for the price of one

Darlington Railway Centre and Museum
Darlington DL3 6ST

SPECIAL OFFER VOUCHER

Two for the price of one

Birkheads Secret Gardens & Nursery
Sunniside, Newcastle upon Tyne NE16 5EL

SPECIAL OFFER VOUCHER

Child goes free with a full paying adult

DIG – An Archaeological Adventure
York YO1 8NN

The Manchester Museum

VisitBritain Official Guides
Terms & Conditions for Attraction voucher

1 Offer applies to normal museum opening days, but not to the museum's special event days.
2 Each voucher entitles the holder to the discount specified by the selected attraction.
3 Valid for use until 31/10/2008 (unless otherwise specified, or if attraction season finishes prior to this). Vouchers are subject to the terms, conditions and restrictions of the selected attraction.
4 One voucher per party will be accepted and cannot be used in conjunction with any other offer. Photocopies will not be accepted.
5 All attractions offering a discount have confirmed their willingness to participate. All information is subject to change without notice and should any attraction close or decline to accept a voucher for any reason, VisitBritain is not liable and cannot be held responsible.
6 VisitBritain shall not accept liability for any loss, accident or injury that may occur at a participating attraction and any dispute must be settled direct with the attraction concerned.
7 There is no cash alternative in lieu of tickets or listed savings.
8 You are advised to check all relevant information with your chosen attraction before commencing your journey.

VisitBritain Official Guides
Terms & Conditions for Attraction voucher

1 Not to be used in conjunction with other offers. Not valid on public holidays. Applies to normal daily castle admission only.
2 Each voucher entitles the holder to the discount specified by the selected attraction.
3 Valid for use until 31/10/2008 (unless otherwise specified, or if attraction season finishes prior to this). Vouchers are subject to the terms, conditions and restrictions of the selected attraction.
4 One voucher per party will be accepted and cannot be used in conjunction with any other offer. Photocopies will not be accepted.
5 All attractions offering a discount have confirmed their willingness to participate. All information is subject to change without notice and should any attraction close or decline to accept a voucher for any reason, VisitBritain is not liable and cannot be held responsible.
6 VisitBritain shall not accept liability for any loss, accident or injury that may occur at a participating attraction and any dispute must be settled direct with the attraction concerned.
7 There is no cash alternative in lieu of tickets or listed savings.
8 You are advised to check all relevant information with your chosen attraction before commencing your journey.

VisitBritain Official Guides
Terms & Conditions for Attraction voucher

1 Offer not valid when pre-booking, during half term holidays or for the Viking Festival (14-18 Feb). Not valid in conjunction with any other offer and not exchangeable for cash.
2 Each voucher entitles the holder to the discount specified by the selected attraction.
3 Valid for use until 31/10/2008 (unless otherwise specified, or if attraction season finishes prior to this). Vouchers are subject to the terms, conditions and restrictions of the selected attraction.
4 One voucher per party will be accepted and cannot be used in conjunction with any other offer. Photocopies will not be accepted.
5 All attractions offering a discount have confirmed their willingness to participate. All information is subject to change without notice and should any attraction close or decline to accept a voucher for any reason, VisitBritain is not liable and cannot be held responsible.
6 VisitBritain shall not accept liability for any loss, accident or injury that may occur at a participating attraction and any dispute must be settled direct with the attraction concerned.
7 There is no cash alternative in lieu of tickets or listed savings.
8 You are advised to check all relevant information with your chosen attraction before commencing your journey.

VisitBritain Official Guides
Terms & Conditions for Attraction voucher

1 This voucher allows one person free entry when accompanied by a full paying adult. Valid until 30 September 2007.
2 Each voucher entitles the holder to the discount specified by the selected attraction.
3 Valid for use until 31/10/2008 (unless otherwise specified, or if attraction season finishes prior to this). Vouchers are subject to the terms, conditions and restrictions of the selected attraction.
4 One voucher per party will be accepted and cannot be used in conjunction with any other offer. Photocopies will not be accepted.
5 All attractions offering a discount have confirmed their willingness to participate. All information is subject to change without notice and should any attraction close or decline to accept a voucher for any reason, VisitBritain is not liable and cannot be held responsible.
6 VisitBritain shall not accept liability for any loss, accident or injury that may occur at a participating attraction and any dispute must be settled direct with the attraction concerned.
7 There is no cash alternative in lieu of tickets or listed savings.
8 You are advised to check all relevant information with your chosen attraction before commencing your journey.

South Shields Museum & Art Gallery

SPECIAL OFFER VOUCHER

Child goes free with a full paying adult

JORVIK Viking Centre
York YO1 9WT

SPECIAL OFFER VOUCHER

Two for the price of one

Thackray Museum
Leeds LS9 7LN

SPECIAL OFFER VOUCHER

Two for the price of one

National Wildflower Centre
Knowsley L16 3NA

Brontë Parsonage Museum, Haworth

VisitBritain Official Guides
Terms & Conditions for Attraction voucher

1 Buy one full price adult ticket and get another ticket of up to the same value free.
2 Each voucher entitles the holder to the discount specified by the selected attraction.
3 Valid for use until 31/10/2008 (unless otherwise specified, or if attraction season finishes prior to this). Vouchers are subject to the terms, conditions and restrictions of the selected attraction.
4 One voucher per party will be accepted and cannot be used in conjunction with any other offer. Photocopies will not be accepted.
5 All attractions offering a discount have confirmed their willingness to participate. All information is subject to change without notice and should any attraction close or decline to accept a voucher for any reason, VisitBritain is not liable and cannot be held responsible.
6 VisitBritain shall not accept liability for any loss, accident or injury that may occur at a participating attraction and any dispute must be settled direct with the attraction concerned.
7 There is no cash alternative in lieu of tickets or listed savings.
8 You are advised to check all relevant information with your chosen attraction before commencing your journey.

VisitBritain Official Guides
Terms & Conditions for Attraction voucher

1 Offer not valid when pre-booking, during half term holidays or for the Viking Festival (14-18 Feb). Not valid in conjunction with any other offer and not exchangeable for cash.
2 Each voucher entitles the holder to the discount specified by the selected attraction.
3 Valid for use until 31/10/2008 (unless otherwise specified, or if attraction season finishes prior to this). Vouchers are subject to the terms, conditions and restrictions of the selected attraction.
4 One voucher per party will be accepted and cannot be used in conjunction with any other offer. Photocopies will not be accepted.
5 All attractions offering a discount have confirmed their willingness to participate. All information is subject to change without notice and should any attraction close or decline to accept a voucher for any reason, VisitBritain is not liable and cannot be held responsible.
6 VisitBritain shall not accept liability for any loss, accident or injury that may occur at a participating attraction and any dispute must be settled direct with the attraction concerned.
7 There is no cash alternative in lieu of tickets or listed savings.
8 You are advised to check all relevant information with your chosen attraction before commencing your journey.

VisitBritain Official Guides
Terms & Conditions for Attraction voucher

1 Voucher valid 1 March to 1 September.
2 Each voucher entitles the holder to the discount specified by the selected attraction.
3 Valid for use until 31/10/2008 (unless otherwise specified, or if attraction season finishes prior to this). Vouchers are subject to the terms, conditions and restrictions of the selected attraction.
4 One voucher per party will be accepted and cannot be used in conjunction with any other offer. Photocopies will not be accepted.
5 All attractions offering a discount have confirmed their willingness to participate. All information is subject to change without notice and should any attraction close or decline to accept a voucher for any reason, VisitBritain is not liable and cannot be held responsible.
6 VisitBritain shall not accept liability for any loss, accident or injury that may occur at a participating attraction and any dispute must be settled direct with the attraction concerned.
7 There is no cash alternative in lieu of tickets or listed savings.
8 You are advised to check all relevant information with your chosen attraction before commencing your journey.

Yorkshire Air Museum, York

win
a full set of official tourist board guides

Keep in touch and WIN a full set of 2007 official tourist board accommodation guides

VisitBritain would be delighted to hear what you think of this guide. Please complete the short questionnaire overleaf and send it back to us.

Questionnaires will be entered into a monthly draw to win a full set of 2007 official accommodation guides.

CUT ALONG LINE

Title First name

Surname

Address

Town/City County

Postcode Country

Mobile Telephone

E-mail

Which age group are you in?

16-24 ❑ 25-34 ❑ 35-44 ❑ 45-54 ❑ 55-64 ❑ 65+ ❑

When do you normally buy accommodation guides? (please tick one box)

- ❑ Easter holidays
- ❑ Before main summer season, ie May
- ❑ Christmas/end of the year
- ❑ Anytime – planning a special occasion
- ❑ Anytime – planning a spontaneous occasion
- ❑ Anytime – planning a holiday
- ❑ Spontaneously purchased

How often do you buy accommodation guides? (please tick one box)

- ❑ Every year
- ❑ Every 2 years
- ❑ Every 3 years
- ❑ Every 4 years
- ❑ Every 5 years
- ❑ Single purchase, ie I do not replace guide

Do you regularly use any other accommodation guides? If yes, which ones?

What do you find useful about this official tourist board guide?

Is there any other information you would like to see added to this guide?

Have you booked any accommodation through this guide? If yes, which one (establishment and region)?

Would you like to be contacted by VisitBritain in future with news, ideas and special offers? Yes ❑ No ❑

Would you like to be contacted by VisitBritain's carefully chosen partners with news of more offers? Yes ❑ No ❑

Please complete, put in an envelope and return Freepost (no stamp required) to:

VisitBritain Commercial Publishing, Freepost RLXU–XLYY–UKLB
Thames Tower, Blacks Road, London W6 9EL

Terms and conditions: Prize draw closes on 31/12/07. The draw is open to adults aged 18+ (excluding employees of VisitBritain and their immediate families, agents or anyone professionally connected with the promotion). The winner of each monthly draw from 01/01/07 to 31/12/07 will win the 2007 edition of Hotels, Bed & Breakfast, Self Catering, and Camping & Caravan Parks.

enjoyEngland™

NE07-RRC